the pursuit of history
Rangers – 1992-98

the pursuit of history
Rangers – 1992-98

Martyn Ramsay

First published 2023 by DB Publishing, an imprint of JMD Media Ltd,

Nottingham, United Kingdom.

ISBN 9781780916538

Printed in the UK

Contents

Introduction

'These could be the best days of our lives, but I don't think we've been living very wise.'
Noel Gallagher

'For every five pounds Celtic spend, we will spend ten.'
David Murray

It was 15 minutes after sunrise on a late-spring morning in 1992 and two men were ensconced at the bottom of a Renfrewshire garden sharing the remnants of the final bottle of champagne. It had been a long night of celebration, one shared with both team-mates and pop stars alike, and Ally McCoist and Andy Goram were the last men standing. Or, more accurately, sitting. 'Andy and I have booked the garden seats for the same time, same place next year, and, hopefully, for the next few seasons after that,' wrote McCoist shortly after. 'You can't beat that winning feeling, and there's nothing about the Ibrox setup which suggests for a moment that it is going to stop.' He was correct, of course. Rangers had just won a double, the league championship being claimed with such style and ease that potential challengers appeared theoretical at best. The 1990s would belong to these players.

The character and story of any decade is never truly bookended by the arbitrary dates that officially start and end it, and the same was true of this one. Many historians have argued, and I would agree, that the 1990s really started with the fall of the Berlin Wall on 9 November 1989 and really ended with the fall of the World Trade Center in New York on 11 September 2001. Cradled between the Cold War and political division at one end and global terror and financial collapse at the other, it was a time – in the west at least[1] – of relative peace and prosperity, growth and pleasure. All the serious arguments about democracy and economics had been concluded – some even suggested that history as we knew it was at an end – and so the politics of this decade were more ethereal; about how we lived, how we spoke and how we treated each other and the environment around us.

In many respects, the 1990s was a long party. Safe, secure and so smugly self-satisfied, it was not a time for sober discourse but for meaningless fun. To borrow a line from Seinfeld, one of the definitive television shows of the era, it was a decade about nothing and, after the turmoil and division of the 1980s and indeed the century as a whole, was there anything so wrong about that? And so it was somewhat true of Rangers. Undisputed hegemony so often carried off with a hedonistic swagger but one that belied complacency and the blissful binds of a warm, familiar sense of contentment.

There is no prologue in this book. That purpose is effectively served by my previous work, *Revolution*, which tells the story of the preceding six years in Rangers' history. One of powerful forward drive and ambition, new horizons and how the foundations were set for a generation of success. At the conclusion of season 1991/92 – the fourth successful title campaign on the spin – one fan was a little despondent about the lack of European progress but was able to console himself with the prospect of a domestic legend that was now visible to the club and fans alike. 'Roll on ten in a row,' he wrote in the fanzine *Follow, Follow*.

It was thought at the time and ever since that Celtic's achievement of nine successive league titles in the late 1960s and early 1970s would never be seen again but even by the summer of 1992, fewer and fewer figures in Scottish football could see any realistic obstacles on Rangers' path to matching and eventually outdoing their rivals. The revolution had established outright dominance at home but now, just as a bigger footballing revolution was about to take shape across the continent, Rangers – thanks in no small part to UEFA's limitation on foreign players – were effectively locked into a path towards the past.

The title of this book could be read in a couple of different ways. First and foremost, it is a positive story about the journey to reach this historic landmark, an obsession which intensified over the decade, but on the other side of the coin is a journey backwards and inwards to settle an old score just at the time that European football was moving at pace towards a new level of modernisation, with a new league and new markets beyond the imagination of the club who started it all, Rangers. It was often a thrilling and enjoyable experience – few moments more so than the season with which we pick the story up – but nevertheless, it was almost always a complex one.

The format of the book is the same as *Revolution*, with six main season chapters diving deep into the detail of the time and six smaller essays that touch on some areas of wider interest. How and why the relationship between Rangers fans and

---

1   Inhabitants of the Balkans and Rwanda may feel compelled to disagree.

the Scotland national side disintegrated. How professionalism reached new levels in the game but struggled at times to take root at Ibrox. The decade produced some tiresome poetry about style over substance and as well as exposing our complicated relationship with heroes and celebrities. There's a look at the player who was ever-present throughout the era and saw his position change arguably more than any other on the field – Ally McCoist – and the endangered species that became the penalty box striker. Finally, a more personal reflection on what it meant growing up as a Rangers fan in this time of all times and how that compares with those who had more perspective when it came and those who never saw it at all.

The cultural impact of the 1990s raises its head throughout the story because it is an inextricably large part. This is a more complicated tale than the one that came before. Graeme Souness, David Holmes and the younger David Murray had a greater degree of agency and clarity of purpose and their stated aims were in sync with what was possible. It was a vision married to the opportunity. Following football's Big Bang in 1992 – television revenues and wages exploding, the draw of smaller leagues reducing and the impact of UEFA's foreigner rule tightening – the bombastic rhetoric from inside the Blue Room became increasingly fanciful. The safer and therefore more inviting target was at home.

To what extent it could have been different is once again the main theme throughout the book. Opportunities and competency fill the equation just as they did between 1986 and 1992. Where those who had shaped the revolution had imposed themselves and their will on Scottish football and beyond – just as those in politics were doing in the 1980s – the 1990s was, as the brilliant modern historian Alwyn W. Turner argued, characterised more by leaders following trends and change that was already happening around them. Borrowing a phrase used by the former chancellor of the exchequer, Norman Lamont, Turner suggested that John Major and Tony Blair might have 'spent the decade in office, but not in power'. There are some parallels with David Murray and Walter Smith during this time, ever playing catch-up outside the parish walls and becoming frustrated with life within.

That's not to say that the success between 1992 and Smith's departure in 1998 – five titles, five cups and a sensational attempt on the Champions League – wasn't welcomed or appreciated. Despite a relatively dull intermission, it was often a source of incredible, intoxicating fun, watching some of the greatest players ever to wear the jersey underline the feeling of permanent superiority. It is just that, as wild as that party was, there was a gnawing realisation that there was a bigger one happening further and further away. To borrow the title of a Britpop hit, it really was something of a bittersweet symphony and, I hope as a result, that it leads to a more interesting book.

Martyn Ramsay
July 2023

Chapter One

The Impossible Dream
Season 1992/93

'To fight the unbeatable foe. To reach the unreachable star.'
Joe Darion

'We've made our mark in Europe. I thought that we were always
a wee bit parochial in the sense that we thought we're a big club.
But I'll tell you what, we're a big club now.'
David Murray, 1993

Walter Smith poured himself a cup of tea, took a seat in the corner of the Rangers dressing room and watched as his players exchanged insults and punches. It was half-time of the sixth league game of the season and his double-winning side had yet to regain their form with only two wins, two draws and a chaotic defeat at Dundee. Now they were a goal down at home to the early leaders Aberdeen – scored by Roy Aitken no less – and those frustrations had finally reached breaking point. Andy Goram had felt that Nigel Spackman had left Aitken in too much space at the edge of the box and lambasted him at the time only to receive not one, but two 'wanker' gestures in return. 'I was apoplectic, in a seethe,' wrote Goram. 'That wasn't Rangers. We didn't publicly point the finger at people.' Presumably loudly berating team-mates in public was fair game but either way, the Rangers goalkeeper nearly took the dressing room door off its hinges at the break. Goram warned Spackman that if he ever did something like that again then he would 'fucking kill' him. Spackman coolly replied, 'Sit down, you fat bastard,' and all hell broke loose as three punches were landed on the midfielder before the team managed to prise the two senior professionals apart.

It was only then that Smith intervened. He had found the right moment where he could remind his players that enough was enough, that their current levels were nowhere near their best and that this had to change. Because of the heightened tension in the room, the warning would have resonance. What happened next didn't just leave the Rangers support spellbound for the remaining 45 minutes but for the rest of a long season. A switch had been flicked that made the team seem unbeatable not only at home but, more importantly on the continent as well. Rangers had helped build the footballing stage of the future and soon they'd be on it, bringing the house down, as television audiences throughout the United Kingdom became hooked on the drama that unfolded, with neutrals in southern England becoming every bit as tense as those Ibrox regulars.

Neither before nor since have Rangers been both as dominant at home and as relevant at the forefront of the European game. The dream shared by generations – to be kings of Europe – felt both so tangible and yet still tantalisingly ephemeral. As lucid and engaging as contrarian arguments may have been over the years, let there be no doubt about it.

This was the greatest season of them all.

* * *

The focal point of the Scottish footballing summer in 1992 was 500 miles east of Aberdeen, in Southern Sweden. For the first time Scotland were taking part in the European Championship finals and for the first time there were five Rangers players in the squad.[2] Mainstays of the successful 1991/92 campaign, Andy Goram, Richard Gough, Stuart McCall and, of course, Ally McCoist were joined by the return of Dave McPherson from Hearts, who was signed for £1m before the competition started. Ian Durrant was offered the chance to go to the pre-tournament camp in Canada but, after a discussion with Walter Smith, decided that it was too soon for him to do himself justice on that stage. A summer of complete rest was enjoyed instead, much to the benefit of Rangers as it would turn out. All five would be in the starting XI and only David Robertson, who had enjoyed such a fine debut season, could feel aggrieved at not making the squad at all.

On the surface, the familiar tale of early elimination and a big win coming too late to make any difference should place this campaign in the same basket as all the rest of Scotland's ignominious summers but that would be slightly unfair. This was the last eight-team European Championship to take place and, with the hosts taking an automatic spot, it meant that seven sides had to win their qualifying group in order to be there. There was no Spain, Italy, Belgium or Portugal there that year and of course the eventual winners, Denmark, hadn't qualified directly and only took their place due to the political exclusion of Yugoslavia. Unlike the

---

2   This is still the most Rangers have ever provided a Scotland squad at a major tournament at the time of writing.

bloated nature of the competition in the 2020s, it was a genuine achievement for Scotland just to take their place in the final eight, especially as the next World Cup in the United States would suggest, ahead of Romania, Bulgaria and Switzerland in their qualifying group.

The draw for the finals could not have been more difficult, even if some of their opponents had new stage names. Scotland were drawn in Group 2 alongside the reigning European champions Netherlands, reigning world champions and now unified Germany, and the beaten finalists from the last time out who started qualification when the Berlin Wall was still in place as the Soviet Union but now, as the old empire creaked towards its collapse, were called the Commonwealth of Independent States. Although they perhaps lacked a bit of dynamism at full-back with Maurice Malpas of Dundee United and Stewart McKimmie of Aberdeen, there was confidence around the central rearguard triangle of Goram, Gough and McPherson, the red-hot form of McCoist with willing runners in Gordon Durie or Kevin Gallagher[3] and something of a midfield diamond comprising McCall, Paul McStay, Gary McAllister and Brian McClair. The optimism was always tempered however, even by the most positive of players as McCoist demonstrated on the eve of the tournament when he said, 'I think that people in Scotland are realistic enough to know that we are not going to win it, but what they would like us to do is go out and have a real go.'

And, over the piece, that was exactly what they did. The opening game against the Dutch was more prosaic and in line with the captain's pre-tournament request to try and be sensible. 'History shows that our old madness doesn't work,' said Gough. 'So let's try and be sane about the thing.' For 77 minutes the holders were kept at arm's length with Marco van Basten, the hero of 1988 who dismissed Scotland as 'all kick and rush', not having a shot on goal. Quality, however, often shines through in the end. The only goal of the game was made in Milan but finished off by the next big thing coming out of Amsterdam. Ruud Gullit, Van Basten and Frank Rijkaard all combined to find the 23-year-old Dennis Bergkamp – for once untracked by Malpas – in enough space to beat Goram. Against Germany in Norrkoping, Scotland were absolutely fearless. Fourteen corners were won to the Germans' two and 12 clear-cut chances were created but to no avail. Germany only needed Karl-Heinz Riedle's clinical strike before the interval and Stefan Effenberg's freak deflection minutes after it to seal a 2-0 win. For all those chances, none fell to McCoist who was marked out of the games and substituted early in all three matches due to his ineffectiveness. A player so in form domestically and vital in qualification was strangely subdued when the tournament reached its upper echelons.

Scotland would beat the CIS 3-0 in the final game, with their opponents going into it still with a chance of reaching the semi-finals, and it was a deserved victory with McStay, McClair and McAllister all on the scoresheet. This was no

---

3   At the time of Tottenham Hotspur and Coventry City respectively.

disgrace. No Costa Rica or Peru. No catastrophic defensive calamity. It was an almost impossible challenge and that suited Andy Roxburgh's side, as he reflected some years later, 'There was no sense of anxiety. We were relishing the idea of playing those teams. We didn't like to have the territory and the ball to ourselves. We played at our best off a tackle.' For a brief moment he had found a side with decent balance, a good team spirit[4] and who were tactically comfortable in being reactive to better quality opponents. It would be a familiar theme throughout the season for Walter Smith's Rangers.

Any feelgood factor around Scottish football generated in Scandinavia in June was almost non-existent by the start of the season on 1 August. In contrast to the positivity and hype around previous seasons, the tone for 1992/93 was generally downbeat. For the first time since the arrival of Graeme Souness, Rangers had gone from most pundits favourites in a competitive race to a foregone conclusion. A price of 3/1 on was the best you could get from Ladbrokes on a fifth Rangers title in a row with Celtic, Hearts and Aberdeen all out at 7/2, 10/1 and 14/1 respectively. Something structurally had now changed so significantly that mere form and injuries could not upset it. The rest of the pack was merely paying lip service to the challenge. Celtic manager Liam Brady bordered on parody in a season preview, 'I said before the start of last season that we would win a trophy and although we didn't I am saying the same thing this time.' It was almost pantomime

The prospect of a 44-game league season was another factor in the waning enthusiasm. The *Glasgow Herald*'s preview played so heavily on the imagery of 'endurance' and 'marathon' that the writer almost sounded exhausted himself before a ball had been kicked. This was a debate yet again in sharp focus that summer due to the planned breakaway of a Scottish Super League. Led by Rangers, Hearts, Celtic, Aberdeen and Dundee United, this was a bid mainly – if not purely – motivated by greater revenue protection, no doubt influenced by events in England earlier in the year. The SSL had four outcomes in mind as outlined by Wallace Mercer: a structure more attractive than the existing premier division, something more competitive, improvement in facilities for spectators, and an increase in financial returns. The latter was projected at £15m in the first three years by way of controlling television, sponsorship, advertising, marketing, and merchandising deals; however, it was never destined to be successful at that stage.

There were bureaucratic issues such as the Scottish Football League's Rule 51 which stated that any players belonging to a club that quits membership would automatically become the SFL's property and could be sold by them[5], not to mention the need to get Jim Farry and the SFA behind the venture in order to be recognised as Scotland's representatives in European competition. None of the

---

4   There were cracks being covered, especially in the relationship between Roxburgh and Gough, which which would not remain closed for long.

5   Even the wording in 1992 makes the Bosman case seem too long in coming.

plans would have a direct impact on the quality of the game, maintaining as it would the repetitive four meetings a season[6] and the stadium criteria – meeting the Taylor Report recommendations – were fantasy for clubs such as Celtic and Hearts, the former being no further forward in getting planning permission for their £100m Cambuslang dream home.

The truth was that the Scottish football economy was no more booming than the nation's by 1992. Part of the previous year's pre-season excitement was down to the fact that ambition was evidently growing and clubs other than Rangers were spending money on English and European talent. Now the recession was hitting and a Price Waterhouse report concluded that all Scottish clubs other than Aberdeen and Dundee United were living 'well beyond their means' and only Rangers could manage that debt due to their commercial potential. There was a sense in the stands and terracing that the game was moving further away from them, even at Ibrox when Rangers paraded 24 top-of-the-range Volkswagens and Audis on the first day of the season, supplied by the new director Ian Skelly.[7] Some fans felt that, with unemployment rising and the economy shrinking for many, such a blatant display of wealth was a little off-key and a sign that the match experience wasn't what it used to be. For many reasons there were clouds overhead north of the border as the new campaign got under way at the same time as the new English Premier League opened to clear skies and an endless horizon.

Walter Smith wasn't overly concerned, however. This was a summer of tinkering rather than surgery, with old faces returning rather than the unveiling of fresh new stars. The McPherson signing was sensible. Rangers had been stretched a little in the centre of defence the previous season and he had enjoyed a good spell with Hearts as well as Scotland and, without question, his nationality was a major positive in view of UEFA's ever-tightening restrictions. Ally Maxwell, the goalkeeping hero of Motherwell's Scottish Cup win in 1991, was brought in as cover for Goram and Smith was comfortable in allowing both John Spencer and Paul Rideout to head down south for £1m between them. It left McCoist and Mark Hateley somewhat exposed but Smith, stung a little by the questioning of his use of youth thus far, was content to allow young Gary McSwegan his chance when it arose. Speaking early in the season he said, 'We were criticised for not giving young players a chance to go into the first team and show what they can do, so we shouldn't be criticised for being willing now to give players that chance. Time will tell whether we are right, but I would hope the necessity of us having to buy backup players from England at £500,000 a time has gone.' Smith still believed that he was lacking something in midfield. A ball player rather than the boundless energy he already had. Someone to replace the gap left by Trevor Steven the previous summer. Ideally, Trevor Steven.

---

6   Albeit the league would be reduced to eight teams so producing a 28-game league season.

7   Skelly had taken up his position in the summer alongside Walter Smith. Hugh Adams had made a very public and recriminatory departure.

It had not been an enjoyable year in France for the England midfielder and the feeling was mutual. With Marseille having yet to complete the payment for the original transfer fee, Rangers always felt they were in a good position to do the deal that would bring Steven home. The French champions initially wanted £3m which the English champions, Leeds United, were happy to pay, but Steven wasn't interested. His stubbornness was initially met with similar obstinacy from Bernard Tapie, the ambitious and charismatic Marseille owner, when he was sent to train with the reserves on Thursday, 23 July and told that he would not feature for them in the friendly with Rangers at Ibrox the following Tuesday night. It was all bluster of course and a deal was done on the Friday evening for £2.4m to bring Steven back. The summer had started with rumours of Lothar Matthäus coming to Rangers and Celtic fans were urged to boycott the *Scottish Sun* when Jim Black reported that Rangers were prepared to buy Paul McStay. Both clubs rubbished the story immediately and ultimately the player, who had said his goodbyes and was expected to move to Italy or England, decided to sign a new deal when only Everton came in with an offer.[8] Overall, there was a relaxed aura of content about what Rangers had at their disposal, even if the pre-season was disrupted with the players who had played in Sweden – the five Scots plus Oleg Kuznetsov and Alexei Mikhailichenko – would only join up after the usual Tuscan camp.

That contentment was disturbed by the final pre-season friendly against Marseille. The 2-1 scoreline flattered the hosts as the French side put on an exhibition of both strength and élan that left both fans and media wondering what chance Rangers would have of reaching the newly formed Champions League in November, such was the gulf in class. It took them an hour but they scored two in a minute from Rudi Völler and Didier Deschamps before Hateley responded with a late penalty consolation. Manager Jean Fernandez was hesitant to talk about his own side's chances of glory – they were top seeds in the first-round draw – but was sure about the fate of Rangers, 'I don't really think they can do well in Europe.' Rangers had been seeded ninth in that draw and were paired with the Danish champions Lyngby. Given the remarkable success of the national side that summer – Denmark won the European Championship after being drafted in at short notice – there was a fair amount of trepidation about another season of European disappointment. As excellent as Marseille were, however, Rangers were some way off it in terms of fitness – such a vital part of any successful Scottish side in continental competition – and, even though Steven started[9], it wasn't a fair demonstration of the creative side of Smith's

---

8   It was an outcome that produced mixed feelings at Parkhead. As much as McStay was loved, there were many, included the manager, who were banking on being able to spend that transfer income around the team. In the end, £1.7m was spent on the Albanian defender Rudi Vata and the West Ham forward Stuart Slater. He would score three goals that season.

9   He would come off with a knock and even his very presence was controversial as he had not yet been formally registered with the SFA. Rangers assumed that he had and played him anyway. Farry threatened serious action but it came to nothing.

team, especially with Durrant and Mikhailichenko on the bench. It was too early to judge.

Unfortunately for Rangers, the season was starting early. With the opening game on 1 August, there would be nine domestic matches played in that month and the rustiness showed. The opening fixtures were benign but it didn't seem to matter.[10] St Johnstone – who had been thumped on the first day of the previous season – and beaten cup finalists Airdrie came to Ibrox in the opening two games and set out a defensive stall that would be replicated many times over the course of the decade. Rangers took full points, winning 1-0 and 2-0 respectively, but it was dull and boring stuff and it wasn't to get much better at Easter Road in an attritional and bad-tempered 0-0 draw.

If Rangers were set to endure stalemates – McCoist said after the opening-day win that it would be unlikely to see the team score as many league goals in this campaign as the previous one[11] – they were given the shock of their lives at Dens Park on 15 August. Simon Stainrod – an eccentric figure, seemingly inspired by Malcom Allison – took a very different approach to the visit of the champions. Dundee were ahead four times in a ridiculous game of serve and volley and, when Rangers couldn't equalise for the fourth time, it marked the first defeat of the season after only two weeks. It would be seven months until the next time that happened but few Rangers fans would have believed it looking on at that defensive display with doubts raised on the radio and the tabloid hotlines about McPherson's return, the quality of Maxwell as a replacement for Goram[12] and, if he was fit, why wasn't Ian Durrant starting games?

The latter question was asked again the following weekend although the mood was slightly better. Celtic had come to Ibrox a point clear of Rangers and stayed that way after a towsy 1-1 draw. Rangers should have been ahead early when a Trevor Steven goal was ruled offside despite Celtic defenders being stood inside the box as Hateley flicked the ball forward for Steven to run on to from outside it[13] but the visitors were the better side for much of the first hour and deserved to take the lead just after the break, albeit from a wild deflection on the cross that landed perfectly for Gerry Creaney. Celtic were unsure and insecure with their advantage and Rangers hunted them down as the match progressed. It was Durrant, on as a substitute, who started the move from deep and finished it with great power in the Celtic box from a Hateley knock-on. Smith's reticence to expose Durrant too much, too soon was understandable but the pressure was building to trust him with a more permanent role.

Rangers had helped themselves to ten goals in the first two rounds of the League Cup – against Dumbarton and Stranraer – but the quarter-final trip to Tannadice

---

10   The *Celtic View* – the official club newspaper – used its front page to highlight the perceived lack of fairness in the two club's first four fixtures, with Celtic away to Hearts and Aberdeen first.

11   In the end they'd manage just the 97 compared to 101

12   He had missed this match with a slight knock

13   This did not make the cover of the *Celtic View*

was a lot closer and needed a Pieter Huistra winner in extra time to earn a place in the last four, after an entertaining but tense 3-2 victory. Mark Hateley missed that trip following a knock against Celtic and he would also miss the visit of Aberdeen on Saturday, 29 August where, for 45 minutes, it looked like more of the same stodgy and insipid league form. Until, of course, the half-time dressing-room fight, Smith's team talk and a tactical switch. Huistra and Mikhailichenko swapped flanks and Durrant was pushed further up to support McCoist. Rangers instantly looked a different side. For the second week running, it was Durrant who forced parity after some nice work on the edge of the box with Brown and Mikhailichenko and simply passed the ball into the net from just outside. When an Aberdeen long ball was cut out, it was Durrant who sprung the counter from his own half, driving forward before releasing McCoist with the outside of his right foot. The number nine wasted no time in scoring his ninth goal in nine games. It was left to Mikhailichenko, the mercurial Ukrainian, to finish it with an impudent first time shot with the outside of his left boot. It was a thrilling second half full of style and passion. For the first time, even more than the Old Firm comeback, Ibrox was truly energised. The tension had disappeared and it was now fun again.

Rangers ended the chaotic month of August in second place, one point behind Dundee United but even by that stage there was little doubt about where the domestic direction of travel was heading.

Europe, however, was a different question.

* * *

Given the exciting and novel drama that would unfold over the course of this season's European campaign, it is often forgotten that it could easily have followed a depressingly familiar path, one that was known only too well to Rangers fans in the years prior as it would do throughout the ones that immediately followed. Midway through the first half of the European Cup first round, first leg at Ibrox, with the match still goalless, Henrik Larsen – scorer of three Danish goals at the European Championship including both in their semi-final win over the Netherlands – clipped a perfect ball from the left hand side which found his team-mate Jan Jürgensen unmarked in the Rangers box. It was a golden opportunity to grab an away goal but the striker froze, timidly heading towards the grateful Andy Goram, who had already had to stick a leg out to stop a Morten Wieghorst effort during a very nervy start.

The Danes, with three European champions in their starting line-up, had one chance cleared off the line before the break but by that time Rangers were already in front. Hateley put his head where many wouldn't in order to divert a low John Brown cross into the bottom corner. His give-and-go with Huistra in the second half was cutely finished by his Dutch colleague and, in the end, the 2-0 lead was well deserved. Even if the early scare had caused more damage, it is more than likely that this particular Rangers side would have had the necessary resolve to bounce back as they had already shown that season and would do so again. It was starting to feel like a team who didn't know when they were beaten. Players would talk privately of 2-0 deficits no longer holding any fear. They had something special by then. A bond that seemed unbreakable. The second leg in Denmark – a 1-0 win from a late Durrant breakaway – was more controlled and serene.[14] There was to be no early European slip-up for Smith this time.

At home, the form was hotting up too. In the eight league games during September and October, Rangers scored four or more goals in six of them, with four being away. There were two 4-1 wins at Motherwell and Partick Thistle and a 5-1 at St Johnstone, a venue that had previously been the scene of frustrating draws or narrow victories. Tannadice too, although it had broadly been a happy hunting ground – except for perhaps Terry Butcher and Gary Stevens – those wins had been hard work, with the odd goal so often being enough. The performance on 26 September was blistering and the 4-0 win was the biggest result there for over 20 years. With Richard Gough injured with a groin strain, Ally McCoist realised yet another childhood dream by captaining Rangers for the first time and the team responded in style with two goals from Huistra, one from Steven and one, inevitably, from McCoist himself. He scored 15 goals in those eight league games, including two hat-tricks and all four in a 4-0 win at home to Falkirk.

By the end of October McCoist had scored 28 goals in all competitions. It was this kind of ridiculous scoring record along with that statement win against United which underlined the wider pessimism around Scottish football that there was no longer a contest to be enjoyed, compounded by the return to national navel-gazing following Scotland's disappointing start to World Cup qualification.[15] Where the league games were close – a scrappy 2-0 win at home to Hearts and a fortunate 1-0 defeat of Hibs at Ibrox – it was clear that Rangers were treading water with bigger matches on the horizon. St Johnstone had to be dispatched in the League Cup semi-final following the Hearts game – a 3-1 win with a McCoist hat-trick of course – and the reason for the lack of focus for the visit of Hibs was almost certainly down to the European Cup second round at Ibrox coming up on the Wednesday. It was, of course, the Battle of Britain and would be the first of five games in the space of 18 days that would sum up the experience of this season very well. Incessant excitement, tension, drama and most importantly, wins.

Only some careless admin prevented Rangers from having to face German opposition for the fourth time in seven seasons. The first-round tie between VfB Stuttgart and Leeds United was an engrossing example of two-legged continental competition. The English champions looked like they had been blown away by

---

14   Especially for the Rangers supporters' bus that was stopped with £250,000 of cannabis on the way home. It had originally travelled through the Netherlands.

15   Scotland lost 3-1 to Switzerland with McCoist equalising early and Gough being sent off late. A drab 0-0 draw at Ibrox with Portugal was to follow in October and, with Italy still to come, hopes of an American dream were dashed from the outset.

three goals in 17 second-half minutes in south-west Germany but the return leg was exceptional fun with swings in first-half momentum finishing in a Leeds onslaught that only just failed to tip the tie over the edge. The 4-1 defeat was still enough on away goals but Christophe Daum, the Stuttgart coach, had chosen to select the Yugoslav defender Jovo Simanić on his bench, the fourth foreigner in the side. What should have been a simple case to deal with before the second round draw – the Germans should have been eliminated immediately – was instead a farce which eventually resulted in a play-off to be held in the Camp Nou, Barcelona. The Rangers squad watched on that Friday night, completely united in who they wanted to win. 'Every single player wanted to get the chance to meet the champions of England,' wrote Gough. 'Not that we thought we had anything to prove to them – but it was an opportunity to prove to a lot of media people in the south that we were something more than a big fish in a small pool. That was going to be important, to be able to wipe the sneers from some faces.' Given the recent record Rangers had against German sides, it was arguably for the best that justice was done in the end[16] and for the media, it was heaven-sent.

With the absence of the traditional Scotland v England fixture for three years due to crowd trouble, this was an opportunity for the British press to relax back into some old tropes and for the hype machine – by the standards of the early 1990s – to be cranked back into gear, especially now with so much at stake in the form of a place in the new UEFA Champions League awaiting the winners. Both the English tabloids and broadsheets hardly gave Rangers a puncher's chance against a Leeds side who, although they had won a title in impressive fashion and had some talented ball players such as Gary McAllister, Gordon Strachan, Gary Speed and Eric Cantona, had yet to win an away match all season and were starting to ship goals from crosses at an alarming rate. There hadn't been this kind of excitement around a Rangers European tie in a generation but it was the Ibrox club who moved to ensure that crowd disturbance wouldn't be part of the story. Leeds managing director Bill Fotherby agreed that it would be a good idea but, along with the police, was sceptical about how it would work. Eventually an agreement was reached so that, with the exception of those intrepid explorers who were willing to seek out tickets and try to remain silent through the drama, the majority of the traditional travelling supporters would have to make do with television.

Except, for the first leg anyway, viewers in Scotland. There were three Scottish clubs in European action that night – Wednesday, 21 October – with Celtic in Dortmund to face Borussia and Hearts taking on Standard Liège at Tynecastle, both in the UEFA Cup. Hearts refused to allow ITV to broadcast the game from Ibrox live as they were at home and wanted to protect their own gate. Chairman Wallace Mercer, while presumably keeping a straight face, justified this stance

---

16   Although the overall record for Scottish clubs against English sides in European competition was hardly encouraging either, with only five victories in 22 previous encounters.

when he said, 'A number of neutrals have been buying tickets for our match and, apart from anything else, we feel that it would be a betrayal of them if they were told later that there was a live showing of a rival game.' How that neutrality data was captured is unknown but Rangers fans without a ticket – Ibrox was cut slightly to 42,000 as UEFA demanded standing sections to be reduced by 40 per cent so there was an almighty scramble – would have to listen to the radio and watch the whole match when it was shown 'as live' following the final whistle.

'When I came out of the tunnel, the hairs on the back of my neck stood up,' wrote Andy Goram. 'The atmosphere was electric. I looked across at my Scotland team-mates Gordon Strachan and Gary McAllister and knew that this was why I had come to Rangers, for games like this: Scotland's champions against England's champions for a place in the Champions League group stages. There was a purity about that game and what was at stake, like boxing's Oscar de la Hoya or Manny Pacquiao refusing the easy way and taking the hardest fight out there.' It really did crackle that night as the players walked out into the arena – the best in Britain – that was built exactly for such occasions, a poignant note given that it was only a week since the passing of the Rangers legend who had done so much to ensure that such a stadium came to fruition. Willie Waddell had died from a heart attack at the age of 71 and, being the only man to lead the club to European success, he would no doubt have been captivated by this particular journey 20 years on. Such modern heights would not have been possible without his foresight and stubborn determination to realise that vision.

In truth the first leg didn't quite live up to the expectation despite the sensational start. All that electricity disappeared in an instant when McAllister shut down the power inside two minutes. Strachan's corner was weak and easily dealt with and perhaps, when the ball approached his international team-mate, there was an expectation that he would take an extra touch. Instead, one would do and it ended up in Goram's top corner. 'What about that wee strike?' McAllister asked McCoist as he made his way back for the restart. The immediate silence was eerie – save for the handful of Leeds fans, including Strachan's father, who couldn't contain themselves and were quickly ejected – but it didn't take long for Ibrox to respond. There was a belief in this side that simply didn't exist when faced with adversity against Bayern, Red Star or even Sparta. As he would do so often over the course of that season, it was Ian Durrant who pushed Rangers back into the game as the tempo refused to relent. It was his corner that was misjudged by the Leeds goalkeeper John Lukic and punched back into his own goal and the pressure didn't stop until Rangers were ahead. Once again it was a cross that Leeds couldn't deal with – this time by Trevor Steven – and Dave McPherson's header could only be parried into the path of the last man Leeds wanted to see. 'What about *that* wee strike, eh?' shouted a gleeful McCoist to McAllister as he struggled to make himself heard over the din of the crowd.

McPherson was rarely on the posters that would adorn young fans' walls but his contribution that season – so often at right-back as cover for the injured Gary

Stevens while Gough and Brown formed a more cohesive partnership in the middle – should not be understated. With the exception of Stevens, Smith had a full-strength side from which to choose that night, but that was a rarity with so many players dropping out for a handful of games at a time or simply, as in the case of Goram from March onwards, those who simply played through injury, his posterior knee ligament damage being so bad that he couldn't train. 'When you're injured, something inside you screams that you can't let the club down, to grit your teeth and keep going,' he wrote. 'You just find a way to cope. The ligament at the back of your knee is the one you can handle if it goes. I strapped it up, but it was agony after matches. It was twice its normal size for the rest of the week until the next match, but I got by.' The bill would be in the post at a later date for this season but no player wanted to miss too many games at a time. The big squad that Smith had, relative to others in Scotland, was a huge factor in being able to manage such a long season. At the end of it, the *Sunday Mail* produced their team of the season based on the star ratings for every league game. Not one player from the all-conquering Rangers side made it. Not only does it highlight the nonsense of match ratings or at least the *Mail's* decision to base the team of the year on cumulative points instead of averages, but it demonstrated that other clubs simply had to keep playing their best players whereas Smith could rotate enough.

Mark Hateley was one player who declared himself fit that night despite some achilles tendon problems but, as he failed to race away and finish a great chance near the end, it is doubtful if he was anywhere near fit in reality. The nervy applause at the end told its own story. A 2-1 win, and the loss of an away goal, might not be enough. It was shared by the English media. 'You can write off Rangers,' wrote John Sadler at *The Sun*. 'They had their chance at Ibrox.' Those famous Scottish Leeds United legends of the past, such as Billy Bremner, Peter Lorimer and Eddie Gray, speculated on just how many goals the Whites would win by in the return fixture. Ian St John finished his television coverage from Ibrox by saying, 'Well, let's hope for England's sake that Leeds do win.' The Rangers, players however, felt otherwise. 'In other circumstances, the normal circumstances surrounding a European tie, they might have been right in thinking that way,' wrote Richard Gough. 'But this was something else. This was different and even though we would not have any supporters with us for the second leg we knew that we could handle the atmosphere at Elland Road and we knew, too, that in an all-British context we could match Leeds. It was not the same as defending a single-goal lead in eastern Europe or in Italy or Spain or Germany. This was on our doorstep and we faced a team we knew inside out. They were not going to surprise us and tactically we knew exactly what we could expect from them.'

Not every English football writer was as dismissive. David Lacey, writing in *The Guardian* on Saturday, 24 October, was making the case for a British league, so taken was he by the drama that he watched play out at Ibrox, 'So far the Premier League has failed to capture the imagination of an English football public not fooled by a change of label and the accompanying hype. A Scottish breakaway league would probably be seen in a similar light. In a few seasons' time, when the bills for rebuilding stadiums come rolling in, clubs could well be searching for a fresh angle to stimulate interest.' He went on to say, with respect to Rangers, something a touch more prescient, 'Their domination of the Scottish League has become a ritual to the point where it may become enfeebling. Unlike Liverpool, Rangers have yet to reflect domestic omnipotence in their achievements abroad. A British League would arguably intensify competition and raise playing standards or at least allay their decline.' As time would tell, he may have had a point.

Four days after the defeat of Leeds, Rangers were in a cup final. 'This was a win which underlined the determination of these players of mine,' said Walter Smith and he could be justifiably proud of such an achievement after such a mental and physical battle so close before it. 'People say that Rangers are stronger and better, but I know we can always compete with them. On our day, I believe we can beat them,' said the Aberdeen captain Alex McLeish during the build-up, in tones more commonly associated with a small underdog talking about the big day rather than a side who believed that it was truly a contest of two equals. It was, however, a more accurate portrayal of the new reality. At the time of writing, there has never been a League Cup Final featuring the two sides since that day as the light in the north faded over the course of the decade. It was also fitting as it was the tenth and final time that Skol would sponsor the competition, and only Hibs the previous season had got their hands on the trophy ahead of Rangers and Aberdeen, with the two playing out some of the most dramatic and enjoyable finals in its long history.

The 1992 version failed to reach the earlier heights and the scoreline – a 2-1 Rangers win after extra time courtesy of an own goal by Gary Smith from a wicked David Robertson cross – doesn't really tell the story of the game. 'Only the last quarter of an hour that Aberdeen worried us seriously,' Walter Smith would later reflect. This came after an equaliser from Duncan Shearer on 62 minutes but Rangers should have been further in front than they were after such a bright and dominant first half, playing on the momentum generated by the win over Leeds. Ian Ferguson rattled the post two minutes before his midfield partner Stuart McCall opened the scoring and it was a goal that spoke to another revolutionary moment in this 'Year Zero' of modern football: the introduction of the back-pass law. It was a FIFA technical report on the Republic of Ireland's 0-0 draw with Egypt at the 1990 World Cup, where the ball was found to be in Pat Bonner's hands for six whole minutes, which finally led to such a significant change in the laws of the game. Mayhem ensued throughout Britain early in this season as goalkeepers who weren't comfortable with the ball at their feet suddenly realised that their chosen profession had changed overnight. After 15 minutes, Theo Snelders suddenly realised that he could not pick up Brian Grant's heavily weighted pass – under pressure from the surging run of Durrant – and he panicked, weakly chesting the ball back out into play where McCall reacted quicker than anyone else. Even when Aberdeen sent the game into extra time and with the loss of Gough and Steven – the injury doubts that were realised during the game – it was still Rangers who were making the better chances and, incredibly, looked to be the fitter side as they toyed with their opposition after going back in front. All three major Scottish prizes now rested in the Ibrox trophy room and the mission to ensure that stayed the same come May by completing the clean sweep in a season was becoming the only remaining domestic interest.

Perhaps the league game at home to Motherwell on Halloween where Smith chose to rest Gough, Steven, Hateley and Durrant was seen as something of a breather in the middle of such an intense fixture list and the performance in the first half an hour was very much in keeping with that complacency. It took an Ian Angus goal to wake Rangers up and they got stuck into the recovery task immediately. The award of a penalty for a foul by Rob McKinnon's tackle on Huistra may have been generous – it looked as if it was just outside the box – and McCoist's second was scrambled home on the goal line, but the second half was much more like it. John Brown added a third with a volley and McCoist finished a ten-pass move – the final four of which were with just one touch – to score his fifth and final hat-trick of the season. It was a genuine contender for Rangers' goal of the season as fans travelled home that Saturday evening. By the end of the Wednesday night that followed, it would be in third place.

For the first four days of November, there was only one thing that anyone associated with British sport was talking about as Rangers prepared to make the short journey south to Yorkshire. In retrospect there is something hollow about the confident assurances that Leeds put out there on the Monday and Tuesday of that week. Big words but ignoring the data that was telling anyone cool enough to read it what was likely to happen. Behind in the contest and having only kept one clean sheet in the 16 games played so far, Howard Wilkinson's pre-match utterances had more than a bit of the British stiff-upper-lip refusal to look reality square in the face, 'It's no secret we have been conceding goals this season and it is a problem, but we will certainly score against Rangers and we will win the tie.' His counterpart was more relaxed and comfortable to let his side do the talking on the pitch, with Gough, Hateley and Durrant back – Steven would miss out. It was Smith's captain that spoke the most and perhaps lobbed up a question for the Leeds dressing room, 'I think it looks as though we will have to get a goal to go through and I would love to see how they would handle it if we were to score very early as they did against us at Ibrox.' Gough would get his wish.

It had all the components of the typical British goal but not necessarily in the right order as the diminutive Ian Durrant provided the flick on by winning the aerial duel with Chris Fairclough for the imposing Hateley to thunder a left-footed shot high into the Leeds net. Two minutes had passed and Rangers had cancelled out the away-goal advantage that many had presumed would be the base from which the English side would lead their inevitable assault. The attacks would come in their numbers – Cantona had a great chance even before Hateley's early goal – but nothing materialised in the way that it had for Rangers at Ibrox, that early response being so psychologically important.

'No game will ever sum up the Gough–Brown partnership better than the second Battle of Britain against Leeds United at Elland Road,' Goram wrote. 'They murdered us, and they had one chance after another, but Gough and Brown threw themselves in front of everything. They were immense. It was a great team display, but I don't think the result would have been achieved with any other central-defensive combination. It had to be those two. They were inspirational.' He was being kind. The folk memory of this match is exactly as the Rangers goalkeeper describes however, upon review, it was he who was the difference as the Leeds attack, especially Cantona, constantly found space behind a Rangers defence that was lacking fitness but overflowing with will. Goram was world-class that evening and season. The best in Britain – even ahead of Peter Schmeichel who, despite a successful summer, was still having the odd difficulty for Manchester United – and perhaps even on a par with Sebastiáno Rossi at AC Milan.

One intricate Leeds attempt was broken down by the Rangers defence in the second half, when John Brown robbed the ball from the feet of Cantona, and one of the greatest Rangers goals got under way. An exchange between Hateley and Durrant left the Englishman rampaging down the left flank on the break, taking the ball and two Leeds players with him. This left Chris Whyte in no man's land when Hateley bypassed them all by delivering a sumptuous cross for McCoist, loitering at the back post, to head home. For all the power of Hateley's opener, nothing that happened in either leg could match the beauty of this perfect counterattacking goal. Voted by fans as the fourth greatest Rangers goal in the *Heart and Hand* poll of 2018, the only thing more mesmerising is the fact that McCoist wasn't broken in half when Dale Gordon came rushing in to celebrate when he was already on his knees.

'Brian, this is just sad,' said Ron Atkinson on co-commentary for ITV. 'Rangers are just playing with Leeds now.' All the confident English assurances before the match had disintegrated. Even some Leeds fans could do nothing but applaud a Rangers performance that was less nervy than a fortnight before and had better players, in better form, at the furthest ends of the park. Cantona finally beat Goram in the dying stages but it was a solitary piece of consolation. Not so much for The Goalie, who had stuck £50 on 2-0 at 20/1 and saw £1,000 disappear through his fingers but, even when he was moaning about it in the dressing room after, he had clearly forgotten the bonus money each player was due for getting through. 'I was still ranting on about this amidst all the celebrations, and Ally just turned to me and said, "We've just won £25,000-a-man in bonuses, Goalie. Will you shut the fuck up about the bookies?"'[17] Alex Ferguson had joined them there, singing and drinking with the players. Presumably having forgiven Smith for poaching his assistant manager Archie Knox, he was never one to let a Scottish win in England go untouched, especially as it would weaken one of his title rivals.

---

17   Accounts vary as to what the figure was. The press reported it to be £20,000. Stuart McCall writes that it was £12,000. Either way, it was substantial for a one-off ties in 1992.

The players headed to Manchester where they persuaded a nightclub owner to stay open all night so they could celebrate properly with each other and some fans who they knew and had made the trip down. The squad returned to the hotel around 6am where there were still Rangers fans up and enjoying themselves. 'There were bodies everywhere, most clutching bottles of champagne in their sleep. It was a bomb site,' recalled Leeds-born Stuart McCall. 'We were due up in a couple of hours so I just took a bottle of champagne and headed for the foyer to take it all in.' Walter Smith arrived down for breakfast and immediately admonished McCall and others for still being on their session. There was a game in 48 hours, of course. 'I told him not to worry, it was only Celtic,' wrote McCall. 'He turned, grinned and said, "Make sure you finish the champers then!"'

There's a famous story of Ferguson popping his head into the home dressing room at Old Trafford to deliver a very quick team talk to his Manchester United side ahead of their match with Spurs. 'Lads, it's Tottenham!' It was all that was required. There is something of that in the attitude shown towards the Saturday after Elland Road. A trip to Parkhead was normally one of the biggest games of the season. A week of intense focus and preparation. Still sweating champagne, Rangers did what they expected to do. McCoist turned provider with a clever header across the six-yard box for Ian Durrant to poke home and Goram was outstanding as usual when required. Rangers were effectively six points clear of Hearts and Aberdeen on Saturday, 7 November, eight ahead of Celtic. Only twice since the arrival of Graeme Souness had Rangers been ahead at the same stage of the season and one of those was only on goal difference. This was starting to be a different league.

On the way to Parkhead that afternoon as Rangers and Celtic traffic passed each other on the roads, one Celtic fan showed his appreciation of the Rangers supporters' bus by 'mooning' through the rear window. Three Rangers fans removed some £20 notes from their pockets and waved them in response. There was no comeback. Celtic, and the rest of the league, were now afterthoughts and also-rans.

As the draw for the first UEFA Champions League was made in Geneva on Friday, 6 November, Rangers were looking to the stars.

* * *

There was nothing new about the November weather in Glasgow as it poured incessantly. There was so much new about that night's match at Ibrox, however. A competition with a new name and branding, even its own Handel-inspired theme music. The logo was eight stars in the shape of a ball, each of them representing the final eight clubs in Europe's top competition. The first eight clubs to walk on to this particular stage. European football in April was guaranteed and Rangers would earn just under £5m, a not insignificant sum when the overdraft was now over £10m. This was where the ambition and speculative investment had been leading and Rangers had been at the heart of making it happen.

Such sums of money were down to a new centralised approach to marketing and media revenue, before the clubs could keep hold of any gate receipts – most of which would be offered as a three-match package deal to ensure it was all up front, lest any of the loyal faithful lose their appetite for dead rubbers in the spring. 'One of the best things that happened in European football was central marketing,' Campbell Ogilvie told me. 'It was a triangular relationship between the club, sponsors and television all working together and that was the whole ethos. Previously you did your own television deal and your own advertising. It was all fragmented. There was a game in Willie Waddell's time as general manager – I think it might have been Cologne in 1982 – where there was a television strike in London so the signal went down. I had to go in 30 minutes before kick-off and tell him that there was no way of televising the match. I got dog's abuse even though I couldn't do anything about the signal going down. We lost £60,000 that night. During the drive home, my wife said that while she was in the Blue Room before the game, she heard some poor guy getting a hard time from Mr Waddell. It was me!'

That kind of arrangement was by now a distant memory. Ogilvie continued, 'The Champions League had this partnership concept. New boards went up around the ground but the police were standing and walking in front of them. The guy from UEFA was going bananas because they were walking in front of all this new advertising. It was difficult for clubs at the beginning because they had their own contracts and this was a new way of doing things but it soon settled down when the revenue came in from the centralised sponsorship fund. Everything was new and fresh, even the music. In the early days the marketing team wanted to change the music just to freshen it up. I had to plead with them not to change it. It was already iconic.'

Rangers weren't just the only British club left in Europe's premier competition – they were the only British club left in any European competition at all. Celtic, Hearts and Sheffield Wednesday were all comfortably dismissed from the UEFA Cup and, on the same night that his old club were enjoying one of its most famous victories at Elland Road, Graeme Souness's Liverpool were turned over comfortably by Spartak Moscow at Anfield. The unseeded group stage draw could have been worse. The media reaction – both in Scotland and in England – now felt that Rangers had a chance of reaching their first European final since 1972, due mainly to the fact that they were not paired with AC Milan, the most imperious side in European football. Added to that was the bonus of avoiding PSV Eindhoven and Romário. It was still a tall order though as summer guests Marseille were due a return alongside Belgian champions Club Brugge and the shock story of the second round, CSKA Moscow, who had sensationally beaten the European Cup holders Barcelona in the Camp Nou when they overturned a two-goal deficit in the space of 17 minutes of football.

Despite the talent within the Marseille dressing room, it was not a happy place by the middle of November. The European Cup was by then an obsession for Bernard Tapie and the crushing disappointment after their defeat to Red Star

Belgrade in the 1991 final was still felt. They had lost some degree of control, such as the increasingly violent form of Basile Boli – although not in the form of league titles where their run of success matched Rangers perfectly – and concern was rising that this indiscipline and disorder would continue to scupper yet another assault on the big prize. A significant reason for that instability could be traced to the increasingly erratic and desperate Tapie. A deal for Diego Maradona in the summer couldn't be done but even then, by 1992 he wouldn't have been a serious difference-maker.[18] On the eve of their trip to Strasbourg in the league, Tapie acted and removed Jean Fernandez. In his place went the club's director of sport, the wily 71-year-old Belgian Raymond Goethals, who managed to guide them to a 2-2 draw despite being down to ten men after 39 minutes. So the French champions did not arrive in a wet Glasgow as the all-conquering juggernauts that they would soon be painted as. Tapie also knew exactly what kind of challenge they would face on the night and the course of the four-month campaign. 'We can reach the final again,' he said shortly after the draw. 'Our only problem is the Glasgow team.'

Walter Smith had his own problems. Rangers had finally stopped winning – just the 1-1 draw at Tynecastle the weekend before – and injuries and suspensions were really starting to bite. With Ian Ferguson suspended and Ally McCoist picking up a knock against Hearts, Smith gambled on the fitness of Richard Gough even though he was nowhere near ready for a challenge of that magnitude. His bench highlighted his problems with availability and tournament eligibility as it included three youngsters – Steven Pressley, Gary McSwegan and Neil Murray – plus reserve goalkeeper Ally Maxwell and, having to be registered especially, the reserve team coach Davie Dodds. Smith's programme notes for the night are intriguing and enlightening, 'My ambitions for Rangers must lead there. The experiences gained this time will help next time around.' On the first night of a new competition, it seemed to strongly suggest that they were delighted to be there but that this season was perhaps too soon for this side.

The common mythology of the game – that Rangers were pulverised on to the ropes for 75 minutes before finding the superhuman strength to come back to do the impossible – is mostly true but it ignores the fact that the early stages were relatively even and Rangers, through Alexei Mikhailichenko, had the best chance of the first half. Gradually, however, the visitors made the bog of a playing surface look immaterial as they moved the ball with speed and purpose. When Gough misjudged a header from a long ball and immediately chased down Rudi Völler alongside John Brown in order to atone for it, he left Alen Bokšić unmarked from the return pass to coolly sweep Marseille in front. When he had to give in to nature at half-time, his young replacement Pressley was desperately unlucky at the start of the second half when his interception got stuck in the mud and Völler

---

18   A deal was closer to bring him from Napoli in the summer of 1989 but the Italian club – and some local entanglements – ensured that it didn't go ahead. Maradona would go on to win another Scudetto the following season.

tapped home the easiest goal of his career. Trailing 2-0 in under an hour, many inside Ibrox wondered if playing six of these kinds of games was worth the hassle and the hype.

Smith's decision to remove Steven for McSwegan with only 15 minutes left to go worked a treat because it brought Durrant back into the midfield where he could be more influential against Franck Sauzée and Didier Deschamps. It was he who picked the ball up from deep and started the move that led to McSwegan's looping header – his first touch in European football – sailing over the despairing reach of a young Fabien Barthez. Rangers were transformed, so much so that supporters were treated to a rare sighting of a Mikhailichenko track-back-and-tackle which brought about the opportunity for Hateley inside the six-yard box, which he was never going to pass up. Bedlam. The match raged on for the remaining seven minutes, with Marseille showing true character in not digging in to see out the storm but taking the initiative and pinning Rangers back. Given the circumstances, it was never going to be an aesthetic classic but it was in the sporting sense. The first night of the Champions League had provided exactly what the clubs and UEFA had gambled on neutral audiences throughout the continent demanding: compelling entertainment.

'I have been enjoying this season but the thing which annoys me most is my scoring rate,' reflected Ian Ferguson the day before the first away fixture of the group. 'I have scored only two so far this season, and I should have had more. I've been getting shots on target, but I've been killing people in the stands and hitting photographers.' Matchday two saw Rangers face CSKA but not, given that it was in the middle of December, in the freezing cold of Moscow. The original plan was to play the fixture in Santander, northern Spain, but eventually they settled on the small town of Bochum in Germany, outside Dusseldorf. In later years, CSKA may not have been allowed to participate at all in this competition. In the week before the opening round they had to take out a front-page advert and apologise for their complicity in domestic match-fixing in recent years. Former coach Pavel Sadyrin, who had left to take over the national team, said, 'When I was coach with CSKA matches were fixed. The outcome was known before the first whistle. This is the team of the military. Some of the players still held ranks there and could do anything they wanted. Money was offered to these players and they could not resist the temptation.' UEFA never blinked but it would not be the last time that they were tested in such a way.

Walter Smith's aim of three points out of the first four – only two were awarded for a win in the competition rather than the more common three – was achieved with a 1-0 victory. It was Ferguson who scored early in the first half – by way of a deflection after the CSKA goalkeeper Aleksandr Guteev went missing at a corner[19] – and Rangers were eventually worthy of full points with the second-half showing but the initial moments were shambolic, with David Robertson having

19   Guteev was hastily drafted in when CSKA sold their first-choice and captain, Dmitri Kharine to Chelsea

to scramble the ball clear off the line in the opening minute.[20] Nervy starts to Champions League away games would be a theme but no damage was done in Germany, much to the delight of the 6,000 Rangers fans who were in attendance, a figure helped by the British Army bases nearby.

In the other group, AC Milan had started with the predictable full house and even then their players were thinking ahead to the final in Munich. The captain Franco Baresi said that the start was 'expected', 'We are a team which has everything and I am certain we will be in the final. When the European Cup began, Rangers were not one of the fancied teams and I have been surprised by their results. Now, though, I believe we will play them in the final. Club Brugge and the Russians are not good enough to win their group and Olympic Marseille are not as strong as before. Rangers would pose problems. When Italy played Scotland last month I found their style of play hard to handle and so did my team-mates. We have the final in sight now but we do not have the European Cup in our grasp despite what so many people are saying. Rangers will be a threat to us.'

This assessment wasn't at all fanciful at the time. The *World Soccer* awards for 1992 placed Rangers as the fifth-best team in the world that year, ahead of Brazil, Argentina, Germany and the Netherlands. Only Denmark, AC Milan, Barcelona and São Paulo were more admired. Walter Smith was voted the seventh-best manager in the world and Ally McCoist was also seventh in the World Player of the Year award, behind Ronald Koeman, Brian Laudrup, Thomas Hässler, Peter Schmeichel, Dennis Bergkamp and Marco van Basten. With the excitement of Europe parked until March, Rangers could focus on managing the domestic challenge over the winter as opposed to going on a full assault as they had to do in previous years. Rangers treaded water from December to March with two draws with Hearts and Airdrie coming close to the opening European ties and three more draws to Airdrie again and Dundee United and St Johnstone at home before it picked back up again. None affected the position of comfort at the top of the table, despite the optimistic noises from Pittodrie and Parkhead that were banking on the continental exertions catching up with the champions.

Injuries refused to subside with Gough missing the trip to Bochum and the return of Gary Stevens being marred by a dreadful tackle by Paul Jack in the 0-0 draw with Airdrie on 1 December that set him back significantly. He would never return to be the same player. When some Ibrox pipes burst before the visit of Dundee United in December and snow hit the north-east later in the month, Rangers were given the mixed blessing of a welcome breather but the prospect of fixture congestion later in a busy season.[21] The postponement of the Aberdeen trip which was scheduled for Wednesday, 16 December was timely given the amount of players that were either out or would have been playing on with injury.

---

20   Trevor Steven started the match at right-back such were the constraints in defence.

21   Rangers had to withdraw from the Tennent's Sixes tournament as the season was simply too congested.

When it was finally played – on Wednesday, 2 February – it was the game that finally killed off any serious conversation about Rangers being dragged into a title race. January had seen Rangers open up a little with some fun and entertaining victories, including a 3-2 success over Dundee United at Ibrox and 4-3 against Hibs at Easter Road, with Hateley and McCoist grabbing five of the seven goals. Neither scored in the new year victory over Celtic at Ibrox, with McCoist sidelined through injury again. Although he was known to be a doubt, only the Rangers dressing room knew for sure, and many lumped on Trevor Steven – whom Smith planned to push forward in his place – to score the opening goal at 16/1. He duly did with a beautiful cushioned header, not unlike his league-winning goal at Tannadice in 1990, after 33 minutes. It would be the only goal of the game as Celtic had all the possession but none of the edge, a narrative that would be well-worn by the decade's end. Rangers were dreadful but, as Richard Gough commented afterwards, there was just a firm belief that they would do what was necessary, 'It's sort of like a rolling stone thing and we are not going to be easily stopped.'

It was the same scoreline in Aberdeen and much the same pattern of play but Rangers were far from dreadful, simply happy to absorb the pressure and strike at the right moment. Aberdeen gave their last throw of the dice all the power they had but it wasn't enough. There was a very late scare when an Eoin Jess shot squeezed through Goram's legs but was smothered on the line by both his backside and then his grateful hands. Goram had been excellent all evening but it was the real Grampian tormentor, Hateley, who struck again with an exquisitely powerful header in the second half. Seven points clear, 33 games undefeated in all competitions, both Smith and Willie Miller refused to concede or expect anything publicly, but no one believed the cliches. The league was over.

So too were the plans for the Scottish Super League, which were scuppered by Celtic's withdrawal from the group of ten to work within the existing Scottish Football League structure to find solutions to the game's problems. The response was bitter as Ian Donald, vice-chairman of Aberdeen, articulated the following day, 'I can't believe Celtic have done this. I feel shellshocked. Celtic have now lost all credibility. At all our Super League board meetings Celtic's Kevin Kelly was telling us his club were in full agreement and committed to the cause. Yet, as one of the five founder members of the SSL they didn't even have the courtesy to do business in a proper manner and we have to find out about their actions only through telephone calls from the press. If this is how they conduct business then they deserve all the criticism they get. I couldn't trust them again, any of them. If Celtic want to become the champions of the first and second division clubs then let them go and play there.'

The SFL's plan was for a 14-12-12 league structure with the Premier Division splitting into A and B after teams had played each other twice (26 games). Following a winter break, Premier Division A would restart on *zero* points and effectively a ten-match day mini league would decide the title. The remaining nine rebel clubs blocked that particular vote but it was over for the breakaway model of control and four leagues of ten was introduced as a compromise for the 1994/95 season. As much as the financial incentive to have greater control over footballing revenue may have been to a struggling club, the need for temporary accommodation while they fixed their stadium may well have been a more pressing concern, not to mention the attraction of being in a smaller springtime fight for the title. Within 18 months, Celtic would get the use of Hampden for a season.

At one stage the next Champions League match in Belgium was due to be played behind closed doors due to the behaviour of the Brugge fans in Marseille. In retrospect, that may have been ideal as the UEFA backtrack allowed for a ferocious atmosphere inside the creaking Olympic Stadium on 3 March. Without Gough, Stevens, Steven, Ferguson and Gordon and with Durrant only making the bench, Rangers were left reeling in the opening stages as Amokachi and Booy both failed to connect with the goal open to them, Hateley heading one off the line and then van der Elst rattling Goram's crossbar. This was all inside the first 15 minutes. Rangers would find their breath and responded in turn, with McCoist hitting the bar. It was Mikhailichenko's nervous clearance that eventually led to the deadlock being broken when Tomasz Dziubinski drilled the ball home. Rangers were superb in the second half however, and created enough chances to win the match. All but one were spurned as Pieter Huistra thumped the ball high into the net to salvage a point. What felt like a disappointment on the night was quickly changed when news filtered through that Marseille – missing Boli, Casoni and Völler – had also drawn 1-1 with CSKA in Berlin. No ground was lost and that rolling stone momentum continued.

Upon reflection it was arguably the most costly night of the season. The opportunities were there to grab a win when Marseille didn't and the pain was starting to take its toll. Goram wouldn't do a day's training that season after his clash with Amokachi left his knee ligament damaged and even the 1-1 draw in Perth the following midweek felt like a struggle with McCoist coming to the domestic rescue once again. The return fixture a fortnight later would be a night cast into both legend and intrigue.

It was back in November, as Mark Hateley relaxed in his room at the Moathouse Hotel the night before a league encounter, that he received a string of calls from a French caller informing him that if he didn't play in the two Marseille games he would be handsomely rewarded. In a 2011 STV documentary on the 1992/93 season, Hateley said that it was not an agent he knew but that 'another agent had given him the number'. According to Hateley in his 2021 book, he was persistent despite him constantly hanging up until he eventually told him to 'fuck off' and thought little more of it. He would eventually tell Walter Smith about the calls at half-time during the Brugge match at Ibrox, by which time he had been sent off.

'There was absolutely nothing in the incident, and that aroused my suspicions that there had been some sort of intervention, and left me with a nasty feeling that the referee had been got at,' wrote Hateley nearly 30 years later. Smith and Knox had to be restrained as they headed down the tunnel. Speaking immediately afterwards, Smith said, 'I thought that both players went for the ball, but I was disappointed by the way the Belgian took the option to feign injury.' Even years later Smith was confused by the whole incident, 'I couldn't work out why Hateley was sent off. I still can't.'

Of all the suspicious incidents during 1992/93 that Rangers fans have clung to over the years, this one stands out more than any other. Hateley had been tangling with Rudi Cossey all night and, right before the break, the two met again as they tried to win a long ball in the air. As both watched on, Hateley landed his right elbow in Cossey's face. The Belgian defender then attempted to grab Hateley in a headlock to which the English forward responded by pushing him on to his back by applying pressure to Cossey's chin with his hand. As both Gary Mabbutt and Paul Gascoigne would testify, the use of elbows was not always punished in 1993[22] but that, and the push to the face, did give the Polish referee Ryszard Wójcik a decision to make by the letter of the law. Hateley would now miss the crucial match in France – a massive loss given his record against Marseille for both Rangers and Monaco – and the initial reaction from the support was that it was a costly overreaction from the official. Hateley's feeling that the referee had been 'got at' when he refused to be – a story that he left out of this 1994 book and that no other Rangers player included in any of their autobiographies before the 2011 documentary – may well have something in it but, as the initial media reaction correctly concluded at the time, he was incredibly foolish for allowing himself to get involved in such a needless incident.

The football that night, on yet another horrible evening in Govan, produced both the sublime and the ridiculous. The Rangers opener and the Brugge equaliser either side of the interval were brilliant examples of passing, movement and finishing. Trevor Steven's pass that split the Belgians open for Durrant to run on to, control with one touch and finish beautifully, is one of the most underrated moments of the whole season. The goal itself would be better remembered if it had not been for what came later in this match and the next tie. When Lorenzo Staelens levelled with an intelligent bit of play – and Marseille were winning heavily at home to CSKA – the situation looked bleak. Not for the first, or last, time that didn't appear to matter to Rangers. 'It might be the biggest fluke in Europe this season, but who cares?' said Alan Parry on ITV as Ibrox was sent into lift-off once more from the unlikeliest of sources.

A man famous for being willing to play anywhere for Rangers, Scott Nisbet had to fill in at right-back at times that season and that was where he popped up as Trevor Steven's cross hit the back of Stuart McCall and spun up in the air. Quite what Nisbet intended wasn't entirely clear but his shape and effort, as a Brugge defender lunged towards him on the edge of the box, was too strong for another attempted cross. He was most probably trying a speculative effort on goal – and

---

22   Both suffered fractured skulls from such challenges.

that was exactly what happened. Later that year Shane Warne would produce cricket's 'Ball of the Century' when he bamboozled Mike Gatting with some wicked leg spin at Old Trafford, and Nisbet's reverse action, aided significantly by a massive deflection, caused the same amount of bewilderment for Dany Verlinden in the Brugge goal as the spin off the penalty area bounce left him stranded and mortified. Nisbet's joy was pure as he headed towards the bench to celebrate. All around the ground, fans did what football fans do: they saw greater meaning in the ridiculous. 'Our name is on the cup!' they claimed. Regardless of the situation, this team just kept finding ways to defy the odds. It felt unstoppable.

But stopped it would be and in possibly the worst fixture imaginable. 'No Limits' by the Belgian/Dutch dance act 2 Unlimited had become an apt anthem among the Rangers support since its popular release in the January. As they made their way into an over-crowded and dilapidated Parkhead on 20 March the last word was changed to 'trophies' as their bitter rivals were reminded who held everything and who hadn't won a pot for four years. It was the Celtic fans, if just on this afternoon, who went home happiest as their side ran out deserved 2-1 winners against a ragged and exhausted Rangers side with the usual litany of missing players and Ally McCoist only on the bench because of numbers, despite him suffering from food poisoning. Tragically, after 30 minutes, he would need to come on to replace the injured Scott Nisbet. Three days after celebrating one of the most iconic goals in Rangers' history, he suffered a serious pelvic injury and would never play for the club again.

After 44 games without defeat, one of the greatest Rangers sides of all time had finally been overcome. It made no difference to the league title race – they still finished the day seven points clear – but that momentum had been curbed, as did the feeling of invincibility and manifest destiny. That game at Parkhead was the 50th match that Rangers had played over the season and it was not yet April. With players either dropping down or playing through barriers that they shouldn't have been, this campaign of endurance was starting to take its toll.

Many were keen to speculate that the Rangers dream machine was finally running out of spare parts.

* * *

There were potentially 15 games left for Rangers in this marathon season but in all reality, even at a stretch, there were only five that really needed full attention and three of those took place within eight days. Such was the level of comfort at the top of the league, Walter Smith's men simply had to keep walking in a straight line until they were eventually presented with the championship trophy. However, to make absolutely sure that they weren't drawn into anything tricky, a defeat of Aberdeen at Ibrox on Tuesday 30 March would do the job. It was 2-0 on the night as Rangers' strength wore away any sense of resistance. The best goal of the night came from Ian Ferguson, a player who was finally able to show his true level of consistency through the season, playing ten more matches than he had ever managed to do previously for Rangers. McCoist grabbed the second and was nearly hit by a golf ball from the Aberdeen end for his trouble but a nine-point gap, with only two for a win and eight games to play, meant that Smith could now focus all his attention on the knockout action.

Down at Turnberry, on the Ayrshire coast, as the Rangers players took well-deserved time out, Smith spoke with the footballing press and, for the first time, was comfortable in talking about the 'treble', 'After such a long run of games it would be nice to finish with the treble. To everybody here it would mean a great deal. All big clubs have historical backgrounds and people remember treble-winners from different eras. If the 1992/93 team could be remembered that way, it would be a big thing for all of us.' Hearts stood in the way of the final as the two met at Parkhead on 3 April[23] and with 20 minutes remaining, that treble dream was at its most fragile. Allan Preston had given Hearts a deserved lead in the second half when he found plenty of space between Gough and McPherson to head home a John Robertson cross from close range. Trying to do just enough and no more – with a bigger game on the horizon – Rangers were punished and looked a touch listless. But, similar to the Leeds game at Ibrox, a mixture of luck and sheer courage would change the script, although familiar actors played the key roles. If the Hearts defence put in as much effort defending Trevor Steven's corner as they did protesting it – it shouldn't have been a corner at all as McCoist's shot narrowly missed any deflection – they might have headed towards the final. Dave McPherson had two chances in the Hearts box, one from his head and the second with his right boot as he scrambled Rangers back on terms. Five minutes later that man McCoist would score the winner when he showed awareness and bravery in equal amounts as he lobbed the ball over his former team-mate Nicky Walker, before being flattened and unable to take the acclaim. It was his 49th goal of the season and his 88th for Rangers in 15 months. His next goal would be back at Parkhead in a cup final. An overhead kick winner no less. All that would be far in the future. That evening, if not the weeks before, the attention was all on that trip to Provence.

It was the biggest Rangers game in 21 years, the club's 160th European tie, and only 1,000 fans were able to get a ticket due to Marseille's intransigence. They wanted the Stade Vélodrome to be the biggest cauldron of noise and colour that they could possibly create as they planned to blow Rangers away as quickly as possible, with Van Halen's 'Jump' used as a final rallying cry. It was effectively a Champions League semi-final and Tapie had been demonstrating his typical calm assurance in the build-up by placing the brilliant playmaker Abedi Pele on the transfer list and boasting to the world about who was likely to be brought in during the summer. His need for control would only grow as the evening progressed.

---

23   Parkhead and Tynecastle were used as the semi-final venues as Hampden was being renovated.

His team did a fine job of establishing that in the early parts of the game. Yet again away from home in this group stage Rangers looked nervous and went behind to a goal that had many defensive culprits but for which, David Robertson took the blame for his poor clearance that Sauzée intercepted and later finished. Yet again, Rangers didn't crumble but instead played their way back into the game, although the more direct route was relatively pointless *sans* Mark Hateley. On 30 minutes they created a golden chance for the golden boot after some brilliant work by Huistra and Durrant but McCoist blazed over the bar. Such an opportunity, coupled with a good penalty shout when Gough was bundled over in the box by Boli was enough for Tapie to try and intervene at the break.

Tapie walked into the office of the Dutch referee Mario van der Ende and asked him if he 'could do anything' for them. It was at this point that he was firmly ordered out of the room by Van der Ende and this commotion was spotted by Gary McSwegan, one of the Rangers substitutes, making his way back inside. 'Fortunately I spoke French,' Van der Ende said in James Dixon's excellent book *The Fix*. 'In my opinion, this was very inappropriate for a club president.' Indeed it was. This was a blatant attempt to begin a conversation about bribery – not a hidden envelope stuffed with French francs in a garden – and it was known to both the UEFA delegate and doping officer, as well as Rangers officials at the time. Tapie went straight from that changing room to his own side's, not to send reassurances to a team with one foot in the final but to berate them, to call some of them unfit to wear the shirt and to actually intervene in the tactical plan by demanding that they adopted a more direct, long-ball plan. Goethals invited Tapie to sack him there and then. It was the madness of the megalomaniac. This was a side that contained the experience of Völler, three players in the peak of their careers in Boli, Sauzée and Bokšić, and three who would go on to define the decade in Didier Deschamps, Marcel Desailly and Fabien Barthez. It was also a side playing its 40th game of the season against a weaker team playing its 54th. It should not have required his input outside of signing cheques for legitimate purposes.

Despite the mayhem around them, the Marseille players restarted with renewed enthusiasm and when Sauzée smashed Goram's crossbar with a free kick, it felt like that it would be more of the same. This was Rangers though and it should have come as no surprise to anyone that the comeback kids would be back in the match soon enough. It was a fabulous equaliser in the end. Trevor Steven, for whom this game should have been made, swung in a pretty average corner that was headed away by Jocelyn Angloma but only as far as the onrushing, unmarked Ian Durrant just inside the box. He met it perfectly. The French camera angle in line with the 18-yard box, which would become *de rigueur* at the World Cup five years later, showed it in its finest light. The definition of power and precision, through a packed penalty area with the outside of his right foot, it left Barthez without a prayer. It was also a fitting scorer of such an important goal, who nearly missed the match due to injury, as he recalled, 'I had staples in my shinbone from an op, but had shaken one off and needed a painkilling injection. The ache in my leg was constant, it was giving me real grief. But I talked Walter into playing me, begged him to let me take the jab. In the morning I only had a 30 percent chance but the needle worked. I was set on playing and I made it.' This was the real comeback season of Durrant's career. That remarkable unbeaten run was started by his goal against Celtic back in August and his goal the following week against Aberdeen sparked the kind of performance level needed to sustain and here he was, on the stage that he may well have been playing on a permanent basis had he not been assaulted, keeping his side on track for the ultimate glory.

Goethals seemed more shaken in the immediate aftermath of the 1-1 draw than he had been before when he suggested that the upper hand was now with Rangers. Beforehand he had said that 'a draw will be enough for us against Rangers', seemingly very sure about his club's chances in the final match in Belgium. Deschamps was a little more honest, 'We believed we were superior in every aspect to the Scots, but events have proved we were too confident. Rangers will be lifted enormously by their spirited performance for their last tie against CSKA Moscow, while we must overcome our disappointment before a far more difficult test against Club Brugge. Pressure is growing all the time to become the first French team to win a European trophy. Our batteries need recharging after such a demanding game against Rangers who, even if they do not reach the final, have proved they are one of Europe's top clubs.' The bookmakers tended to agree. Rangers – at home to the bottom side in the group – were placed as marginal favourites to be in the first Champions League Final.[24]

With the league all but secured bar a massive swing in goal difference, the momentum kept moving towards that final night at Ibrox on Wednesday, 21 April. There was a tension infused with the excitement that evening, more in keeping with the Leeds game than the previous two group matches. It really did come down to this, with one ear on events in Brugge. Rangers got off to a rip-roaring start with Richard Gough powering a header straight at Plotkinov in the second minute. As soon as the crowd had settled there was an eerie silence as the news no one wanted but everyone feared, slowly came through from Belgium. A dreadful pass out of defence allowed Marseille to spring and when Bokšić was released through on goal, he made absolutely no mistake. The news of an equaliser never materialised but then, neither did a Rangers goal with McCoist missing three huge chances and Steven and Brown going exceptionally close later on. As the referee's whistle pierced the air as well as the dreams, the tears flowed along with the blood and the sweat. It was a heartbreaking night at Ibrox for anyone who believed in sporting destiny. Marseille would go on to win that final against Milan, with Basile Boli making the difference by ensuring a half-fit Marco van Basten never found his rhythm – it would be a selection that would haunt Fabio Capello – and the glancing header which secured the trophy.

---

24   It was not known as this at the time but retrospectively applied. In 1992/93, the Champions League only applied to the group stage and the 1993 final was just the European Cup Final with no marketing logos or special ball. It was the following season that it lasted from the groups to the Final and hasn't changed since.

As Marseille celebrated, there were some developments in Paris that would soil this team and this season for some time. The French champions were going for their fifth title in succession as well as their first European trophy and that denouement was causing Tapie some stress. Ahead of Paris Saint-Germain, but only slightly, they would play the capital side following the final and would go to Valenciennes the weekend before, a team who were fighting relegation. Getting involved in that kind of struggle only days before the biggest match in their history wasn't ideal so Marseille made moves. Valenciennes had a couple of ex-Nantes players (Christophe Robert and the man who scored the winning goal of the 1986 World Cup Final, Jorge Burruchaga) and Marseille had one – Jean-Jacques Eydelie – who had done a sterling job on Gianluigi Lentini during the final. He was told to sound out his former team-mates if they would be open to going easy so that Marseille could rest some players and enjoy a quieter game as a whole. A reward of 250,000 Francs was on offer. Even though it would likely send their side down, Robert and Burruchaga agreed, although the latter claimed that he changed his mind and tried as normal. Eydelie also approached a player with whom he had played at Tours, Jacques Glassman. He was not so amenable and eventually blew the whistle, starting a chain reaction that would leave Marseille stripped of their championship, relegated and consigned to disgrace, while Tapie was sent to prison.

But what of the Champions League title? Contrary to popular wisdom and many Rangers books on the era, Marseille were never stripped of their crown, despite the growing suspicion and outright allegations of similar behaviour in the 1992/93 Champions League. There have been four main areas of interest that have exercised Rangers fans ever since the truth began to unravel over *L'affaire VA-OM* and James Dixon makes a strong argument as to why each allegation was, ultimately, somewhat insignificant. Firstly there was the claim, made initially by the CSKA manager Gennadi Kostylev[25] – and suggested contemporaneously on Radio Clyde by Davie Provan – that they had been approached to lose the return fixture in the Vélodrome following the tight 1-1 draw between the two sides in Berlin two weeks previously. This, however, was Marseille's easiest game of the group, one which they were always likely to win (the size of score was not relevant to qualification given the head-to-head rules) and would it not have been more likely and rational, to fix the tricky away tie with some key players missing? Secondly there is the claim made by Mark Hateley that the Polish referee in the home tie with Brugge accepted the kind of offer that he rejected, and sent him off unfairly. Again, this is a tough one to argue given the incident itself. Thirdly, that the CSKA players were 'incentivised' by Marseille to give their all at Ibrox but that was normal practice on the continent at time – it is not match-fixing, it is literally doing what any side is supposed to do; try really hard – and anyway, the most glaring Rangers chances that night were off-target, not kept out by a goalkeeper on a mission. Finally, as was alleged by the Romanian national coach of the time, Cornel Dinu, in

---

25   He later recanted, as did others whom Tapie leaned upon to do so.

his 2019 autobiography, that he acted as an intermediary between Marseille and the Romanian referee in the Brugge v Marseille tie, not to yellow card Boli, who would then miss the final. He also claimed that Tapie had told him that thanks to Goethals, 'I took all the necessary measures to prevent the Belgians from causing us trouble.' Goethals had been found guilty of match-fixing while coach of Standard Liège and had worked with the Brugge coach Hugo Broos while at Anderlecht together. The Marseille goal is a comedy affair that would alert any modern-day investigators but Dixon was at pains to point out that Brugge were trying in that match up until the final whistle, creating many chances. The finishing of those chances however, is perhaps more in question. Crucially, even if an equaliser was found, it was Rangers who didn't hold up their end of the bargain that evening.

One important issue with such a focus on the efficacy and rationale behind these claims – Tapie was hardly a model of cool and composed decision-making that season – is that it misses the question of intent. As with Hateley's phone call and Tapie's intervention in the referee's room against Rangers, that action was bad enough. Finding a motive for such intervention doesn't matter nor does the result. As Eydelie wrote in his autobiography, 'Cheating had become second nature. We were all solicited at one time or another to make a call to a former team-mate or a friend.' It is almost inconceivable that there were no illegal approaches or agreements during Marseille's European triumph but at the time, neither UEFA nor Rangers decided to pursue it then or later, once the truth about the domestic situation was clear. UEFA had no appetite to go back into that when the Brugge allegation was made in 1995 alongside an attempt to fix the win over AEK Athens in 1989 and the European Cup semi-final first leg away to Spartak Moscow where Tapie had paid over two million francs for 'television rights' but which was later admitted by those involved to bribe the Spartak players. Tapie was said to have handed a note to a journalist before the game with instructions to only open it after the final whistle. It simply read 3-1, which of course, was the nature of the Marseille win.[26] In truth, Marseille shouldn't have even been in the 1992/93 competition.

Rangers officials knew about Tapie's visit to the referee's room but didn't feel they had the sufficient evidence with which to move it further. Perhaps if they had at least lodged the concern, they would have found out the exact verbatim of the conversation but it really wasn't in the nature of the club to complain to officialdom about anything. A 'dignified silence' – except when they had a manager who got up early each morning just to practice being confrontational – was the general policy when sensing that something might not quite be cricket. Also, this is the elite group that Rangers wanted to join. They wanted to be mixing with these clubs and owners for the rest of the decade, shaping football from the inner circle. Being a whistleblower was not going to aid that ambition. It took Hateley nearly 20 years to talk about his story and Dinu nearly 30. It was a time where this behaviour was more accepted from

---

26   There is much more detail and insight into the extent of the Tapie regime in Dixon's book which is strongly recommended.

certain parts of the continent. Marseille themselves would point to a very dubious goal from Benfica that stopped them facing Milan in the 1990 European Cup Final as justification for fighting fire with fire and indeed the Milanese themselves, on the final day of Serie A – the weekend following their disappointment in Munich – were involved in something similar. Needing just a point to clinch the title, they did exactly that courtesy of a 1-1 draw with Brescia. It was an extremely passive game for a title-clincher and when Demetrio Albertini scored, with just eight minutes on the clock, there was an incredible equaliser just a minute later when both Paolo Maldini and Franco Baresi seemed to be playing in slow motion. A point for Brescia would keep them up and, in turn, relegate one of Milan's great rivals Fiorentina. Joe Jordan, on co-commentary duty for Channel 4's *Football Italia*, called it out immediately, 'Milan have let them score there. Baresi didn't seem bothered.' A new footballing era it may have been but old habits die hard. As Dixon excellently summarised in his book, 'A week either side of the Champions League Final both its participants had been involved in fixing matches. One was punished, one was not.' The full scale of the one who was punished will never be truly known but part of it is still felt by a generation of Rangers supporters to this day.

Rangers still had trophies to tidy up and ensure that it remained a season that would be tough to match. However, they would have to do so without the golden boy. As Scotland's World Cup qualification went from being merely inauspicious to an outright disaster in Lisbon, where they were hammered 5-0 by the Portuguese, Ally McCoist suffered a broken leg. On target for an incredible 60 goals that season, the form of his life was suddenly over. McCoist would be back and would continue to pop up with memorable goals in big games for club and country, but he would never get close to reaching these heights again. A Rangers player who would be centring his focus on club only was Richard Gough. At the end of May, after tensions in the relationship between himself and Andy Roxburgh simmering for years following an altercation on the plane home following a defeat where Gough wanted to read a book instead of joining in with Roxburgh's party games, things finally gave way when the manager chose to play up the stand-in performance of Brian Irvine against Estonia in a way that seemed to snub the Scotland and Rangers captain. Enough was enough – under the current management at any rate – and after 61 caps Gough had played his last game for his country. The split – after a season where Gough missed so much football so as to prioritise Rangers – said something about the increasing tension between the nation's biggest club and itself.

At Broomfield, Airdrie, on Saturday, 1 May – ten days after the heartbreak against CSKA – Rangers won their fifth league championship in a row. It was McCoist's young deputy Gary McSwegan – one of a youthful quartet including Neil Murray, Steven Pressley and David Hagen who played 58 games that season between them – who grabbed the only goal with a nice controlled lob. It was a record that brought Rangers in line with those standard-setting days from the Bill Struth era, when his side managed five in succession between 1927 and 1931. It was now that the media started to look ahead to other records, more specifically Celtic's nine from the late 1960s and early 1970s. It was once widely accepted that Scottish football would never see such a run again but now, just over the potential halfway mark, such was the feeling around the chasm that had opened up between Rangers and the rest.

It left Smith and his team nearly an entire month effectively without competitive football until the Scottish Cup Final on 29 May. Rangers won two and lost two of their remaining league matches but the 1-0 defeat up at Pittodrie was not a portent of things to come. At Parkhead on a warm late spring afternoon, Rangers won the cup in the first half through sheer power more than anything else. Neil Murray scored the first, via a deflection, but it was a fair return for a debut season that generated a lot of optimism. Unsurprisingly it was Hateley who got the second through a blend of clever passing between Huistra and Durrant and a sheer force of will as he bore down on Theo Snelders with the ball falling to his left foot. It was as if the Aberdeen goalkeeper was a hologram as the ball simply travelled through him at great speed. The celebrations of the players, right on half-time, said it all. It was done. There was a late scare when a Lee Richardson goal brought Aberdeen back – and any thoughts about what Rangers could have done to AC Milan should be tempered by the energy levels on display in the later stages of that game – but the day, and the season, belonged to Rangers. 'We couldn't let them down,' said a tired Gough on the field as the Rangers fans basked in the sunshine of a treble win at the home of their great rivals. 'There was no way we were losing today's game.'

It belonged to Smith as well. Arriving on the scene as the assistant, he was thrown into the big job in difficult circumstances and stood there, wearing the now famous navy blue cardigan, as a winner of six out of the seven domestic trophies available to him and had taken his side as far as they had ever been in Europe's big competition. As speculation mounted around the future of his predecessor, after a torrid season at Anfield, it was Smith who was guiding Rangers to new heights and making the job look very easy.

Just how far could he go? That clear blue sky seemed to be the limit.

* * *

There have been better footballing Rangers sides than this one. There are arguably two better in this entire era. But there was never a Rangers team as loved. Incredibly successful and with no shortage of quality moments, it was the grit and spirit that endeared them most to a generation of fans who prided that more than anything else and where the youngest weren't quite totally seduced by what they saw on *Football Italia* or thought they knew it all because they had guided Northampton Town to Premier League glory on *Championship Manager*. In the current perspective, where the lives of footballers have long been seen as being beyond the reach of the paying public, here was a group of players who seemed to enjoy this success as the support would do if they had the talent. They worked hard, they played hard and they knew all the words. There was a connection with the ordinary fan that has arguably never been as strong since.

Winning all four in 1992/93 was an unlikely dream rather than an impossible one. Given the margins involved, one more goal in Belgium or in France, could have seen Rangers in the final and we shall never know the levels that they could have summoned for one last push against a Milan side who were strangely put together on the night. It really did feel possible for the thousands who were on that journey. An exciting dream but still a tangible destiny. It was only made possible by that team bond, without which those comebacks would not be possible nor would the willingness to suffer the mental and physical pain for one another. 'The team that drinks together, wins together,' the captain would famously say. Team spirit in both senses of the word.

Instead, the impossible dream was the hope and expectation that such a season created for the future. Unlike the two other comparable modern-day equivalent campaigns – in 2007/08 under Walter Smith's second spell of guidance, where they reached the UEFA Cup Final in Manchester only to lose to Zenit Saint Petersburg, and then the penalty heartbreak in the 2021 Europa League Final – this did not feel like a one-off to many. The supporters knew that Smith's second bite at it was one of those runs, never to be repeated. It *had* to happen that night. In 1993, it felt like this is where the club was supposed to be. Where it had been promised by Souness and then Murray. It was part of the plan.

The problem with the approach that created this romantic adventure was that it could only ever be short-term. The heroes were broken – literally in McCoist's case – and many would have to be repaired or rested in the coming season. More long-term, the team bonding approach to success was never going to last the race against an increasingly professional sport. Again, the necessary Scottish identity of the Rangers side would become more at odds with the continental standard.

No one was listening to that in the summer of 1993, however. After what that season brought, it understandably felt that the good old-fashioned British pluck could compete with the very best. After all, the cup winners couldn't beat Rangers. This side had nudged the door to the promised land ajar. This season was very close. Next time it would be closer.

No one could have anticipated that very soon the same door was about to be slammed shut.

Chapter Two

Lads

'We ended up once on a three-day bender in Glasgow with Gazza and the Rangers football team. We hired a boat to go to an island in Loch Lomond, and I remember waking up in a forest at five o'clock in the morning with Sara Cox and Trevor Steven all huddled together in a ball of human flesh because it was so cold.'
Will MacDonald, television producer

'I was looking for some action. But all I found was cigarettes and alcohol.'
Noel Gallagher

Covent Garden. The cultural heart of London's West End. It is late on a Friday night and people are spilling out on to the streets. Opera-goers have been thrilled by a new production of Verdi's *Aida* while lovers of ballet were enraptured by Darcey Bussell in *Sleeping Beauty*. There's another kind of dance going on now, however. A busker has struck lucky as £20 notes continue to fall into his hat as long as he continues playing the requests on his clarinet. Like a human jukebox, he provides the soundtrack to a large conga dancing its way around him. It is headed by none other than Walter Smith, leading his staff and players as they let their hair down during a particularly stressful part of the season. In the morning, those up quickly enough grab what's left of Ally McCoist's eight tickets to the Five Nations rugby union clash in Cardiff between Wales and Scotland. The instructions from the assistant manager Archie Knox back in the capital are clear: get to the pub first thing. Some make it back that evening, others straggle back in the morning, vowing never to touch alcohol again. Davie Dodds still has his ginger 'See You Jimmy' hat on. 'Some place that, Dublin,' he said upon his arrival.

Rangers were tensing up – a surprise home defeat to Hearts had created a bit of a wobble – and Smith knew what his boys needed. It worked. The two games after their trip were away to Aberdeen and Hibs and both were won as Rangers got back into a groove that would take them to the championship, their eighth in succession. 'The team that drinks together, wins together,' Richard Gough famously said. It is a quote that many players feel was unfairly overused. 'If we were smashed as many times as we're supposed to have been we'd have been too blitzed to pick up the trophies,' wrote Ian Durrant once he had left Ibrox. 'But there is truth in what Goughie says. We used those times together to sort out any backbiting or problems that there were and emerged as a TEAM.' Stuart McCall wrote that Smith 'had a great feel for when to take us out of the limelight', adding, 'It brought us together and I will always believe that the way the manager came out with us and could be one of the lads was a masterstroke rather than a mistake.'

Greater resources and better players will be the decisive factor in winning football matches more often than not, but there is no doubt that there are still those crucial moments – especially away from home or when hit by important injuries – where champions need more than that. The spirit that Smith and Knox created within the Rangers dressing room – helped in no small part by the consumption of spirits – powered that side on to wins that would have passed quieter teams by. McCoist, in Neil Drysdale's book *Silversmith*, said that Smith 'fostered a shared purpose among all the guys, he knew when to shout and when to crack a joke, and it was brilliant going into the ground every morning and knowing that we were all joining forces again. Nothing beats it. Nothing. That sensation of waking up on Saturdays and getting myself psyched up for three o'clock – and the banter, the ribbing and the wind-ups which are part and parcel of the daily training routines – and then hearing the mighty roar when you step out of the dressing room. At Rangers, under Walter, everybody was pulling in the one direction, and you forge bonds which are never broken when you live like that with a group of people for any length of time.' It was the X-factor that kept a group of winners hungry for more but it was the necessary trade-off that created one of the biggest discussions of the era.

A couple of pages before McCall's account of the weekend in London, he recounts the aftermath of a Champions League mauling by Juventus, 'It showed just how far away from the best we really were. We were not good enough, that was the realisation.' No dots, however, appeared to be drawn between the two stories nor was there evidence of much self-reflection within the dressing room at the time about whether Ajax or Milan players were also upside down in kebab shops during the business end of the season. Later McCall relays a similar team day out at the races in the April of the following year, 'Not surprisingly none of the foreign lads were among the dozen or so out that day, which says a lot about the different attitudes there are.' No analysis, no questions about who is right or wrong, the story just flows on to the next anecdote. These cultural differences seemingly accepted in much the same way as the weather. *It's like that here, you see.*

Such tensions would grow as the number of foreign players grew and, when that cohesion and 'one for all' spirit was called upon at the final hurdle, it wasn't quite what it once was.

Fans talked about it too. At the start of the 1994/95 season, after an enjoyable World Cup spectacle in the United States and the outlay of between five and six million pounds on two Champions League winners, 'Rantin' Robert Burns' wrote a satirical piece in the first of that season's editions of *Follow, Follow*. 'Fearing' that all of this technically sound and secure football he had been watching all summer could catch on at Ibrox, he said, 'These new players are going to be sending out the wrong signals to our potential stars of the future. The little blighters will be wanting the ball to their feet during games, and then afterwards, instead of heading off to Victoria's[27] or a close in Springboig according to choice, they'll be sitting in Caffe Qui drinking espresso and discussing existentialism and that would be a crime wouldn't it? If loads of the bevy and women was good enough for [Jim] Baxter then it should be good enough for these ponies, they'll regret it in later life when it all starts to catch up with them.' It was a piece that nicely summed up the tension in the middle of the 1990s as the pace of Rangers' modernisation slowed dramatically just as there was an explosion in professionalism and sports science on the continent. Signing top players is one thing, building a working environment that suits them is another, and it wouldn't be long into that season before that incompatibility for some was laid bare.

As the years went by and the gap between Scottish and European success was more and more evident, there was a realisation that 1993 had been the last chance rather than just the start of a brave new challenge. Winning the biggest prize was now something of a chimera and it was then that the vitriol on the dressing room culture started to rain down. The antics in the hotels and clubs after that victory at Elland Road – with just two days' preparation before a trip to Parkhead – became a cheeky part of a legend when it seemed that anything was possible and an example of inherent unprofessionalism when reality finally dawned.

For the Christmas of 1991, Ally McCoist was employed by Tennent's Caledonian Breweries to 'rap' on their drink-driving awareness campaign. An audio warning where McCoist adopted a mid-Atlantic brogue to spit lines such as 'Hello windscreen, meet my face!' was sent to radio stations, pubs and clubs in order to try and make an impact on a younger audience. Five years later, hours after Oasis had played on the banks of Loch Lomond, McCoist was stopped by a police patrol car at 4am after leaving the Glasgow nightclub Archaos, and was found to be over double the legal limit. McCoist, by then an MBE, blamed it on the foreign beers he had been drinking and didn't think he'd be in excess. Only the week before, he had poked fun with mock outrage at Aberdeen players who had been caught out on a pre-season tour, 'Their appalling behaviour has left me shocked and saddened that fellow professionals can behave in such a way.

---

27   Victoria's was a Glasgow nightclub and was the most notorious haunt frequented by footballers at the time.

Drinking binges on a pre-season tour. Late nights. Furious managers. Warnings and fines. It all sounds like the Dons are in pretty good shape to me.' It's how we do it here.

Andy Goram had already been banned for the same offence the year before and the bad behaviour extended into the private lives of players who were public property. Goram, Gordon Durie, Stuart McCall and that unlikely lothario Davie Dodds were all on the front pages for extra-marital reasons. And then there was the arrival of Paul Gascoigne and all that came with him, most pointedly the Channel 4 documentary that really opened up a can of worms in relation to Rangers' dressing-room culture.[28] Some fans, embarrassed by the fresh Champions League disgraces, suddenly found their Struthian[29] morality and took to the pulpit to condemn the players for living as they themselves did.

None of this was an exception in British football at the time of course, but if it wasn't Rangers leading the way then it was perhaps Arsenal. They had more flair under George Graham than they get credit for but the '1-0 to the Arsenal' tag stuck for good reason. A tough side who won titles in England and a European trophy between 1989 and 1994, they worked hard and played hard. The 'bonding sessions' known as the 'Tuesday Club' were infamous as they were regular but they enabled serious problems. Captain and leader Tony Adams would eventually confront his alcoholism as would midfielder Paul Merson – alongside a cocaine and gambling addiction – who once remarked that he was stunned when he heard that Ryan Giggs was eating his toast without butter so as to potentially make physical gains. For his team, the equivalent was reducing their intake by a couple of pints.

What happened next at Highbury, in late 1996, was effectively what was required at Ibrox years earlier. Arsène Wenger – a relatively unknown intellectual who was managing in Japan – changed Arsenal and in turn, British football. Alcohol, chocolate, chips, burgers, bacon rolls and sugar with tea were all banned. Boiled vegetables, fish and chicken – with no seasoning – were now in. There was resistance, doubt and some squad workarounds but his training methods quickly ensured buy-in from a group of players for whom it was a cultural revolution. A Premier League and FA Cup double was secured within two years and the other top-flight clubs had to move with the times. Ultimately it was a combination of players and manager but, while the influence of stars such as Dennis Bergkamp and Patrick Viera strictly adhering to the instructions was important, the direction had to come from the top. Foreign imports at Ibrox may well have refused to indulge in drinking sessions at the wrong time in a season and even questioned the

28   Even when the signing was first mooted, one contributor to the fanzine wrote, 'Paul Gascoigne I simply find hard to believe. With his knees and the relentless nature of the premier league how many games would Rangers get out of him. Quite apart from the thought of Gazza and Goram hitting Victorias in tandem. For that amount of money is he really worth the gamble?'

29   Bill Struth was the first legendary Rangers manager and set standards not just for success on the pitch but behaviour and deportment off it.

wisdom of it, but when some of those sessions were being led by the manager and when players were stopping in a cafe for a cup of sugary tea and a bacon roll on the walk to the training ground, there was little chance of their idea of professionalism taking off.

A drinking culture was no less accepted at British football clubs in 1990 than it was in British society as a whole. What the mid-1990s brought however, was another gear change entirely. Far from just being accepted as a grimy reality of British life, it was now celebrated. The era of the 'lad' had begun and football took centre stage, intertwined so closely with music, fashion and comedy. The first edition of the spectacularly successful 'lads' mag' *Loaded* described its purpose as 'dedicated to life, liberty and the pursuit of sex, drink, football and less serious matters'. Football, not long since a social pariah in British society, was now cool and an intrinsic part of 'Britpop', the explosion of exciting new British music, with Oasis in particular keen to wear their support of Manchester City so visibly on stage. Everyone now had to have a team, including those who wanted to become prime minister. Tony Blair professed a long-held love for Newcastle United and that he fondly remembered watching the hero of the 'Toon', Jackie Milburn, play. As Alwyn Turner pointed out in his excellent book on the 1990s, *Classless Society*, and others did in the pages of *Follow, Follow* at the time, Milburn had left Newcastle only a few weeks after Blair's fourth birthday. Blair was, like John Thomson's character in *The Fast Show*, a phoney, but it had to be done in order to stay in touch.[30]

The two most ubiquitous figures in British football during the period were arguably two stand-up comedians rather than players. David Baddiel and Frank Skinner would later be synonymous with 'Three Lions', the massive hit song they helped write for Euro '96, but it was in 1994 that they first sat down on a sofa in their mock-up studio flat for *Fantasy Football League*, which aired late on a Friday night on BBC2. Two blokes, enjoying some beers – ironically non-alcoholic for Skinner, who had been sober since 1986 – wearing replica shirts with jeans, talking about football and taking the piss.[31] *Lads, lads, lads!* Women were seemingly only part of the picture if they knew the offside law, were happy to get the pints in or where there was the possibility of sex at the end of it. 'Basically, when all's said and done,' joked Skinner in 1994, 'I'm just drawn to sluts with big tits.' A year later the Liverpool striker Robbie Fowler, by then the most exciting young English attacking talent around, was asked by a magazine about his 'type' of female partner and what chat-up lines he used. 'As long as they've got a fanny and breathe,' was

---

30   It sometimes wasn't enough for those who genuinely were fans. John Major really was a Chelsea supporter and once sent a note down to Chris Patten in a cabinet meeting asking if he would like to join him that Saturday. Patten sent it back asking who they were playing and received a curt response which said, 'If you don't know, you can't come.'

31   The extent of that humour was pushed to uncomfortably racist limits with their treatment of the misfiring Nottingham Forest striker Jason Lee, but only in retrospect. Baddiel apologised nearly 30 years later when it was retrospectively considered to be in bad taste but the contemporaneous reaction was to laugh along to 'He's got a pineapple on his head', to the Sunday School tune of 'He's got the whole world in his hands'.

his response to the former; 'Do you like jewellery? Well, suck my cock, it's a gem,' the latter. A world away from the courteous, PR-polished output today but deeply characteristic of this brash, hedonistic culture – where the lads were eventually joined by the ladettes – of which football was such a central part. Rangers – with some shine still left on their late-1980s Souness glamour, enhanced by capturing Britain's attention in 1992/93 and then signing the ultimate British footballing lad in Gascoigne – were a part of the chic. Robbie Williams came to watch and posed in the top and Chris Evans – drinking pal of Gazza – wore the Adidas-manufactured Rangers training kit, alongside his producer Will MacDonald, on the riotously popular Channel 4 show *TFI Friday*. Rangers were cool at a time where Britain was too, for the first time in 30 years. What serious chance then of its homegrown players with plenty of money in their pockets and mingling with rock stars, denying themselves a part of the zeitgeist and staying at home doing sit-ups? What weight did a few reactionary voices in a fanzine have when so much of the support were living that life and watching Rangers win trophies? So typical of the time, it was a great deal of fun in the moment when men were sold a fantasy that growing up was optional, but there was a price to pay eventually. British football had talent but, like lad culture made manifest even in the mainstream, such as BBC1's *Men Behaving Badly*, it was not full of serious people.

How different could it really have been? As further chapters will recount in detail, the optimism and pride felt by Rangers fans about their place in Europe in the summer of 1993 would be eroded by humiliation and disappointment. How much better could it have been was one of the main talking points of the decade. In terms of winning the Champions League, 1993 was the last opportunity for that. All things being equal, Rangers needed better technical talent and the UEFA limitations rendered the sufficient quantity an impossibility. If the Scottish Premier League breakaway had happened in the very early 1990s instead of 1998 then there is a chance that far greater marketing and buy-in from Sky would have been possible at a time where more clubs were performing at a better level and the Premier League hadn't yet taken off. Even riding on the coattails of that supernova would have generated revenue throughout the Scottish game at just the right time but it didn't happen, and a backwater status was ensured.

Still, things could have certainly been better. More consistent performances, tighter margins, perhaps qualification out of a group or two. The biggest factor within the control of Rangers to aid that was an appointment of a different manager when Graeme Souness left in 1991 or possibly in 1994 when the reality under Walter Smith first became apparent. This would have risked the pursuit of nine and ten however, and was simply not going to happen. Smith was bankable to at least equal the record such was his grip on the Scottish game. For all the angry talk that some fans gave about ambition and professionalism by 1995, any such move would have caused uproar. For all the idealistic talk about wanting Scottish players to adapt and show more technical assurance and flair, it was the foreign imports who were quickly criticised for not showing enough Scottish characteristics. In other words, if they didn't run around a lot, they were lazy and simply wouldn't do. A journalist writing in *Follow, Follow* under the pseudonym 'The Dowanhill Hack' penned a piece in the spring of 1996 when Rangers were linked with the Swedish winger Jesper Blomqvist, 'It now seems that any pretence towards the great European dream is being quietly dropped. If cut-price Scandinavians can keep us ahead of Celtic so be it. People are being asked to pay fancy prices for Falkirk and Caley Thistle while in Champions League terms they are being sold a pup. It's just not tolerable.'

The writer was correct – European ambition was by then all lip service – but it is doubtful as to whether the support were much different in reality, despite some loud proclamations. In an ideal, fantasy timeline, Graeme Souness would have realised at the end of 1989/90 – after the evisceration by Bayern Munich and his unwillingness to back technique over strength in the middle of the park – that he had reached the end of his revolution and it was time for someone to start a new one at Ibrox. A second phase of modernisation – Wengerian even – with further implementation of professional practices while the earlier Souness ones were still fresh enough and before the pull of domestic sequences became a factor and Rangers were caught in a never-ending bind of winning the league in a manner to which they were suited, in order to qualify for the Champions League for which they were not. We have to deal in reality, however, and Souness was never going to make that admission and nor were the club or support able to remove themselves from the tractor beam of settling history.

There's an old phrase used in Washington that is apt for those who were running and watching Rangers in the 1990s, 'All politics is local.' Yes, failures in foreign policy and wider ideology may create a lot of noise and protest but people only vote with their feet when their jobs and immediate community are impacted. Perhaps one conversation summed this up better than anything else, a perfect distillation of what was known and understood but also ultimately excused and forgiven. Walter Smith, so the story goes, was bemoaning one of these European nightmares the day after one of the more gruesome results when he was in conversation with prominent fan and businessman – and later Rangers director – John Gilligan. 'I don't care about Europe,' Gilligan told the manager. Somewhat taken aback, given the visceral reaction in the media, Smith asked why not? 'Because I don't work with AC Milan fans,' came the response.

Chapter Three

The Hangover

Season 1993/94

'£4m? That's an awful lot of money for a sub.'
Mark Hateley

*'Having a British spine made us tougher. But we were maybe not
as sophisticated football-wise; it was more direct.'*
David Murray

Even by his own standards, Jim White was excitable as he paced around the
Scotsport studio, still hours before it was time to go on air. 'We've got the
biggest story of the season,' he beamed gleefully. It was Sunday, 17 April 1994 and
most of those in attendance at Ibrox the day before would have to have taken a few
moments to guess what it might be. Admittedly the bar wasn't particularly high on
a relatively unremarkable season in Scottish football. The Duncan Ferguson thing?
Thousands who were there didn't think that there was anything in that! Not so,
when slowed down and zoomed in apparently. 'He's in big trouble.'

And so he would be. More trouble than could be dished out by the SFA at
Park Gardens, Glasgow. 18 months later, Ferguson would be sentenced to three
months in prison for his head-butt on Jock McStay at Ibrox that afternoon. By
the time he was sent down he was no longer even a Rangers player. It had been the
transfer that dominated the summer of 1993 and broke the record between two
British clubs. David Murray spoke about it as taking Rangers to the next level,
after going so close only a few months before, 'This is not necessarily the end of
the spending. We are the biggest club in Britain and people had better realise it.
There's no limit to our ambition.' There is a hint of self-aware insecurity about

'people had better realise it'. Rangers had beaten English competition for this signing and Murray made mention of having done so before, as if the landscape was the same when Terry Butcher and Trevor Steven had first arrived, which of course it no longer was. Regardless, this was another transfer coup and show of successful ambition. It would, however, turn into an abject failure.

When it came to Ferguson, Rangers were in a bind of their own creation, seemingly unable to possibly let the opportunity pass. In terms of profile he was almost perfect. Young, Scottish, talented and from a Rangers family, he was exactly the kind of player that the club felt they needed to sign. He was a difficult personality, sure – by that time Ferguson had one criminal conviction and another pending – but in Walter Smith, Rangers had one of the best man-managers in the business. The problem was that it was a transfer that needed to happen that summer, at a time when Rangers already had a player in Ferguson's mould, who was in the form of his life. Although aged 31 and with his next birthday fast approaching, Mark Hateley was hardly at retirement age and had just enjoyed a blistering two seasons. With Ally McCoist still recovering from a broken leg there was simply no way that Rangers were cutting their losses on the other half of their alchemic duo and resting all of their goalscoring responsibility on the shoulders of a 21-year-old with so much still to learn. Similar in style, the two couldn't play together. Similar in personality, neither would accept a season of apprenticeship and phased retirement.[32] It couldn't work and, with no hope of a Scottish rival meeting Dundee United's valuation, in hindsight it was perhaps one best left to the new English Premier League.

If Ferguson's season was something of a nightmare then he wasn't alone in a Rangers dressing room full of broken, bruised and exhausted heroes with understudies who were woefully inadequate. Hateley, however, responded with extraordinary power to have the season of his dreams. It may not have been the tall centre-forward who was billed to steal the show but, for Rangers' sake, it was just as well that one of them did.

* * *

The signs were ominous as soon as Ferguson arrived at Il Ciocco. On the team bus to an open-air disco for a night off during the strenuous efforts of pre-season, the newest arrival declared to a squad that had just been a couple of goals from immortality that he was there to take them 'to the next level'. According to the account given by Stewart Weir, a reporter based there with the *Evening Times*, to Alan Pattullo in his excellent book *In Search Of Duncan Ferguson*, this was not received with warmth. It was Durrant who took the first bite, 'You, you big skinny drip of water. You're only here so the big man can have a day off now and again,'

---

32   On a Scotland tour North America a 20-year-old Ferguson had told Pat Nevin – an experienced and skilful international and nearly 30 years of age – 'See you, son, when you get the ball, give it to people who can play.' This was not a character likely to be a passive learner for a year or so.

Ferguson hit back with his scoring record at Dundee United. It was Durrant again with the volleyed return, 'You've won fuck all apart from your BP Youth Shield and Forfarshire Cup – I could play keepie-uppie in a telephone box with a beach ball and you wid'nae get a kick at it.' The new boy's final effort was to say that it was more Dundee United who didn't win anything, not him. This time it was Davie Dodds who very forcibly finished the rally, 'Dundee United never won anything? Dundee United never won anything? I've got two League Cup medals and a Scottish championship medal, and I played in a European Cup semi-final. And Dundee United never won anything? It's because of the likes of you that Dundee United haven't won anything!' It made little in sense in reality but a point was made nonetheless as the bus roared with laughter. In Weir's opinion, an early tone had been set, 'Given how Ferguson had been put in his place, it was clear to me that the Rangers squad were far from convinced they needed him.'

Weir was also a first-hand witness to the effect it had on Mark Hateley as the two forwards tried to out-do one another in a training exercise involving some passing work in midfield and then connecting with a cross. Ferguson copied Hateley nearly every step of the way until he failed to make contact at all with a poor cross. An early victory for the incumbent. According to Stuart McCall, as soon as they arrived back in Glasgow, Hateley, who he said was genuinely stunned when the news of the signing came through to their Tuscan base, changed his training number from 14 to ten, the latter having been earmarked for Ferguson. 'You could tell there was an edge between them. Mark was just determined to keep that shirt. Mark felt he still had some good years left in him and picked up the gauntlet,' wrote McCall.

The chase for Ferguson's signature had hardly been a quiet one. Rangers had been fined £5,000 in the January of 1993 for attempting to make an 'illegal approach'[33] with both Gough and Murray being very public in their intentions. Indeed, it is said that the player was whisked to Ibrox by both Gough and McCoist after Scotland duty to be shown around, even to the extent to where he would sit in the dressing room. With memories of 1986 and the tussle over Richard Gough still vivid, Jim McClean – now no longer manager but still chairman – and Dundee United were clear that they were not interested in selling to Rangers. Ironically, the race really stepped up after one night at Ibrox, where Ferguson was excellent for Scotland in a friendly against Germany. The world champions won 1-0 but the legend of 'Big Dunc' was born when he attempted an audacious acrobatic effort at the Broomloan Road end. Starting the move with instant chest control and spraying it out wide to the left, he made his run to the far edge of the box where his first time overhead kick was executed perfectly. Legend is the correct word to use because, years later, even the official SFA account of Ferguson's international career – as well as a

---

33   The act of 'tapping up' or in other words, the act of offering a job opportunity to another adult, must be one of the most draconian offences in football.

thousand folk memories – records the effort crashing off the crossbar when, in fact, it was superbly saved by Andreas Köpke. Ferguson's performance that night – in a rather fetching salmon Scotland shirt – took the discussion from a local wrangle between two rival clubs and into a wider market.

Bayern Munich were said to be keen as well as interest from England. In the end, Leeds United made a deal for £3.25m which, it was understood, included an agreement not to ever sell the player to Rangers. Indeed, by 3 July, they were confident that they had a deal in place with Ferguson too when they released a statement saying, 'Ferguson is happy and ready to sign and there will be a press conference on Monday. After five weeks of talking, it looked as if the deal would be called off, but the player is now ready to join us.' Even by midday they had realised that they were premature. McLean and Dundee United had been trying everything to push Ferguson to Yorkshire, but ultimately he wouldn't budge. He only wanted one move and his current employers were forced to face the reality. The reality for Rangers was paying a premium – the likes of which Souness initially refused to do – of £500,000 more than the fee agreed with Leeds, plus another £250,000 if he played 150 times for the club.[34] One suspects that Murray was only happy to do so in order to break the British record – technically this deal was worth £4m and therefore more than the other big British signing that summer, Roy Keane's £3.75m move from Nottingham Forest to Manchester United – and McLean could offer up a big kitty to his new manager, the Croatian coach Ivan Golac. Around £700,000 of that fee was used to sign Gordan Petrić.

Ferguson's big introduction was delayed – appropriately as it would turn out – by a hamstring niggle, a hangover from an injury suffered at the end of the previous season. Rangers' hangover was by then being fully felt. On 4 June Andy Goram underwent surgery in Los Angeles for an injury that had stopped him training since March. Finally it had to be fixed and the appropriate rest allowed. The quality of his replacement, Ally Maxwell, would be a consistent issue throughout the season and how Goram dealt with the lay-off ensured that the SFWA Footballer of the Year and SPFA Players' Player of the Year in the summer of 1993 would find himself in a very different situation the following year. With Goram and McCoist out for the start of the season, it meant that the third member of that exceptional trident, Hateley, would be relied upon heavily. Even those who had made small but memorable contributions to that Champions League campaign would never play for Rangers again. Scott Nisbet's groin injury at Parkhead had started to spread to his hip and three specialists advised an early end to a career – at just 25 years old – in order to prevent longer-term damage. The man who started the heroics, Gary McSwegan, was sold to Notts County – then in England's second tier – for £400,000 on 26 June and Dale Gordon joined West Ham for £750,000

---

34   The initial Rangers offer was £2.5m. The extra payments were structured accordingly: £100,000 after 50 games, another £100,000 after 100 games and the final £50,000 once Ferguson reached 150 appearances.

a fortnight later as Rangers prepared the way for a new forward and brought in over £1m to help finance it.[35]

Another notable absence in the summer of 1993 was Richard Gough but this time it was in relation to Scotland and was entirely through choice rather than enforced by injury. On 1 June, Gough declared his international career over as long as Andy Roxburgh remained in charge of the side. The final straw was comments made by Roxburgh about Gough's replacement, Brian Irvine, after a World Cup qualifier win over Estonia. Gough had pulled out of that squad after a mammoth season with Rangers and a Scottish Cup Final coming up on the following weekend. Roxburgh said, 'Brian Irvine is really impressing me and he has a great will to play for us. Who knows which players will come in and make themselves indispensable. Irvine is so dependable and last night he was starting to order people about during the game and I thought, "This guy is really settling into this." Young players need reliable, steady influences around them and Irvine is like a rock.' Encouraging comments for a young debutant perhaps but not for a 28-year-old with no great international future ahead of him.[36] No, it was a pointed reference – to Gough in particular – about footballing priorities and, once the treble had been completed, Gough made his decision.

It had been a decision long in the making. Gough wasn't impressed by the methods of either Roxburgh or Craig Brown, after working with Jock Stein and Alex Ferguson in the Scotland setup – Roxburgh's name was a joke to Graeme Souness for example – and this antipathy never softened. He had no time for Roxburgh's card games on a long flight to Saudi Arabia, was exasperated by Brown's obsession over deportment rather than coaching[37], enraged at Roxburgh's misleading use of the press in relation to his injury at Italia '90 and a European Championship qualifier against Switzerland, frustrated at players being played out of position so that the manager's favourites could remain and finally there was the infamous night in Lisbon where Scotland were hammered 5-0 by Portugal and Roxburgh's team was set up to play against a side without their key man, Rui Barros, whom Craig Brown was reliably informed by a local taxi driver would miss the match. Ultimately the Rangers captain viewed the national set up as something well beneath what he was used to at Ibrox. The tension between Rangers and Scotland, one that had been brewing since the revolution, was entering a new phase.

If pre-seasons can foretell the pattern of the coming campaign then the on-field performance of 1993 was something of a clunky bellwether. Rangers were outclassed by Kevin Keegan's Newcastle United at Ibrox for Ally McCoist's testimonial, Hateley scoring in a 2-1 defeat, and he had been on the scoresheet when Rangers met Sunderland at Roker Park the week before. The result on the

---

35   Fraser Wishart would come in on a free transfer to provide cover at right-back given Nisbet's loss and the delayed return of Gary Stevens.

36   He would play five more times for Scotland.

37   Brown would paint the tape on player's socks so that they matched the colour of their kit.

park was a 3-1 win but the fan violence off it was what made the headlines, leading to a furious response by Murray in the aftermath. Thirty-five arrests were made and three people suffered knife wounds in the first 'friendly' visit to England in seven years. 'This will not be tolerated by a club which has worked so hard to improve its image on the international stage and the image of Scottish football in general,' said the Rangers chairman. 'It is not on and, as soon as we identify those who have been arrested and charged, they will be informed by the club that they are no longer welcome at Ibrox or at any other stadium where Rangers are playing. It is not a subject for debate, it is final.'

* * *

'Certainly, we would not accept the Champions Cup if Olympique [Marseille] is stripped of it. If allegations against the French team are proven, then we would ask UEFA to repeat the Cup final, this time against Rangers. It would be a fair solution.'

So said Silvio Berlusconi on 1 July in an appeal to UEFA to take decisive action as the fallout from the Marseille scandal continued apace. In reality it was never quick enough. The decision to prevent Marseille from defending their trophy was only taken at the 11th hour, with AS Monaco taking their place in the competition when Paris Saint-Germain refused on commercial grounds. They were never stripped of their title and a play-off never took place but it didn't stop a brief summer of dreaming what might be. Quite what an injury-ravaged Rangers would do to a Milan side who would go on to win the Champions League in some style is questionable but it was still an argument from the old season that raged just as the new one commenced.

If talk of a Munich replay was just an attempt to keep the exciting spirit of 1992/93 alive, then hopes of adventure were dampened by Walter Smith before a competitive ball had even been kicked. 'It is vital that I do everything to ensure that this club's success continues,' Smith said on the eve of the opening game at Ibrox against Hearts. 'Everything has become muddled with winning the treble, but I don't think everyone really believes we will do so again, as though it is automatic … I can't say to you that the entertainment level of the team's performances will improve this season. I might want that to be the case, but the Premier Division won't make it possible. Having to play 65 games plus international matches demands too much of the best players and the best teams, and although there will be good matches, some great goals and moments of excitement, I can't say Rangers will be more entertaining to watch this time around. You see, brilliance needs a fresh mind and Scottish football, the way it has been developed, dulls the brain.'

It was not exactly inspiring stuff but typically honest in terms of the reality of another 44-game league season that would be punctuated with great but brief moments and perhaps an exercise in managing expectations given that Smith could only top the previous campaign by getting to the Champions League Final, an incredibly tall order in itself. The comment about a 'fresh mind' is intriguing. Smith had been Rangers manager for just over two years and had lifted six trophies. What more was there to re-invent in an attritional slog where he knew he held the overwhelming stockpile of firepower? For much of the following two years, and perhaps beyond, this pre-season comment would be most apposite.

The tone for the season was set by an opening-day win that saw very little in the way of good football, another casualty to add to the list – this time Stuart McCall – and a Mark Hateley goal that made the difference in a 2-1 win. Even the nature of Hateley's goal had a sense of poetry to it that summed up the battle that Rangers faced. 'That was pure anger, that header,' Hateley told me. 'Craig Levein literally tried to break my leg on the halfway line ten minutes before. For the next ten minutes I could not wait to put the ball in the net or break him in half. That was the only thing that was going through my head. The header that day, I wasn't even looking to head the ball, I was looking to smash Levein. He ducked out the way and the ball hit me on the head.'

There wasn't much more rhythm to be found in Perth the following Saturday where Rangers yet again scraped to a 2-1 win, with Richard Gough having to atone for a defensive error that gave St Johnstone an early lead by crashing in a header before Ian Ferguson scrambled home a second-half winner. Naturally, he was soon carried off with an injury but not one that ruled him out of the first trip to Parkhead seven days later. A match where his namesake also made a long-awaited appearance.

Considering his lack of competitive action, Duncan Ferguson was very bright in his Rangers debut, testing Pat Bonner from outside the box on two occasions but it was a match where both defences smothered any creativity in a 0-0 draw, although it is debatable how much variation in Rangers' play was expected with both Ferguson and Hateley leading the line. With newly promoted Kilmarnock coming to Ibrox the following weekend, the conditions were ripe for the new boy to get off and running. 'I fancy Rangers to win by a few today and for Ferguson to open his account,' said Derek Johnstone – a man who knows the importance of getting a goal early in your Rangers career – on Radio Clyde before the game.

Ferguson couldn't have gone much closer. A first-half shot fizzed just wide and then he nearly opened the scoring early in the second but his left-footed effort hit the far post. Perhaps the anxiety about Ferguson getting off the mark transferred to others but yet again Rangers were poor and this time, sensationally, they were punished. Tommy Burns's side were value for their 2-1 win, where they were ahead twice with a Stephen Pressley header sandwiched in the middle. It was surely a proud moment for the young defender at the time but few outside of his family remember it due to his late error when he dithered on the ball in his own corner, lost possession and Kilmarnock snatched a winner through a face from Rangers' past in Bobby Williamson. If Ferguson's effort had been inches to the left then history may well have been so much different with the big signing off and running, perhaps adding a second as Rangers strolled to a comfortable victory.

However, as seductive as sliding doors are, it was never likely to be a smooth process. On the Monday morning after the Kilmarnock defeat, Ferguson was convicted of assault for the third time, following an incident in an Anstruther hotel in November, with the sentencing scheduled for the middle of September. A record signing facing a spell in prison and a 19-month unbeaten record at home shattered all before August was over. It was clear that this was going to be a very different season for Rangers, fine margins or not.

* * *

'It was a sad summer and we must ask ourselves if this is only the tip of the iceberg.' Dark clouds hung over the continent as well as Govan as the UEFA president Lennart Johansson addressed the media at the first draw for the new season's competitions. Match-fixing at Marseille, Warsaw and Łódź as well as a fraud investigation hanging over Dynamo Kiev made for some pretty grim weather around Bern, where UEFA were based. 'I am still convinced that these were exceptions but one never knows. There are a lot of rumours and so much money is involved in the game that certain people forget the difference between good and bad. We must be more careful how clubs are governed,' said Johansson. Nevertheless, he declared the inaugural Champions League a success as the central funding pot made sure all football associations were handed at least £220,000 from the extravaganza, adding, 'I very much respect the major clubs for accepting the rules of the Champions League. If they had run their own affairs they would have made more money from television and advertising. This provided us with the means to help restore the balance between the rich and poor. I am absolutely certain that, if we do not continue this assistance, a crisis will arise and this must be prevented.' Earlier in his speech, however, Johansson had lamented the rejection of his plans to combine the Champions League and UEFA Cup into one bigger league structure with three qualifying rounds and then four groups of four teams providing the quarter-finalists, thus drawing three or four clubs from certain leagues into the one competition. 'Many people within the game are anxious to know how the future will look. I can accept that my original idea is only in the fridge waiting to be taken out at the right moment, for the working party will reach the same conclusion as I did,' he said. Ultimately they would. In 1994 the competition would use the four groups to decide the last eight, with only one qualifier, and in 1997 the Champions League began the admission of clubs who hadn't won their national title. The door was now fully open to something that looked more like a European Super League but would blow Johansson's 'balance between rich and poor' out of the water.

The draw brought both good news and bad for Rangers when they were pitted against the Bulgarian champions Levski Sofia, whose last entry into Europe's premier competition had been five years earlier, when AC Milan hammered them

7-2 on aggregate. The more concerning outcome was that Rangers were unlikely to be seeded if and when they eased through to the next, and crucial, qualifying round. With a seeding of nine, they were one outside where they needed to be but a potential opportunity was opened up when Marseille were finally prevented from defending their crown on 7 September.[38] 'We would be very disappointed if we got through our first round to discover that another team had overtaken us into the top eight seeds,' said club secretary Campbell Ogilvie at the time, with the prospect of Paris Saint-Germain taking their place, with a lower coefficient than Rangers. It was all, in the end, entirely academic.

'I would be loath to put him into a game like this without any match practice,' said Walter Smith about Stuart McCall, two days before the first leg at Ibrox on 15 September. McCall, after all, had just undergone a hernia operation less than a month before. Not only would he play, he would captain the side as the musical chairs in the Ibrox treatment room showed no signs of stopping with Richard Gough being the latest with another muscle injury, this time the groin. Sky were there to cover the game, with Andy Gray providing viewers with a tour of the stadium where he both used to play and stand. Some fans decided to watch in his company rather than go to the game as a slightly sparse Ibrox welcomed Rangers back into European action after the heroics of the previous season. Saving their money for the more glamorous games to come perhaps.

Levski's scout Ivan Tichanski – his full title was head of international dept and public relations – had been unimpressed when he watched Rangers snatch a late draw at Dens Park ten days before but admitted that he expected the Scottish champions to 'show a different face' when their tie came around. It wouldn't be far removed. Hateley had said after that match, 'Ideally, I'd rather be playing with my old partner. We have proved we get goals together,' and the mis-match up front between himself and Ferguson continued at Ibrox that night as Rangers were too often direct.[39] The artillery fire created problems however, especially for the Bulgarian goalkeeper Oleg Morgun, with all three goals coming from cross balls that he should have dealt with. Dave McPherson and, of course, Hateley profited, the latter with two. Crucially it was Gough's absence that caused the fatal issues for Rangers. Twice a two-goal lead was halved when the defence couldn't defend rudimentary attacks. Both full-backs – David Robertson and Gary Stevens – were the last men to be asked to take care of the final balls into the box but there were countless issues surrounding the moves and Ally Maxwell should have done a lot better with Daniel Borimirov's header that first pulled the visitors back into the tie. Even the reaction around Hateley's second that made it 3-1 – a very quick response to the fist Levski goal – was that the expected minimum cushion had

---

38   It should be said that this decision was made before investigations had been concluded but the French authorities had already demoted Marseille and UEFA used the cover of the allegations being bad enough to damage the game's image.

39   Ferguson could be forgiven for having his mind elsewhere as the outcome of his court case was due the following day. He was on probation for a year.

been restored and that Rangers could coast through the rest of the evening. It was an evening of complacency that didn't end there. Those fans who had their season tickets in the Club Deck had a form to apply for the second round land on their doormat the day after the match in Bulgaria. By that time Rangers were out.

'If we play our own parts properly, they have nothing – on the evidence of the first match – to suggest they have a great deal which should worry us,' said Stevens. At least he was confident. There were signs in the 2-1 home win over Hibs on the Saturday that Stevens was recapturing some of his old form, and Smith was relieved to have him back, especially as Robertson was injured for the trip to Bulgaria. Just as one key player returned, another departed and Fraser Wishart deputised at left-back.[40] In truth, Stevens wasn't too far wrong. Despite Levski getting that crucial goal in the first half – Nasko Sirakov having far too much time and space to get his shot away – parity on the night and the advantage in the tie was regained right on the stroke of half-time when a Stevens cross was nodded home by Ian Durrant at the back post. Both goalkeepers had work to do in the second half but it wasn't a game played with the kind of urgency one might expect with so much on the line. Maxwell in particular made two very good saves, the first from Nikolay Todorov seemingly so crucial. The next time Todorov had sight of goal, Maxwell wasn't given a hope in hell.

With less than a minute of normal time remaining, Walter Smith was furiously urging his players to keep their shape and see out the tie. Rangers in fact had a corner as he barked his orders not to push too many men up for it. Instead of playing it all the way back to keep recycling it until the whistle, the ball came back to Durrant in the corner, who did what most Scottish players would do and swung in a cross. It was dealt with easily before Levski won a foul and built one final attack. A long ball was won in the air and the second ball was gathered with similar ease before it was laid into the path of Todorov 35 yards from goal. 'He looked up and you could sense he was ready to have a go and didn't have a hope,' wrote Ian Ferguson. 'A goal seemed so unlikely that I can remember saying to myself as he lined up, "Go on, shoot, shoot," and then he did and he could never have struck a ball better in his life.' It was an incredible strike, in off the underside of the bar, in the final seconds of the tie but the damage was done by such a careless performance at Ibrox. After the never-ending glory of 1992/93, it was a jolt to players and fans alike. 'As Alex Ferguson used to tell his players at Aberdeen when they went out of a tournament early – all we had to look forward to on a Wednesday night now was *Coronation Street*!' said Ian Ferguson. 'And that was no kind of consolation after the heady atmosphere which had surrounded Ibrox when we had played Leeds and Marseille.'[41] Trevor Steven described it as a

---

40   Davie Dodds took his place on the bench once again for this European tie. It was becoming the surest sign of Rangers struggles' with injury.

41   It provided Scottish football with a much-needed moment of schadenfreude as the all-conquering Rangers were finally brought down a peg or two. Some got a little carried away, however. When the Radio Clyde DJ 'Tiger' Tim Stevens, in his other role as the stadium announcer at Parkhead, asked the Celtic support to observe

'catastrophe' and 'morale-shattering', 'We felt a bit sorry for ourselves and a bit down and the league performances suffered a little bit around that time.'

A 'little bit' is quite the understatement. From the 0-0 draw at Parkhead in August to a 2-2 draw at Tynecastle on 3 November where they were 2-0 ahead, Rangers won only three league games in 12, by far the worst run of league form in the Souness and Smith years and something that fans wouldn't see again until late 2005. There were 1-1 draws at Dens Park, where the equaliser came late and soon after Dundee were down to ten men, and Stark's Park, where it took a Raith Rovers own goal to put Rangers in front before getting a deserved leveller soon after. The visit of Partick Thistle brought about the same scoreline although Mark Hateley should have added to his brilliant free-kick equaliser but saw his penalty saved by Andy Murdoch in the second half. It was yet another game where the direct style was criticised for being too blunt and obvious, with the responses from teams at the lower end of the league being slicker and easier on the eye in comparison.

Smith reacted the following Saturday, with the home leg against Sofia in midweek being the final straw for the Hateley-Ferguson partnership, as he dropped his new signing and replaced him with the promising 17-year-old Charlie Miller. Given the casualty list, Smith had few options but to give a reserve player his debut at Pittodrie, with a Rangers team badly out of form and craving experience, was perhaps a sign of muddled thinking and there was arguably evidence of stress in his post-match comments. When asked about Ferguson's place on the bench, his only explanation was, 'I pick the team.' When asked about the worrying form, he muttered something about his players needing to do less talking and more playing. Rangers were beaten by half-time as Aberdeen roared at them from the outset and were 2-0 up inside 35 minutes with Eoin Jess rampant and involved in both goals. Again, Maxwell was at fault for one – he spilled a Jess strike to the feet of Duncan Shearer. Again, Pressley was involved in a calamity as he put through his own net for the second. Again, Rangers were dull and heavy-footed whereas their opponents were sharp, accurate and incisive. Defeats at Aberdeen can happen but worse was to follow 18 days later on 6 October when Motherwell came to Ibrox, one point ahead of Rangers in the league table. It started well enough, with some better movement and composure in the first half and a brilliant Ian Ferguson strike in the second to give Rangers the lead. Then, with only 13 minutes remaining, it fell apart. Young Colin Scott – the stand-in for Maxwell who was the stand-in for Goram[42] – could do very little as dreadful marking and mistakes on the ball gifted Tommy McLean's side both points. Rangers were seventh after ten league games and the magic and excitement of the previous season was fading fast. After the draw against Raith, one fan was heard to shout, 'Why don't you resign, Smith?' Even at a club as demanding as Rangers, it takes quite a nosedive

---

a minute's silence for Rangers following news of the result, he was promptly sacked.

42   Maxwell had a virus.

to erode such outstanding credit but this was a run of form simply unthinkable five months before. When woven into such wretched form, the season's European exit is easier to explain.

How then, does one explain the form in the League Cup, which took place at exactly the same time but was exciting, dramatic and, ultimately, successful? The early rounds lacked the usual festival of goals as Rangers could only manage one at home to Dumbarton and two away to Dunfermline but the quarter-final at home to Aberdeen was where the action really started. Coming straight after the defeat by Kilmarnock, the pressure was starting to build but Rangers were ahead in less than one minute. Hateley's knock-on from Gough's long ball fed in Durrant who was fouled by Brian Irvine in the penalty area after only 12 seconds. Hateley composed himself before sweeping the ball home. Smith had opted to leave Duncan Ferguson out for the first do-or-die game of the season and Durrant's advanced role was far more effective. Aberdeen hung on, however, and had a penalty of their own in the second half when Gough was slightly out of position and wrestled Scott Booth to the floor, and Joe Miller levelled things up in an entertaining game. 'Big Dunc' was introduced late on but couldn't prevent extra time where Rangers were the better team. He was involved in an audacious chip of Snelders that had the Dutch goalkeeper scrambling to save and it was bright but brief evidence of what he could do when he was involved in more intelligent play. By that time Rangers were already back in front with another goal immediately after the whistle, as the Ferguson who had really been making the early headlines – Ian – smashed home a left-footed shot from the edge of the box after only a minute of extra time. There was still a nervy edge at times that night at Ibrox but more football from Rangers in 120 minutes than there had been in the six games they had already played that season as they took their place in the League Cup semi-finals, which they hadn't missed out on since 1980.

The draw for the semi-finals was conducted live on *Reporting Scotland* and pitted the Old Firm together. The only issue being that Hampden was still being renovated and, with no suitable alternative stadium in Glasgow, Walter Smith and Celtic's assistant manager Joe Jordan would have to toss a coin to see which ground would be used, albeit split 50/50 for 'neutrality' purposes. Jordan won the toss and it was announced that Parkhead would host before Smith declared that this toss was just to see who got to call the real one. Jordan did, lost, and so Ibrox would be cut diagonally for a classic cup tie on 22 September.

Once more, the game came straight after a bad result – the 2-0 defeat at Aberdeen – but this was a Rangers side that looked unrecognisable. Like the previous round, there should have been a very early penalty but Bonner's challenge on the onrushing Hateley somehow remained unpunished but it didn't deter a first-half performance that had invention and pace, but no reward. Perhaps the frustration got to Pieter Huistra as his-fresh air swipe at Tom Boyd following the breakdown of yet another promising move resulted in a deserved red card. The ten minutes that proceeded it was the only sustained period of pressure that

Celtic enjoyed but, as so often at crucial moments since 1989, they could not capitalise. When Mike Galloway attempted to deal with the ball in the left corner like Paolo Maldini, the game turned as Durrant robbed him before rolling it into the path of Hateley who tapped in from close range, releasing an outpouring of relief from half the stadium. Despite the tiredness and turmoil, Rangers were in yet another final, where they would face league leaders Hibs at Parkhead on Sunday, 24 October.

It is tempting to explain this good cup run – in the context of such a dismal period in general – to be the work of individuals showing their prowess at big moments. Hateley definitely, Ian Ferguson too and also Durrant, so often a big-game player, who opened the scoring in the final after 55 minutes with a delightful goal. But that would ignore the genuinely good team performances in both matches against Aberdeen and Celtic where even beleaguered individuals like Maxwell still came up with good saves at key moments. The football was far better and more focused than in the disappointing fixtures around them. Durrant's goal was the work of two different give-and-go moves through the centre of the pitch that split Hibs apart with ease but it was the nature of the winner that gives credence to the initial argument that Rangers had players who simply popped up with something brilliant when it really counted and none more so than the ultimate talisman himself.

'He is a lucky bastard. He is sure to go through life like that, so there's no point me spoiling it,' said Walter Smith after the match, still shaking his head in disbelief. Rangers were worthy of their lead but the old frailties were never too far from the surface and the match was squared when Maxwell got caught in no man's land to collect a weak pass by Stevens and McPherson ended up heading the ball into his goal. With his side rocking, Smith looked to his bench for someone whose very presence could still inspire his team-mates to something great. Ally McCoist had made his first start for five months at Stark's Park on 2 October but a slight reaction had delayed his second until the 2-0 win at home to St Johnstone on 16 October, a week before the final. Although he had forced the own goal against Raith, he understandably lacked sharpness and Smith didn't feel it was right to start him so, with Duncan Ferguson also now on the treatment table for the foreseeable future, he opted for Durrant's forward role to begin with. 'He had shown enough to suggest that he could come on and make an impact,' said Smith after. 'But I didn't think of this.'

'This' was the type of cup-final winner that can usually only be found in comic books. Less than 15 minutes after replacing Huistra, the cup was won in the most dramatic fashion. David Robertson's throw-in, coming through the low, dying sun, could only be flicked on by Steven Tweed but beyond the control of anyone in a crowded penalty area before it entered the vicinity of McCoist. He was still facing Robertson on the Main Stand side touchline as he jumped to chest the ball back up into the air before turning 90 degrees to the left to meet it on the way down with an overhead kick. There were four Hibs players within three yards of

McCoist, at all four sides, but they were simply witnesses to history. Jim Leighton – the 35-year-old whose career renaissance had been the focus of the pre-match build-up – was caught in two minds but the arc of the shot into the side netting was likely to have him beaten even if he had stayed on his line. It was the kind of comeback that only McCoist could deliver as his late goal ensured that he broke the record for most League Cup winners' medals[43] and his joy was unconfined. As was that of his team-mates. This was not just an important goal in a cup final; Ally was back, and no embrace was longer than the one between himself and Hateley, reunited at last. A cup win coming on the back of two league wins in a row, the first of which a very impressive 3-1 victory at Tannadice, and now their lethal partnership back in action. A corner appeared to have been turned.

Waiting for them was a Celtic side who had outdone themselves in the calamity stakes by managing to have an even worse start to the season than Rangers. Their 2-1 defeat at St Johnstone on 6 October meant that they only had two wins to their name from their opening ten league matches (and none at home) and it was enough for Liam Brady to call things quits before he faced a very difficult AGM later in the week. Assistant Frank Connor managed to steady things with a narrow home win to bottom-of-the-table Dundee and then a 1-1 draw away at league leaders Hibs. On the Tuesday before the trip to Ibrox, they got their new man through the door. Lou Macari, a former Celtic and Manchester United hero as a player who had a mixed career at that point as a manager[44], was handed the unenviable task of managing the football club while the holding company stumbled from one shambles to another. Waiting in the wings was a Scottish exile in Montreal, Fergus McCann, who had put together a proposal worth close to £20m to bail Celtic out of their ever-worsening predicament and re-energise their fortunes both on and off the park[45] before recouping his investment and leaving in five years time but it was described as 'fantasy' by the Kelly and White family pact that was clinging on to power by their fingertips. McCann's credentials as a big Celtic fan were also embarrassed when it was apparent that he wasn't aware that the Old Firm League Cup semi-final was even taking place. They were more and more resembling a cartoon club and no one gave them much hope in the build-up to the third encounter of the season.

With just over 20 minutes remaining, this poor game summed up the season so far for Rangers. Hateley had picked up a knock in the cup final but played on regardless, Stevens pulled a hamstring while covering for a goalkeeping error, Trevor Steven eventually had to make way following a large cut in his face and

---

43   This was his eighth; he would pick up his ninth and final one in 1996.

44   Macari's career in management started with promise as he guided Swindon Town through the lower leagues but he was forced to leave his next job, as manager of West Ham United, when it became known that he had previously placed a £1,000 bet on his Swindon team to lose to Newcastle United in the FA Cup. The FA called it a 'foolhardy misdemeanour' but it is inconceivable that a manager would work again in the climate of the current day.

45   This involved over £8m of his own money and some from other investors as well as a public share offer for fans.

Ally McCoist was in the right place at the right time to bundle the ball in to put Rangers ahead. A poor performance with yet more injuries but an individual picked up the baton when required. This is a pattern which is all well and good until another individual drops it.

It was Maxwell. Rangers had the lead for only three minutes when Pat McGinlay lofted a speculative ball into the area which the goalkeeper came out positively to claim only to then fumble it upon landing. Gerry Creaney was arguably the man who put him under any kind of pressure but the ball landed right at the feet of John Collins, who seemed to take an eternity to compose himself, toy with the scrambling Rangers defenders and dink it in with the outside of his left foot. The unthinkable was to happen in injury time as Collins whipped in a corner from the right-hand side. Maxwell jumped but was never close and Brian O'Neil was left to head home from two yards out. Maxwell got the blame for that one too – he would have taken the blame for unemployment and NHS waiting list figures at this stage – but the fact that O'Neil was allowed to get in front of John Brown and Stuart McCall so easily shouldn't go without remark.

Rangers would lose to an inferior Celtic side on occasion throughout their period of dominance – mostly in the final meeting of the season when nothing was left at stake – but to lose one at home in such a precarious stage of the campaign to a side this poor, new manager bounce or not, was a big shock. 'It is not championship form,' Richard Gough remarked, without much need, afterwards. When he was pushed on Maxwell, all he would say was, 'Everyone saw what happened. Bad mistakes were made.' There is always a desire for a scapegoat but the problems Rangers had were much more than just Maxwell. Leading 2-0 with less than 20 minutes to go at a soaking-wet Tynecastle the following Wednesday night, they contrived to take only a point. And yet, despite this woeful form, they were only three points behind Aberdeen that night, back in fourth place behind Hibs and Motherwell. It was a situation that underlined the overall balance of power. Rangers were at their worst for years and were still in the hunt for the title. Before Graeme Souness, the quality at the top would have pushed Rangers well behind a pack that was too good to be reeled in. Years later – when the interminable two-horse race was established – that kind of form would finish a title push in November. At this moment in time, however, it was a mere grace period for Rangers to cope with some injuries.

No other Premier Division club could find the consistency with which to punish Rangers for their hangover. No other Premier Division club could find over £1m to reinforce the challenge with a striker from Tottenham Hotspur.

* * *

As much as Jim McLean was something of an underrated forward-thinker on the training ground, it is impossible to imagine him stopping a drill and taking his players to smell the flowers around them in Camperdown Country Park. If Mark Hateley was Scottish football's star man that season then there was no doubt as to who its best newcomer was. Ivan Golac was passed over for the Celtic job when they opted for Liam Brady in 1991[46] but was an eventual hit with the media, desperate for some colour in a pretty grey landscape, when he replaced McLean in the summer. His Dundee United side could be anything on any given day and he was a surefire source for good copy. Sometimes they got carried away and Golac had to rein the press in when they quoted him in the build-up to the trip to Ibrox on 11 December as saying that Rangers were 'on the slide'. 'How could I say Rangers are on the slide with the resources they have? Their reserve side could easily live in the Premier Division,' Golac argued. He did, however, suggest that the juggernaut could be caught, 'People talk about how much Rangers dominated in the past but it is different this season. Rangers are still good, of course, but others have got better. You can tell that by the closeness of the league. People don't want the same team running away with everything every year. And Dundee United will definitely be in at the finish.' Big talk for a club who were seventh in the table at the time of asking.

Twenty-one minutes in, however, many were conceding that he had a point. Indeed, barely 20 seconds had elapsed before the writing started to appear on the Ibrox walls. Smart running by Paddy Connolly on the left gave him enough space to find Dave Bowman from 12 yards out as Ally Maxwell grasped in vain to stop his header setting the match on fire. Connolly's pace was the undoing of Rangers' defence once more as he collected a simple through ball to give Maxwell no chance on 16 minutes and then Craig Brewster tapped in from five yards after a comedy of errors in the Rangers box. 'The easiest goal I have ever scored,' said Brewster afterwards. Maxwell and co. would give Laurel and Hardy a run for their money in presenting him with an easier one before the season was out. McPherson and Gough came off injured with yet more muscle damage after the second and third goals respectively – given the difference in movement, it would be fair to say that they weren't 100 per cent to start, indeed Gough was rushed back for the fixture – and Ian Ferguson was sent off after spitting at Gordan Petrić (the Serb's elbow on the midfielder was not seen). According to Golac in the aftermath, with his side still seventh but only three points behind Rangers at the top, 'We are on our way to the top of the league.'

At the time it might have been viewed as the epitome of this Rangers season; a fourth home defeat, more defensive calamity, further injuries and now some indiscipline to boot. With only three points separating seven sides in the middle of December and with Celtic only a point behind, it would also make a mockery of any claim to Rangers' superiority and Celtic's catastrophe. When the media complained about the overall quality on offer, Walter Smith took umbrage, 'If we were well ahead in the table, the critics would be saying it was boring and the game needed challengers for the title. Now there are four teams at the top, Rangers are

---

46   Golac, while assistant at Partizan Belgrade, was required to step into the hot seat for his side's second leg of a Cup Winners' Cup first round tie against Celtic in 1989, because of illness. In a sensational game, Celtic won 5-4 but went out on away goals.

considered poor and so is every other team in the league. People will have to make up their minds one way or the other. Either they want a level competition or they want one side or other, be it Celtic, Aberdeen, or anybody to run away with the league. You can't have your cake and eat it.' This notion of a tight contest was a mirage, however, as league tables can often be. That 3-0 defeat was the only loss in 31 games for Rangers between 3 November and 26 April and the signs of that recovery were already visible before the visit of United.

'There were no decisive battles in World War II,' wrote the historian Phillips O'Brien. In his view the traditional use of set pieces acting as turning points is illusory. The superior Allied resources and planning was always going to prove critical. And so, in the midst of this apparent dogfight, only one club had the power to make the difference. On 23 November, Smith finally got a player who Rangers had tried to sign five times previously, when Gordon Durie arrived at Ibrox from Spurs for £1.2m. 'Money and timing' were the reasons Smith gave for the deals falling through previously, starting with Graeme Souness's attempt to bring him up from Chelsea, but the time had been right for several weeks since Durie swore at manager Ossie Ardiles when he was substituted in a League Cup tie against Blackburn Rovers, precipitating a fine and the chance to train with the youth team. A Rangers fan, Durie jumped at the opportunity on this occasion and with it, Rangers were assured of experience, work rate and some much-needed goals.

The impact was almost immediate as Durie's support allowed Rangers to deliver two statement wins against the young pretenders surrounding them. His movement at Ibrox against Aberdeen on 1 December allowed Hateley the space to torment goalkeeper Michael Watt once more as his two powerful goals sent Rangers above Willie Miller's side up into the top spot. When Rangers travelled to Fir Park the following Saturday, the hosts could have deposed them with a win but it was Durie who grabbed one in each half to send his side two points clear, albeit with a game more in the bag than both of their opponents that week. The response to the United defeat was a 4-0 win away to St Johnstone with all four goals coming from headers.[47] The aerial route provided Rangers with 30 of their 74 league goals that season – over 40 per cent – and ten per cent higher than the previous campaign. Only an injury-time penalty for Hearts at Ibrox at Christmas prevented another win courtesy of Hateley, in imperious form as he bullied a young Davie Weir among others, to grab two more goals in a 2-2 draw. Rangers sat in second place on Hogmanay, one point behind Aberdeen who had 31 points and ahead of Motherwell and Celtic who had 29 and 28 respectively but who had both played one game fewer. The table presented a tight and competitive picture as the new year trip to the East End lay in store.

Although still beleaguered off the pitch, Lou Macari's side were unbeaten on his watch and he talked up the chances of the title during the festive break, saying

---

47   Two from Hateley, one from Durie and one from Trevor Steven who managed to head home with the ball on the ground.

that he didn't think that there was 'any real gap' between the teams in October. Jim Traynor, in his preview for *The Herald*, said that it was 'impossible to see Rangers taking even a point from Parkhead' but his match report would end up significantly different. Apparently, by the time he penned that, 'It was never on to believe [Gary] Gillespie and [Dariusz] Wdowczyk could put the frighteners on a player of Hateley's confidence and power.' Macari had reminded his defenders at their Seamill base what to expect and how to respond. Apparently there were some nods, belying the nerves and fears that the current, fragile optimism could evaporate in a matter of seconds. Sixty-four to be precise. Rangers had already managed to squeeze Alexei Mikhailichenko through the Celtic lines but Bonner was quick to react before launching the ball downfield. When it came back, he was faced with the thunderous power of Hateley bearing down on him after beating an incredibly high offside trap. The outcome was never in doubt and so a season seemed to turn. By the third minute it was two. The build-up play was actually very nice but the space afforded to Rangers was criminal as Neil Murray ran through a space that could have been filled by half of the travelling support. His shot was blocked but Mikhailichenko – of whom it was said previously let the fixture pass him by – was quickest to react as he drilled it home. Just before the half-hour mark he made it three. Hateley won the first header from a Stevens cross, Durie won the second ball but the contact was weak and Mikhailichenko was somehow left unattended in the six-yard box to prod home.

Later in the year Smith put that crazy half an hour down to the vagaries of derby football. 'Like me, Lou would not have been able to give you any reasoned analysis of how that had happened to his team on the day,' he wrote in his autobiography. 'I mean, Lou had organised the Celtic defence, had got them working in a way that meant they were not losing many goals, and yet before they could get to grips with us they were out of it … That's what puts the game in a category of its own. And that's why its appeal will never fade. I just don't think you can exaggerate the effect the game has on the players involved. There is so much passion, so many emotions are poured into the game that the tension is almost unbearable. Unless you have experienced this at first hand, it's hard to accept just how different these games are from all the others you play. It's almost as if some outside force takes over for the build-up to the game and the match itself. There are times when you feel as if things just move beyond your control. That's why players make mistakes they would not make at other times, why managers get over-excited and why the rivalries will never die.'

It was at this point, however, that tensions reached very different levels. Celtic fan Martin McCallum was able to run on to the field of play and confront Ally Maxwell but was stopped with purpose by John Brown and Richard Gough.[48] And then the home vitriol was turned upon the real culprits of the piece, who

---

48   McCallum was sentenced to two months in prison on 25 January. 'I was drunk,' he said. 'I wanted to be banned.' It was little wonder.

were sat up in the directors' box. A member of the Rangers party was cut on the face by unfriendly fire as coins, pies and Mars bars rained down on the Celtic board from the main stand. It was arguably the nadir for a club kidding itself on that it was at the same level as their oldest rivals and could remain there. A John Collins goal right after the break gave the home support hope but Rangers saw out the threat before the forgotten Ukrainian, Oleh Kuznetsov, volleyed in from the edge of the box to make it four. A Charlie Nicholas consolation didn't spoil a very happy new year for Rangers players and fans alike. Not for the first time, Celtic's form nosedived after a stinging Old Firm defeat – they would lose their next two games and draw the following three – but perhaps this was their darkest point as the board could only stumble on for a matter of weeks before Fergus McCann finally took control. With no sporting interest remaining, boycotts and protests could be intensified and a last ditch promise of a share issue was rejected, with the chairman of the fans' group, Matt McGlone, questioning what would stop David Murray and every masonic lodge in the country from exploiting it and taking control. It was a festive joy for Rangers and, although there would be more to come, the cartoon cavalcade at Parkhead was nearing its end. Rangers would soon have to work harder to remain in pole position.

In the meantime Rangers were adept at manoeuvring themselves out of the congestion and then out of sight. A crushingly dull 0-0 draw at Pittodrie on 22 January suited them perfectly as it kept them top, before a run of seven league wins on the spin that ended the chase in any meaningful way. Once again Durie was at the heart of it, scoring two in a 5-1 win over Partick Thistle at Ibrox, the first in a 2-0 win over Hibs, the winner in a 2-1 win away to Raith, the final goal in 4-0 home rout of St Johnstone and the equaliser at home in a vital match against Motherwell on 5 March. Four points behind Rangers, and with a game in hand, this was realistically the last chance for Tommy McLean to keep his side's dream alive. It looked promising when Paul Lambert drove high into the Rangers goal in the second half but Durie responded – with the help of a deflection – to turn the tide. It was his driving run in injury time that led to John Philiben's handball and a gift from the penalty spot that Hateley was never likely to pass up. Fittingly, Motherwell and Aberdeen would draw that game in hand, leaving Rangers five clear with 12 matches remaining.

By this point, it wasn't only Durie's introduction that was making a difference. Rangers were starting to look like their old selves again with heroes returning from the shadows. Andy Goram was rushed back a little earlier than anticipated to play in the win over Hibs on 12 February, McCoist had recovered from another operation – this time a hernia – that had kept him out since December, and Smith now had a full group of regular defenders from which to pick. With Duncan Ferguson now back in the squad – over 20,000 fans turned up to Ibrox to see him score an equaliser in an Old Firm reserve match in January – only Ian Durrant's absence was notable as McCall and Ian Ferguson showed signs of their old chemistry and Trevor Steven was rolling back the years as well. McCoist and Hateley got the band back together at Tynecastle with two super goals in a 2-1 win and it was that ultimate talisman again who popped up very late in the game at Firhill to grab a dramatic winner in the rain. Undeterred by his reprimand for speaking publicly about transfer targets, David Murray said that Rangers were 'likely' to bid for Gary McAllister in the summer, a remark that drew an official complaint from Leeds United. Rangers heroes coming to the fore when it mattered in the early springtime and the chairman talking about summer targets, Scottish football was correct to ask what had really changed.

Once again we should beware the transient illusion that football often produces. Goram lasted for just under two months before breaking down again during a 0-0 draw at Tannadice, and Smith was increasingly tetchy about his side's attitude. After a poor performance at home to Aberdeen where Rangers were pegged back after an early lead to draw 1-1, Smith stopped his players talking to the media. 'The players have been hearing and reading too much about the league having been won. They are only human, and this sort of thing has taken the edge off their play,' he said. But when the media changed tack, Smith wasn't happy with that either. The prospect of a 'double treble' was on as Rangers needed a replay to get the better of Kilmarnock in the Scottish Cup semi-final, the first games at the new-look Hampden Park. The first game was an awful 0-0 draw and the second act wasn't much better as Rangers needed a Hateley double to rescue it after finding themselves behind against Kilmarnock yet again. When the reviews were less than fawning, Smith reacted by returning to a familiar gripe. 'It seems to be assumed that the only reason we have been successful is because the general standard is bad,' he said after the game. 'That is not the case, because Rangers players have had to work really hard to achieve what they have done in recent times.' Echoing his pre-season predictions, he went on, 'When people look at our team now, they are expecting something which is very difficult to achieve. It is unfair to expect sparkling performances every game. We have had to overcome a lot of injuries and a physically demanding programme, and our players deserve an enormous amount of credit for sustaining the level of success that they have.' As ever, there was something in both arguments. Smith's Rangers side were physically and mentally shattered but they found reserves to ensure they got what they needed when it mattered. However, the apparent closeness in competition earlier in the season shouldn't mask the fact that it was a dull season of Scottish football.

One obvious exception was, of course, Mark Hateley. The equaliser that night was dubious – both for offside and whether or not the ball crossed the line – but the second was once more all about Durie's industry and Hateley's instinctive awareness. It was his 30th goal in all competitions that season as he was the undisputed SFWA Footballer of the Year and the SPFA Players' Player of the Year, the first Englishman to be recognised in such a way. Unfortunately for Rangers, it was the last goal that he would manage to score.

What happened the following Saturday could have been the perfect link between two eras of Rangers' history. On 16 April they defeated Raith Rovers

4-0 at Ibrox to go seven points clear at the top with only 12 points left to play for and the man who was supposed to take over from Hateley in the long term finally got off the mark. Less than a minute into the second half, with the score at 2-0, Duncan Ferguson broke free on the left and clipped a beautiful strike into the corner of the net. The relief was palpable and Ferguson was booked for his over-exuberance. In an ideal world this would be an ideal time at which to turn over to a new chapter. Hateley had carried a team on his back as his young replacement adjusted to life at a big club and regained his fitness and then, just as he himself was tiring, the baton could be passed over.

In the real world, however, what Ferguson did in the first half was more important. It effectively ended his Rangers career.

* * *

'The fans are bound to get impatient, but I'm feeling just as bad as them,' said Duncan Ferguson in the profile on him in that afternoon's matchday programme, where he would get a rare start as Hateley was rested on the bench.[49] Patience was starting to wear thin among the loyal throngs, not unreasonable after such excitement surrounding the transfer, but it was his off-field behaviour that was causing as much tension as his lack of on-field substance. One particularly impassioned plea in the February edition of *Follow, Follow* said, 'Really he has to grow up and stop acting like an overgrown spoiled five year old. You owe us all a great debt. Start delivering off the park if you cannot deliver on it. This club has much more to offer you than you can give it.' Perhaps that fan was one of thousands cheering his name early in that second half. In retrospect, it may have been better for all concerned if he wasn't on the pitch at all by then.

It was around the 35th minute that Ferguson was tussling with the Raith right-back Jock McStay – cousin of Celtic captain, Paul – in the corner between the Main Stand and Broomloan when the referee Kenny Clark blew for a Raith free kick. As he turned away to look upfield, presuming that the kick would be taken quickly and without fuss, it would be a strange and costly presumption to make. McStay appeared to look back at Ferguson and, in the striker's opinion, began to 'square up' to him. Ferguson got his retaliation in early as he charged forward towards McStay, leaving him on the floor holding his face. 'I tried to show some aggression. I misjudged my distance and collided with his head. I was clumsy with my head.' Words given not in the post-match media debrief or in an interview years later, but in court as Ferguson found himself yet again charged with assault. It was the moment that changed his life.

If Clark had been looking where he should have been looking at the time or if his stand-side linesman Jim O'Hare acted on his initial thoughts that the

---

49   Hateley would later play at centre-half that afternoon, one of the other options mooted as a way of extending his career as well as fitting both into the same Rangers team.

lunge looked 'pretty bad' and raised his flag then perhaps the sense of immediate sporting justice would have negated the pressure for a different kind. According to the then vice-chairman of Rangers, Donald Findlay QC – who couldn't represent Ferguson at the initial trial as he was there in the ground and was technically a witness – 'There was an enormous media clamour. I have no doubt that the police and the fiscal reacted to this.' There was no formal complaint made by McStay or Raith Rovers and indeed it was a Glasgow publican, Dick Barton, who may have started that particular ball rolling when he sent a letter to every police station in the country, demanding action.

Neither manager made much of the incident in the immediate post-match media round. In fact Walter Smith missed the whole thing as he was on his usual walk down to the dugout from the directors' box where he preferred to take in the early stages of every match. The interviews that both players gave were far more impactful on public opinion, amplified by the television footage slowed down by *Scotsport* the following day. McStay's initial priority was to prove that he hadn't dived or overreacted to the kind of trivial coming together that happens every weekend in British football. In order to do this he spoke with his friend and *News of the World* journalist Kenny MacDonald out on Edmiston Drive after the game, pointing to a cut on his lip as proof of contact. Speaking to Alan Pattullo years later, McStay said, 'What I think did for him [Ferguson] in the court was the club doctor's report. There was a cut above my lip, it confirmed.' What was curious about that at the time and still, nearly 30 years on, is that the best picture of the incident proved that Ferguson's contact was clearly on the left-hand side of McStay's head, near his ear. Only the subject of a Picasso masterpiece could suffer direct damage to their lips with that kind of contact. It would have made no material difference to the eventual outcome – it was a head-butt with deliberate force – but it did add to that immediate media storm, from which the legalities arose. Ferguson, famously media-shy, only spoke with *Rangers News* and a young Fraser Mackie who was starting out in an in-house publication as many football writers do. Ferguson had a celebratory can of McEwan's Lager[50] and said, 'The boy made a bit of a meal of it,' before the two toed the party line by talking only about his joy and pride in scoring his first Rangers goal with his family watching on. When the wider press latched on to the quotes, it made for a wild juxtaposition in the context of the dominant media narrative of the week. 'Hope you are proud of me, Dad!' was *The Sun*'s headline, saying that the strike was 'overshadowed by the one that left Raith ace McStay with a bust lip'. This simply wasn't fair and apparently the nation demanded action.

Nearly three weeks later, Ferguson was formally charged and the following week the SFA banned him for 12 games.[51] If the wider media pressure was enough to persuade the Procurator Fiscal to get involved with a sporting matter

---

50   Rangers' shirt sponsors from 1987–1999.

51   Rangers immediately appealed, so Ferguson was able to feature for what was left of the season.

then the context surrounding the eventual hearing, in May 1995, was equally as unhelpful to Ferguson. By that time he was an FA Cup winner with Everton, but 1994/95 had been a notorious season in English football with match-fixing allegations, transfer bungs, sleaze, racist language and, on 25 January 1995, the ultimate barometer when Manchester United's Eric Cantona lunged at a Crystal Palace spectator with his foot after being subjected to a torrent of abuse on his walk off the field following a red card. Cantona was eventually given community service after an appeal against a custodial sentence, but at least this involved a member of the public. Violence on the football field was nothing new and, as many commentators as well as Rangers and Ferguson's legal team made clear, far worse had occurred without the law getting involved.

A few weeks after the event, the Scottish Junior Cup Final (held at Ibrox and shown live on STV) between Glenafton and Largs had multiple incidents of violence including punches and a head-butt and even more famously, in August 1994, two Hearts players – Graeme Hogg and Craig Levein – were involved in an on-field fight during a pre-season game away to Raith Rovers[52] where the latter ultimately broke the former's nose with a left hook. Video evidence of both was used but, in the end, dismissed by Sheriff Sandy Eccles who said that the examples were 'irrelevant' because they 'took place in play and immediately from continuing play, unlike the present case'. Except, that the Ferguson case was exactly the same in that the match was stopped immediately before the incident arose and the damage a lot less severe. 'Looking at the TV film of it, it didn't look as if it was done in the heat of the moment,' Eccles explained to Pattullo, suggesting some degree of pre-meditation on Ferguson's part for an act that preceded a tussle that occurred literally seconds before it. Given that he had three previous convictions for assault and, by the time of the hearing, one for drink-driving, it should have been no surprise that Ferguson was sentenced to prison if and when he was found guilty for assault. However, it rankled for many Rangers fans at the time that it had gotten that far given the more violent sporting comparators. For Findlay, Ferguson was a sacrificial lamb at a time where there was public pressure for footballers to be held to the same standard as the man on the street. He quoted from Voltaire's *Candide* when making that point in Patttullo's book, 'Dans ce pay-ci, il est bon de tuer de temps en temps un amiral encourager les autres.' It is good to kill an admiral from time to time, in order to encourage the others. Ferguson would play and score for Rangers again in the following season but only a handful of times. It is always tempting, for narrative reasons, to use a flash incident as the turning point in a career or life but, with Ferguson's character and his rap sheet by then, it would have likely happened on another day if not this one. It did happen this day however, and after Raith, the end for Ferguson at Ibrox was nigh.

There was still business for Rangers to complete as this exhausting season limped to a close. Fittingly it was Dundee United who visited Ibrox for a Scottish Cup

---

52   Jock McStay watched from the bench.

Final dress rehearsal in a week dominated by what should happen next to the man who left one club for the other in July. A quick glance through the records would suggest another business-as-usual 2-1 home win and another two important goals for Gordon Durie as Rangers cruised to title number six but there was more to it than that. United took an early second-half lead when Christian Dailly converted a Jerren Nixon cut-back and then they should have had the opportunity to make it two when Dailly was taken out by Dave McPherson in the box only a couple of minutes later. Referee Jim McCluskey waved play on and Rangers capitalised with two headers by Durie which took his tally to 12 goals in 20 league games, highlighting once more the importance of that winter purchase.

Ivan Golac opted for sarcasm as a way of dealing with the opportunity which he felt his side had been denied, 'I understand completely the decision. The referee was four or five yards away and in line with what happened. Yes, it is very difficult to make a decision in those circumstances. I am still convinced the decision would have been different if it had happened at the other end.' By that time he had been riled by Walter Smith who had said that at least Dundee United 'had played' when they came and won 3-0 in December, 'If they don't put men up the park they lose.' The Croatian's response was pointed, 'I read that Walter Smith had not seen the Duncan Ferguson incident because he was on his way down from the stand. If he thinks we didn't play well he must have been in the tunnel. If we had scored a second goal with the penalty there is nothing Rangers could have done to change things. Our players are angry and even more determined to win the cup final. That is how I want it to be. We will emerge stronger as a result of this.' They would do but no one inside Ibrox could have possibly known that Rangers were just about spent nor that they had witnessed, on 23 April, the final victory of the season. Even the chance to seal the championship at Fir Park three days later was passed up as Motherwell defeated Rangers 2-1 for the second time that season and ended a 22-game unbeaten run. On it went until the following Saturday where the title could be won – if other results went Rangers' way – at home to Celtic. However, it would be an Old Firm game with a very different atmosphere.

Damage caused by Old Firm fans at the home of their rivals was nothing new but the level carried out in the Broomloan Road stand during Celtic's previous visit on 30 October was higher than ever as more than 800 seats were ripped out or broken. When the club complained more vigorously than ever, the Celtic response set in motion a chain of events that led to unprecedented action. Not only were Celtic not prepared to pay for the damage – the previous understanding was that it was the responsibility of the home club to ensure crowd safety and behaviour was upheld – one of their directors, Tom Grant, denied any malicious intent and blamed the damage both on 'exuberant fans' celebrating victory or them trying to avoid queues by climbing over seats. Given that both Kilmarnock and Motherwell had taken big supports to Ibrox and celebrated dramatic late winners in recent months without anywhere near that level of damage, Rangers were in no mood to accept excuses.

The reaction was predictably extreme. 'David Murray has me feeling ten feet tall at the moment,' wrote one notoriously cynical contributor to *Follow, Follow*. 'Thank you, thank you, thank you,' he continued, for 'sticking by the Rangers fans and their club'. 'Stand By Our Man' was the editorial headline in that edition in February 1993, with Mark Dingwall signing off the piece with, 'Thank you David Murray – for finally burying the myth that anyone needs a strong Celtic. STAND FIRM.' All the main football writers – Alex Cameron, Alan Davidson and Ian Archer at the forefront – felt that it would denigrate the greatest derby in the world (one they had poured scorn over for its unsavoury elements for years), with Davidson going further by saying, 'Rangers were nothing without Celtic.'[53] The importance of a 'strong Celtic' had been a subject that had dominated the back pages for some months by this stage as the club teetered on the brink of disappearing, with most columnists backing the rebel bid to oust the board. Even when Fergus McCann finally took control, more work was to be done according to Gerry McNee – the self-styled voice of Scottish football which one would assume is a title that suggests impartiality – in his column in the *Sunday Mail* during March of 1994, 'This has to be said, there are at least four people who still have to go. I won't rest until they do. For the best part of six years, I have campaigned here and elsewhere to help bring down a Celtic board rotten to the core.' 'Campaigns' are common for local reporters in a one-team city, such as with Newcastle United during the Mike Ashley era, but less so in a divided town and remarkable for a man who saw himself as a truly national voice. It would be akin to Martin Tyler banging a weekly drum about how the Glazer family were running Manchester United and evidence that the concept of 'fan media' isn't as new as many think.

McCann made a peace offer to Murray privately, which he then made public in the week of the game, stating that neither he nor his directors would attend, 'If the supporters are not welcome we consider we are not welcome either. Instead we will be here for the reserve match. Rangers fans will be able to come here, too, and we will let them have a seat.' His offer was a surcharge on Celtic tickets sold only to fans who provided names and addresses, payment for any extra stewarding or policing required, an independent inspection before and after and a promise to pay for any damage. Crucially there was a refusal to pay for the original damage and so Murray remained unmoved, as McCann would surely have known he would be. However, it was a cute use of the media in the days before a game where Rangers could win the title against Celtic and should have been an early sign that Murray was facing a very different opponent across the city.

Perhaps if Rangers had scored early, it would have been different, but they couldn't and it was a strange and flat atmosphere, despite the balloons and streamers, made flatter still by a John Collins free kick that gave Colin Scott no chance and alerted stewards to Celtic fans who had managed to somehow

---

53   One Celtic fan, a Mr Pat Devitt from Erksine, wrote to the Herald to say that if Celtic fans couldn't be in the ground then the match should be forfeited and his club given the points.

secure a ticket. Rangers huffed and puffed and eventually got an equaliser when Mikhailichenko's deflected shot spun over Pat Bonner and into the net. But even then, there was no late charge to finish the game off in style. It was clear that there was very little left. Some pundits suggested that Rangers were choking with the prospect of an historical 'double treble' tantalisingly in reach. 'Losing our nerve? Us? Not a chance of that happening,' said Stuart McCall immediately after the game. Perhaps not nerve – this was a side who had come through tougher tests – but energy, almost certainly.

Rangers celebrated their sixth successive title at Easter Road on Tuesday, 3 May with a 1-0 defeat and with it not being technically won at all. While it was conceivable for Rangers to stumble to defeat in the final two games – in the end they lost 1-0 at Kilmarnock and drew 0-0 with relegated Dundee at Ibrox on the final day – it was fairly unlikely that Motherwell were going to claw back a goal difference deficit of 18, so even Walter Smith allowed his side an early celebration. Injury and illness kept Durie and Duncan Ferguson out and the Hibs goal came from a defensive error by Richard Gough. It was almost the perfect way in which to seal the 1993/94 title; an under-strength, error-strewn defeat on the same night that their closest rivals lost as the country shrugged at yet another league flag being hoisted above Ibrox Stadium. And yet, when Smith wrote his autobiography later that year, he was very proud of this triumph. That title, he said, 'gave me more satisfaction than any of the other trophy wins we have had. This was a long, hard slog for the players.' It was done, he continued, 'despite a crippling series of injuries which would have crushed lesser teams. Andy Goram was out for most of the season. So was Ally McCoist. And Ian Durrant. The team was chopped and changed, and yet the players delivered. It's hard to tell just how much they had been drained by the efforts of the previous season. Certainly, there were stress injuries which affected us during the season. And mentally there must have been a tremendous strain. The constant pressure, the never-ending demand for success must have taken its toll.

'I'm not trying to make any excuses here. I don't think I have to make excuses for players whose names will go down in history. I'm simply pointing out the kind of pressures which they went through. There was no time for them to relax. No time for them to sit back and say "haven't we done well" – it was on to the next game, the next competition, the next challenge. For them to have kept themselves up for such a period of time was incredible. For them to have taken the title once more, after all the early season problems and the lingering worries which hit us, was amazing. You won't find me criticising them because, at times, they didn't show the same style as they had the previous season. Winning last year asked for different qualities from the players. It wasn't just about their footballing ability, it was also about the physical and emotional reserves they had left to draw on.'

Smith wasn't being disingenuous, he was genuinely proud of this one. Ever protective of his squad and their achievements, this was a very different kind of success than the ones he had been used to thus far as Rangers manager, which were either dramatic or sensational. Champions need to grind too and, as with the League Cup and those key league games at Parkhead at the turn of the year, Aberdeen at Ibrox in December and twice against Motherwell in December and March, this side could and would turn it on when absolutely required. As fans made their way to Hampden for the Scottish Cup Final, they were aware that Dundee United would pose problems once again but believed that Rangers would surely be ready for them. As one fan remarked in the fanzine in April, 'As we come to the end of another treble winning season (nobody really expects the Teddies to let Arabs[54] finally win something do they?) the standard of football on display has been awful.' The two themes of the season wrapped up in one complacent line; Rangers were well below their best but when it comes to silverware, there was a strong assumption that this machine would grind up anyone in its path.

As it would turn out, those brief season highlights were the exception rather than the rule. There was no lack of effort on the day – Rangers dominated, especially the second half – however the creative responsibility was just landed on too few – almost wholly on Mikhailichenko in the latter stages – and even Hateley lacked the power and presence that he had so often demonstrated. Golac named his team the day before – as Smith sweated on fitness doubts – and made it clear that his side would have a go. 'We will attack Rangers' weaknesses,' he said with confidence. 'I'll play three up front to stretch their defence, but I hope others in my team also will get forward. I want to attack with six and seven players rather than defend with that number. We are all confident and believe there is no reason why we can't go to Hampden and win the cup.' In truth, they were far more reactive than proactive but their dangerous press would ultimately bring reward. Rangers were unlucky to have a McPherson header cleared off the line but fortunate not to concede a penalty when Ian Ferguson appeared to knock Alec Cleland off balance in the box, all of this in the opening ten minutes.

In the end, the main takeaways were all too familiar. Injuries? Of course. Trevor Steven – who had been at the heart of that spring revival – didn't make it and Gary Stevens went off after 25 minutes. Selection issues? Tick. Smith gambled on some McCoist magic once more but he looked way off the pace, with the ball refusing to stick and the Rangers manager ended the season in exactly the same way that he proposed to start it before being forced to ditch those plans, with both Hateley and Ferguson up front. The combination didn't work that day either. Mistakes? The biggest of the season and there were no prizes for guessing who was involved. Dave McPherson was a late doubt but was just passed fit to start and was arguably one of the best Rangers players over the course of the 90 minutes but, just over a minute after the restart, he was given a choice to make when Craig Brewster had flicked on a long United ball into his path. Seconds earlier he had seen Andy McLaren press Neil Murray hard over on the touchline and, with Christian Dailly chasing him down, he opted not to give Murray another test and instead made the short pass back to Ally Maxwell. In this instance however, Murray was in a lot

---

54   'Arabs' was a nickname for Dundee United, used by their fans originally before more common use.

more space than he had previously and McPherson was looking in his direction as he went to take the ball. At the last second he changed shape and went the other way, putting his goalkeeper under more pressure than Murray would ever have received. Maxwell was one of many goalkeepers who were struggling with the new back-pass law – then nearly two years old – and, where others may have feinted one way and kept possession, he just decided to kick it as hard as he could. Sadly he directed it straight at the onrushing Dailly. For a brief second he appeared to have smothered the danger when it bounced back at him but not for long as Dailly regained possession and tried his luck from a very narrow angle. The ball hit the post and span back into the path of Brewster who had sensed the danger long before and he won the cup from two yards out.

'Until Saturday, Rangers were threatened more by their own peculiar lethargy than anything their opponents could do. No one took advantage. No one could, because no one was capable,' opined one columnist on the Monday morning. 'Frankly, I'm glad it's over. The longer it dragged on the more damage was being done to Scottish football's reputation.' Despite a remarkable sequence of eight domestic trophies out of ten since he took the job and one fabulous European run, Walter Smith was under no illusions about the level of criticism that would come his way as a result of this defeat. The juxtaposition of watching AC Milan eviscerate Barcelona in the Champions League Final just a few days before[55] wouldn't have helped lighten the doubt that Rangers were a tired and blunt force. His side had failed to win any of their final six games and were victorious in only three out of the last 12. The final gap was three points over Aberdeen but no one had truly convinced themselves of a title race, even with Rangers winning only half of that season's league fixtures. Smith knew that big action was required and when he called for Andy Goram to meet him in his office, the goalkeeper knew that he was in trouble. In truth, he had no idea just how much.

* * *

Smith had repeated himself more than once before he stood up to shake Goram's hand and wish him well for the future, telling him, 'Andy, your chance is gone now. That's it. I wish you all the best, but I won't be backing down on this. Good luck.' The players were in for their final session of the season after which the manager would speak to them all individually before their summer break. If it was a simple chat about a fitness regime and weight expectations for the restart then it would be done in Smith's smaller office near the dressing room. If it was more serious than that, then players had to go to the manager's office up the marble staircase with all those imposing figures from history looking down on the conversation. It was Davie Dodds who came into the dressing room, instructing Goram, 'Goalie, he wants you now … upstairs.'

---

55   An un-fancied Milan won 4-0 against Johan Cruyff's 'Dream Team'.

Although Goram had broken down once more at the start of April, there were still hopes that he would return for the season's close but he knew that there was no chance of this. Despite Smith being increasingly concerned about the impact of Goram's lifestyle on his recovery, he felt the best chance of his goalkeeper getting fit was with a restful break with the family in the sunshine, so he ordered him to go away somewhere nice. Even with his back still causing problems, it was the kind of break Goram needed, until the very last day where he met his old Oldham Athletic team-mates and ended up missing his flight home and being stranded without his family on Tenerife for another week, during which time he ended up breaking the cheekbone of a Dundee United fan in the week who had been taunting him about the end of his career. As the media got a hold of it and a myriad of flashbulbs met Goram's eventual arrival back at Glasgow airport, it was one thing that Smith didn't need in the run-up to that fateful final. Goram was to pay the price, alongside Stevens, Huistra, Kuznetsov and Wishart among others as he made his transfer list known the week following the defeat. He was in tears – a broken man – as his life appeared to spiral out of control.[56] He begged for another chance but Smith wouldn't entertain it, telling the press that it was a 'regrettable' decision but the only one that he could make after what he called 'disagreements about how he [Goram] should handle his training after coming back from injury'. Smith's first signing – the man who had become his colossus – was heading for the exit.

By the time Richard Gough lifted the Premier Division trophy on that final home game against Dundee, it was clear that the title was beginning to feel a lot like Easter for Rangers fans; they weren't sure exactly which date in the spring it was taking place but they knew that it definitely would. A4 sheets of cardboard were left on every seat with a '6' on it to hold up at the presentation. Thousands were turned upside down to make '9', the real objective now. For many fans it felt like a banal waiting room for that season to come, going through the motions of picking up the necessary titles in the meantime. Truthfully, it was becoming boring.

Smith saw drastic action as the only way to reinvigorate the whole project but it was one thing telling the world who he thought was no longer required and another replacing them with the kind of players who would reintroduce some colour to the increasingly grey backdrop of Scottish football. Fans had been discussing that very topic for months and back in February one cantankerous contributor to *Follow, Follow*, 'The Major', suggested the usual Scottish names such as Alan McLaren, Eoin Jess and Gary McAllister before writing, 'Looking further afield, I note with great interest that AC Milan are selling Brian Laudrup who I think could be a sensation at Ibrox.'

Now, there was a thought.

---

56   On the Friday after the Scottish Cup Final, the Abbey National Building Society announced that they had instigated court proceedings against Goram for mortgage arrears.

Chapter Four

Identity Crisis

'Most people are other people. Their thoughts are someone else's opinions, their lives a mimicry, their passions a quotation.'
Oscar Wilde, De Profundis

'It's shite being Scottish! We're the lowest of the low. The scum of the fucking earth! The most wretched miserable servile pathetic trash that was ever shat on civilisation. Some people hate the English. I don't. They're just wankers. We, on the other hand, are colonised by wankers. Can't even find a decent culture to get colonised by. We're ruled by effete arseholes. It's a shite state of affairs to be in, Tommy, and all the fresh air in the world won't make any fucking difference!'
Irvine Welsh, Trainspotting

With 15 minutes remaining, Hearts were shell-shocked. They had gone nearly two years without defeat at Tynecastle and had welcomed a Rangers side – humiliated at home to Hamilton Accies in the Scottish Cup the previous week – fully expecting to dent their title hopes. Now here they were, 4-1 down. An unlikely scoreline that day in February 1987, it would have been an absolutely unthinkable one a year before. So too the reaction of the home support. As Graham Roberts swung in a free kick, some of the Hearts fans who were still there broke into a song of patriotic defiance. 'O Flower of Scotland' could be heard in the background as Rangers worked the ball along the edge of the box before Davie Cooper fed McCoist to score number five. A direct reaction to a characteristically tough performance from Roberts, most likely, but it was almost certainly a challenge to the visiting faithful too. Once thought to be the bedrock of the Scotland support, the next decade would see a drift away towards ambivalence and outright antagonism. Their team might be winning today, they might well win this title and many more, but they were no longer truly Scottish. They were now something else.

Quite what that identity was had been an issue bubbling under the surface of Scottish life for a generation or so. Thirty years before, there would have been little hint of tension. With both colours of government committed to full employment and supporting traditional industry and the memories still strong of standing shoulder to shoulder with those from all corners of the union against fascism, there was little need to challenge the compatibility of feeling both Scottish and British. The question of separation was redundant when, in the words of academic and author Sir Tom Devine, the two major parties had 'presided over an unprecedented increase in personal incomes, living standards and health care in these decades. Westminster had delivered to the Scots where it mattered most, in jobs, wages and welfare.' Given the strong party loyalty on religious grounds – the Conservative appeal to the Protestant working class was a major reason for its relative success in Scotland[57] and Scottish Labour was very quickly seen as the party for the Irish Catholic diaspora – few would have expected it to change so quickly.

But change it did. The general election in 1970 was the first time that Scotland didn't vote for the same party that ultimately gained power. Coming only three years after the election of the first SNP MP[58], it was a sign of the coming divergence. When that number rose to 11 seats in 1974, the new Labour government were forced to open up the question of Home Rule. However, it should be noted that, even at the SNP's 1970s electoral height, support for independence was only 12 per cent. It was a tactical tool used to show dissatisfaction and to try and force some leverage and that need only intensified in the following decade as Margaret Thatcher replaced full employment with beating inflation as priority number one and actively sought to manage the already terminal decline of heavy industry, with devastating effects on the associated communities in Scotland. The apotheosis of this was the trial run north of the border of the Community Charge – known better as the 'Poll Tax' – which Devine argues, more than any other policy, 'drove home the message to many Scots that they were being ruled by an alien government. On the eve of its introduction, the leaders of the three largest Scottish churches condemned the tax as 'undemocratic, unjust, socially divisive and destructive of community and family life.' This sense of alienation inevitably led to an unstoppable demand for devolution which was eventually passed into law following the referendum in September 1997. Standing firm against federalisation

---

57   The Conservative and Unionist vote in 1955 was the last time there was a popular majority in Scotland for any party in a general election. In 1968 almost 40 per cent of Protestant manual workers in Dundee voted Tory compared to only 6 per cent of their Catholic colleagues. Even by the height of Thatcherism in 1986, 46 per cent of the members of the Church of Scotland voted Conservative.

58   Winnie Ewing sensationally took the Hamilton seat from Labour in a by-election.

and warning the nation of the doors that it would be opening, was none other than the vice-chairman of Rangers Football Club, Donald Findlay QC. He led the 'No-No' campaign and many placards could be seen at Ibrox for a League Cup tie against Dundee United and a reserve league game against Celtic.[59] From the very top of the club to the support, Rangers were part of the story.

It should hardly be surprising that one of the bastion institutions of unionism in Scotland would be so embroiled in the debate and, as was the case with the socio-economic issues of the late 1980s, this was a debate that was regularly played out in the pages of fanzines as well as on buses and in the pub.[60] The first mention of it in *Follow, Follow* comes from 'The Wee Prime Minister' shortly before the 1990 World Cup as he outlined his fears that English hooliganism would further tarnish the reputation of the Union Flag. Indeed it was an emblem already under attack at Ibrox from the club's very own head of security, Alistair Hood, of whom it was said 'epitomises the maxim that "work expands to fit the time allocated to it"'. 'For all Rangers fans the Union Jack stands for something more than merely the team's colours. But rather what the club represents,' he pleaded. 'The sight of the Rangers end in full swing, with the flag high, is a living testimony to the continuity of our Scottish and British heritage. A love of Queen and country that no other team can match and which has spurred our club on to triumph after triumph. It is this which makes all of us responsible for getting the message across before the World Cup begins, that England has its own flag which Englishmen can be proud of or denigrate as they see fit. The Union Flag represents the United Kingdom, not just the English part of it. Apart from perhaps the Belfast City Hall and the Palace of Westminster I can't think of another place in the United Kingdom where the sight of the Union Jack streaming out in all it's glory can fill my heart with more pride than when it flies over Ibrox Stadium. Long may it continue to do so.'

As is almost always the case – especially when tribal rivalry is involved – when tensions start to appear, extremes are easily found. From April 1991 the Scotland team and its supporters became regularly referred to as 'Jacobites', the inference increasingly being that simply supporting the national side was akin to being a fully fledged adherent to separation, political dissidence and the restoration of the House of Stuart. With so much caricature, points were easy to score, even if the back-and-fro in every edition got tiresome very quickly.

At first there was a discomfort with the increasing level of anti-English sentiment associated with the 'Tartan Army' in the early 1990s, especially with the recent influence and importance of anglo imports at Ibrox. 'Let's face it, if all we Scots can think up to be proud of is hatred for the English then what hope have we got?' lamented 'Rantin' Robert Burns' in that same April edition. 'Flower o Scotland? Count me out. I'm as Scottish (and not ashamed of it) as the next yin,

59   The referendum asked the Scottish public two questions: firstly, if there should be a devolved parliament and, if so, should it have tax-raising powers?

60   The tensions of Thatcherism and Rangers are discussed in my previous book, *Revolution: Rangers 1986–92*.

but I'd rather sing a national anthem which celebrated something positive about our country, our people. Like what? I hear you cry. Well, like "Freedom, Come All Ye" for example. No, I know you've never heard of it, but whose fault is that?'

A similar discomfort was felt by other Rangers fans around the overt loyalty to the union and creeping British nationalism, fuelled in no small part by a need to show support for the loyalist cause in Northern Ireland. In September 1991 the use of an outstretched hand while singing 'Rule Britannia' or the national anthem was first picked up on – and not favourably. It has been defended since as a 'Red Hand' salute but the fascist connotations were immediate and the condemnation in a fanzine letter by Carol McPherson, soon after the sad death of former Rangers great Willie Thornton, was clear, 'My message to those fans who indulge in these pathetic and childish antics is simple. Take yourselves and your fascist propaganda over to the banana-throwing idiots at Parkhead and leave the rest of us to get on with watching the football. Unlike that fine ambassador Mr Thornton, you don't deserve to wear the colours of Rangers.'

Contrary to popular belief, there were, and indeed are, Scottish nationalists within the Rangers support and this position was also made apparent at the time. Alan Kilpatrick noted his bemusement and disappointment with the wide affection towards the union within the fanbase. In the summer of 1992, he wrote, 'I find it hard to believe that any intelligent, democratically minded Scot can openly and cheerfully support this one sided, unfair, Union,' before providing his type of history lesson. And so the tartan touch paper was lit, with just about every issue released within the time period of this book, containing some kind of comment on it. 'Big Mac' wrote, 'My pride in being British and belief in the union means I see Scotland as part of a nation but not as one,' before suggesting that his increasing apathy towards international football could be resolved by having a United Kingdom side to get behind. 'The Major' questioned any notion that the Rangers support and Tartan Army were as in sync as they once were by asking, 'Why is there no flags of a Jacobite nature, e.g. St Andrews, Lion Rampant at any Rangers game if we're all so patriotic? Why does every away support bar the Beggars try and taunt us with their Scottish flags and songs? Would they do that if we were all Jock Tamson's bairns?'

The riposte by 'MacDougall', otherwise known as Professor Graham Walker, was both swift and strong. Although admitting that the sheer numbers of Rangers fans feeling solidarity with Scotland was now history, he was keen to highlight that the love affair with England was almost certainly one-sided before moving on to his wider rebuttal, 'And as for the saltire and Lion Rampant being Jacobite flags, tell it to the Covenanters! These national emblems have, of course, been the flags of the Protestant churches which have always resisted the erosion of Scottish identity. While we're on religion, some comment is required on The Major's remark that he has more in common with an English Protestant than a Scottish Catholic. I'd be interested to hear The Major's idea of what an English Protestant is. If, for example, said English Protestant was an Anglican and serious about his religion, then he would have more in common with a practising Catholic than with a practising Presbyterian. I doubt if the Major has a clue about the distinctive reformed religious traditions of Scotland, and how the nation struggled over the centuries to defend the more democratic and less ritualist nature of those traditions.' Walker then moved on to Scottish football's other identity crisis in order to paint the debate in a slightly different light, 'Then there is the small matter of the Celtic fans' allegiance. The Major states, without realising the significance of his words, that only Celtic fans do not taunt us with Scottish flags. Of course they don't – they have traditionally been unenthusiastic about Scottish patriotism because they perceive it as hostile to Catholic Irish extraction. However, irony is lost on The Major. This factor – of Celtic fans' contempt for the Scottish national team – should be reason enough for Bears to support it. All people like The Major are doing is displaying the same persecution complex as the Tims. Let's rise above the small-mindedness of the Farrys of this world.'

Nevertheless, the disintegration of the relationship between the Rangers support and the Scottish national team during the 1990s is irrefutable. Journalist Andrew Marr once described the position of the union at the turn of the 21st century as two slices of pizza being pulled apart, held only together by strings of cheese. At times, especially viewed through such a cartoonish lens, the majority of the Rangers support were seen as that mozzarella.

Perhaps of more interest to this story than the political and historical aspects was their manifestation in the actual football and it leaves us with one key question to answer. Were the footballing flashpoints indeed just a fig leaf for this constitutional schism or was it in fact the football that was the main driver in the first place? Whatever the answer was, the impact of the Graeme Souness revolution on it appeared to be immediate, as Campbell Ogilvie – club secretary throughout the period – recalled, 'The club in the early '80s used to have allocations for Scotland games. The members' section at Ibrox would always be clambering for tickets for the games with England. When we started signing the English players, I noticed there was a change in the interest. There wasn't the same hype around it. Why, I don't know. I just know that the demand for these tickets was considerably less.'[61]

There may be some substance to Ogilvie's initial suggestion as to why interest for some faded so quickly. The English arrivals were taken to the heart of the support very quickly and, under the laws of football fandom which state that one's enemy's enemy has to be one's friend, there was an overt show of defiance. Replica England tops were visible at Ibrox throughout that first Souness season and many fans revelled in defending their new heroes, whose welcome to away grounds in

---

61   If there was a reduction in applications from the members, it wasn't evident in the overall attendances in the match between Souness's arrival and 1989, when the fixture was canned. There was a gradual impact, however. Hampden would never see 74,000 at a Scotland game again, as it did for the 1986 World Cup qualifier against Spain. Only 27,740 bothered to turn up for the key Euro '92 qualifier against Switzerland in October 1990, while there were 62,817 at the Old Firm League Cup Final 11 days later. Even if the opposition was San Marino, only 35,170 took up the opportunity to celebrate qualification for Sweden in September 1991. Over 5,000 more attended Hibs v Dunfermline at the national stadium the next month.

Scotland was often less than hospitable. 'English bastards!' was a common greeting on Scotland's terraces, less the subject of op-ed pieces than ones with religious connotations it must be said.

However, the bigger reason is almost surely one of bandwidth, both economic and emotional. The 1990s saw the club – the big club at least – become more prominent than the country, leading to the 21st century where the World Cup was supplanted by the Champions League as the ultimate stage in the sport. The lottery of birth no longer mattered, the pinnacle of club football would be one where all the world's greats could and would be tested. With Rangers games becoming both more expensive and attractive, for many families there wasn't the ability to do both and as such, Scotland lost out. And, with the clubs taking increasing primacy in the hearts of supporters, it was natural that rivalries grew more intense and therefore cheering on opposition players or sharing a common cause with fans from other clubs became more difficult. It is interesting that the volume and repetition of the national identity discussion in the fanzines reached new levels from 1992/93 onwards. A piece in the *Sunday Times* in January 1993 said, 'Rangers' position is unique. In no other European country does one club stand out from the rest as much as Rangers do in Scotland. In most other countries, the leagues are structured for the benefit of the top clubs, whereas in Scotland, it is almost the other way around.' Rangers had bigger ambitions than the national game and were not weighed down by bureaucrats in the boardroom and technocrats in the dugout. Rangers were bigger than Scotland, their fans loved it and opposition fans hated it. This could never make for a comfortable relationship.

Perhaps the height of the changing power dynamic was exemplified by David Murray's attempts to make Ibrox the national game's home. With Hampden being partially renovated during the qualification process for the 1994 World Cup in the USA, Ibrox played host to three qualifiers against Portugal, Italy and Malta and a friendly against Germany. Murray first courted this move in early 1991 when Ibrox hosted a friendly with the USSR, at a time when the future of Hampden Park itself was in serious doubt. Did the authorities need to spend millions on a stadium when Glasgow had a modern venue right there? Why not, instead, put money where all the talk was, and invest instead in grassroots and youth development? The reason was evident fairly quickly. Attendances were not good with Ibrox half-full for the Portugal game and only reaching a majority for the others by way of free tickets for school kids. With Rangers fans losing interest, Celtic supporters rarely having it and the rest begrudging putting more of their own money in the coffers of a club who were already a domestic leviathan, it was always destined for failure. Tom Shields wrote in his *Herald* diary that Ibrox could not be the future, 'It is not, we can assure you, the prejudice of someone who, even if he had been the Jim Baxter of the South Side as a boy, could never have played for Rangers. It is not even being faced with the prospect of having to say the words "A Blue Nose Burger, please" if you fancy a snack. It is not the thought that a tenner from each £20 goes into the Ibrox coffers so they can buy even better players. It is not having to listen to the Murray International brass band. It is nothing to do with ancient rivalries. No, it is simply that however commodious the Parc des Huns might be, it will never replace Hampden as the national stadium.'

Andy Roxburgh, who had previously complained that the Portugal game had been overshadowed by press questions about the upcoming European Cup tie between Rangers and Leeds United – a sign of the times if ever there was one – suggested that Scotland failed to beat Italy because Ibrox was effectively a neutral ground. Ibrox would play host again to a friendly against Denmark prior to the World Cup in 1998. Brian Laudrup was booed around a stadium where he was normally a god. Any notion of harmonious coexistence was by then a dissonant farce.

If the die was cast earlier by the changing political dynamics, the abrasive arrival of Graeme Souness in 1986 hastened the Rangers support down that road. As detailed in my previous book, he took a deliberately antagonistic approach towards the SFA, the media and the opposition and in so doing carried a large part of the Ibrox fanbase with him in seeing the rest of the Scottish footballing community as the enemy. In a series of interviews in his final season, after an almost constant war footing had taken its toll, Souness was still labouring the point. In one conversation with BSB's David Livingstone, when questioned about the lack of cordiality in Scottish football and his role in it, he was quick to bounce the blame back, 'This carpet is blue and there would be people out there who would argue the point. Everything to do with Rangers, in some people's eyes, is wrong and that is something we'll just have to get on with.' A month after his departure, the day after that particular title race had reached its dramatic conclusion, he was still as adamant when he spoke with Livingstone again, 'There's a line in a song that Rangers supporters sing that "no one likes us, we don't care" and I really, really believe and I've felt it more and more this season than I've ever felt it. There is such an anti-Rangers feeling within Scotland, within Scottish football, that they are up there on their own … They're up against it up there. Jealousy is a terrible thing. People who are jealous take it to bed with them. It must be like a big cancer sitting there.' The sense that the Scotland side, and more importantly their fans, were small-time and chippy was undoubtedly a part in the growing antipathy. One contributor wrote in 1991 about his disaffection with the national side, 'If you've seen one picture of some tartan-clad gummsy drunk from Caldercruix booking his ring into a fountain you've seen 'em all.' The Tartan Army weren't a serious football support, they were just small club tourists looking for a party.

This antagonism was given plenty of oxygen as footballing matters presented fans with many opportunities with which to play out that club v country battle. Richard Gough's fallout would be followed by David Robertson and Duncan Ferguson. There was Craig Brown's unnecessary dithering over Andy Goram and Jim Leighton and his underuse of Ally McCoist. Players like Ian Ferguson were felt to be unfairly under-capped because they were Rangers players and then were the targets of abuse after bad results, his final cap coming in Monaco when Scotland drew 0-0 with Estonia in a re-arranged match where some fans made their feelings known as the players trudged off the pitch. As Colin Calderwood went to applaud them, Ferguson was having none of it, saying, 'Don't clap they cunts, fuck them.' His diplomacy was caught on BBC Scotland microphones and another storm ensued. 'I think it was a sign that the Tartan Army does not contain as many Rangers supporters as it once did,' Ferguson later wrote. 'Mostly the Tartan Army, these self-styled "best fans in the world" come mainly from areas outside Glasgow and are supporters of other Scottish teams rather than Rangers. So I suppose that being an Ibrox player was another reason for me to get it in the neck but I was not prepared to take it.'

It would be naive to suggest that this kind of situation was peculiar to Rangers and Scotland. At around the same time, there was a very similar kind of fault line opening up south of the border. In 1994 the former Tottenham Hotspur and England player Alan Mullery appeared on the ITV discussion show *Sport In Question* sporting a rather ostentatious Blackburn Rovers jacket. They were vying for the Premier League championship with Manchester United at the time and when asked about his sartorial choice, he replied, 'Well, everyone wants them to win, don't they?' Anyone But United – ABU – became a dominant theme around English football in the 1990s. It had little to do with the autonomy of Scotland in a political union, but the comparisons with Rangers were obvious. The biggest clubs in the United Kingdom, dominant, brash and successful, they were also the most hated.

There were other similarities, too. The absolute glee shared by the rest of the footballing nation following European exits[62], the lengthy bans for Alex Ferguson and Eric Cantona and, although Walter Smith was never as obstructive as Ferguson was about international duty of his players, he wasn't slow in letting them know where their priorities should lie. Stuart McCall wrote in 1998, 'On the Scotland front Craig Brown had taken over as boss. The first game under him was in Italy and I went there on the brink of signing a new deal for Rangers. The last words Walter Smith told me were, "Don't come back here injured or else!" He wasn't anti the Scotland team, he just had a lot of players returning from international duty with knocks and was sick of it. I went with a dead leg and could have pulled out, but I wanted to play and I was fit enough to start. But Dino Baggio landed on my ankle in the last minute and I was in pain and had to miss the next Rangers game. The gaffer blanked me for weeks after that. Although my injury was minor it was another problem for him and the contract talks went on ice. Nothing was mentioned about

---

62   It should be noted that fans such as James Peacock, would write letters to newspapers as he did on 25 August 1994, complaining that other supporters were not behind Rangers in Europe, 'I really cannot comprehend the mentality of someone who actively supports the European opposition, as Mr Thomson unquestionably indicates he has done. Apart from anything else it is hardly the action of a Scot, and given that Rangers are representing Scotland in the tournament by virtue of being the Scottish champions.' These fans were then were also quick to point out that the victory over Leeds United wasn't one for Scotland but one for Rangers and Rangers alone.

a new deal for months. I think it was the boss's way of letting me know who paid my wages. He never stopped me going on Scotland duty, but the message came through clearly. The contract came through eventually in December. I missed several Scotland games later, but they were down to genuine injuries.'

In England, the hypocrisy of those same haters to then depend on Manchester United players whenever an international tournament came around, only – in the case of David Beckham in the summers of both 1998 and 2000 – to use them as an easy scapegoat when their dreams were not realised was not lost on United fans. Too pervasive and too important were club loyalties that aligning two mutually exclusive feelings proved too much for many. Rob Smyth, a United fan and football and cricket writer for *The Guardian* among other outlets, noted that the mood within the fan base changed after 1993/94, was accelerated by the Cantona affair and then went 'into overdrive after the Beckham thing'[63], 'Euro 2000 was the first one where I can remember not being happy that they lost as such, but being vaguely amused. I wasn't invested at all. It's never been a consistent thing but there have been times where I've found it absolutely hilarious when they've gone out, I've really enjoyed it.'

In a way, it is much like an appreciation of the arts, where the willing suspension of disbelief is necessary in order to fully enjoy what is being offered up to the audience. International football demands all fans of big clubs to park their loyalties and biases at the door on their way into the stadium or the pub to watch the game. In order to experience international football properly, as any supporter should, one must pretend that grudges and divisions don't exist for 90 minutes. The most perfect crystallisation of this occurred at Hampden Park on 10 June 2017 with what could be called the 'Griffiths Test'. England were in tenuous control of a World Cup qualifier with only three minutes of normal time remaining when Celtic striker Leigh Griffiths turned the game on its head with two brilliant free kicks in the space of a few minutes. Bedlam at Hampden and in homes and hostelries across the country. Griffiths had enjoyed a fine season at Parkhead almost as much as he had the two victories at Ibrox during the campaign. After the 2-1 win in December he tied a Celtic scarf to the goalposts and then in May, he humiliated Rangers even further in the 5-1 battering by appearing to wipe his nose on the Ibrox corner flag. All's fair in love and war, of course. It is the nature of rivalry.

However, for Rangers fans gripped by the dramatic finish on that warm 2017 afternoon, there was quite a predicament. To experience the match as any football fan should – wild hugs with strangers and adulation for the conquering hero – they had to leave their Ibrox allegiance to one side. To shower praise on a man who had rubbed their noses in defeat and share embraces with those who may believe their club to be dead – or wish that it was – generates a great deal of

---

63   David Beckham was sent off in England's World Cup second round game against Argentina in 1998, for a petulant kick at Diego Simeone. When England lost on penalties, he became the ultimate scapegoat. There were effigies of him on fire on the first game of the following Premier League season.

cognitive dissonance with which to work through. Many couldn't then as they hadn't through the 1990s, as United fans couldn't after France '98, and so the pretence was dropped. Some felt ambivalence, others a wry smile, when Harry Kane – captain of England for the first time – popped up in injury time to steal a point. More and more supporters were unable and unwilling to forget their true love, even for a brief fling.

What then of the contemporary support? Instead of being fuelled by envy at Rangers' success in the 1990s, the more recent decade has been shaped by gleeful gloating at their failure. The bloodlust around Rangers' demotion to the fourth tier of Scottish football in 2012 with a divisive independence referendum campaign thrown in for good measure two years later did not help the cause of fraternal goodwill. Recent studies have shown a complex picture. Much was made of a 2018 examination of the official Scotland Supporters' Club with over 20,000 members which found that Rangers was still the number one club represented ahead of Aberdeen, Celtic, Hearts and Hibs in that order. No figures were published but it is understood that the top line was 14 per cent, still a significant drop from the days when the Rangers support was believed to have provided the Tartan Army with two thirds of its soldiers and probably shouldn't be too surprising that the biggest club in the country – even with its issues with the rest of the nation over the last three decades – would still provide more fans of international football than the provincial clubs.

When *The Athletic* surveyed more than 8,000 Rangers fans in 2020, it wasn't a ringing endorsement for the national team and its footballing establishment; 76.2 per cent cared significantly more about club football than international football and on a scale of one to ten, with one meaning 'if they lose I am not affected at all' and ten meaning 'it defines a significant part of my life', two thirds chose ten with respect to how much they care about Rangers being successful and 46 per cent chose one when the question was asked about Scotland. Over half stated that their support for Scotland had decreased significantly since the events of 2012 and over 90 per cent felt that the relationships with other clubs had declined in that time. What was perhaps more interesting was that only 37 per cent felt that being a unionist was an important part of a Rangers fan's identity while nearly three-quarters felt that nationalism was something that was synonymous with the Scotland fan base. For 'them' there was the overt political posturing, for 'us' it was simply a case of club matters first.

One curious point, given that this poll was conducted in late 2020 with Scotland on the brink of qualification for the delayed European Championship the following summer, was that two-thirds claimed that qualification for a major tournament wouldn't change their support for the national team. The noise around that summer – with at least one new generation of Scottish supporters able to properly 'plug in' to these global events for the very first time – suggested that declaration may have wavered, especially with a younger section of fans more interested in being part of any relevant football contest and, if not nationalist, then at least less overtly unionist than their forebears. More rigorous work is perhaps needed on this question and the general tensions that international football presents all over the world.

Regardless, the picture is significantly different than it was when Rangers signed the Scotland captain to be their first player-manager and the world view of the support was turned on its axis. An increase in the depth of the fanaticism only turned up the dial on cynicism and tribalism. The rise of the big clubs and their ascendancy to the top of the game itself brought with it a level of professionalism that faded the old romantic era. There was a loss of innocence in the 1990s. There was also no more need for pretence.

Chapter Five

God Complex

Season 1994/95

'Brian, how come you are so good?'
Jim White

'God gave Davie Cooper a talent. He would not be disappointed with how it was used.'
Walter Smith

Walter Smith was sitting in his office, bristling at the meeting he was just about to have. It was early in the September of 1994, just days after the infamous 'Week from Hell' where his side had failed to qualify for the Champions League, had lost to Celtic at Ibrox and were eliminated from the League Cup – a trophy to which they almost had exclusive rights – by Falkirk. Now Smith had to summon his star signing back from his home country for crisis talks.

Two months earlier, down the corridor in the Blue Room, David Murray sparkled as he introduced Basile Boli to the Scottish media. There had been more expensive signings certainly – one at double the price the year before – but in the chairman's opinion, none as good. This was his 'biggest'. He was going to be the difference in Europe for a Rangers side who couldn't afford to miss out on the elite stage again. The fourth estate were in no doubt that this was the most exciting signing in Scottish football for many years and the front pages of first editions of the fanzines bore his picture. The player seemed to agree. He could have gone elsewhere – Genoa, Tottenham or Arsenal – but he chose Glasgow, not because he 'liked the town' but because he wanted 'to play at the highest level and that is the European Cup'. In order to be successful at that level he said, you need 'skill, experience, good tactics, and good players' but felt that Rangers were 'capable of it'. Ironic then that, so soon after arriving, he would be telling a very different story to the press.

Or did he? That is what Smith sought to get straight. Describing Smith's tactics as 'crazy', he also lambasted his new colleagues' attitude before the crucial tie with AEK Athens as 'all wrong', by saying, 'You just cannot go about winning such an important game when you are having a laugh in the dressing room half an hour before the kick-off.' It was a major embarrassment for Smith when he needed it least but apparently it was all lost in translation – not for the first time with a new foreign signing – and all just a big misunderstanding. Ultimately, it never worked out. For the second season in a row, the marquee signing was a disaster who didn't fit in.

Fortunately, however, there was another signing and, although he arrived with slightly less fanfare, he would go on to become a Rangers legend. Season 1994/95 shared many of the characteristics of the season just gone; injuries, players forced to play out of position, cup disappointment at home and abroad but it had one shining light. Set under grey Scottish skies in the foreground and the brightness of a very enjoyable World Cup in the back, it was a year where the subject of entertainment and individual flair dominated conversation. One where the Rangers support worshipped the birth of a new god and mourned the loss of an old one.

* * *

Given what he would go on to do, it is jarring to imagine Brian Laudrup being very much secondary on that summer's bill. It should have jarred more at the time given what he had already done; a European champion both at international and club level, he had been voted the fourth-best player in the world by *World Soccer* 18 months previously. The signing of a 25-year-old with that pedigree in 2023 would draw crowds covering Edmiston Drive all the way back to Paisley but perhaps there are several reasons to explain the relative nonchalance in 1994. Firstly, Rangers fans expected big signings every summer so the notion itself was not a novelty. Secondly, the summer speculation concerning Rangers and Laudrup initially centred around his older and more distinguished brother Michael, who was leaving Barcelona. The *Herald* reported in the wake of the Scottish Cup Final defeat to Dundee United that a bid from Rangers was 'certain' but he eventually joined Real Madrid instead. Finally, by Laudrup's own admission, he was at something of a crossroads in his career and had hated Italy, with the 'frightening' fans and stifling tactical rigidity. Despite winning the Champions League with AC Milan a few months before – Laudrup didn't play in the final but did manage seven appearances in the competition while on loan there from Fiorentina, who had been relegated in his first season in Serie A – there was a sense that he had failed there and that his career was now stalling. Even his new team-mates were initially underwhelmed. David Robertson speaks of coming in at half-time during one of the early pre-seasons friendlies thinking, 'This guy is not as good as people make out.' It would soon change, as Robertson admitted, 'It turned out that we weren't as good as he was and we had to catch up to him. He was making passes that I simply wasn't reading. But as time went on I knew that if the ball got to Laudrup, I could make a run and nine times out of ten he would find the pass to me. He made our lives so much easier.' Rangers brought Laudrup and his family over to see the city and the more rural surroundings that they hoped he would call home, but never pushed the player into the deal. Smith and Murray's patience was rewarded. Together, it is doubtful if they spent £2.5m more wisely.

They spent slightly more on Basile Boli, but then they were far better acquainted. Boli had featured twice against Rangers for Marseille in 1992/93, had scored the winner in that season's Champions League Final and was a notoriously physical defender as Mark Hateley and Stuart Pearce would testify. While Smith was clearly looking for creativity, Rangers still had Alexei Mikhailichenko, Pieter Huistra and Ian Durrant on the books with Ally McCoist returning soon and, even if Hateley had been worn out by the previous season's exertions, there was still the possibility that Duncan Ferguson could come good, legalities depending. The real gaping hole in the side that summer was unquestionably in the heart of the defence, with such porous play being incompatible with another European run and something that would provide a real risk in the domestic cups if not the league championship.

The purchase of Boli provided a solution of quality, with the first edition of *Follow, Follow* that season adorned with a picture of the new defender under the headline 'The Terminator Has Landed'. Just as with the headline signing the previous summer, however, there were issues both on and off the park that cooler observers should have highlighted. For most of his time at Marseille, Boli had played in a three-man defence – he played sweeper for the majority of that spell, including in that Champions League Final – and, where he did play in a four, he was the on the right-hand side of central defence. Smith had therefore bought himself a headache if he didn't go to a three, as his captain Richard Gough was immovable from that position through choice. Boli, whose English was nowhere near as fluent as Laudrup's, struggled to integrate himself as well and, years later, Hateley wrote of his scepticism at the move, 'I saw Basile as nothing other than a bully and feared that once the typical Scottish strikers got stuck into him, he wouldn't want to know. I was proven right.'[64] Few were making such pronouncements at the time, however. His talent was not questioned, especially not when there were other features for the press to remark upon. In his column the week that Boli signed, the celebrated Scottish diarist Tom Shields wrote, 'The signing by Rangers of Basile Boli, the talented black defender, is good news not

---

64   The Danish defender Marc Rieper was another defensive target that summer but Brøndby wouldn't budge enough on their valuation. At Boli's unveiling, Murray confidently said that he expected that he would arrive eventually. In retrospect, this may have been the better priority.

only for the Ibrox club. It transpires that Mr Boli is eligible to play for Scotland. His great-great-grandfather had Scottish blood in him. He ate a member of David Livingstone's expedition.' Welcome to liberal Scotland.

And what of those existing Rangers players whom Smith promised to rid himself of? Very little, at least quickly. Of the bigger names[65], only Oleh Kuznetsov left that summer, on a free transfer to Maccabi Haifa, as names like Gary Stevens, Pieter Huistra and Fraser Wishart would have to wait until later in the season to depart. In the end, there was no dramatic departure for Andy Goram. Smith was candid throughout the years that, if the right offer had come in, then Goram would have been sold; he wasn't playing games. Goram, too, knew exactly that and it was a mixed reaction of both a dent in professional pride and personal relief that none came in. Injuries and professionalism were no doubt a factor in that but Goram was in no doubt as to what the overriding reason was: his height. In Peter Schmeichel and David Seaman the Premier League was moving towards goalkeepers who were well over six feet tall, whereas Goram was very much not. He was given a stay of execution and used it very wisely, getting himself into the shape of his life by the end of the summer camp. He had seen the post-season team trip to Canada – a mixture of fan event, McCoist testimonial dinner and Durrant stag do – as his farewell and his behaviour on the first night there was predictable. 'When the hangovers had cleared,' Goram wrote in 2010. 'Bomber [John Brown] and Durranty sat me down for the heart-to-heart that in many ways saved my Rangers career. Bomber said to me, "What you have done to the gaffer is a joke. Now you either tell us to fuck off and go your own way and we never see you again, or you can screw the nut, get yourself fit and be ready for pre-season if the chance is still there for you. We don't want you to go."' His efforts were obvious – including going for the Perrier water approach at Durrant's wedding[66] – and he was taken off the list before the action started back for real.

The pinnacle of the pre-season – after the usual Italian training camp and a low-key tour of Denmark – had been in the planning for months. The Ibrox Tournament, which commercial director Bob Reilly felt could become the 'most prestigious event in Britain' once it was up and running on an annual basis, would see Rangers pitched at home with Manchester United, Newcastle United and Sampdoria, with two semi-finals taking place on the Friday night and the winners and losers facing off the following afternoon. So much about the event was indicative of the prevailing moods. With the Premier League two seasons in, Rangers were desperately clinging on to a sense of relevance in British football and especially wanted to prove themselves on the field against a club with whom they believed themselves to be in rivalry off it. If Rangers and Manchester United were at war, it was a cold one as a competitive encounter had never been seen before but it was most likely something that Rangers saw as more important than

---

65   Chris Vinnicombe and Stephen Watson left too.

66   Until Smith himself told the players to inform Goram that he was allowed a few beers as he was a 'right boring bastard' without a drink.

United. Sampdoria represented Italy's Serie A, the greatest league in the world, but arguably Newcastle represented something increasingly more important: entertainment. Their thrilling start to life back in England's top flight had given Kevin Keegan's team that 'Entertainers' tag and it was something that fans wanted to see more of. The World Cup that summer in the United States had confounded the pre-tournament fear-mongering by providing a tournament set in constant bright sunshine with fun, excitement, surprises and bags of individual stars, maestros like Roberto Baggio, Hristo Stoichkov and Gheorghe Hagi who drove their team on with class rather than sweat. A Scottish review of the tournament was almost funereal. 'In the beginning,' it opened, 'there was a longing to see Scotland be part of the World Cup carnival of colourful supporters and exciting players, but in the end the feeling was one of relief that our players were not there. Scotland would have been out of place in America. The World Cup finals, which were brought to a close in Pasadena yesterday, were a celebration of football. They were about skill, goals and entertainment. All qualities which have been banished from the Scottish game.'

One fanzine wag wrote a piece on style and professionalism in a dour and unhealthy Scottish game by joking, 'I hope our players have studiously ignored the dubious "talents" on view in the States. "Talents" like the properly weighted pass, defenders being comfortable with the ball … either foot … ridiculous. These things, if imported into the domestic game, could ruin our traditional Saturday afternoon entertainment. What we want are full-backs who are adept at trapping a ball further than I can kick it, and they can do this with either shin! We don't want our game tainted by centre-backs who insist on passing the ball to a player of the same team, such fancy continental stuff might work for Brazil, Italy, Sweden, Bulgaria, Romania, Germany, Holland, Mexico, Norway, USA, Nigeria, Saudi Arabia and the Uncle Tom Cobley Works XI, but we must retain our distinctive indigenous skills. There must always be a place for the big donkey who can only kick with one foot, and that only sometimes, and who, rather than playing a simple square or reverse pass to a colleague, wants to excite the crowd by punting the ball as far up the park as possible.'

Rangers were successful – and a continuation of that in Scotland was not in doubt – but how they did it and how much it mattered was starting to become an issue as the wider footballing horizons were opened to the support. Rangers and Manchester United did play on the Saturday, as planned but not in the final, as had been hoped. Rangers, despite being 2-0 up on Sampdoria, were outclassed in a 4-2 defeat but the crowd were eventually pleased as Newcastle won the English encounter on penalties. Alex Ferguson and Steve Bruce both complained about the hostile reception they had received and this only intensified on the Saturday as Rangers – with a completely different starting XI save for Ally McCoist – won the third-place play-off with a David May own goal and got the added bonus of an Eric Cantona red card for a wild lunge on Steven Pressley[67]. 'Rangers are a club with ambition,' Ferguson said. 'Their directors and manager have great ambitions, but their support doesn't live up to these ambitions. The supporters are not big time.' He added that the behaviour of the fans was 'stupid and pointless' and said, 'If they are going to boo every good team which comes to Ibrox for friendlies then teams might stop coming.' Sampdoria beat Newcastle 3-1 in the final but Rangers fans felt that they had won the real tussle, the 'Battle of Britain'. Any thoughts of superiority outside of Scotland, however, were an illusion.

It had been known for months that the first competitive game of the season would be a Champions League qualifier, a few days before the league season started. And yet, when the draw was announced, Brian Laudrup knew that Rangers were likely to be going another season without playing at the elite level. Speaking at the end of the season he said, 'After just four weeks of preparation, we weren't up for it, we weren't ready, because of new players coming in.' It was, in his immediate view, 'one of the worst teams we could get'. The team was AEK Athens, with that all-important early first leg to be held in the intimidating cauldron of the Nikos Goumas Stadium. Old foes Sparta Prague had been avoided, as well as the in-form unseeded side Hajduk Split, but there were easier matches to be had such as Servette, Maccabi Haifa, Vác Samsung, Silkeborg and Avenir Beggen. Even the first leg at home might have given Rangers the opportunity to grow into some form before the trip to Greece but there is no early season evidence to suggest that it would have been material.[68]

It is hard to overstate just how much of a mess the first leg, on Wednesday, 10 August, was. Off the field, Rangers players and officials were hit by bottles and the 700 travelling fans by flares, some of which set fire to a flag in the Rangers section.[69] On it, saw one of the worst nights that a Walter Smith side had given in European competition. Remarkably, Basile Boli was suspended following his booking in the 1993 final – Marseille of course hadn't competed in Europe the following year – but Smith still used a back three regardless. Although ageing, John Brown was deemed good enough to be an option on the bench as was Dave McPherson. Being left-footed, Brown would still have been a better option than Gary Stevens, a fantastic right-back in his prime but whom Smith had put on the transfer list, he was certainly not accomplished enough to play on the left side of a back three. Twenty-one-year-old Neil Murray at right wing-back was another bizarre choice if Smith wanted to use Stevens. A four with Murray or Ian Durrant in midfield appeared the more sensible option. Rangers were absolutely ripped apart in over 90°F and had Andy Goram to thank for keeping the score down to

---

67   Incredibly this meant that Cantona was suspended for the first two games of the English Premier League season. It wouldn't be his last ban in 1994/95

68   Even the rest of the draw was as difficult as it could be. UEFA drew the eight qualifying ties at the same time as the four Champions League groups so every qualifier knew which group they would go into should they be successful. Rangers, AEK, Casino Salzburg and Maccabi were drawn with the holders AC Milan and the eventual winners that season, Ajax, who would go on to defeat their fellow seeds in the final.

69   AEK would be fined £25,000 by UEFA.

the eventual 2-0 defeat, with Dimitris Saravakos scoring both on his AEK debut, seemingly unaffected by the lack of squad gelling in the same way that Laudrup was, who barely noticed the ball all evening. 'I tried the wrong defensive tactics for the game, and in the first half they didn't work,' said Smith later. A system that players had never played in before is a risk in any game but one away from home, in such an important tie, where Archie Knox had already briefed him about the dangers that would be posed, would prove to be extremely costly.

Laudrup's welcome to domestic football in Scotland was quick and hard as he was dumped off the ball by Rob McKinnon after only a few minutes of the opening league match of the season at Ibrox, against Motherwell.[70] No foul was given but he didn't complain, got up and changed the game. First, his cross was headed home by Mark Hateley just before the interval but, when Motherwell equalised with an early second-half penalty, the game was running away from Rangers, piling on the pressure so soon after Athens. With three minutes to go Laudrup carried the ball from the edge of his own box to the edge of the opposition's and laid it into the path of a team-mate to sweep home the winner. Fans and press alike should have been talking about the great Danish performance for weeks but there were two reasons why they didn't. Firstly, the attention was on who scored it. Duncan Ferguson, still allowed to play for the time being, had shown something early that gave hope that there might be a recovery in this career move after all. The post-match narrative was dominated by the bad-boy potentially turning good. Secondly, what was about to come ensured that no Rangers player would be talked about glowingly for some time.

Rangers despatched Arbroath from the League Cup easily, Ferguson grabbing a hat-trick in a 6-1 win, before making slightly heavier weather of the trip to Firhill on the Saturday with Hateley's effort and an own goal just about ensuring they kept up the winning league start but everything was focused on the return of Athens to Ibrox on Wednesday, 24 August. Smith called on the fans to play their part and Basile Boli told the *Sunday Mail* that it could be 6-0. He might not have known then, however, that he would be expected to play at right-back. 'The manager phoned my old boss, Franz Beckenbauer, who had played me on the right before, and you all saw what happened. But I was not the worst player on view,' Boli reportedly told *France Football* in the interview that caused all sorts of problems at the end of the month.

Boli played on the left side of central defence, with Dave McPherson over at right-back on the Saturday against Thistle, but Smith said after that the switch wasn't a gamble because Rangers 'had to go for it'. However, there was no real sense to playing a centre-half/sweeper with little pace at full-back instead of in the position in which he had excelled at the very top. With the Hateley-Ferguson combination being used yet again – it looked for most of the game that Ferguson was expected

---

70   No longer under the management of Tommy McLean. Alex McLeish was now in charge in his first managerial role.

to play on the left of midfield, with Gordon Durie running off to Hateley's right alongside Laudrup – it was a muddled and insipid evening. The atmosphere prior to kick-off was sensational and may have been remembered alongside Kiev, Parma and Leipzig had the Greeks not killed the tie just before the break.

It was a devastating defeat. Levski Sofia could be written off as just one of those things, the capricious nature of knockout football, but this signalled something far more worrying to any Rangers fan or chairman who expressed a belief that being a major European force was something that could be consistently realised. Laudrup said on his first day that he thought it could happen but perhaps 'in two years'. He was being kind. The result was a shock to the outside world – with the 1992/93 heroics still fresh in the mind – with Ajax coach Louis van Gaal saying, 'They are one of the biggest clubs in Europe and I was convinced they would go through their preliminary round. I had even begun studying their players and had not paid any attention to the Greeks.' But it was the manner which was telling. If there was a footballing cloud in the USA that summer then it was surely Greece[71] so what did that say about Rangers? Van Gaal's countryman and rival Johan Cruyff noted in the aftermath, 'I have always had a soft spot for the Scots. Their enthusiasm for the game is infectious and their players probably have the best spirit of any in the world. But while Scottish football can be entertaining, all too often the quality of play is not of the required standard … There are too many hod-carriers and not enough creators now. You cannot have 11 of them in a team and be successful. The Scots concentrate on strength and physique, whereas I have always picked players for their skill.' Over £5m spent and notions of grandiose tournaments, Rangers were playing the part of a big European club but it was now becoming purely an act.

The BBC's Chick Young travelled to Ibrox on the Thursday – the morning after the defeat to AEK – for the usual pre-game interview for the following evening's *Friday Sportscene*. What was eventually broadcast was nothing like the first attempt, which became a VHS legend in the 1990s and a YouTube hit for the next generation. What followed spoke volumes about the kind of pressure Smith was under and has to be presented in full verbatim.

Young: Two of the disappointments on the park were the big-money signings from Europe this summer, Boli and Laudrup, would you go along with that?

Smith: I'm not answering that.

Young: Well what I'm trying to say is that you've gone out and spent at the highest level. But is the standard of play in Europe higher again? And are you going to have to match the AC Milans and pay these types of fees?

Smith: I'm not following your line of questioning.

Young: Well, you spent £5m Walter, in the summer on good players, but these players are seemingly not good enough at the highest level in Europe.

---

71   They were abysmal and finished the group stage with no points.

Smith: I don't think you can say that. How can you say that? I mean, they've just came to the place in't they? You've got to give everybody a chance to settle in. Are you saying that Boli and Laudrup cannae play in Europe?

Young: No.

Smith: Boli's won a European Cup winners' medal, for fuck's sake, you cannae say he's no a good enough player to play in Europe. That's fucking stupid, innit?

Young: Well, at the end of the day…

Smith: Well that's what you're saying. You obviously cannae say that Boli and Laudrup cannae fucking play. I mean, Laudrup played seven out of ten games for AC Milan last season, and Boli played in the team that won the European Cup, and the only reason he didn't play last year was because his club were banned. You cannae say they cannae fucking play in Europe. For fuck's sake!

Young: At the end of the day

Smith: Have you been up all night working that out? They're no good enough to play in Europe? That's your fucking words to me?

Young: No, no,

Smith [to the cameraman]: Nae wonder you're fucking laughing, Billy. Jesus Christ.

Both men stumbled to complete their sentence then Smith then shouted down the tunnel, where the interview was taking place, to the oncoming Archie Knox.

Smith: Archie, come and listen to this fucking interview. He's coming out with worse shite than ever.

Knox: I'd have him out of here on his fucking arse if it was up to me.

Smith [back to Young as Knox disappears]: Come on, you cannae be fucking serious.

Young: All right, I presume you want to start that bit again. The Rangers fans, what I'm trying to get at are the Rangers fans are demanding…

Smith: Your questions to the chairman last week were fucking shite as well. If we had a bad night last night, then you are having a fucking horrendous one the now.

Young: You did have a bad night.

Smith: That's what I said to you.

More inaudible back and forth.

Young: But would you agree that the two of them didn't play well?

Smith: That does'nae mean they aren't good enough to play in Europe. Surely they have fucking proved on many occasions before. Fuck sake, I mean that's just silly stuff you've come out with there.

Young: OK, I gather that you're not happy with that. Let's start again. What I'm trying to get at is…

Smith: That'll go down well at the Christmas fucking party I'll tell you.

Despite the evisceration that would become entertainment in years to come, Young had some fair points. Laudrup and Boli were poor, although in the case of the latter he could have asked the manager why he was played out of position. His language in the follow-up question about the two not being good enough at that level was a little clumsy but it was a fair line of inquiry. Boli hadn't played there for a year. Was he over it? Laudrup had struggled in Italy. Was this evidence why? And, even if both were still at their peak, was the obsession with individual talent ever going to be enough in an increasingly intelligent team sport? Did Rangers have the money to buy enough and would UEFA ever allow them to all play, even if they did?

At least there was domestic business to come, the level at which was becoming more and more relevant. Celtic were due to arrive at Ibrox on the Saturday – and this time with another new manager. Lou Macari was an early casualty of the Fergus McCann regime and Celtic opted for another old boy who was having a more convincing start to football management at Kilmarnock. One of the surprise packages of the previous season, Tommy Burns had done a good job blending some very old faces with young talent and now it felt right to go where he considered home. Two points behind Rangers already, the visitors were expected to be happy with a draw. Unlike the previous encounter, the Celtic fans were back behind the Broomloan Road goal. Just like the previous encounter, John Collins whipped in a free kick to give Celtic the lead. Smith played four centre-halves, with only Gough in his rightful position (although McPherson had at least played at right-back two years before) and the midfield engine room of Ferguson and McCall was showing signs of malfunction.

There was no deflected equaliser this time and McStay made sure of the win with a low drive which went in off Goram's right-hand post. Ibrox boiled over. Smith and the players received a torrent of boos and, according to Neil Drysdale of *The Scotsman*, one fan made his way close to the directors' box to call David Murray a 'fucking cripple'. It was starting to put the previous season's difficult opening into perspective and even more so when Falkirk came to Ibrox on the following Wednesday on League Cup business. It was fully presumed that this would be the night to give Rangers the opportunity to get back on the rails, in a competition that they loved. It bore witness to Brian Laudrup's first goal in blue but, sensationally, it was sandwiched between two Richard Cadete strikes to give Falkirk – under their manager Jim Jefferies – their first win at Ibrox since 1926 and knock Rangers out of the League Cup before the quarter-finals for the first time in 14 years.

The 'Week from Hell' – three defeats at Ibrox to three sides who shouldn't have troubled Rangers – quickly became the greatest source of entertainment in Scottish football in years as rival fans and pundits lined up to take shots as well as rival players, such as Andy Walker, when he joked on Radio Clyde about a new pressure group in Scottish football, called Gers For Change[72]. Fans raged on phone-ins to say that they wouldn't be renewing their season tickets and a Church of Scotland minister described the purchase of Boli as Rangers going out to buy a 'black pudding'. Smith would never have used language like that but did have had

---

72   'Celts for Change' had been a fan pressure group at Parkhead before the McCann buy-out.

more choice words when news reached him about an interview that had appeared in France where his defender currently was, recuperating from a minor hamstring strain. 'Get back here!' was the message that was returned.

This was arguably the biggest crisis in Smith's managerial career.

* * *

Laughter filled Glasgow's Royal Concert Hall as Donald Findlay held the Rangers AGM in the palm of his hand. It wasn't a meeting without criticism around the management of Athens or that last week of August but it only really amounted to why didn't McCoist or Durrant start in Greece. With no concerted and prepared block of pressure, these meetings gave room for the more obscure and eccentric questions among the standing items such as away ticket allocation and how fans were treated when they travelled.[73] One shareholder in particular questioned the money that the club received for Trevor Steven in 1991, with reports in *Rangers News* and the *Daily Record* being £500,000 apart, the inference being that Rangers were fraudulently hiding that money. Murray invited him to come to Ibrox to look over the documents of that transfer and then Findlay quipped, to great acclaim, that there were 'no biscuit tins' at Ibrox, a clear reference to the frugal and slightly shady popular reputation of the previous Celtic board. Therefore before any critical analysis of the club's planning could get under way, the support was brought onside by a clear comparison with their great, but catastrophic, rivals. It could always be worse.

Murray was eventually pressed to explain the level of debt which now stood at £8m – the impact of two consecutive years of European failure – but he was relaxed, saying that the overdraft facilities could go to £14m if required but that Rangers didn't have a cash crisis. In fact, there had been another player in the door by that point when Alan McLaren was signed from Hearts for £1.6m plus Dave McPherson in late October. In order to get the player that Smith had arguably needed for over a year now, he had to bring some cash in and so began the attempt at a big autumn sale. The first player out the door was one that had been expected for some time. After a short loan period at Tranmere Rovers, Gary Stevens signed permanently for £350,000 and so another piece of that original Souness dream disappeared. His final two years were painfully frustrating as injury took hold but his first four should never be forgotten and his departure was a reminder of those exciting times where Rangers could buy the best British talent in their position. For nearly double that money, Steven Pressley's transfer request and demands for first-team football were met by Coventry City but it was when Smith himself drove two players down to Goodison Park for moves that fans really sat up and took notice.

---

73   On the this occasion the latter really exercised Murray who was furious with the facilities being offered to the Rangers support on a recent trip to Tynecastle. Filling in the corners at Ibrox and putting in screens where they could 'beam back' away games to a packed stadium appeared to be the response but was never likely to get permission.

In early October, the original deal with Everton – who were struggling at the bottom of the Premier League – included three players. Trevor Steven and Ian Durrant would be sold for £3m and Duncan Ferguson would go on a three-month loan period to get himself match fit and regain some confidence as uncertainty continued to hover over him. Smith wanted to get both McLaren and Marc Rieper through the door to try and create a new defence upon which his new creative superstar could sit, but that would definitely mean recouping this kind of money before it was possible. It never happened in the end. The move for Steven – who hadn't started a match that season as he tried to recover from a calf injury – was ditched as Everton didn't trust his reliability, even though he was a famous old boy. They also got cold feet on Durrant and, remarkably for someone with that level of talent and experience, he was given a month's loan to prove himself to Mike Walker who didn't even know where he played. 'Here I was,' wrote Durrant, 'just, two years after all the glory of the Champions League with 11 caps for my country and this guy didn't know me from Adam.' Durrant wrote that he felt the need to jump at the chance because he was concerned at the time that his career was plateauing in Rangers' reserves but he had started six out of 11 games before the move and four of the last six in addition to one substitute appearance so it was hardly an exile. It is not an explanation that stands up. The reaction from the support was filled with sadness and shock, especially when it was a Rangers side hardly overflowing with creativity. More than that, he was one of them. 'The important goals always, always, saw him make straight for the terraces,' wrote Mark Dingwall in *Follow, Follow*. 'He is our hero, and we are his people.' Despite playing well – Everton rose six places in that time – Walker told Durrant in a disco one night that he wasn't being kept on. As enraged as Durrant was at the manner of it, it was really what he wanted to hear and he was immediately back in the Rangers squad upon return.

If the loan that was supposed to become permanent didn't work out, the loan deal that wasn't did. According to Durrant, Duncan Ferguson transformed himself at Goodison Park. From an early encounter against Arsenal where he dominated Tony Adams, the Everton support took to him in a way his boyhood favourites didn't. Back in August, Rangers won their appeal with the SFA meaning that any ban – 12 games or otherwise – couldn't be imposed until the court hearing had passed, lest it prejudice the case.[74] This allowed some space for Ferguson to flourish at Everton and eventually the loan deal was made a fixture, with a small profit for Rangers on top. A case of what if but ultimately the right move for all parties as Ferguson realised some, if not all, of his potential and became a club legend.

Durrant's reception when he came on as a first-half substitute at Ibrox against Partick Thistle on 5 November was as warm as his comeback from injury all those

---

74   It is worth noting that the appeal panel was chaired by the Liberal Democrat MP Menzies Campbell QC and there is probably no coincidence that better legal understanding and independence helped come to the correct decision.

years earlier but even he knew by then, that there was a new Rangers legend being firmly established. It is a notoriously tough crowd to please. Rangers fans tend to create monuments to players out of plywood instead of carving them into stone, just so that they can set fire to them upon witnessing a poor performance or hearing post-career opinions that don't match theirs. In the case of Brian Laudrup, any slow start affected by that deeply disappointing period was more than matched by the rapid pace at which the fans took to him into the autumn. Even the most cantankerous and cynical of fanzine contributors – 'The Govanhill Gub' – was quickly besotted, 'From everything I have heard and read, perhaps the four greatest Rangers players this century up to now have been Davie Meiklejohn, Alan Morton, Willie Woodburn and Jim Baxter. While I have loved listening to the stories of these legends, there has always been a touch of sadness or perhaps envy is the word I am looking for on my part. In that I have always wondered when I would get to see a truly great player. My longing is over. Just as 30 years ago, my old man would have been arguing with his old man that Baxter was better than Morton. I will quite simply state that Brian Laudrup would walk into any all time Rangers XI … Quite simply for me, Brian Laudrup. HERO YOU COMETH AT LAST!'

Rangers faced Hearts at Ibrox on Sunday, 11 September – the first game after the 'Week from Hell' – four points behind the early leaders Celtic. Eleven games later they were six points ahead of them and two ahead of that season's challengers, Motherwell, at the top of the league. In every one of those games – win, lose or draw – Laudrup had a hand in at least one of the goals. There was an assist for Hateley in that first game against Hearts, two assists in a 2-2 draw up at Pittodrie, a corner for a Boli header at Easter Road, a pass laid into the path of David Robertson in a 2-0 home win over Kilmarnock, pressure on Motherwell that lead to a John Philliben own goal in a 2-1 defeat at Fir Park and then the cross which led to a penalty at Tynecastle converted by Hateley in a 1-1 draw. There were only four goals in that run of games but the very nature of them – in addition to the constant endeavour and creativity – ensured absolute devotion.

Laudrup's first league goal came at Brockville, Falkirk, where the other summer signing had already got his first of the season – Boli bundling home in the first half. Laudrup's goal was actually a relative rarity – a direct free kick – which caught the goalkeeper off guard with its movement and was whipped into the centre of the goal. His second was one of those worth the ticket price alone and something that Rangers fans had longed to see for years. They were 1-0 up at home to Dundee United on 1 October thanks to a Hateley goal in the first half but, as a very open game wore on, they were riding their luck. Jerren Nixon had hit the bar and then Craig Brewster was given yet another gift courtesy of a defensive mess – this time the ribbon was tied by the captain – but, unlike at Hampden, his effort was lifted high over the bar. With three minutes remaining, Neil Murray stopped another United advance, fed Laudrup on the halfway line and, similar to his run and assist on the opening day of the season, he just drove at pace deep into the heart of the United defence, gliding past a tackle from Gordan Petrić before lashing the ball high into the net from the edge of the box. It was a stunning goal but more than that, it was one that Rangers fans hadn't been used to seeing. There were many long-range screamers and intelligent team moves since the Souness revolution in addition to tonnes of penalty-box opportunism and aerial prowess but something like this – truly individual – had been a rarity. Not since Davie Cooper had Rangers fans witnessed a player take possession deep in the pitch and not immediately seek out a team-mate, whether five yards away or 50. There was a majestic sense of ownership to this goal which in turn feels like evidence of magic, from which heroes are born. If anyone still retained a hint of the melting scepticism about the younger Laudrup brother then his third league goal would be the end of all that.

The build-up to the second Old Firm match of the season had been busy for both clubs. Celtic, having signed Phil O'Donnell from Motherwell the previous month, were forced to pay Kilmarnock £100,000 for 'tapping up' Tommy Burns while former manager Lou Macari was suing for unfair dismissal, taking action to the point that Rangers couldn't pay Celtic the gate money they were due from the League Cup semi-final at Ibrox as Macari's lawyers had managed to arrest the club's account. That cup fixture had proved to be a much-needed boost, however, as they beat Aberdeen in extra time to reach their first final in over four years. The league form was of more concern, with only two wins in seven following the victory at Ibrox and none at all in the four previous games, including two defeats on the spin to Hearts and Falkirk. Nevertheless, the fact that they had booked their place in that final against Raith Rovers was enough to get Burns excited. 'We could play Rangers right now,' he said after fumbling open a bottle of champagne the following day at the launch of a new club shop. 'Reaching a final after so long has given the club a fantastic boost. The players are so up after having beaten Aberdeen that they could play any time now.' Not for the last time, it was evidence of an over-emotional manager getting lost in his own dreams.

Walter Smith finally got his man on the Tuesday before the game. Four days earlier it looked like the deal was off for good as the agent for both Neil Murray and Dave McPherson demanded too much from Hearts as part of the deal that would bring Alan McLaren to Ibrox. In the end it was sorted out, although it would just be McPherson and £1.6m travelling east. The direction of the Rangers bus was more south than it was east for this fixture due to Celtic's agreement with the SFA to swap with Queen's Park for the season, as the much-needed renovation work commenced at Parkhead. It was met with righteous anger as many clubs had been forced to forgo transfers in order to get their own grounds in order in the early 1990s, so as to comply with the Taylor Report, while Celtic did relatively little until it was too late but any outrage fell on deaf ears as the governing body could bring in more income than they ever could in a normal season.[75] A strange setting then for an Old Firm league game at a ground traditionally neutral.

'The be-all-and-end-all,' said Burns as he stood next to Smith being interviewed by Jim Delahunt of STV on the trackside while the teams warmed up. Smith agreed but with a greater sense of calm and suggested that this was more the case for those watching, external and not integral to the drama. Being in the middle of the maelstrom required a cool head and none were much cooler than Brian Laudrup as Burns presented him with the league's Player of the Month award for October. 'I'm very much looking forward to this game,' he said, not trying to hide nerves, but with genuine anticipation such was his personal form. It was the best performance of the season by a Rangers side who just clicked when it mattered. Burns said afterwards that he felt his side 'controlled the first half', a 45 minutes where Rangers scored twice, had one chance cleared off the line, where Murray missed a sitter and where Hateley should have been awarded a penalty. Celtic did score – a brilliant equaliser by Paul Byrne – but this was true balance in action. For all the excuse-making around needing time to gel and build chemistry, McLaren, Basile Boli, Fraser Wishart and David Robertson had hardly met one another before putting on a fantastic defensive display, while Goram was alert whenever he needed to be. With McCall and Murray tenacious in the middle, Smith opted for width on both sides with Laudrup and Huistra providing support to Hateley and young Charlie Miller. It was the latter two who combined for the opening goal – Miller robbing Tom Boyd before threading the ball through to Hateley who rattled it home with his first touch – and then Laudrup and Robertson on the left worked Celtic open to give Hateley an easy second to put Rangers back in front. If Laudrup's pass to Robertson was quietly impressive, his run through on goal to make the game safe was absolutely sublime. Doing it in this fixture counts double and when he grabbed another goal and remarkable assist against Partick Thistle the following Saturday, where he twisted the right-back into all kinds of shapes before crossing right on to Hateley's head, he was confirmed as an Ibrox god. The worship was inspired by Mike Myers' cult hit *Wayne's World* – 'we're not worthy!' – as fans bowed down in appreciation to salute the next gift of celestial delight.

That match against Thistle on 5 November was notable for another reason beside Laudrup's latest masterclass. It was the one and only time that season – in 42 games – where Walter Smith was able to select the same starting XI as he had done in the previous fixture. This collegial inconsistency may explain why the rise to the top was more protracted than it could have been with draws at Pittodrie and Tynecastle from winning positions a particular frustration. The 2-1 defeat at Motherwell was well-deserved in a game – and that ludicrous purple strip – where Rangers never got going but the defeat by the same scoreline at Easter Road on 8 October arguably told a more accurate story about the schizophrenic nature of

---

75   In his book published around this time, former Celtic chairman Michael Kelly suggested that a deal was done in principle with the SFA from 1990 should the club need the use of Hampden.

that season's team, typified by Boli. His early header to put Rangers in the lead was stunning, as were many of his blocks and tackles as Hibs tried to get back into the game. But he was posted missing for the Hibs winner and was sent off soon after for his second needless and reckless booking. This was also the moment where Smith indulged Hateley's career extension plan by opting for him to drop back in at centre-half instead of moving McPherson along and using Murray at right-back. Laudrup was pulling as many strings as he could, the rest of the field self-harmed on a regular basis, but this was still far from vintage.

And that is perhaps why Donald Findlay could joke and charm his way out of serious inquiry and attack by the time the AGM arrived in the middle of November. When asked why, instead of the Saturday, Rangers chose to play Aberdeen on the Friday night of the weekend of the League Cup Final, which Ibrox would host on the Sunday, Findlay answered, 'We've got to keep the pitch in good condition to give Raith Rovers every chance.' More laughter in the hall and much, much more as Celtic were pinned back in extra time before contriving to lose to Jimmy Nicholl's side on penalties, the vital one being missed by Paul McStay. Celtic's barren run continued, any Rangers deficiencies were covered by a genius and thus, complacency remained the order of the day.

* * *

The adulation for Brian Laudrup wasn't limited to the Ibrox fanbase. The Scottish media had no choice but to lavish praise on a foreign import, the likes of which they had never seen before in their game. Saturday evening radio ran out of superlatives, in December the *Sunday Mail* likened him to the best type of 'Power Ranger' which was the number one toy that Christmas and then, later in the season, STV's Jim White delivered a line in a television interview – on the prompt of his director to truncate the original question – that created a lifetime of fawning, sycophantic parody. The first part of the question is almost entirely forgotten but provides a context that makes better sense. 'What can you say to up-and-coming youngsters, Brian, everybody wants to know about your appetite for the game and the skill factor,' White started, before going on to finish by saying, 'How come you are so good?' The ultimate softball perhaps but it rather summed up the general reception for a player who appeared to have arrived from space but who, in his skill and grace, had hints of what Scotland felt it once used to produce: the supremely talented individual who played with carefree abandon.

Not everyone was a fan of course. One letter to the *Herald* in January asked the media if it was possible to 'water down their adulation of Brian Laudrup just a little … This constant and extravagant eulogising of his talents simply focuses unwelcome attention on our own low level of attainment, and we are already too well aware of our deficiencies in this area … The man is unquestionably gifted, but as he continues to prance and cavort among the ranks of the inept, let it be recognised that while his game may be on a higher plane, he is not from another planet.' Laudrup's medals and accolades prior to arriving in Govan may be testament to achievement at a higher level – and he would go on to win the FIFA Golden Ball in what became known as the 1995 Confederations Cup where Denmark defeated Argentina in the final – but there was a strain of truth among the curmudgeonly appraisal. Laudrup had already turned down a move to Barcelona to effectively replace his brother and did so without much consideration. 'So you prefer to play against Falkirk on a Tuesday night than go to Barcelona?' a surprised Walter Smith asked him when they met at what is now the Crowne Plaza Hotel on the banks of the Clyde, to discuss the offer. 'Absolutely,' replied Laudrup, desperate for the easy life with all the freedom that he could ever ask for on the pitch. Perhaps the most telling comment came from that arch critic of Ibrox, Ian Archer, in one of his *Sunday Mail* columns in December 1994. After devoting so much space to extolling the Dane's virtues and how it was good for the Scottish game, he finished by writing, 'Still, it would be nice to see some hulking defender dump him in a heap before the season is finished. That's part of our game too.'

It certainly was but just how comfortable the Scottish footballing public were about this reality was starting to change. One of the most prominent football writers advocating violence as the way to match sporting artistry was just one example of the deepening sense of insecurity and increasing isolation that Scotland was feeling, just months after the first World Cup in a generation in which they hadn't featured. Years later, Andy Gray would raise that level of macho insecurity with his comments about Lionel Messi having to prove himself against Stoke City in the lashing evening rain but this was essentially the same point: your skill is all well and good but we have a culture and a climate that can bring you down to our level. When Rangers and Laudrup visited Kilmarnock on 10 December, even that glimmer of hope disappeared. 'The thing about these foreigners is this: they are all right with their slick tricks and fancy skills when they have a bit of sunshine and a nice park. Wait until they get to Rugby Park on a dreich, soaking December afternoon. Then we'll see,' wrote Jim Traynor in his *Herald* match report on the 2-1 win. 'We did, too. And what did we get? We got slick tricks and fancy skills. For so many years we have managed to kid ourselves that the inadequacies of our own lot are as much down to the kind of weather and surfaces they have to tackle in a typical Scottish winter. When we play summer football, things will be different. Ah, well, it was a comforting argument. But it holds as much water as the marvellous Kilmarnock pitch did on Saturday. Brian Laudrup splashed through it with wonderful control, breathtaking skill, and enough strength to last the day.'

This inferiority complex wasn't helped by access to live Champions League football during the week and from the greatest league in the world on a Sunday. England wanted to be the greatest but Manchester United's chastening experience in the Camp Nou in November, when they had been beaten 4-0 by Barcelona, was a reminder that in terms of quality they weren't there quite yet. In terms of drama and sheer entertainment, however, they almost certainly were. After two seasons of saturated coverage, Scottish football fans – whether they enjoyed the live matches on Sky or the revitalised highlights on the BBC's *Match of the Day* – struggled not to be drawn into the soap opera of the Premier League. It too had a recently reawakened sleeping giant as its dominant force but, unlike Rangers, Manchester United had some genuine competition for the championship. The 'glory hunters' could hitch their wagon to United and the rest could root for exciting challengers like Kevin Keegan's Newcastle United or Kenny Dalglish's Blackburn Rovers, but it was becoming impossible to remain ambivalent, especially when the season turned on its axis on the evening of Wednesday, 25 January 1995, when Eric Cantona launched himself at a Crystal Palace supporter with his out-stretched leg as he walked along the Selhurst Park touchline after being sent off. That event, and the subsequent ban, provided a huge twist in a brilliant title race that went to the wire and saw United, briefly, knocked off their perch by Dalglish. Scotland lacked the drama, the characters and the quality. When Rangers beat Hearts 1-0 at Ibrox on 21 January with no strikers and after a poor performance, one match report opened with, 'Stop the nonsense now. Just tell Rangers they can keep the premier division championship trophy. But let's hold the ball for a minute. Someone has to take stock of what exactly is going on in our game. Frankly, it has become so one-sided it is embarrassing. Nothing, absolutely nothing, any other team can come up with will prevent Rangers from winning their seventh successive title.' The piece ended by saying, 'Rangers' supporters might enjoy winning the title all the time, but no one else will, and the game will suffer.' Dominance had led to drudgery.

How that came about – the inevitability of a seventh consecutive title before 1994 was even out – was anything but. After two 1-1 draws away to Hearts and at home to Falkirk, Rangers did what they had done so often in the past, and went on a winning streak that destroyed the mirage of a title race. In the previous season it was a seven-game stretch in February and March that took Rangers from level-pegging to six clear, with only two points for a win. The introduction of three points for a win for 1994/95 was designed to produce more entertainment and discourage sides from booking in for bed and breakfast when they visited grounds like Ibrox but when the champions got into a stride, it made the impact even more explosive. Rangers held a two-point lead before struggling Aberdeen visited on Friday, 25 November. By the time they left Fir Park on Hogmanay, the gap at the top was ten. The league was over before the bells.

Ally McCoist scored his only goal in an injury-hit season, courtesy of a Laudrup assist of course, to defeat Aberdeen who were staring down the face of a relegation battle. On Sunday, 4 December, live on STV, Rangers travelled to Tannadice where Ivan Golac had promised the media that a 4-0 hammering awaited them. 'I wish he would shut up. All he is doing is making our job harder. Walter Smith won't need to wind Rangers up, our gaffer has done it for him!' a United player confided in a journalist at the time. Despite the cup win, the Golac schtick was wearing thin and Rangers rose to the occasion by putting on one of their best shows of the season. Laudrup was at the heart of it, starting and finishing a move for the first which saw him toy with two United defenders before curling in beyond even more bodies. Huistra fired in a second before Laudrup again produced a perfectly weighted pass for Ian Durrant to knock home and underline his return. The Rangers support made Golac very aware of what they thought of him and his predictions. He would be gone by March.

Next up was that ballet on the water in Kilmarnock, with McLaren getting his first for his new club before Laudrup defied expectations and cultural norms with a run through the puddles and around the goalkeeper to make the points safe. 'He is a very special talent,' said Gough later. 'There was I telling our lads to make sure we made no mistakes at the back and to be careful about their passing, and he pads up and starts to run with the ball on that surface. He amazes me.'

The captain himself was on the score sheet as he and Mark Hateley struck early at home to Hibs on Boxing Day before the trip to Motherwell on the final day of the year. The only side that could realistically stop Rangers, Alex McLeish's men needed a win to bring the gap down to four points and they gave a good account of themselves, pulling level early in the second half. But they were still a long way short of being a team on a mission to put the question to rest as early as they could. Stuart McCall had been asked on the morning of that game why he hadn't scored yet that season and felt it was worth his friends having a bet on him at 28/1. He duly delivered by getting on the end of a Huistra ball to put Rangers ahead before Laudrup scored one of the oddest goals of his career to re-establish that lead two minutes after being pegged back, his arching shot hitting the post before rebounding off the back of goalkeeper Stevie Woods and into the net. Yet again, he turned creator just to be absolutely sure, feeding Durie with the perfect chance to finish the match and, realistically, the title. A 'big-game mentality' was how McLeish described Rangers afterwards and it was something that he admitted his side lacked. Speaking at the end of the season, McCall reflected on the importance of the win by saying that the celebrations 'because it was New Year's Eve, carried on for a few days'.

It was probably no exaggeration if the performance in the following game was anything to go on. On Wednesday, 4 January Rangers hosted a Celtic side who had just won their first league game in 12, a run that included three defeats and eight draws. Despite going in front from an Ian Ferguson goal in the first half, Rangers were fortunate to take a point in the end as Celtic were flooded with a brief sense of belief after Paul Byrne's equaliser. It was a slack performance where even Laudrup ended up on the periphery and this match started another Rangers trait which was becoming as familiar as those powerful title-winning run of victories: an injury-hit period of easing up once the hard work had been done. Andy Goram was injured playing for Scotland in Greece just before Christmas and his rushed recovery ended in disaster at Firhill on 7 January when he went down and wouldn't be seen again for the rest of the season.[76] Ally McCoist suffered similar setbacks both away and at home to Dundee United and wouldn't start a

---

76   He was replaced by the usual mixture of Colin Scott and Ally Maxwell plus, later in the season, the experienced former Dundee United goalkeeper, Billy Thompson.

game post-December and even the warhorse of 1993/94, Hateley, played only one game between Hogmanay and April Fool's Day because of an 'untreatable deep-lying pelvic injury'. This meant that Rangers played several matches in January and February without a recognised striker and then had to use Durie and Laudrup – who preferred to use the channels in very different ways – as the focal point. When Charlie Miller was sent out to do some work with schoolchildren on the astroturf complex opposite the stadium just before Christmas, he corrected one question from an eager young fan who asked what it was like playing up front for Rangers, 'I'm not playing up front, I'm playing in midfield.' Perhaps then he was, but it wouldn't be long before he too was asked to do a shift in an unusual position to help the team through the remainder of the course. Described by Hateley years later as the 'best player I had ever seen at that age. Bearing in mind I had worked with Paolo Maldini when he was 16, that shows how highly I rated Charlie', the dominant presence of Laudrup on this season shouldn't allow the job done by both Miller and Craig Moore – 18 and 19 when the season began respectively – to be forgotten, especially in such a challenging environment.[77]

Walter Smith received further reinforcements in late January – once the Duncan Ferguson deal was finally sealed – as Rangers spent £750,000 releasing both Gary Bollan and Alec Cleland from a contract hell at Tannadice.[78] This provided Smith with some more defensive cover but it was the blunt edge in attack that caused him the most headaches in early 1995. Rangers could only manage four wins in the first three months of the year and one of those was a 3-1 victory over lower-division Hamilton in the Scottish Cup third round. Incredibly the five draws and three defeats in the league not only did no harm to the title challenge, the lead was actually increased to 12 points by the end of March. One of the wins was a 1-0 home scoreline against Hearts by way of a very early Miller goal which gave rise to the exasperated newspaper report referenced earlier on the following Monday. There was a comfortable 3-0 win at home to Kilmarnock on 25 February but the other victory was more notable. Rangers came from 2-1 down to beat Falkirk at Brockville on 14 January without Laudrup, or indeed Andy Goram, Richard Gough, Basile Boli, Alexei Mikhailichenko, Mark Hateley and Ally McCoist. It was Pieter Huistra who started the comeback with a fine goal – his second of the game – and it was his last before moving to Hiroshima at the end of the month. Stuart McCall was ready to pounce in the final seconds to grab the win and show that Rangers had muscle memory and nerve to collect full points, even when their maestro was off on international duty. Cue more groans and self-reflection in the match reports, 'Just look at the Premier Division table. Take a good look … study the positions and points carefully, and then say Scottish football is heading in the correct direction. How can the domestic game be in good health when Rangers,

---

77   Miller would go on to be named SPFA Young Player of the Year. Jimmy Nicholl would win the Manager of the Year award and Laudrup – who else? – won both the SPFA and Writers' Player of the Year prizes.

78   Bollan had taken Dundee United to court over the legality of his contract duration, a policy by Jim McLean that was becoming a running joke in Scottish football.

who by their own manager's admission have not been functioning at a particularly high level, are now 14 points clear of the rest?'

The 16 dropped points in the period demonstrates that Rangers were not a well-oiled machine but the paucity of the rest of league ensured that they were still an unstoppable force over the course of the season. There were stumbles, however. Aberdeen, who had sacked Willie Miller and replaced him in the dugout with Roy Aitken, started that new era by beating Rangers 2-0 at Pittodrie on 12 February. Only two points off the bottom of the league, it was a very disappointing defeat for Rangers, regardless of the historical danger that the ground possessed. Smith was furious that two excellent penalty claims were turned down at key stages of the game – referee Jim McCluskey conceded later in the week that he was wrong on both counts – but Aberdeen had more about them on the day. As did Hearts at Tynecastle on 18 March when they deservedly won 2-1, where Laudrup's goal would be on any showreel if it hadn't been a consolation. It was their victory over Rangers there a month previously however, that provided the biggest gut punch since August. The Scottish Cup fourth round tie was played on the Monday evening, live on TV, and it had much in common with the previous season's final, with Ally Maxwell at fault for the two Hearts goals before the break, the latter again coming as a result of a pass back to his feet where he panicked and picked it up. The resulting free kick led to a corner from which McPherson scored. Rangers responded well though and were level within a few minutes of the restart with Laudrup and Durie grabbing two quick goals. Most expected a Rangers win from that position, including the neutrals at home, but those old frailties returned soon enough. Jim Bett's shot from the edge of the box was accurate but not overly powerful and Maxwell could only parry it out straight to the feet of the predatory John Robertson. A fourth on the breakaway simply rubbed it in. Rangers, for the first time in five years, would have to make do with 'only' the league title but at least it was an enjoyable ding-dong battle that provided some much needed entertainment for the wider viewing public.

And that viewing public, more often at home and consuming football at their convenience as work and lifestyle patterns began to change, was a significant factor behind the inward sense of self-doubt that characterised mid-1990s Scottish football. The annual new year Old Firm game barely merited the traditional name, moved as it was at the behest of Sky, to 4 January. With only two sports channels in those days – and Sky Sports 2 not operating at all times – the north London derby took precedence over the Glasgow one on the traditional 2 January slot with both Manchester United v Coventry and Queens Park Rangers v Chelsea more attractive to the broadcaster the following day. It caused a great deal of uproar, with one supporter concerned that the time may soon be arriving whereby Rangers would be live on television up to eight times a season. Among the hysteria of that fanzine piece was the salient point that any 'local support many teams have left will be eaten into as kids identify more with the teams which appear regularly on TV, TV appearance money will concentrate in fewer hands making it even more difficult for other clubs to compete'. What happened internally in Scotland was replicated when we consider the nation's place in the bigger picture. Not only was television coverage highlighting the difference in quality and entertainment as a product, it was creating a difference in finance. Tommy Burns was beside himself with excitement as Celtic – boosted by the upcoming share issue that would raise around £13m – managed to do a deal for just over £1m for the Dutch striker Pierre van Hooijdonk in mid-January. In the same week, Manchester United spent £7m on Andy Cole. Rangers had barely managed to spend that much across five players that season and the prospect of even Scotland's biggest club investing that kind of money in one asset was unthinkable. In more ways than one, just over a year from Rangers breaking and holding the British transfer record, England was now a very different league.

It was somewhat poignant that, as Scotland pondered its place in the game, its last true artist decided to retire. Davie Cooper was never slow throughout the end of his career to complain about the kind of fare that was being dished up for the paying public, often likening matches he had just played in as war rather than sport, where skill and expression were subjugated by physicality and fear. Approaching 39, it was time, while back at his first club Clydebank, to hang up his boots.[79] 'My appetite hasn't gone,' he said. 'I still love the game – but I'm not able to do the things I did before. It's time to make way for a younger player.' Given that Cooper was about to start filming an STV football training series for kids called *Shoot!*, a new chapter in his career was expected to open up. Positive news then, that this particular voice – whether through coaching or punditry – could still be heard in a national game that badly needed to listen to it. For it to be lost immediately wouldn't simply be a shame. It would be a tragedy.

* * *

If you were to read any popular history of modern Britain, you will most likely be told that until September 1997 it was a buttoned-up and emotionally repressed nation, unable to show public displays of emotion whatsoever and certainly not grief. After one tragic evening in Paris nothing was the same again. Since then it has been a country much more in touch with itself, one where shrines to dead heroes would become commonplace. And yet, two and half years before the death of Diana, Princess of Wales, and admittedly on a different scale to the palaces of London, the flowers and scarves poured from the Ibrox gates out on to Edmiston Drive. At this club of all clubs, renowned for its stoicism and deeply held suspicion for sentimentality. All that seemed to have changed. Whether at lunchtime or deep

---

79   Cooper was due to have his final game at Ibrox on 1 May where he would line up in Scott Nisbet's testimonial, which would see Rangers stars past and present play one another. Graeme Souness was the manager of the International Select and his reception back in the dugout was frosty. He said it would be the last time he managed any team. 'I really don't have a lot of interest in the game any longer and managing a club does not hold any particular appeal for me,' he said on 20 April. On 21 May, he was appointed as manager of Turkish side Galatasaray.

into the night, men, women and children gathered to leave something behind and to take it all in. Where the only noise to be heard was the passing of a car or the catching of a tearful breath.

Rangers had said farewell to legends in recent years – Willie Waddell and Willie Thornton to name but two – but this was different. Those were old men from a distant time. For many standing in silence on that cold, damp March weekend, it felt like Davie Cooper had still been playing for Rangers the previous week, such was the vibrancy of his legacy that had been captured and replayed in every news bulletin for days. It hit hard not just because it was a shocking and tragic loss for a relatively young, fit and healthy man but because his talent could have seen him jettison Ibrox quickly but his heart ensured that he couldn't. 'I think the continent may have suited me with the amount of time you get on the ball,' Cooper said in his final interview. 'But I don't look back. I was a Rangers supporter and I spent the bulk of my career at the team I loved. You take your chances. I had a great career. I've enjoyed every minute of it.' Cooper's celebrations were always in sync with the everyman supporter. He was from those terraces. What he had often just done seconds before, however, was as if he was from another world.

On Wednesday, 22 March, Cooper was out on the astroturf pitches next to Broadwood Stadium, the new home of Clyde FC, near Cumbernauld, where he was showing 14 youngsters how football should be played. Shortly before they began filming a new session for a television show due to go out in the summer, he suggested to his 'co-star' Charlie Nicholas that they should go for a pint afterwards. Minutes later Cooper lay on the floor, motionless. One of the crew eventually shouted, 'OK, Davie, the joke's over.' When blood appeared from his mouth it was clear that the situation was infinitely more serious and he was quickly rushed to Monklands General Hospital before being transferred to the Southern General's Institute for Neurological Sciences. Early signs were not good as stunned fans tried to digest the evening television and radio bulletins but their shock was nothing compared to Cooper's family and former team-mates, as Ally McCoist struggled to convey the message over the phone to Ian Durrant, before making his way to spend the night close by his bedside.[80] It was in the middle of the following morning, in a small lecture hall on the hospital campus, that the consultant neurosurgeon Garth Cruickshank delivered the news everyone had feared. Davie Cooper had suffered a subarachnoid haemorrhage – bleeding between the membranes lining the brain that can occur without any hint of warning – and because of its nature, a successful operation was never an option.

The reaction – whether from former team-mate or foe, media or the ordinary fan – was almost universal: Cooper was a quiet introvert who shunned the limelight that he could have hogged, a player who often refused to deal with the media in his early career leading to the 'Moody Blue' tag but who warmed to it in later

---

80   Updates on his condition were announced on the tannoy at Easter Road where Cooper's other former club, Motherwell, were playing Hibs in an understandably lacklustre affair. Manager Alex McLeish was just one of many tough professionals who would speak to the media through tears the following day.

life, showing his dry wit and keen observations as a pundit. He was one-footed, terrible in the air, poor in the tackle and slow in a foot race, but that all became completely irrelevant once he had the ball at his left foot. There were hints of green and yellow among the sea of blue as the tributes piled up outside Ibrox Stadium. Cooper never hid his love for Rangers and all that went with it, and wouldn't even politely entertain a bid by Jock Stein when he was still at Clydebank, yet there was a deep respect for his ability in death when far too often there wasn't in life. Almost every written or spoken tribute had another commonality: will Scotland ever see the likes of Cooper again? Paul McStay spoke of a skill 'sadly missing in the Scottish game just now' and Chick Young finished his piece for *Sportscene* by calling him the 'last of the great wingers … God bless you Davie, I know not when we'll see your likes again'. The Rangers fans too – so often consumed by the final score and nothing else – appeared to be gripped by self-reflection. The club's historian, Robert McElroy, opened his tribute to Cooper with the great American sportswriter Grantland Rice's famous quote, 'For when the One Great Scorer comes to mark against your name, he writes – not that you won or lost – but how you played the game,' and even the most cynical of *Follow, Follow* contributors was caught by it all when 'The Govanhill Gub' finished his tribute by saying, 'Is Rangers Football Club today, a club going for seven leagues on the trot, any better off than when the absolute shambles of a club we were ten years ago that had Davie Cooper and nothing else? Winning isn't everything. It has taken the tragic death of David Cooper to make me realise this.' In a season where the questions of skill and entertainment dominated the conversation, Cooper's death underlined it with as much force as one of his free kicks.

Walter Smith and Ally McCoist led the mourners at the funeral, where crowds were ten deep as the hearse passed by. McCoist bravely got to the end of his eulogy, describing Cooper as a 'remarkable talent and a fine, fine man', but it was Smith, as it was so often, who found the perfect words. 'God gave him a great gift,' he said. 'But I don't think he could be disappointed in the way it was used.' As it happened, Rangers were not due to play between Cooper's death and the funeral, but they were back to business on 1 April. Smith deliberately invoked Cooper's memory by pleading with his side to go out and wrap the league title up in style. They duly delivered.

It took 11 seconds before they took the lead at Tannadice against a Dundee United side, under the new guidance of former Rangers reserve coach Billy Kirkwood, who were being dragged into a dogfight with Aberdeen to stay in the league. How the New Firm had fallen. So soon after an impeccable minute of silence, Gordon Durie found himself free of the United defence and lifted the ball cutely over the onrushing Kelham O'Hanlon and the travelling support had only eight minutes to wait before Alan McLaren scored a sensational free kick to increase the pace of United's downward spiral. The 3-2 victory over Aberdeen at Ibrox the following Sunday had a sense of fun and adventure that had been badly lacking all season as Rangers were dragged back from two goals up to 2-2 at half-time before Hateley's return saw him head in a winner. Laudrup was involved in everything, passes found their man, and Aberdeen were left bottom of the Premier Division table. They would win their next league game at home to Celtic on 15 April and, in doing so, they confirmed Rangers as league champions before Smith's men took on Hibs at Ibrox live on STV the following day. Somehow, with five minutes remaining, the match was level at 1-1. Rangers had been terrific in the build-up but perhaps lacking that cutting edge in the final third. Justice was done in the end, however, as Durrant and Mikhailichenko both scored beautiful goals to give the title party some energy.

As Smith reflected on his fifth successive title as manager, and his side's seventh, he was having none of Rangers being involved in a national counselling session, 'I feel aggrieved at times that this club is not given credit for what we are trying to achieve here. We are attracting almost full houses to our home games and are trying to bring good-quality players to the club, the kind of players that people want to watch. Yet we are dragged into this talk about a country in crisis. I don't think it's fair. It certainly does not reflect what we are doing at Ibrox.' Once he had finished the now customary caveats around injuries and saluted the best performers that season, he moved on to the real matter at hand, 'Every year we have won the title, my admiration for what Celtic achieved in going nine years in a row grows. It was a tremendous achievement and all we can do is hope that we can match or maybe beat it.'

It must have been wearing for Smith to achieve a league title and having to admit himself that it was just a small part of something bigger that now had to be won. Like reaching what you assumed to be the summit of a mountain and then seeing it stretch out beyond the clouds. His captain too made mention of the task at hand while also suggesting, with a degree of mischief, that his side were there already, Richard Gough admitting, 'I think you have to examine the two achievements. Obviously, nine titles in succession was a marvellous thing for Celtic – but that was in the old First Division. This time you are looking at seven Premier Division titles in succession. In my view there is a big difference and I think it is a record that will last a very long time.' Given that half of the old First Division was part-time, it isn't a ridiculous point to make but Gough knew that it wouldn't hold any water in this city. As much as the obsession with that target was intensifying, it wasn't yet the ultimate goal for the supporters. At some level, it was assumed that it would be at least equaled anyway – Rangers were even money to make it nine and 6/4 to go one better – but better football and European success was now a must, especially given that seeding for the following season's Champions League qualifier would be more advantageous. Fans openly discussed whether it was worth renewing their season tickets given the show on offer with one very blunt in his honesty that summer, 'I have succumbed to the temptations of Sky TV and now have the power to watch games with more verve or simply switch channels if they show the lack of interest like that in the recent Old Firm game.' The match in question was an awful 3-0 defeat at Hampden on

7 May which saw goalkeeper Billy Thompson sent off, as Rangers phoned in the remaining four games of the season. 'Tactically we are a shambles,' wrote one fan. 'The manager has to get it right next season or he should be told to step aside and make way for fresh blood.'

Bold talk but it was increasingly unrealistic that Murray would make any kind of decision on Smith's future while the odds of domestic success remained so good. European fortunes had to change, however, but who were the players that would facilitate that? On the morning of the league coronation, the Sunday red tops were alive with the prospect of Dennis Bergkamp coming to Ibrox from Internazionale but the story never had the legs. The eventual £7.5m fee that Arsenal paid should have explained why not. You could have made an XI from the names Rangers were linked with in the tabloids at the end of the season. Mark Bosnich, Stephen Wright, David Weir, Alan Stubbs, Stevie Crawford, Jonas Thern, David Platt, Dennis Bergkamp, Gary McAllister, Florin Răducioiu and Tomáš Skuhravý, with Jesper Blomqvist, Scott Booth and Dougie Freedman on the bench. Given that the majority of the names were foreign, Rangers would still struggle to put an XI on a Champions League stage that would be technically proficient enough to seriously compete. David Murray, however, like many British club chairmen, was speculating that the days of the foreigner rule were coming to an end. In the April of 1995 a relatively obscure Belgian player called Jean-Marc Bosman was deliberating over whether to accept a settlement agreement with UEFA and other governing bodies or proceed to the European Court of Justice where his case of breach of contract under the Treaty of Rome was due to begin, with clubs all over Europe waiting to pounce on UEFA should the decision go against them. He would choose the latter and, in so doing, change world football for ever.

A relaxation was unlikely to occur before the new season and, even if it did, how were Rangers to finance such an improvement in a squad with few valuable assets that they would wish to sell? Murray was clear when answering those questions from the supporters. There was a five per cent increase in season ticket prices across the board which was designed to bring in £8m that summer as well as offering fans to buy into what he called 'Ready For The Future', where they could pay a one-off figure of £399 which would go into a player transfer reserve fund as well as 'Blue Heaven' which would help fund the filling in of the two corners on either side of the Govan Stand bringing the capacity up to 51,000, installing two of the biggest screens in Britain so he could show away games at Ibrox and turning all the seats in the stadium blue.

Wanting between £10m and £12m to spend on players in the summer of 1995, Murray called it a crossroads and said, 'We have now to go through a major transition as a club. We are going to spend another £4m on the stadium by August, following on the £33m already spent on it, and a net £14m spent on players. We have to go to our supporters to seek additional funds. Not all of them can afford that and there will be some who will be cynical about this, but no one is being forced into it and we would hope there will be those who wish to do so.'

The £399 payment would give a fan the right to buy the season ticket for their seat at Ibrox for the next 25 years, their name on the seat, a certificate recognising their contribution, the right to transfer their seat within their immediate family, ten per cent discount at Rangers' shops and the Argyle House restaurant and a free weekend ticket worth up to £40 for Rangers' pre-season tournament when Tottenham, Steaua Bucharest, and Sampdoria were due to visit Ibrox. Murray's gift for taking money from fans wasn't limited to the ordinary punter. In April, he persuaded the Edinburgh property developer and Rangers supporter, Ian Russell, to spend £1m to become an 'associate director'. The title held absolutely no power whatsoever – it was debatable whether even a full directorship did by that point – but, in Murray's words which were presumably delivered with a straight face, 'It is another form of sponsorship. Associate directors will be a sounding board for the directors – these are Rangers people and they can give us their thoughts.' Regardless, there was a renewed energy with respect to raising funds. Everyone at the club knew that the two years of treading water were over. Big changes were required in the squad.

* * *

But just how healthy is this God Complex? Not the mock worship in celebration or 'Godrup' pressed on the back of the new home kit, but a system no more advanced than 'give the ball to Brian' and where thousands started to look forward to seeing one player play a team sport. The two played in very different circumstances, but both Davie Cooper and Brian Laudrup were expected to carry a team on their backs, too often the only creative outlet at Ibrox. Gifted heroes with carefree spirits are fine – indeed they are necessary – but a dependence on one player is never sustainable in the long term, as better sides isolate them and leave the rest exposed. Perhaps the British obsession can be traced back to the cartoon hero Roy Race. 'Don't worry about working hard at creating a system lads, Roy will bail us out.' Or Bryan Robson. Or Brian Laudrup. That season's Champions League Final, held in Vienna, told a more modern story about visionary heroes. Rinus Michels and Arrigo Sacchi were not direct combatants – they were likely watching on in the stands – but their ideas and their coaching legacies were going head to head as Ajax defeated AC Milan 1-0 to be crowned kings of Europe. Two of the strongest XIs to take the field in football's most prestigious game and not one player – no matter how good – who stood tall among them all. It was a lesson in the direction of travel at the top level. Technical excellence was required all around the pitch.

It was more than likely going to be the case in Scotland too, relatively speaking of course. Even by their recent comic standards, Celtic were unlikely to lose to lower-division opposition once again in their second cup final of the season. In a tense game with so much to lose, they edged out Airdrie 1-0 – new boy Pierre van Hooijdonk with the only goal – to win their first silverware since 1989. So much reliance on a single player – even of the class of Hateley or Laudrup – would no longer do. It was also the first campaign since 1987/88 where Celtic had got the better of the Old Firm head-to-heads and the ease of the final win of the season gave them hope that a corner had been turned and that their precious nine-in-a-row record could be preserved. A newspaper advert welcoming applications for season tickets at the new and improved Parkhead said, 'Celtic winning the Tennent's Scottish Cup is only the beginning. We are back on form.' Rangers simply had to react and buying one or two quality players alone wouldn't be enough. They had to fit into a better system on the park and be surrounded by players who could go more than a month without serious injury. As it would turn out, despite the buzz around their place, it would be nearly two years before Celtic defeated Rangers again and the best part of three before they did it in the league.

Walter Smith was often agitated by transfer speculation even though it was a normal part of the job. In the summer of 1992 he rolled his eyes at the link to Lothar Matthäus, suggesting that, if the media was going through the Ms then perhaps Maradona would be next. He duly treated the weekly list of new names around this time with the usual straight bat. All except one. On Friday, 5 May the *Daily Star* ran yet another fanciful transfer link but by the Monday, Smith had been forced to confirm that a deal was in place with the player's club. It was now all about the man in question. Not since Maurice Johnston six years before – not Brian Laudrup, not Basile Boli, not Mark Hateley or Duncan Ferguson – had Rangers been close to signing a player who generated so much thrill and cynicism in equal measure. The spark that would re-energise this dressing room or another expensive liability, both in body and mind? The debate raged all summer long both for those who were excited and for those who were frozen in fear. Before the season was even out, Rangers were making a huge statement of intent.

Gazza was coming.

Chapter Six

Roundheads and Cavaliers

'**Complaining about boring football is a little like complaining about the sad ending of** *King Lear*: **it misses the point somehow.**'
Nick Hornby, Fever Pitch

'*They are going to watch the final on television, with their philosophy.*'
José Mourinho on Ajax, 8 May 2019

It had been the most enjoyable season for the neutral in five years but by the halfway stage of 1995/96, Celtic still found themselves that little bit behind their rivals. With two defeats and a draw in the three Old Firm matches that had already been played, they were four points behind the champions going into the busy festive period. 'The team across the city can maybe get away with grinding out results,' Celtic full-back Tosh McKinlay told the *Daily Record* in December. 'But we've been brought up on pure football.' Rarely has there been such insight into the Celtic state of mind. In other words, 'Sure, we *could* win titles by winning the big games by small margins but it simply wouldn't be accepted. We either win beautifully or not at all.' With only one trophy so far in the decade, the answer was more often not at all.

'Cavalier football' was a phrase that echoed through Scottish football radio phone-ins and newspaper columns in the 1990s. An emotional insurance policy and a psychological crutch of consolation, it reached its zenith during this particular season with many former team-mates of Tommy Burns using their punditry pulpit to preach the true gospel. Yes, yes, Rangers kept winning the key matches but that was all balanced out by the lives of the poor being enriched by watching their side spray 247 passes from one side of the pitch to the other in an entertaining score draw against Kilmarnock. Some things are more important than mere results, after all. When one future Celtic signing described his new manager as 'the kind of man you read about in the Bible', it was perhaps a sign that the messianic narrative had reached its limit.

It all pre-dated Burns, of course. The mythology of the Lisbon Lions – Celtic's European Cup-winning side of 1967 who were all born within the circumference of the centre circle at Parkhead – was built mainly around the fact that they overcame the great defensive wall of Internazionale and Helenio Herrera's *catenaccio*. Given the overpowering monochromatic need inherent within so much football writing, defence was beaten by attack, pragmatism by flair, bad by good. The almost certain offside nature of the Celtic equaliser was blurred by the broadest of historical brush strokes. Even Liam Brady's Celtic team – the one that famously went unbeaten for 14 games – was hastily given the tag of Scotland's 'best footballing side' and imaginary points for style were awarded alongside the real thing. It all came to a shuddering halt on a night where style didn't matter as Rangers – playing with ten men for 84 minutes in horrific conditions in the Scottish Cup semi-final – gritted their teeth, reorganised, took their one chance and with it, their place in the final.

If Celtic – and Aberdeen for a few years in the late 1980s and early 1990s – were the dashing Cavaliers then Rangers had to be painted as the Roundheads.[81] Dull, prosaic, Cromwellian protestants up to no good with their penchant for clean sheets and titles where even the reports of excellent performances were underlined by a suspicion that Walter Smith would cancel Christmas, given half a chance. Pat Nevin – the former Chelsea and Scotland winger and later BBC broadcaster who has cultivated a reputation as football's leading intellectual and high priest of indie chic – was once reported as saying, 'If there were only 99 Scottish clubs, Rangers wouldn't make my top 100.' The level of romantic narrative arc at Ibrox was insufficient.

It wasn't wholly true throughout the match reporting of the time nor the transfer speculation – newspapers still had to sell to the dominant market of Rangers fans – but the commentariat too often indulged the caricature, the inflation of certain chosen characteristics and the minimising of others. The towering central defenders, tough-tackling midfielders and powerful strikers were front and centre when sketching Rangers, with the stylish and creative wingers – a lineage that runs through the history of the club from Alan Morton to Brian Laudrup – pushed to the margins. Jim Baxter was immortalised at Wembley playing for Scotland rather than any trophy won for Rangers. He didn't fit the script. In 1995/96, Graham Spiers lamented in *The Herald* the fact that Laudrup and Gascoigne weren't Celtic players and if they were, the league would have been won with weeks to spare. Spiers perhaps typified the entire mindset with two reports in

---

81   Cavaliers and Roundheads were the names given to both sides of the English Civil War (1642–1652), where the parliamentarian forces (Roundheads) defeated those loyal to King Charles I (Cavaliers). The monarchy was restored in 1660 under Charles II.

the December of 1995. Both Celtic and Rangers handed out heavy thrashings of Hibs, just three weeks apart, and his accounts were somewhat different in tone. 'Celtic simply played lavishly here … Theirs is an increasingly convincing cause. Someone whispered it last night: Celtic for the championship?' was his takeaway of a 4-0 win at Easter Road. When Rangers won 7-0 after Christmas, he wrote, 'An inspired Rangers, yes of course, but what an embarrassment for the Scottish game to have this murderous scoreline adoring its season … some of us were cringing amid the ringing celebrations.' The brave spirit of the rebels and the crushing inevitability of the empire.

Caricature lies at the very heart of rivalry, however. The extremes become part of the story and are often indulged in the same way by both sides. Even to this day there is a tendency for Rangers fans to romanticise spirit over technique and more creative players have to start their Ibrox careers like Laudrup did, lest they build up a bank of distrust whereas an early display of energy and endeavour can delay the final judgment on ability. Being something other than mere results – be it style or political identity – can sustain a support through leaner and more comedic times. In the early part of the decade, when Celtic were borrowing floodlight bulbs from Queen's Park, attempting to convince fans that upgrading the toilets amounted to significant investment and, with signings such as Carl Muggleton, sounded as if they were competing more with *Sesame Street* than Serie A, the focus has to shift elsewhere. As David Brent – the comic creation of the next decade but one based on observations of the 1990s – would later say, that was 'the real quiz' It didn't halt the comedy, however. When Celtic lost to Raith Rovers on penalties in the 1994 League Cup Final, one fan called BBC 5 Live's famous phone-in *606* to complain that it was unfair. Instead it should be the team who breaks the deadlock in extra time – the brave and fearless poets – that wins.[82] John Paul Leach, one of the new voices on the emerging Scot FM, suggested that Celtic's purchase of the German midfielder Andreas Thom – in the same summer as the arrival of Paul Gascoigne – was 'the most significant signing in the history of Scottish football'. Also a stand-up comedian, it is doubtful if his Edinburgh Festival set had any lines as funny as that. Poetry without substance quickly leads to parody.

There were Rangers fans, both at the time and now, who believe that the binds of this rivalry were counterproductive. Not that success was anything to be dismissed, but that by being effectively defined by Celtic and what they once achieved in a league that contained part-time opposition – which the quest for nine and ten championships in succession clearly did – was something of a trap that kept the club locked in the small time, just when the game was growing exponentially to another stratosphere. There is a great deal of truth in this but it ignores the reality of the situation that Rangers found themselves in – fans overwhelmingly demanded it – and the nature of rivalry itself. It is always a

---

82   It is important to note that when FIFA and UEFA adopted this point of view with the 'Golden Goal' from 1996 it too often led to sides barely crossing the halfway line such was the paralysis that making one vital error gripped them.

duality to some degree. 'Celtic really are in an awful state and it's bad for the whole Scottish game. Nobody finds it even remotely funny,' wrote Alex Cameron in the *Daily Record* in September 1993. Thousands would have strongly disagreed with his assessment but the argument that Celtic needed to be saved because Scottish football needed both clubs to be healthy was another consistent trope used throughout the decade. A year later, Ally McCoist spoke similarly in the *Sunday Post* when he said that Rangers 'needed a strong Celtic'. As the following chapter and beyond will demonstrate, he was absolutely correct but Rangers fans with longer memories bristled that they didn't recall too many pundits and players pleading the Gers' case in the dark years of the early 1980s. It wasn't true – many editorials lamented the inertia in both the Rangers boardroom and dugout – but that it wasn't at the same volume and regularity could be explained by the number of scribes and pundits by the mid-1990s who had Celtic leanings and the fact that, with both Aberdeen and Dundee United posing a genuine challenge back then, there simply wasn't the need. A more relevant comparison was the lack of demand for healthy competition in Scotland post 2012.

In that same season of 1995/96, Celtic had a contemporary bedfellow in Newcastle United. Kevin Keegan's 'Entertainers' were the darlings of the casual viewer up and down the country, with such an array of attacking talent and overload in approach. It was this ethos that led fans in voxpops outside of St James' Park to say that they would rather see their team lose 5-4 in an entertaining game than win 1-0 in a duller affair. In the March of that season, after a 12-point lead had been eroded to just four, Newcastle welcomed the other United, of Manchester, enjoyed most of the ball, huffed and puffed a great deal, but lost 1-0. Newcastle United won the hearts and minds. Manchester United went on to win the championship. That Keegan's side scored seven goals fewer than the champions was ignored just as the romanticisation of this Celtic team chose not to dwell on the fact that they scored nine fewer than Rangers, played in 11 draws – nine of which were either 1-1 or 0-0 – and when nine of their 24 wins were settled by the margin of one goal.

There is plenty of precedent for this kind of story in football. Individual careers fêted without a great deal of major honours with which to support them and endless paeans to those who nearly made it but were beautiful in failing. Think of 1970s football and almost certainly the Dutch national side comes readily to mind. Much loved and respected, they won nothing despite coming close in two consecutive World Cup finals. In their defence, they can point to the gift of 'Total Football' – a fluid and technically superior way of building a team – that influenced the world and the success in the European Cup of Feyenoord and Ajax from 1970 to 1973. It is still a little harsh on the West German side who were in 1976, somewhat ironically, a penalty away from three consecutive international successes after winning the European Championship in 1972 and the World Cup two years later. They could also point to club triumph with Bayern Munich's hat-trick of European Cups coming directly after the same Ajax feat. And yet, most respect is grudging if it exists at all.[83] They spoiled the fun and stopped what could and, more importantly to those writing the folk songs, *should* have happened. The same was true for Paolo Rossi and Italy in 1982; his three goals being lost under a stampede to eulogise the Brazilian side that lost. The need to venerate style over substance wasn't contained within football either. The 1990s produced one of the greatest snooker players to have ever picked up a cue as Stephen Henry won all of his seven World Championships in the decade. The overwhelming contemporary hero of the time, however? Jimmy White, who lost in the final five times in a row. The Whirlwind caught the imagination, the winner took the rest.

Fast forward to the middle of the 2010s and you can find evidence of where this argument ultimately led. On 22 April 2014 José Mourinho, in the first season of his second spell in charge of Chelsea, took his side to Madrid for the first leg of a Champions League semi-final against Atlético. Neither he nor his counterpart that evening, Diego Simeone, were known for valuing the aesthetic over the outcome, therefore a cagey first match was always likely. The goalless draw that ensued was not a spectacle but the reaction on Twitter told an interesting story. More than the predictable criticism of the game as a form of entertainment was a sense of neutral entitlement. 'You owe me and everyone who watched that an apology,' wrote @ Eoin_98, an Arsenal fan, on Twitter, while the Canadian journalist Campbell Clark posted, 'Chelsea set out to remove all fun from football. zzzzzzzzz.' All of this missed the point that if you were a Chelsea or Atlético fan, you were most likely sat on a knife edge all evening, such was the importance of just one moment of skill or error. The game is for the two clubs involved and their fans first, and detached viewers a distant second. This isn't like buying tickets to watch *Hamilton* and discovering on the night that one of the performers has suddenly forgotten how to rap. And yet the viewer at home was more likely to point to their bill and ask more for their money. Sport – especially the version that was honed and shaped into a television show in the 1990s more than by any other decade – was now theatre and those paying the subscriptions were demanding more bells and whistles, ignoring the fact that sporting tension, that perilous state which actual theatre can only dream of producing, is the greatest drama of all.

It wasn't long until their wishes were granted as the Champions League in particular started to produce knockout ties with the most remarkable swings in momentum from 2016 onwards. In the spring of 2017, Barcelona came back from a 4-0 defeat at Paris Saint-Germain to win 6-1 in the Camp Nou before the following year letting a 4-1 home-leg lead slip when they faced Roma in the Stadio Olimpico. In the semi-final stage in 2019, both ties were wild. Liverpool overturned a 3-0 deficit when they defeated Barcelona at Anfield by four goals in the second leg and Tottenham were dead and buried in Amsterdam – 3-0 on aggregate with just over half an hour of the tie remaining – and managed a last-

---

83   There was perhaps, admittedly, another reason why an outpouring of love and admiration for Germany in the 1970s wasn't forthcoming.

gasp equaliser on the night to go through on away goals. Sitting in the television studio was a dismissive José Mourinho who, it appeared with a degree of pleasure, eviscerated the ultimate philosopher club for not shutting the game down when they were in full control. The Champions League era of Mourinho, Simeone and Rafa Benítez had been supplanted by the adventure of Jürgen Klopp and the atheistic beauty of Pep Guardiola hence it should be no surprise that the average number of goals in a Champions League game rose by nearly half a goal in the eight years after that stalemate in Madrid compared the eight seasons which preceded it. Was this a victory then for the Cavaliers? Was this a restoration of flair?

Like the original story of Roundheads and Cavaliers, appearances would suggest so but it may be misleading. The monarchy may have been restored in 1660 but eventually under far greater and increasing control by parliament. More and more elite-level games appeared to be more expansive and free but there was method in the mayhem. As the bigger clubs hoovered up the best attacking players then it made practical sense to deploy them with full support. This has arguably been a pragmatic positivity – much like English cricket under the leadership of Brendon McCullum and Ben Stokes, despite marketing phrases such as 'brand of cricket' – it simply has made sense for some teams to take the game to the opposition with more aggression than before. It has not been beauty for the sake of it.

And so too with Rangers, as the next chapter and beyond will show. The general narrative died down after season 1995/96. For a start, it was clear for those with Celtic at heart that this ethereal fig leaf couldn't cover reality for much longer. They had to get tougher, smarter and more physical. And it became too ridiculous for most writers to label a Rangers team who would play the way they did that season – and would later do so at times under Dick Advocaat and Alex McLeish – as brutish and functional. Smith's answer in that all so crucial summer of 1995 was to find a blend that provided that most desirable state of all: balance. He added one more Cavalier to join Brian Laudrup and surrounded them with a stable framework of Roundheads.

There was pragmatism underlining the poetry. As there always should be.

Chapter Seven

Number Eight

Season 1995/96

'Gascoigne has to go. There can surely be no argument about that. Not long after he signed, I forecast he would not be at Ibrox next August. Rangers must not wait that long.'
Gerry McNee, Sunday Mail, 10 December 1995

'Slowly walkin' down the hall, faster than a cannonball.'
Noel Gallagher

'Fucking show me how good you are,' Alan McLaren challenged his team-mate as the clock ticked down on the penultimate game of the league season. Seconds later he won the ball midway inside his own half and it bobbled to the feet of the man he had so recently been berating. He had already shown how good he was – earlier in that game and throughout the long season – but now he was tiring and had been pleading with Archie Knox to take him off. Natural instincts took him past two players and by the time he reached the halfway line, he was fuelled by a title-winning destiny. Ibrox had seen Brian Laudrup do similar 18 months before – with more grace and panache – but somehow this was even better. The concept of football as a team sport was left redundant for the nine seconds that it took for Paul Gascoigne to win the league, with no one else seemingly able to get near him as he hustled and bustled his way through the heart of that Aberdeen side.

Another title won by a heavy reliance on a different individual talent? That is certainly the popular mythology of 1995/96. This was Gazza's season. A mercurial, unpredictable genius. A man who seemed to thrive on chaos on and off the park, who dominated the front pages as often as the back, who on the pitch gave fans things they'd never seen, but off it didn't exactly help the increasing unprofessionalism of this Rangers squad. A scenario where Trevor Steven would awake at 5am on a small island on Loch Lomond hugging an MTV presenter and a Channel 4 producer in a 'ball of human flesh' just to stay warm, is unthinkable without Gascoigne's arrival. So too is the renewed vigour that Rangers showed to deal with their first title challenge of any kind in five years and the first from Celtic in eight. It was, so the story goes, all about him.

In reality, however, it wasn't. For all of Gascoigne's anarchy, the true story of the season was actually one of reliable stability. A season where five Rangers players played over 40 games – Gascoigne, the new back three and Andy Goram – and six other key figures made over 30 appearances. It was the first time for years where a first-choice XI could trip off the tongue with ease. Not to mention the story that would change football for ever, the breakdown in relations between the Scottish champions and the national team and the work permit that could have changed so much. It was a season that could demand its own book.

No, this was more than just a maestro's masterclass. Gascoigne may have been the brightest spark added to a Rangers dressing room since Graeme Souness, but if he had just been plugged into the same system and environment that Smith had been persisting with then this season could conceivably have ended with nothing and a legacy ruined. It was another signing that summer, a change of formation and some better luck with injuries that ensured that Smith could put together his best ever team. It was how Smith housed his new genius that made the difference and created something so rarely associated with the Englishman's life story: balance.

* * *

Somewhere in the affluent suburbs of Rome, in early May of 1995, an England international was driving around his back garden on a quad bike trying to run over his overweight friend, as Walter Smith pressed his doorbell. Upon being told who it was, Paul Gascoigne stopped his chase and drove around to meet his visitor. 'What are you here for?' he asked. 'I'm here to see if you'll sign for Rangers,' Smith replied. 'OK.' 'What do you mean?' 'I said I'll sign for you.' And a couple of months later, he would.

Gascoigne would have known exactly why Smith was there, however impromptu the visit was. His time with Lazio was coming to an end and he was aware that a few clubs were interested including Rangers, Chelsea and Aston Villa. He had no interest in living in London again so discounted the first two assuming it was Queens Park Rangers and not the Scottish champions. When that became clearer, his interest was immediate. The two men had met briefly in Florida on holiday the year before and had shared a telephone call before Smith took the gamble on door-stepping the midfielder and capitalising on those early positive nosies. 'Drink that beer and don't talk,' said Smith as he outlined his plans. 'I thought, this is all right,' Gascoigne wrote in 2004. Negotiations between Rangers and Lazio didn't take much longer as the Italians made some money on their original investment and quickly agreed a deal for £4.3m. It was Gascoigne's management team that ensured that the situation became more protracted than he or Rangers would have liked, with Mel Stein – the player's principal manager – involved in a financial scandal in the USA of which he was later cleared. Nevertheless, by 17 May, the *Corriere dello Sport* was running with a quote from the man who was being chased around Gascoigne's garden, Jimmy 'Five Bellies' Gardner, 'Il suo amico Jimmy Cinquepance è convinto che alla fine Gascoigne si sistemerà a Glasgow.' Gardner was 'convinced that in the end Gascoigne will settle in Glasgow.'

Although official confirmation wouldn't come until July, Gascoigne was in the Blue Room to meet the press on Sunday, 4 June. 'I have looked around now and sorted out one or two little details with the chairman and I will sign a three-year contract with the club in July,' he announced. 'I won't be doing it before then for personal reasons, which I don't want to go into at the moment. But everything has now been settled. I didn't take a lot of persuading, because I know just how massive this club is. Take a look at that stadium and you know what Rangers are all about.' Those personal reasons could have been Stein's legal problems or the fact that his girlfriend Sheryl had informed him that she was pregnant, news that Gascoigne did not take well. 'My first thought was, oh shit. That's the last fucking thing I need,' he wrote years later. Yeah, I know it was horrible. It's not the way to behave when your girlfriend says she's pregnant. I know that, don't tell me. I should have given her a hug.' Either way, it was an early sign – not that it was really needed – that Rangers were taking on far more than just a footballer.

No one was more aware of this than Smith. 'When you take Paul Gascoigne, you take him knowing what you're taking. There's no use complaining about it afterwards,' he said in Roger Hannah's 2017 biography of Archie Knox, *The School of Hard Knox*. 'You sit down and say to the rest of the guys, "Look lads, we've brought him in. He'll probably get away with a bit more than the rest of you but he'll win us football matches."' From the outset it was clear that this didn't just mean domestic matches. Both Gascoigne and his prospective chairman were keen to reference the ambition to return to the Champions League and how this move was a big part in ensuring that. 'We want to get back to these Champions League nights we enjoyed three seasons ago. We all want that,' said David Murray that Sunday. 'We want it for this club, but we also want it for the whole country, because we want to raise the standard of the game in Scotland.'

If Smith needed Gascoigne for greater things, then so did Terry Venables. The first appearance in the Blue Room was a flying visit, during his involvement with England in that summer's Umbro Cup – a preparatory tournament in advance of the following summer's European Championship. Gascoigne had played in a nervy win over Japan the previous day and would play a controversial part in a lucky 3-3 draw with Sweden later in the week, where he broke the nose of Magnus Erlingmark with a flying elbow. Brazil won the cup at Wembley the following Sunday with a 3-1 win over England – an eighth cap and a goal for a young talent on the way to PSV Eindhoven called Ronaldo – but Gascoigne's late substitute appearance gave life to an England side struggling without him.[84] Watching on from the Royal Box was a footballing king. 'He looked to me like a player who can change the pace, the rhythm,' said Pelé. 'England did not have anyone able to direct or influence the midfield. There was no thoughtful player.' Nor had there been one in the centre of a Rangers midfield that had lacked that consistent vision for years now. After 14 operations in four years, it was a gamble that had to pay off.

Despite rumours of a late attempt by Manchester United to hijack the deal – which prompted the United chairman Martin Edwards to rubbish the claims on 28 June – Gascoigne was finally paraded in front of 2,500 fans gathered outside the main door on a baking hot July afternoon. What was commonplace in Italy – Gascoigne himself had encountered it on his arrival in Rome as had Diego Maradona and Roberto Baggio – wasn't really a thing in Britain at this point. Newcastle United would do similar the following summer with Alan Shearer but the kind of mania that was engulfing Glasgow wasn't seen when Roy Keane turned up at Old Trafford two years earlier or when Stan Collymore broke the British record that same summer when he completed his £8.5m move to Liverpool from Nottingham Forest. Some Rangers fans had gathered at the same door six years before when news of Maurice Johnston's signing broke, but mainly to confirm that they weren't having hallucinations. This was all very Mediterranean and it had the weather to match as he walked around the metal perimeter fence shaking hands with children and adults alike, many of whom had the peroxide blonde haircut as an homage to their new hero.[85] 'It's nice to feel wanted again,' Gascoigne said as he took in the fervent adulation. One journalist moaned that 'he's only a bloody footballer' and in doing so completely missed the evidence in front of his eyes. No, he wasn't. There had been signings more controversial and more important in Scottish football since the Souness revolution but none as 'big', not before nor since.

'I'm not here just to recapture the form I have shown before, I'm here to do more,' Gascoigne promised the world on his official unveiling. With so many injuries and a notoriously chaotic lifestyle, this was by no means assured. On his last day of training at Lazio he arrived already half-drunk with a Lucozade bottle full of wine and mockingly got on one knee in adulation to the Czech coach Zdeněk Zeman – a relationship of mutually held frustration – before falling over laughing and passing out. Alan Bokšić had to carry him off the pitch. After Sheryl had informed him of his impending fatherhood, he 'stuffed his face' with burgers and ice-cream in Las Vegas while suggesting an abortion. And yet, he more than

---

84   The difference between English and Brazilian football at the time was nicely underlined at half-time when the Notts County player Andy Legg was on the pitch, demonstrating his remarkable skills. If the game was played in the Maracanã the crowd would expect ball juggling. That day, the skill was an attempt to beat a long-throw record, which he duly did.

85   One Glasgow barber claimed that he had 300 requests for the same haircut already.

balanced this excess with hard work. 'Normally I would be coming back from holiday with five or six chins,' he said at that July press conference. Incredibly, not this time. The six months of recovery work had paid off and Stuart McCall was one of a few new team-mates who was taken aback by how slim and in good condition he was in, 'miles ahead' of him in the pre-season runs. What Gascoigne needed more than anything now was games of football and Rangers ensured that their preparations catered for his needs with some behind-closed-doors games at home and a tour of Denmark. In Scandinavia, Rangers would see both the good and the bad as Gascoigne moved the ball around with ease and invention, curled in free kicks but was too often wild in the tackle and prone to reaction when he himself was the subject of close attention. The referee in the final tour match – a 2-1 win over Hvidovre where Gascoigne scored a stunning goal – Peter Mikkelsen, himself FIFA's number one official in 1991 and 1993, shared a warning with the travelling media circus: he'll need to curb the temper or he'll be sent off early into the new season. Twice Gascoigne reacted with his elbows after tackles from behind and, if it was anything other than a friendly, he would have seen red. This tendency for self-defence was unsurprising given the fractured cheekbone that he had received from the elbow of the Netherlands' Jan Wouters at Wembley in 1993. When the friendly schedule reached Ibrox however, and the tournament began with Sampdoria, Steaua Bucharest and Tottenham – with whom Gascoigne played and was involved in an on-field fight in a pre-season encounter at Ibrox in 1989 – there was a lot more controversy to come.

Rangers won the event on this occasion, beating Steaua 4-0 and defeating Sampdoria 2-0 in the final, displaying far more fluency and cohesion than at the same stage a year earlier. As an added bonus, the new star had scored – a simple goal from a Brian Laudrup pass – and Walter Smith should have expected many a column inch on how his side was set fair for the new campaign with two exceptional players reading each other's movements so quickly. 'I fear that Rangers will discover that signing Gascoigne was a mistake,' said the MP for Carrick, Cumnock, and Doon Valley, George Faulkes on the Monday morning, and later in the week Lawrence Donegan suggested in his piece for *The Guardian* that 'the last thing' the Northern Ireland peace process needed was a 'blond crop-haired footballer putting his talented foot in it'. Gascoigne's new team-mates had set him up for a fall by suggesting that if he wanted to ingratiate himself with his new support – as if that needed any further work – he should mimic the playing of a flute in an Orange band in a post-goal celebration. It went down well with those in the stadium – *Follow, Follow* released a colour poster of the image in the first edition of the season – but sparked controversy among those who did not have Rangers at heart.

The club's immediate response was confused. Secretary Campbell Ogilvie said the story was 'blown out of all proportion' on the Monday and added that 'Walter Smith will deal with the matter as he deems fit' but then, as the story grew in notoriety, Rangers banned the BBC from Ibrox on 1 August because they had shown footage of the incident on *Reporting Scotland*. Embarrassingly for Rangers, due to the friendly nature of the game it was not widely available footage and was owned by the club and the production company Cameron Williams. So, in effect, Rangers had sold the images to the BBC and then flew into a huff when they used some of them. The matter was quickly resolved but the whole story was indicative of several things. Firstly, sensitivity and sensationalism around the sectarian issue was changing quickly. Two years before, Rangers' players – most notably Andy Goram and John Brown – did the exact same action at the Scottish Cup Final and it had been a running in-joke that when they crowd asked a player to 'give them The Sash' the player either had to produce the flute charade or be mocked for 'not knowing it'.[86] Secondly, Gascoigne himself simply brought a new kind of intensity that would ensure a more extreme reaction than had any other new signing indulged in the same way. Many columnists shared the perfectly fair observation that the man was typifying the growing culture of celebrity in 1990s Britain. Rangers had Paul Gascoigne, the brilliant and irrepressible footballer but with it they had to manage the alter ego – Gazza – and the media circus that this attracted. Finally, the issue said something about the growing hype around offence. It was the end of the week before *The Guardian* suggested that it could derail the peace process but the original piece from the game by Glenn Gibbons didn't even mention the incident. Rangers fans dismissed their own humour as entertainment but often got upset by provocative genuflection – as good a comparison on the other side of the divide as you can find – and treated stories such as Aberdeen supporters installing screens showing Rangers clips in the urinals of a local pub so that they could literally piss on their rivals, as evidence of dehumanising the Rangers support and, in the words of one fanzine contributor, 'celebrating their Auschwitz mentality'. Humour wasn't what it once was and football's clown prince would need to be mindful of that.

Of much more importance to Smith was how to manage the footballer rather than the jester. 'We want to give Gascoigne and Laudrup freedom,' said Smith on his arrival in Denmark. 'We want them to have the opportunity to express themselves, to show what they can do. When you have players with their skills, then you must try to build your team around them.' In order to do that he was now preparing to use the 3-5-2 that he had naively toyed with in Athens and which Graeme Souness had planned for in 1990 before injury and arguments forced his hand. 'Coaches do not really impose tactics or systems on players,' he said, curiously. 'The type of players who are available tends to dictate the style of any team.' One could argue that coaches buy players to fit their system and in that sense, Smith did so. Stephen Wright's pace and industry as a young right-back at Aberdeen would allow the manager to utilise the same kind of player on both sides, with another Aberdeen alumni, David Robertson, doing the job on the left.

86   It may well have started, ironically, with Maurice Johnston. When hit by a pie from the Celtic end at Ibrox as he went to retrieve the ball for a corner, it was said that he very quickly mimed some flute playing, to inevitable umbrage.

Celtic were left empty-handed in the chase for Gordan Petrić from Dundee United as Smith added a necessary component to any three-man defence: a genuine ball player. It is understandable that Gascoigne stole this show that summer and is remembered accordingly but the acquisition of Petrić should not be undervalued. If Smith had brought Gascoigne into his existing 4-4-2 – one that was defensively creaking and leaving an ageing Richard Gough badly exposed – and allowed him the same freedom as Laudrup, this season could well have ended in disaster for Rangers. If Italia '90 and, later, Euro '96 told us anything, it is that the best of Gascoigne is highly correlated with the use of a 3-5-2. One exception was the diamond 4-4-2 that Venables used in the excellent 4-1 win over the Netherlands at Wembley but in the opening game of the finals – a 1-1 draw with Switzerland – Paul Ince was badly exposed as Gascoigne went wherever he wanted to, leaving huge gaps behind. Give him some ballast, however, and the expression was more likely to pay off. The industry and protection of Stuart McCall and Ian Ferguson was just as important, as was the use of Petrić and McLaren[87] around Gough, who would go on to have an outstanding two seasons at the heart of this Rangers team; his team. In that sense it was far more than spending big on memorable names and including them on a team sheet. Smith's only significant tactical alteration in his first term as Rangers manager was hugely significant. He was building some balance.

It wasn't built cheaply but then, David Murray was only delivering on his promise. Rangers spent just under £10m that summer – a remarkable total in the context of previous summer outlays – funded in part by the £2m the club was able to recoup on Basile Boli who went to Monaco[88], but mainly from the additional reserves brought in from Murray's extra finance scheme and season ticket uplifts. Almost £5m was generated by the controversial 'Blue Heaven' project, with another £8m coming from 34,000 season tickets. When the corners of the stadium were finally filled – at a projected cost of £4m – it would take that number to 39,000 holders and another 6,000 on the waiting list.[89]

Where Smith had used that money wisely in buying players who suited his new support structure, he had less luck and sound direction in attack. The talismanic Ally McCoist had managed only nine games the previous season for a return of one solitary goal and therefore it was felt that Smith needed to find a long-term replacement for a legend who may well have run his race. By the end of June, Rangers were very publicly stating that they were chasing one of Romania's World Cup stars, Florin Rǎducioiu, even though the player was adamant that he was not leaving Espanyol. At Gascoigne's unveiling Murray reiterated his expectation that Rǎducioiu would, with the help of former AC Milan team-mate Brian Laudrup's persuasion, become a Rangers player. A month after the interest first broke, and

---

87   Hearts were the only side in Scotland who played with this formation before this summer so McLaren was another who was well-suited to it.

88   Ally Maxwell also left the club, to Dundee United for £250,000.

89   Both corners were due to be finished by January but would not be until the following season.

with a £2.7m fee agreed between the clubs, Rangers finally gave up. Răducioiu ticked a lot of boxes for Smith – intelligent inside and outside the penalty area, clinical, with a great scoring record for Romania and especially with Brescia in his first year in Serie A (13 goals in 29 games) – but his lack of interest in coming to the UK should have killed the chase early.[90] Two days after Smith closed the door on a month-long saga, another hero of the 1994 World Cup who plied his trade in La Liga was in Glasgow to sign for Rangers. Oleg Salenko was the joint-top scorer in the United States, although all five of his tournament goals famously came in the one group match against Cameroon. His seven goals for Valencia would suggest he was more the answer to a pub quiz question than a player ready to be a long-term heir to the greatest ever Rangers goalscorer.

Nevertheless, this was arguably the most exciting summer since 1986. The greatest English talent of the decade, a cultured defender and young prospect both proven in the Scottish Premier Division and some international glamour from one of Europe's top leagues. A Mr Sharp from Motherwell wrote a letter to the *Herald* which simply said, 'There was no mention of Rangers Football Club on the back page of *The Herald* this morning (1 August). Is this a mistake?' 'The last two seasons have not kicked off with fans in such high spirits,' wrote Mark Dingwall in the opening editorial of the season. Optimism, yes but, with painful memories still fresh, there were nerves too.

Smith travelled to Switzerland on 12 July for the Champions League qualifying draw wary of three teams who were lurking, unseeded – Steaua Bucharest, Dynamo Kiev and Hajduk Split. For once – and for the time being – the draw was kind, with Rangers being paired with the lowest ranked club in the hat, Anorthosis Famagusta of Cyprus. Once again, both legs were played before Rangers kicked a league ball and, despite the evidence of vibrancy in pre-season, the tension was obvious. Anorthosis played the expectations game well by talking about trying to avoid a huge defeat at Ibrox. In truth this could easily have been another nightmare for Rangers and one which seriously tested Murray's resolve around the future of Smith, with the league saga coming so close to completion. Gascoigne and Laudrup were bright and aggressive in the opening minutes, the Englishman having a blistering free kick saved, but after the early onslaught the Cypriots could and should have scored with all of their four clear-cut chances. Smith started with the three-man defence but, without the unavailable Petrić, it opened the door for the forgotten man of Ibrox, Brian Reid, Graeme Souness's final signing who hadn't turned out for over two seasons.[91] Two of the chances were dragged wide and Andy Goram was to thank for keeping out the other two, one of which was from Ivan Todorov who had sunk Rangers two years earlier in Bulgaria. On a warm summer's evening, Rangers toiled in their new red and white harlequin change strip. McCall hit the bar not long after the hour mark and the introduction of

---

90   Răducioiu's eventual move to West Ham the following summer was made famous by the allegation from his manager Harry Redknapp that the player was out shopping with his wife when he should have been at training.

91   Reid lasted for 45 minutes as Smith replaced him with Durie and back to a four.

Charlie Miller for Ian Ferguson increased the intensity. Two minutes later the goal finally arrived. Gascoigne split the deep defence to release McCall, whose cut-back was swept in by Gordon Durie.

Such was the impact of that summer's heatwave, the temperatures in Cyprus two weeks later didn't create the same cauldron that Athens had. Rangers weren't a great deal better on the night although Miller should have had a first-half penalty and missed a good chance in the second, when put into a great position. Goram had to make one excellent save to keep the advantage and much was made of him pulling out the Scotland squad for a vital European Championship qualifier in Greece the following weekend because he wasn't 'mentally attuned' to give everything for the national cause while trying to avoid injury and be available to ensure his club qualified for what was increasingly becoming the biggest stage in football. A stalemate on the night was enough and Rangers were finally back among the big boys. They would find out soon enough just how high those levels had been lifted in their absence.

On the face of it, the opening three league games showed much to be happy about. Three wins, seven goals, none conceded, Miller picking up where he left off the previous season, McCoist back on the scoresheet alongside new partner Salenko, it was the first time Rangers had won the opening trio of league fixtures in ten years although, with Kilmarnock and Raith Rovers at home and Falkirk away it was hardly the toughest of starts. Despite the positives, the narrative was still around Gascoigne and the objective onlookers were far from convinced. He came on for the last half an hour at Brockville and the *Herald* match report on the Monday was heavily caveated, 'He was good in that late stint, strolling around with the arrogant, self-confidence that marks the extra-special player, spraying passes with either foot, side-of-the-foot flicks, chips over defenders' heads, and cheeky back-heels – in fact most of what is available in his natural repertoire. Whether he will be able to do this at pace for 90 minutes at higher level again will not be answered until he achieves proper match fitness. The problem for Rangers is that Gascoigne has become the main man on the park. Everything is fed through the Englishman, and already his colleagues accept that he is the team's general, seeking him out with every midfield area pass, moving aside to let him take the ball and acknowledging his authority at set pieces. This is fine and will be beneficial if the ex-Lazio player achieves the stamina required for the stresses of the Scottish season, not to mention European cut and thrust, but until that is established, the jury must stay out.' With an Old Firm league and cup double around the corner, and both games taking place at the new Parkhead, there was a sense that the verdict was ready to be delivered.

It had been a tough summer for Celtic as they tried to kickstart their metaphorical rebuild to reach the pace of the literal redevelopment of the stadium, which still had two stands behind the goals to complete as the new season kicked off. Not only did they miss out on Gordan Petrić to Rangers, Marc Degryse and Dmitri Radchenko slipped through their grasp and David Ginola led them a merry dance to engineer a little more money from Newcastle United. Given that Fergus McCann had promised fans that the 'lion's share' of the £14m share windfall would go on players, the pressure was being felt. He went into print in *Celtic View* to complain about the press treatment of the inactivity by effectively pointing to the players that they had spoken to and that £4m had been spent the previous season on Phil O'Donnell, Pierre van Hooijdonk and Tosh McKinlay. Peter Grant underlined that in a summer preview when he said, 'Every year big clubs need players to freshen their squads. The fact that we attempted to secure a world-class player like David Ginola underlines Celtic's desire to bring the best here. In the end he didn't sign, but just as important for us is that John Collins has agreed to stay. Pierre van Hooijdonk, Phil O'Donnell, and Tosh McKinlay will be like new players for us next season as they have never played for the club at Parkhead before. Even old-timers like me agree it will be great to be back playing at home.'

Casting an eye over players is very different to getting them through the door and the *Herald* ran a mock telephone counselling session hosted by McCann – the likes of which had been put on for teenage girls that summer when Robbie Williams left Take That – with one example being: 'Q. But when can we look forward to seeing some top names at Parkhead? A. Basically, when Rangers come to play us. Meanwhile, we are introducing an exciting new feature into the match programme. It is called Fergus's Fantasy Football. From a long list of players, fans can select the Celtic team they would have liked to see play in the hoops if only I wasn't too miserable to meet their wage demands.' German forward Andreas Thom was persuaded to make the move, however, for just over £2m from Bayer Leverkusen. He had been nicknamed 'the Phantom' by the Bayer fans due to the fact he went missing when it mattered.

The first of the two Parkhead clashes was a League Cup quarter-final on Tuesday, 19 September. Rangers had moved through the gears with relative ease against lower-division opposition – Morton and Stirling Albion – but this was a bigger test of Smith's new side, with two derbies in 11 days, especially when the protective midfield layer was not available to him for the first tie. The Rangers side that evening may well have been the most attacking line-up that Smith ever deployed in such a fixture. It had Goram and the back three of Gough, McLaren and Petrić which was now settling well in addition to Robertson and Wright as the wing-backs. With McCall and Ferguson not yet ready for action, Smith had little choice but to opt for a midfield three of Gascoigne, Miller and Laudrup, with McCoist and Salenko up front together. In reality it looked more like a 3-4-3 with Laudrup completely free between those lines, which resulted in one of the most open Old Firm cup ties in recent memory and a genuinely enjoyable spectacle, if there can ever be such a thing for those watching on with deeply vested interests. Smith had noted the new optimism around Celtic – returning home and starting a new era – and impressed on his players that these two fixtures were the most important derbies for ten years. Here was a chance for

Rangers to lay down a psychological blow with a statement of their own, 'You may feel that the times are a-changing but we're still on top.'

The pressure was on Smith following early Champions League disappointment (more of which later) and on Gascoigne, with tabloid frenzy about his private life a constant feature. Rangers were impressive in the first half, with three great chances to take the lead, but Celtic took hold of the early stages of the second, Goram saving brilliantly from a Collins free kick and Gough launching himself to block a Van Hooijdonk shot after he had spun past Petrić, early signs that the new setup worked well for the captain. It could even be argued that the same block would not have happened if he was still part of a flat back four and allowing Gough those few extra yards of depth was to prove so valuable over the next two years. The only goal came with 15 minutes remaining and was the result of a combination of an Old Firm veteran and debutant. McCoist's predatory awareness at the back post hadn't left him as his career began to enter its final phase and he was in the perfect spot to head home Gascoigne's cross. The match reports still noted that Gascoigne had been quiet throughout the game – bookies were taking odds on the minute that he would be sent off – but even if he had only touched the ball once in the entire 90 minutes, that particular touch, a first-time flighted ball that took out the Celtic goalkeeper and defence with tantalising perfection, was worthy of the bottle of champagne and sponsor's cheque alone. With his shirt untucked, it was a level of vision and execution that no other player on the park had.

By the time Rangers returned, they were behind Celtic in the table. The 1-0 defeat at home to Hibs on 23 September was a bit of a freak result – Rangers should have had a penalty when Salenko was fouled inside the box but got a free kick and Hibs won with a penalty against the run of play that was actually outside the box – but the possibility of Celtic going four points clear at this stage of the renaissance was one that had the media enthralled in the build-up. Again the pressure was on Gascoigne who, in the opinion of the *Sunday Post,* had 'a lot to learn from Paul McStay'. If the subject matter was discipline then it was a fair comment as Gough had to settle him down at half-time while he was on a booking. Smith's only concern was getting him further forward and in both respects, he duly delivered and silenced the critics for that weekend at least. Rangers were already ahead by that point thanks to the unlikely source of Alec Cleland, filling in for the injured Robertson at left-back. With both McCall and Ferguson back to give Smith the kind of support he most desired, the game had more of the traditional 'harem scarem' feel of Old Firm clashes with Celtic again having most of the ball but none of the composed edge to make it count as the extra defender was always there to make the difference. Cleland's intelligent header just before the break was all the work of Salenko, coming deep to take the ball, using skill and patience to get himself into more space before delivering a beautiful cross on to the wing-back's head. The Russian international was involved again for the second, being a focal point for McCoist to run off of before the arch marksman returned the favour from the previous week by sending through a perfect pass which Gascoigne finished without breaking stride. The moment that had filled the dreams of one half of the city and inspired the fretful nightmares of the other, had arrived and provided an early iconic image of the season. There he stood in the foreground, the number eight and global superstar while in the background there was scaffolding and white vans. A stark reminder that Celtic still had a lot of ground to make up.

The columnists had to change their line of attack as it was fast becoming clear that Gascoigne was going to fill his boots in Scotland, especially in this new Rangers setup. Some had predicted that the pace and chaos of the Old Firm atmosphere would be too much but in two touches of a football he had made a mockery of that. The media needed another platform now, on which their prophecies of doom could be proven correct and the greatest footballing test of them would suit just fine. How would Gascoigne and the rest fare on their return to the Champions League?

* * *

'Campbell Ogilvie, please take a bow!' So ended a piece in all of the Champions League programmes for matchday four. 'One of the nice things about this season's UEFA Champions League is that Campbell Ogilvie is back,' it started. 'On every matchday we should go to his office on the first floor of the Main Stand at Ibrox Stadium in Glasgow and hang a "Welcome Home" banner over the door.' Ogilvie, the piece rightly impressed on readers throughout the eight European cities that evening, was responsible for all of this. It outlined how his initial vision was rejected and explained how he then modified it down, translated it into various languages and actively door-knocked and campaigned until he made a case that was convincing enough to get the ball rolling. Now, in 1995/96, with its four groups of four leading to a quarter-final knockout stage, UEFA had eventually been led back to his original concept. It was just three days under three years since Rangers secured qualification for that very first Champions League. For many that evening, it might have felt like three decades.

Walter Smith wasn't indulging in cliches when he gave his reaction to the group stage draw in Geneva on 25 August. 'Just pleased to be there' was a genuine source of relief after the agony of the two campaigns that had been and gone, but he still remained 'satisfied'. There is no question that he could have been happier. Rangers have reached this stage of the competition on 11 occasions at the time of writing and have only ever faced a tougher draw twice – in 1999/00 and in 2022/23. They avoided the holders Ajax in 1995 but that is where luck deserted them. Juventus were the early favourites for the title – correctly as it turned out – and, in Borussia Dortmund, they were joined by the next toughest seed. The German champions were a developing side but would go on to win the following season's crown by beating Juventus in the final. Nantes, Spartak Moscow, Porto and Blackburn Rovers – now without Kenny Dalglish – were the other seeds who were unfortunately avoided; the latter two would fail to make it out of their groups. Aalborg, Legia Warsaw and Grasshoppers were some unseeded names who would have been a more appealing prospect than old foes Steaua Bucharest. It wouldn't be a sunny walk in a friendly park this time around.

The sense of excited optimism on Jim White's face as he introduced Rangers' return to the big time in that opening match was in sharp contrast to the despondency with which he delivered his closing comments to camera. Rangers were six minutes or so from a fine and respectable 0-0 in Bucharest. They had defended well and both Trevor Steven at half-time and then Terry Butcher in commentary, as a slow match rambled on, commented on how little Steaua had managed to get beyond their back five. As Daniel Prodan sliced a long effort wide, Butcher was sure that Andy Goram would be happy to see more of those and how the match was so obviously heading for a draw. After another Goram save from a Constantin Gâlcă free kick, Prodan got one a lot closer. One could argue that Petrić could have been more intense in closing down the Romanian defender as the corner was diverted to the edge of the box, but the finish – the kind of 'once in a lifetime' efforts that Rangers were becoming sick of seeing whenever they visited eastern Europe – was unstoppable. Smith, fans and media alike were all in agreement about what was missing, and it wasn't just Alan McLaren for the latter stages after he was sent off for violent conduct.[92]

'Retaining possession is our biggest problem,' said Smith immediately after the match. 'We are defending well, but the main disappointment was the way we gave the ball away, and because of that we never started to play, which meant we couldn't begin to carry the game to Steaua.' Because of McCall and Ferguson's lack of availability, this was not exactly a Rangers side lacking ball players. Gascoigne, Miller, Durrant and Laudrup all started but all were ineffective as long balls boomed over their head and, whenever they did get on the thing, lacked the confidence and awareness to use it properly. This was to become a theme of the autumn and an enduring one in Scottish football to this day.

'It's going to be hell for Dortmund. Gazza is going to give the Huns[93] a right seeing to,' reported the German newspaper *Bild* on 27 September, its source being a 'prophezeit mir ein zahnloser Alter in der Horseshoe Bar'. In English, 'a toothless old prophet in the Horseshoe Bar'. It was very much the approach favoured by most, if Rangers were to get back into the competition. As the Dutch referee Jaap Uilenberg blew the first whistle, the players were serenaded with the theme from *The Dam Busters*. 'They won't like it up 'em!' In the end, Dortmund coped but not without moments of anxiety. The tie had similarities with that first night on this stage, against Marseille in 1992, with Rangers showing a lot more bravery with and without the ball than they had done in Romania and having to get back on

---

92   McLaren would be given a further three-game ban on top of the automatic next match, but it was reduced to two on appeal.

93   The more traditional German 'Hun', one presumes, rather than the more common epithet that is used around Scotland to describe Rangers fans or protestants.

level terms twice – with goals from Richard Gough and Ian Ferguson – to draw 2-2. What's more, Gascoigne was brilliant, his best performance in a Rangers shirt (until the following Saturday at Parkhead at least) with Dortmund appearing to accept that he'd do whatever he liked in the middle of the park and that they were best closing down the space available for other Rangers players hoping to receive his passes. The result was no disgrace but it was clear in the manager's programme notes that he had targeted as close to maximum points as he could get from Ibrox. 'I would ask you all to get right behind the team and hopefully we can give you the result we all want,' was how Smith closed his message.

On 20 occasions in the previous season – one regarded as being characterised by domestic toil plus Laudrup – Rangers played in front of more than 40,000. On that night, the first night back in the Champions League, the attendance was 33,209. That can partly be explained – especially the huge gaps in the Broomloan Road end – by Dortmund originally asking for 3,000 tickets but only using 1,300 and not giving the two blocks back in good time, and also a period in Champions League history where attendances in general struggled as the novelty of consistent live football on television kept people at home before the draw of the spectacle that they were watching created a bigger demand to actually be there. Mainly, however, it was blamed on David Murray. The same seat which cost £12 on a Saturday was £27 for the visit of Dortmund. Season ticket holders could get three-match packages which cost £63 at the cheapest, with some in excess of £70. 'I thought it was a reasonable attendance given the circumstances,' he said, refusing to acknowledge that this was the key factor in the Ibrox match average being down almost a quarter for one of the biggest games of the season. It wouldn't be the last time that this tension between maximising the revenue so as to afford the best players and marginalising what Rangers called the 'grassroot support', would be so evident. Welcome to modern football, in more ways than one.

On 19 October, at Winchester Crown Court, the jury hearing the trial of Rose West – one of the most appalling criminal cases in British legal history – were due to leave and visit the site of her former home, 25 Cromwell Street, Gloucester, where the bodies of nine young women and girls had been unearthed. They were under strict instructions from the judge, Mr Justice Mantell, not to discuss the case. Any other topic was permitted, he said, before suggesting, as an example, 'a rather depressing performance by Rangers last night'. Even in the most horrific of circumstances, Rangers' show in the Stadio Delle Alpi was still considered to be bleak. The story of the season overall really isn't one of injury-hit disruption, but if there was a short spell that seemed so redolent of campaigns just past then it was the six weeks of October and early November. Laudrup limped off against Dortmund with an ankle injury that kept him out until 19 November, Robertson, Miller, Goram and Ferguson all had some time out around the same time and crucially, Gascoigne wasn't fit enough to travel to Turin, the site where his tear ducts opened and his life was changed for ever. With the suspension of McLaren and the loss of his two best players, Smith had a selection nightmare ahead of the toughest match of his managerial career. In hindsight, he may have re-arranged the deckchairs slightly differently, perhaps with John Brown joining the three man defence, allowing Craig Moore to go into midfield and support McCall and even using a natural midfielder like Durrant in there with Salenko on his own, in a 5-4-1. (A younger Mark Hateley could have spearheaded such an approach better but by this point this part of his Rangers career had come to an end as he joined QPR with a minimum of fuss in September.) In the end the midfield three consisted of Gordon Durie, Stuart McCall and Alec Cleland with McCoist and Salenko up front. Within seconds, it was obvious what kind of night Rangers had in store as Goram was forced to make a spectacular double save in the first minute. After further onslaught, the Italians went ahead in the 15th minute when Fabrizio Ravanelli's free kick was deflected past Goram. Two minutes later, a cross ball was able to pass beyond six Rangers players in the box and still find Antonio Conte who pounced to double the lead. The roof was caving in. Before the match, Jim White asked the studio guest Alex McLeish about the prodigious young talent Alessandro Del Piero. A fine prospect, McLeish agreed, but he was confident that Richard Gough and the Rangers defence would have enough to deal with him.

For Rangers fans at this time, Miller represented the future, although not necessarily on this occasion, you understand. At 19 years old he was far too young for a big club with high expectations to rely upon. But definitely, at some point down the line, he would grow into the role and become a great Ranger. That worldview was somewhat shattered in Turin that evening as a 20 year old Del Piero tormented Rangers. His high, dipping free kick from near the corner flag took out everyone including the impressive Goram and made it three goals in eight minutes. The second half was in a slightly different gear but Del Piero was almost in exhibition mood when his exquisite Cruyffian drag back made a fool of Alec Cleland in front of a watching continent. The wing-back's revenge two minutes was typically Scottish as he scythed down his young opponent and immediately headed straight off the field. The fourth Juve goal, by Ravanelli with 14 minutes left, typified many of Smith's issues. Moore attempted a long hopeful ball for Salenko but Ciro Ferrara acted quickest, intercepted and set the white-haired hero Ravanelli on his way into plenty of space. Gough scored a deflected consolation three minutes later but there was no hiding from the footballing reality. 'Tallies 4 Wallies 1' was *The Sun*'s headline the next morning.

Pundits called on Rangers to evoke the spirit of Marseille on that big opening night when Juventus returned. 'The slow game doesn't suit Rangers,' said McLeish in the pre-match build-up. Yet by the break Trevor Steven – one of the other injured players – was bemoaning the lack of possession and control. What was it to be? Passion or cool? A focus on spirit or technique? The postmortem, not just on Rangers but Scottish football as a whole, kicked off after the final whistle at Ibrox, as further humiliation was heaped on with a 4-0 defeat. One letter to the *Herald* scorned Rangers, and other Scottish clubs, for even trying to play the continental sides at their own game. No, 'even if our top teams filled every position with an assured ball player there is no certain prospect that they would be able to effectively use these particular skills through a wet, windy, cold, and muddy Scottish winter and win our league championship'. Instead we should never deviate from a game based on 'speed, pace, and athleticism and getting the ball quickly from one end of the pitch to the other'. An opinion piece followed the Ibrox fixture that took a different line, 'Passing the ball should be easy for anyone who calls himself a professional footballer, yet the trouble British teams experience with this part of the game is astounding. Teams like Rangers and Celtic have to decide what exactly it is they want. If they are content with a Scottish title which guarantees them the opportunity to try to qualify for the Champions League that is fine, but they should say so and make it clear they are interested only in the riches available through qualification. However, if they believe they should be more than bit-part players at the top level then they have to admit they are way behind schedule. They must rethink their strategy, because the current one is not working, even though Rangers' Murray insisted yesterday, "There will be no change in our policies."' In 2023, the same conversation is taking place.

A more fascinating insight was offered by the legendary Hugh McIlvanney in the *Sunday Times*, as Smith allowed him complete access on the evening of the game and the following day. He likened the result to a Tarantino movie, 'Rangers and Celtic were not merely done in – they were blown away. Their pride was splattered all over the fancy palaces they have built to house the central traditions of one of the world's most passionate football cities.' As he left Archie Knox huddled over sheets of paper in the small manager's room, McIlvanney took in the Italians' warm-up at close quarters and concurred with Smith's assessment of their muscularity and fitness. 'Did you see the thighs on the likes of Ravanelli?' Smith asked him the next day. You were looking at players who are far, far stronger in terms of muscle development than anything we've got. We have always assumed we would have to struggle to compete with the technique of the best continental teams but that we would have a physical advantage over them. One of the key lessons for me in these matches with Juventus is that we are lagging behind physically now and that puts us in really deep trouble.'

Smith went on further on the same theme, 'When I watched Milan-Juventus recently, I found it as physical a game as I've seen in a long while. Players on both sides put themselves about to a tremendous degree. But they were so fit and strong that they could do that, and harry the opposition mercilessly to regain possession, while still applying their old standards of touch and control when they had the ball. For years, when those sides lost possession they were intent on defending with numbers behind the ball but now they will press and harry with terrific speed and vigour, refusing to give you a moment's respite. Their new levels of strength and fitness enable them to play more effectively under pressure than our fellas can, and to stand up to hard challenges far better than they used to. The gulf in technical capacity is widened because they have made themselves superior athletes. I feel a change in our approach is essential. We must scrap all our assumptions about having a physical edge and realise we have, in fact, a serious deficit to make up. Obviously, we must go on striving for improved technique but that will be harder to attain than the physical improvement and, in any case, it won't help us sufficiently if we don't get fitter and stronger at the same time. I don't mean a sleeves-up and get-intae-them attitude. I'm talking about a scientific approach to giving our players the athletic capacity to apply whatever skills they have to the maximum.'

The scientific approach specific to Juventus may not have been one that Smith would adopt. Rumours of doping have long since blackened the legacy of that Juventus win with a successful prosecution being overturned at appeal but with haematology expert Giuseppe D'Onofrio testifying in court that he was 'practically certain' that two Juventus players from the mid-1990s had taken the banned EPO and 'very probable' than seven others had, based on his analysis of the blood samples. Regardless, it was undeniable that legitimate strides in sports science were taking the continental game into the distance and leaving the traditional dependence on pluck and isolated individual talent, way behind.

The scoreline that night is slightly more misleading than the first tie. At 1-0, and with Rangers playing far better than they had in Italy, Petrić hit the post with a header only for Juventus to immediately spring into action, resulting in Moreno Torricelli bursting away to make it two and, again, something of a collapse ensued. There was no Goram to provide heroics in the second half that night due to injury and no settled back three, as Petrić was caught between two stools for the first goal. Also, Stephen Wright's knee injury that night was not one of the minor niggles that were keeping some key players out for a few weeks during this time, but one that would effectively finish his Rangers career. A crying shame on another depressing evening. 'Tallies 4, Wallies OUT' ran *The Sun* after this one. It wasn't strictly true – incredibly, Rangers still had a chance of qualifying for the next round with two games left – but everyone knew it was all but correct. Regardless, Smith was far from amused and ejected the newspaper's Kenny McDonald from a subsequent press conference.

The supporter reaction to both Juventus ties was very revealing. There was an edition of *Follow, Follow* out to press following both matches and the difference in tone was stark. Although Mark Dingwall noted that the defeat in Turin was a 'footballing lesson', he maintained that the 'players didn't disgrace us and they didn't disgrace themselves'. Juventus were a class apart, they were always likely to win and these were the games required to push and develop Rangers. The first line of edition 51, published in November 1995, read, 'There comes a time when the whole operation of a club needs to be looked at,' before finishing with a suggestion that the fanzine should start its own 'think tank' to rival the SFA's ongoing reflection into the ailments of the national game. The tone throughout is sombre, with some demanding change in the management team, especially Archie Knox and Davie Dodds, and, while there weren't calls for Smith's head – as there were elsewhere in the support – there was at least fair warning. There were suggestions that Rangers should tempt Fabio Capello from AC Milan and oversee the footballing operation at Ibrox while also having guys like Jimmy Nicholl, Alex McDonald and Tommy McLean – all former Rangers players in Scottish managerial roles – involved in any new setup, thus perfectly exemplifying the irresolvable tension between demanding continental sophistication as well as hardline tradition. What is important to note is that there was still genuine hope of a result against Juventus in Glasgow and it wasn't purely down to the return of Gascoigne and a shock 4-0 defeat that Juventus had suffered at the hands of Lazio on the Sunday. With two home games back-to-back, many felt that Rangers could still progress. Given the fact that they had only lost a European match at Ibrox four times in the previous 20 years and with the biggest margin being 3-1, this wasn't as ridiculous a notion as it may seem. The result in Turin wasn't too far removed from what happened in Belgrade in 1990.[94] These things happen. But Ibrox was a different matter. What happened there on 1 November was a loss of innocence and a realisation of just what status Rangers actually had. The courage and spirit of 1992/93 was a different world now. It was an aberration. For many, any ambition to win the biggest prize in club football – an aim synonymous with the revolution of 1986 and one that was directly referenced at Gascoigne's unveiling – died that night as the true impact of the shifting tectonic plates of the game was brutally realised.

Despite Goram's excellence in the next match and Gascoigne's stunning solo goal – his first in European competition – Rangers were pegged back by Adrian Ilie's intelligent move and finish in a night that killed the theoretical hope. Steaua's passing and movement for the goal and plenty of their other chances in the 1-1 draw, highlighted what was missing from the home side and it was underlined by the Romanian manager, Dumitru Dumitriu, afterwards when he said that there was no point in having players like Laudrup and Gascoigne if no one else was on their wavelength or was capable of doing something themselves. Gascoigne's goal, which came from him having no options as he collected the ball in his own half, wasn't the kind of thing that could be relied upon every week. Yet again it was the need for a team of technicians and not just a couple that was being so viscerally highlighted.

The leading school of thought is that this campaign deserves its place in Rangers' 'Hall of Shame' that sadly characterised the 1990s following 1993. Given the double Juventus humiliation, that is understandable but it is perhaps harsh upon reflection. A Juventus side that would go on to win the tournament and be in the following two finals was more than capable of giving that kind of under-strength Rangers line-up a heavy beating. Two entertaining draws against the imminent champions of Europe was no disgrace which left the real disappointment being only one point against Steaua. Criticism was justified – although a late stunner

---

94   Rangers were hammered 3-0 by Red Start in the second round, first leg of the European Cup. It could have easily have been a lot more.

was hardly new to the Rangers' European story – but it was not on a par with AEK and certainly not in the same league as some of the failures still to come. It would be the new year before this side settled and found consistency and one can only wonder how much of an improvement on three points they'd have made without that autumnal disruption or if those lesser lights would still have dimmed on the big stage, looking in vain for their two gods to do the difficult work on their behalf.

On this footballing mountain – the highest peak in the sport – those gods can be sacrificed as easily as they are exalted. And so it was in the freezing cold of Dortmund on 6 December. Gascoigne had started well, a beautiful ball after ten minutes that split the German defence and led to Laudrup opening the scoring, but a Dortmund recovery only created mounting frustration. He was booked in the first half for a heavy challenge on Andreas Möller and then, with Rangers 2-1 behind, berated the Spanish referee for not giving his team a penalty, leading to a second yellow. Gordon Durie warmed the frozen travelling support a little by grabbing a late equaliser but the focus was all on the Englishman. Gerry McNee could hardly wait for his column in the *Sunday Mail* to come around in order to go to town on Gascoigne. 'He badly let down team-mates who battled for the club's damaged pride. He also let down a manager he claims to admire. He made much of that admiration of Walter Smith when he arrived at Ibrox. In Dortmund he stabbed him through the heart,' he wrote with characteristic hyperbole, after demanding that he should be sold as soon as Rangers could find a buyer. Even the more sedate *Herald* pondered if this could continue much longer. It wrote that Gascoigne 'appears destined to be torn between greatness and disgrace. It is a pity, but so far he has been more trouble than he is worth to the Ibrox club and the Scottish game in general.'

By this point of the season, it was a more of a consensus view than is often remembered. Smith's comments following Dortmund that 'the player will have to look at himself because his dissent is happening too many times' was as far as he had gone, even when dismissing rumours of a sale to Chelsea a matter of weeks before or when dealing with Gascoigne's imploding private life.[95] Even fans who had been strong defenders of the player in the pages of the fanzines and tabloid hotlines were losing patience. 'Walter Smith should be banging his head off the dressing room wall,' one wrote. 'His discipline is appalling, he vanishes far too often in games for my liking and also is playing far too deep to hurt the opposition.' As ever with Rangers, 'noise' around the team or an individual player is amplified or subdued by results and the European struggles did nothing to help Gascoigne's cause, even if he, along with Goram, could point to credible individual performances. Domestically, it was also proving to be the stickiest part of the season, although some of that was more a matter of perception than reality. Between the win at Parkhead at the end of September and the final group game

---

95   Another story of Sheryl ending the relationship surfaced before the Juventus match at Ibrox.

in Germany on 6 December, Rangers went from being one point behind Celtic to four clear at the top of the league and much of that was driven by Gascoigne, with three brilliant solo goals in that time, the best being a super driving run and finish at home in a 4-1 win over Hearts that would be far better remembered if it wasn't for all the others.

It would have been better remembered at the time had it not been for other aspects of his game dominating the conversation. One of those good league results was a 1-0 win up at Pittodrie on 7 October when Craig Moore grabbed the only goal in a scrappy performance where a renewed Aberdeen, following their relegation scare, were more than worthy of at least a point. Unfortunately for Rangers, they would exact some revenge soon enough, first, at Hampden where Aberdeen had only got the better of the Gers once in the last ten years. Like in Turin seven days previously, injuries left Rangers with such temporary lack of balance – no Laudrup, Robertson, McCall, Ferguson and, crucially for this one with the earlier defensive solidity up in Aberdeen in mind, Gough – although it was very revealing about where Ian Durrant now sat in the pecking order as he could only make do with a substitute appearance when Rangers were crying out for natural midfielders instead of Moore and McLaren popping up to support the increasingly frustrated Gascoigne. He suffered a bad challenge from Paul Bernard and acted, yet again, with the elbows. He was booked – it could have been worse – but, as a result, was subdued and was hardly seen in the second half. Aberdeen got themselves into a two-goal lead thanks to a Billy Dodds double. The first had a bit of fortune in the bounce of the ball working for Dodds and against Brown but the second was a disgraceful goal to lose by a defence who, domestically, had enjoyed their newfound strength. It was an evening, and a spell of games, that demonstrated that this may well have been technically Smith's best team but that all the parts had to be there for them to shine. They would later in the season but, even though Salenko managed a late goal, a treble that was there for the taking disappeared.

When Aberdeen visited Ibrox on 11 November, the result was marginally better but the consequences arguably far worse. It was a horrible game played in horrible weather and Aberdeen, Eoin Jess in particular with a fantastic opening goal, were the better side. Salenko was once more the man to rescue something from the encounter but neither goal was the talking point following the final whistle.

It was Gary Bollan – another makeshift selection – who set the tone with a bad tackle on Joe Miller following a loose touch. The referee John Rowbotham chose to deal with an over-the-ball tackle with studs showing through the use of an informal warning. It might have been better if he had chosen a card. Seconds later, with passions high, Gascoigne was held back by John Inglis and a free kick given. Whether the frustration was with the close attention or with the fact play wasn't allowed to flow with Gascoigne still in possession wasn't clear but he immediately turned to head-butt the Aberdeen defender in the ribs. Again, no action was taken at the time and, in the second half, when Gascoigne furiously rebuked Rowbotham for being penalised for the use of his arm on Stewart McKimmie's face, he was subbed for his own good. There was no real danger in the 'rhino' action but, in the post-Duncan Ferguson world, fears were real that yet another high-profile Rangers signing would be heading for the dock. The Procurator Fiscal were also called upon to look at three other players – Dodds, Brown and McLaren – for an incident late in the game. There was a spate of events around this time as well. Alan Lawrence of Hearts had head-butted Craig Moore and there were two other incidents in the lower leagues. Both SFA and the law were most probably aware that if the high-profile case was taken seriously, then there were others that must join. The courts weren't troubled and Gascoigne ended up with a two-match ban in December[96] but it understandably led to fears from fans and smug 'I-told-you-so' columns in the Sunday papers.

None of this was new. Gascoigne's career had hung by a thread – and ligaments – after his wild performance for Spurs in the 1991 FA Cup Final. The margins between beautiful footballing genius and reckless harm were razor-thin. Gascoigne – a man weighed down by crippling anxiety, insecurity and hypertension – was seemingly only truly happy with a ball under control at his feet. When that possession was threatened, he could react dangerously. Speaking the following week while on England duty, Gascoigne tried to explain, 'I went out on Saturday nervous because I didn't want to get beaten. I am trying so hard, I am blaming myself for everything. Everybody wants us to get beat, and every time we do they slaughter the team. The lads are feeling it. If they're going to look at the video of the game, then the Scottish FA should also look at the video evidence of some of the decisions given against us. I don't think people realise how much pressure we are under. I'm not saying I'm victimised, but sometimes I feel I need a bit more protection.' When the dust settled, a short ban was easily absorbed by Rangers. Rowbotham however, – a FIFA referee at the time – was heavily criticised. In years to come, he wouldn't make the mistake of leniency again and in so doing, may have arguably diverted the course of history.

'After all the publicity about the bad aspects of the Scottish game it would be nice to think that the focus would now move to the more positive things we saw today,' said Walter Smith following a draw in his side's next league game. There was very little moralising after that one, just an exhausted appreciation for one of the best Old Firm matches of the entire era. Celtic couldn't afford Rangers to stretch their lead to seven points so threw everything at the hosts in a match of momentum swings, controversy, six goals that stood, one that should have and an incredible save that overshadowed everything else. Both sides were at full strength with all key players back fit and both were in front and behind at points before the match ended 3-3.[97] The flair players all turned up with Laudrup scoring on his first game in two months, Gascoigne creating two goals and Andreas Thom and Pierre van Hooijdonk bookending the fixture with a goal apiece.

---

96   The incident and others in that match led eventually to the use of television evidence to support retrospective action in Scottish football.

97   Celtic took the lead twice to go 1-0 and 2-1 in front and then had to equalise to take a point.

However, two moments that didn't lead to goals are most remembered. With Rangers 1-0 down, the renewed partnership of Robertson and Laudrup down the left cut open the Celtic defence. Unusually, it was Laudrup the provider on this occasion as he exploited the space between Jackie McNamara and John Hughes with a pass that saw Robertson run past both players to pick up, before steadying himself and finishing well. In the background of the television pictures showing both men celebrating, referee Hugh Dallas – making his Old Firm debut – had his hand raised. Fans inside the ground quickly realised that, for some reason, the linesman on the Govan Stand side had raised his flag for offside.[98] The stadium announcer, Bill Smith, called the goal as did STV's commentary team of Gerry McNee and Charlie Nicholas and their producers. Viewers at home were led to believe that the match was all square for ten minutes as the on screen scoreboard continued to say 1-1. McNee explained that he missed the complete lack of a restart from the centre circle as he was concentrating on the monitor replays of the goal. It was a farce in more ways than one but Laudrup's equaliser, shortly after some technician had to change the score back, restored parity for real and set both sides on course for a classic.

Celtic's second was from the penalty spot and some criticised Goram's inability to keep it out despite guessing the right way. After McCoist had brought Rangers level for the second time, Goram made a save that will be talked about for many decades to come. Thom's endeavour was stopped by Gough and McKinlay's resulting cross was perfect as Van Hooijdonk was placed right on the six-yard line to make it 3-2, a third blow that Rangers were perhaps unlikely to recover from. Somehow it didn't land. The Dutch forward did everything right, shaping his body to let the cross do the work and setting his aim to the other side of the diving Goram. And yet, his reflexes were enough to block it with his outstretched right arm. For anyone watching – at the game or at home – there was almost the need for a double take, as if they had just watched a phenomenon at work. Which they had. Rangers got their noses in front courtesy of a McKinlay own goal before Van Hooijdonk finally got the better of Goram – for now – and a nation sat back to catch its breath.

It had been a tumultuous two months following the win at Parkhead. The Champions League reality check and the frustration of a missed chance at Hampden provided further cacophony around the Gazza circus and in doing so, placed more pressure on the manager and squad. However, Rangers were 11 league games undefeated and four points clear when they visited Tynecastle on 2 December. It was Gascoigne's last league game before his domestic ban commenced and he signed off in style with a goal and a maestro's performance as Rangers won 2-0. The doubts still remained, however, and the fact that he would go on to be the undisputed player of the year says a great deal about his skill and

---

98   The linesman was on the opposite side of the incident. A Mr Horan previously, it was alleged, of the Methill Celtic Supporters' Club. Proof that conspiracy theorists are not completely confined to one side of the divide.

resilience as well as his manager's guidance and pastoral instinct. When Gascoigne phoned on Christmas morning to complain about loneliness, he was soon picked up and brought into the Smith family home for dinner. He would repay that love and kindness – which is really all that Gascoigne ever needed – in a matter of months. Perhaps the Aberdeen fiasco at Ibrox – arguably his most reckless day on the park for Rangers – wouldn't have happened at all if Smith had been in the dugout. Instead, that weekend he was in the warmer climbs of South America to watch another player he felt could make that vital difference at the top level. If, of course, he had all the paperwork in order.

* * *

Of all the European capitals that have played host to the landmark moments in footballing history, Luxembourg City is almost certainly the most surprising. But it was there, on 15 December, that the game's most pivotal moment since 1992 arrived. Arguably we are still waiting for one as powerful. Finally, after a protracted legal case that took most of 1995 to hear, a judgment was made on C-415/93 that would be for ever known more commonly as the 'Bosman ruling'. The entire business of the sport would be turned upside down 'all because', one Scottish journalist wrote, 'a Belgian took the huff'.

Even if that were true, he had every right to take one. In 1990 Jean-Marc Bosman was coming to the end of a two-year spell at Standard Liège which hadn't been a satisfying experience. With a better contract on the table from the French club Dunkerque, a way out was possible if, of course, Liège agreed to let him go for free or worked out a reasonable fee. Bosman was at the end of his contract but could still be held by Liège if they didn't get what they wanted and so, in turn, he was cornered. Liège demanded a fee of £500,000 (four times what they paid for him) while also forcing a new contract on him which paid him four times less. Speaking to *The Guardian* in 2015, Bosman said, 'I didn't accept this procedure. I was suspended by the Belgian federation because I didn't want to sign. But if I didn't re-sign I still belonged to Liège and I didn't accept this. I missed an opportunity to earn much more money at another club.' It was effectively ransom – one Dutch MEP called it 'slavery' – and it was entirely illegal under the Treaty of Rome.

As the hearing developed over the summer and autumn of 1995, apocalyptic warnings were never far away from the sports pages. One major assumption was that freedom of contract meant that transfer fees as a whole would be banished and not just when a contract was allowed to expire. What is notable is the figures purportedly there to support footballers were not exactly welcoming of any reform to the system. Speaking in July, the Scottish Players' Union leader Tony Higgins said, 'The problem we have now is that if Bosman wins this case, there are major problems for the game. Essentially it would mean that whenever a player's contract with a club ends, he is a free agent. He can go anywhere and the club is not compensated. I don't believe that is right.' His counterpart in England,

Gordon Taylor, appeared to be more concerned with clubs having the value of their assets wiped out like a footballing Wall Street Crash. Two perspectives that are very indicative of how players were viewed at the time; purely commodities. It is tempting to imagine how history would have looked if Liège had not been so intransigent and had done a deal with Dunkerque but it was something that would surely have been tested at some point. UEFA's argument was always effectively that football (and sport in general) was different to any other business, purer as it was than mere commerce. This of course flew directly into the wind that was blowing by the mid-1990s, one where the Premier League and the Champions League were all created to maximise revenue. There was a bullish and quite astounding attitude from UEFA to the challenge, with president Lennart Johansson saying, 'You will all have heard of the European Union and the increasing influence of Brussels. UEFA is far bigger than the European Union. We have 49 members whereas the EU have only 15. The latest interference concerns the transfer system and the rules on non-selectable players which are both key elements in the regulatory structure of football. We cannot tolerate this continued interference.' It was a hubris that would soon come crashing down.

Bosman sought a remedy from a contractual nightmare and £300,000 in damages but what he helped to produce was a truly transformative moment in the sport. There could now be no transfer fee at the end of a player's contract, nor could a player be held at a club until one was forthcoming, and the use of quotas on foreign players – whether in European competition or in domestic leagues – would soon be a thing of the past. The balance in power swung from the clubs to the players (and agents), with a massive increase in salaries at the top end of the game and huge signing-on fees going some way to replacing transfer fees for those players in that situation.

It was a decision that changed the face of football but what for Rangers? The club broadly welcomed the outcome as ridding European football of maximum rules on foreign players had been something it had campaigned for since its introduction. As Scottish football fretted unnecessarily about the majority of its clubs going amateur without the ability to receive transfer fees, Donald Findlay correctly surmised, 'It seems to me that if something is judged illegal, then it is precisely that.' The consequences were just something that all clubs and bodies would have to live with. Walter Smith was happy to see the decision go in Bosman's favour but still stressed that it was important for Rangers – and all clubs – to retain something of an authentic identity. More foreign players, yes, but still with a broad Scottish base which, in effect, would be a voluntary quota system, still as technically limiting. The maximum rules were ended for the following season's UEFA competitions but by that time the market attraction that Rangers held was more limited than it once was and that game of catch-up would be ultimately futile, not to mention ruinously costly.

Bosman was less a single revolutionary event than an extension of the deregulation that started with football's Year Zero in 1992. The strength of television markets would draw the best of the talent with higher wages and the ability to all play together for a collection of 'super clubs'. When France arrived in England for the European Championship in 1996, 18 of their players plied their trade in Ligue 1. Two years later, when they welcomed the world and became champions themselves, only nine of the squad of 23 played at home. On Boxing Day of 1999, Chelsea became the first English club to field a starting 11 filled entirely with foreign talent. How different the landscape could have been had the law acted immediately is one of the biggest 'what-ifs' in Rangers' history. The timing of the ban – when the club was at its most powerful and the biggest in Britain – could not have come at a worse moment.

Back in the real world, Rangers toiled somewhat without Gascoigne's invention, a 1-0 home win over Partick Thistle and a 0-0 draw at Fir Park on Tuesday, 19 December, a game shown live on Sky and which meant that the gap at the top was now only two points. But with the freezing weather and lack of undersoil heating meaning that Celtic couldn't play again in 1995, Rangers had the chance to produce some scoreboard pressure before the next Old Firm clash on 3 January and, with Gascoigne back, they duly did. A 3-0 win over Kilmarnock on Boxing Day was followed up by the visit of Hibs to Ibrox – the only opponent to have beaten Rangers thus far in the league – on 30 December, a game that was billed as the battle of Scotland's two goalkeepers, Andy Goram and Jim Leighton. As it would turn out, one would have a considerably busier day than the other.

Boos rang around Ibrox at half-time but this wasn't for an underperforming Rangers side in danger of being victim of another shock defeat; instead they were all for the referee Dougie Smith – in charge of his first league game at the stadium – and deservedly so. With Rangers 2-0 up and getting back into full flow, Gascoigne made a meal of a great opportunity to make it three when he drifted too far wide of Leighton and the chance was wasted. Upon picking himself back up he noticed the referee's yellow card on the pitch, picked it up, ran over to Smith and comically branded it to him, as it had been done to Gascoigne so often in the season thus far. A festive joke but one that Smith felt had embarrassed him and – with so much pressure on referees to hammer the Englishman following Rowbotham's failure – he immediately booked the midfielder for real. Players of both sides as well as Jock Brown on commentary found it farcical and the clip was the source of widely shared derision about the state of the Scottish game. Gascoigne had been involved in another incident with his arms – entirely accidental on this occasion – which had passed without warning so perhaps this had played on Smith's mind too but it was the attention on Rangers' star man that was becoming ridiculous. It didn't derail the football, however as Rangers were imperious. Slightly lop-sided as Smith opted for Ian Ferguson to fill a gap on the right wing-back role, it mattered not as the movement was matched so often with the passing. Durie came deep for the first goal when he released Charlie Miller and he would go on to help himself to four goals of his own in a performance that Smith described as 'as good a 90 minutes as we've ever turned in' and had some early hallmarks of an even better one that would end the season on a glorious high. Gascoigne got one of the others in a 7-0 evisceration and it was yet another sublime bit of individual brilliance that was now becoming a collection. Eight points clear, albeit with two more games in the bank, the pressure was back on Celtic when the two sides met again at Parkhead four days later.

Celtic had been in good form before the winter intervened, a 4-0 away win at Hibs on 9 December being the highlight of their run. This was the game, after three without success, that many said Celtic had to get right. Burns was somewhat despondent when he made his way into the press room afterwards. 'When I pass away,' he said, 'it will say on my tombstone, "Andy Goram broke his heart." I think he is the best keeper I have seen for … for … for ever.' Goram had been magnificent in a tense but still open 0-0 draw that couldn't possibly match the energy of the previous tie. His close-range save from Andreas Thom was the highlight although many reference the fingertip he got to Phil O'Donnell's long-range strike which diverted it safely on to the post. When Pierre van Hooijdonk crashed into him while he had the ball safely in his grasp it was merely another episode in a growing personal battle that would reach its zenith later in the calendar year. Gough was brilliant too as this strong defensive unit held out but we should be careful in writing this match as yet another chapter in this growing and tedious narrative of beauty against brawn, Roundheads against the Cavaliers. Celtic had the edge on territory but Rangers made the best chances and could easily have won the match and perhaps settled the league championship before most fans were back at work. Salenko was both unlucky and wasteful on two occasions and confused on another when referee Les Mottram overruled the linesman and allowed play to continue after he had flagged for offside. Brian Laudrup ran out of steam in a breakaway with a weak shot – he wouldn't repeat that the next time he visited – and Gascoigne so nearly secured the points with a free kick that crashed off the bar with only four minutes remaining.[99]

Celtic could have easily buckled but they made up the ground with their two games in hand and Rangers in turn responded to the chase with two 4-0 wins away to Falkirk and at home to Raith Rovers, leaving the gap back at two points with parity on games played by 13 January ensuring that a real title race was on. The Ibrox win may have seemed routine but it was special for one man in particular. After 21 minutes Ally McCoist took the ball at the edge of the box and curled it into the top corner to put Rangers in control against Raith but also to become the club's greatest ever goalscorer, breaking Bob McPhail's 57 year-old record of 230 league goals. The feat was 'the one he wanted most of all' and the emotion was obvious as McCoist carved his legend further into the Ibrox stone. Up in the

---

99   The match was odd in that the teams attacked in the 'wrong' direction. Traditionally they would attack into the end housing their support in the second half but, for some reason, this was swapped by Celtic that evening. The match was preceded by a valiant attempt at a minute's silence for the 25th anniversary of the Ibrox disaster, with Fergus McCann leading both managers out into the centre circle with wreaths. It was inevitably interrupted.

directors' box, the 90-year-old McPhail looked on approvingly. 'It couldn't have gone to a nicer fellow,' he said as McCoist's wait finally ended. Legend or not, however, McPhail's presence in the posh seats wasn't the reason so many camera lenses were turned towards it. There that day, it was hoped, was an Ibrox scoring legend of the future, sat next to his impossibly glamorous wife.

Mário Jardel was perfect. Rangers had struggled to replace Hateley and now, with McCoist nearing the end of his time, Smith was desperate not to lose any potency in attack after years of enjoying plenty. Big and strong, Jardel could replicate Hateley's presence but he also combined that with a predatory instinct around goal. With the 'big man/little man' double act on the way out of fashion, the Brazilian was a strike partnership all by himself. The £2.7m deal for the player was announced in late November at a time when the club were able to confirm Champions League profits of £4m and a new kit deal with Nike commencing in 1997/98, where they were paid £7.5m up front. His final game for Grêmio, for whom he was on loan from Vasco da Gama and had scored 41 goals in 49 games, was against Ajax in the Intercontinental Cup at the Olympic Stadium in Tokyo on 28 November. Grêmio lost on penalties – Jardel missed two good chances in the stalemate before being substituted – but excitement was high. The *Herald* reported that he 'should join Rangers within the next month or so and it looks certain that work permit problems won't affect the giant striker, who apparently has dual nationality, like so many of his countrymen. Only last week, Porto played five Brazilians against the French champions Nantes in the Champions League. All of them had Portuguese passports, and if that also applies to Jardel, as seems certain, then he is a Common Market resident and can play in Scotland without a work permit being necessary.' 'Apparently', as it would turn out, was very much the operative word.

Rangers were assured by Jardel's representatives that a passport would be no problem due to the fact that his supermodel wife, Karen, possessed one. Instead, it soon became clear that it was very much a problem. Without parents or grandparents being Portuguese, it was actually a lot more difficult than was commonly assumed for Brazilians to obtain one and Jardel didn't have such family ties. In January Rangers were therefore forced to admit defeat and go down the work permit route to get him in for the crucial months and years ahead. The immediate issue there was that the Scottish League was only allowed ten spaces for non-EU players on permits and they were all taken. Rangers held one, for the Russian Oleg Salenko, so very quickly work was under way to free that up. A straight swap for Peter van Vossen – a Dutchman and therefore a holder of that prized EU passport – from the Turkish club Istanbulspor was the proposed solution. Players like Stuart McCall suggested that Salenko never mixed with the squad enough, that he would come in and go home, and therefore was always destined to be at Rangers for just a short time. However, the notion that Salenko was a flop is very harsh. He played 20 games by the time he left in January and scored eight goals which is hardly a disaster. It is hard to believe that Smith would have cut him loose with that kind of return – plus some important link-up play at crucial times – without other administrative imperatives on his mind.

Even with Salenko's departure, the chase for the work permit was far from a done deal. The permits were non-transferrable so Rangers didn't have the right to hold on to Salenko's until a new target came along. In releasing it, the Scottish League was required to alert any other clubs about the space, should they seek to fill it too, and then it would be a battle over who could make the most convincing case to the Department of Employment. Given that permits were normally supposed to be granted to players who had played in 75 per cent of their national team's games in the two years prior to application – and Jardel had precisely zero caps for Brazil – any case that Rangers made would have been up against it. In the end it was Kilmarnock and the 22-year-old Ghanian international Sammy Adjei who halted the move. Adjei was only a trialist who lasted just over a month at Rugby Park, but it was enough to derail the hope. By the time the space became available again in March, Smith had more attacking options and was content to come back to Jardel another time but he never did and the moment passed.

Often fans and pundits place too much emphasis on the importance of one transfer deal, as if the magic bullet to success in a team sport is always just a cheque and a handshake away, but the case of Jardel and Rangers is almost too tempting to pass up. It is unlikely that he would have spent more than three seasons at Ibrox but that may have been enough to make history. 'I don't have to spend the rest of my career in Scotland,' he said after the Tokyo final, 'but while I am there I will make sure the club and their supporters are satisfied with my performances. No other club offered as much money as Rangers. The salary is much bigger than I imagined I would earn. I do not know very much about Scottish football except that it will be cold and wet. But when you are to be paid such a wage there is no point in moaning.' Hardly the words of a man wanting to put down roots for the rest of his career and, with the likes of Ajax's Danny Blind bemoaning the move, saying, 'It is a shame he chooses to join a physical team like Rangers and puts money before football,' the eventual lure of somewhere more glamorous would have been too much. Archie Knox later suggested that when Jardel trained with the Rangers squad during his visit in the January of 1996, he seriously underperformed and 'couldn't trap a bag of cement' with other players suggesting that it was never a move destined to be a success. This, despite the rain in the west of Scotland, is difficult to accept.

Jardel would move to Porto in the summer of 1996 and play for three clubs where the red tape wasn't as stringent as it was in the UK. In his seven seasons at Porto, Galatasaray and Sporting, he played 198 league games and scored 205 goals. Missing out on Brazil's 2002 World Cup-winning squad, when he had reason to be hopeful, was a dreadful blow which, in conjunction with his marriage collapsing, sent his career into a downward spiral of drug abuse, weight gain – 'Lardel' became his new nickname – and constant injury.[100] At that time however, he was an incredible talent but didn't get that vital international recognition because of phenomenal forwards ahead of him such as Romário, Ronaldo, Rivaldo, Bebeto and eventually Ronaldinho. In Scotland it is difficult to imagine him not being a sensational addition who, while the Champions League would have demanded more around him, would have ensured domestic dominance for as long as he stayed fit and happy.

'I can look at this as more of a hiccup than a crisis,' said Walter Smith after the visit of Hearts on 20 January. It is doubtful if even Jardel could have saved the points on a freak day where Rangers looked at their calamitous worst from the two seasons before. A defence that hadn't conceded a league goal in eight games looked as if it hadn't met one another before as the Hearts youngster Allan Johnston ran riot with a hat-trick in a stunning 3-0 win. Without a flu-ridden Gascoigne, Rangers were dull in attack but it was just one of those rather complacent days in defence that was pounced upon by a youthful Hearts side under Jim Jefferies that was starting to show signs of future promise. As news of the rout worked its way down the A77 to Kilmarnock, where Celtic were playing, they would have known that they had an opportunity to go top of the Premier Division if they could only find a goal. That they couldn't perhaps tells a story of a side who would continue to freeze when the chance presented itself. Defeats make the headlines but so often draws are the silent killer of championship hopes in Scotland and Celtic's 11 that season were terminal.

Highland League side Keith provided a chance for Rangers to get that defeat out of their system and they took full advantage with a 10-1 bodying in the Scottish Cup third round tie, moved to the neutral venue of Pittodrie. Clyde made them work a little harder in the next round but it was still a comfortable scoreline in the end with Peter van Vossen finding his first Rangers goal in a 4-1 victory, although the focus was firmly on an engrossing league championship race. Gascoigne's return from illness brought some magic and mischief in equal measure as Rangers took the points in their next two league games but Smith was forced to discuss discipline and referees yet again. At Firhill, Gascoigne dominated proceedings, scoring two brilliant first-half goals in a 2-1 win. Subjected to taunts about his weight, he jumped the advertising hoardings and celebrated in front of the huge Rangers support behind the goal, making an enlarged belly shape with his arms. Referee Jim McGilvary felt compelled to book Gascoigne for leaving the field of play, even though there was no danger of incitement. He was sheepish in administering the law and perhaps used leniency later in the game as the midfielder's arms and elbows were used to protect his possession of the ball yet again. Seconds after landing one on the face of Billy Macdonald, the Thistle number eight tried to clean the legs from his opposite number and saw red. Cue more hysteria in the press about Gascoigne's treatment – both too harsh

---

100   With that passport finally secured because of his time in Portugal, he had an unsuccessful stay at Bolton Wanderers in 2003 but it was the red tape again that foiled an earlier move to Manchester United in the summer of 2000, after Ruud van Nistelrooy had seriously injured himself ahead of his proposed move that year.

and too light – and it was enough for McGilvary to retire immediately citing the impossible pressure being placed on Scottish referees to control matches.[101]

When Gascoigne was fouled for a Rangers penalty against Motherwell at Ibrox the following Saturday – with 13 minutes remaining and the match poised at 2-2 – he was booked for celebrating. McCoist rolled the spot-kick home to take the points but Smith had reached the limit of his patience. 'I have difficulty in understanding why Paul Gascoigne is being booked week after week,' he said after the match. 'I have not said anything up until now about the situation, but last week he was booked for celebrating a goal and this week he was booked again for celebrating after a penalty had been awarded in his favour. I have criticised Paul Gascoigne and he is no angel, but neither he nor Rangers are asking for anything in the way of special treatment. All we want is for him to be treated just the same as any other player. There was a recent incident when the Celtic players went en masse to the fans at Tynecastle and no one was booked. I am not complaining about that, because players should be entitled to celebrate goals. All I am doing is pointing out the difference in the interpretation by the referees. Players should be able to express themselves in tense games, when goals are scored or penalty decisions given, without being cautioned. This only seems to happen to Paul Gascoigne.' Referee scrutiny was nothing new in football but the levels during this season were considerably higher than throughout the years of comfortable Rangers dominance and would be a sign of things to come as the claustrophobic era of the two-horse race took hold.

With the pressure intensifying and the Scottish Cup tie against Clyde being played on the Thursday, Smith took the opportunity to take his squad down to London for a spot of bonding. A night out in Covent Garden ended with Smith himself leading a conga around a busker playing requests was followed up by some making the train journey to Cardiff for the rugby international with Scotland – not all made that evening's train back – but Gascoigne yet again was at the heart of the drama as his argument with his estranged partner continued until she went into labour on the Saturday. Gascoigne – still unable to process the reality of fatherhood – was in his home town of Dunston where he had fled in a rage after being told he wasn't wanted anywhere near Sheryl. He found out about the birth of his son, Regan, in the newspapers and only made contact two weeks later where it created a thaw in the relationship which led to both moving up to Scotland as Gascoigne finally found a house to call his own in Renfrewshire.[102]

Whether or not that was ideal preparation for a tricky spell of fixtures is up for debate but there is no question that the kind of team spirit that it helped to create was a factor as Rangers kept their nerve. Another Celtic draw on 10 February had extended the lead back to three points but when Rangers took to the field on the live television clash at Pittodrie on Sunday, 25 February, Celtic's 4-0 home win over Partick Thistle had put them level at the top of the table. It was a big question

---

101   Thistle chairman Jim Oliver demanded that the game be replayed. It wasn't.

102   The *Daily Record* covered the story by asking residents, 'Do you want him for a neighbour?' and asking local pubs and curry houses if they would be 'barring' Gascoigne.

to ask Smith's side, still without the injured Gough at the heart of the Rangers defence, but Brown and Goram provided the answers as they hung on to a one-goal lead until the end. The man who provided it? Gascoigne, of course. When Laudrup was flattened by Brian Irvine in the box, he displayed nerves of steel from the spot to keep Rangers in front.

In a winter of seismic change in the world of football and with a missed opportunity to secure years of glory, Rangers kept focus on the here and now. With Gough to return soon, a familiarity would be brought to a team that was now poised to secure a deserved double but there was still a lot of work to be done as the media excitement about an actual title race grew in its crescendo. It wasn't just the league championship that was creating the buzz, however. Paul Gascoigne had divided Scottish football fans since his arrival, with Rangers supporters both defending and praising him at every opportunity against the rest. Usually the opposition would be fragmented on club lines but on 17 December, at the International Conference Centre in Birmingham, the fates aligned to provide a tantalising encore to a production where there was only one star performer. Even if Gascoigne disappointed half of Scotland by driving Rangers on to success, they'd have their chance to unite against him when Scotland played England at Wembley on 15 June in Euro '96. How united the Rangers support was however – with hero pitted against hero – was another matter entirely.

* * *

'The national team is stronger than Juventus, remember.' A fan had written to Craig Brown at the beginning of May with one simple question, 'Why do you not pick Richard Gough for Scotland?' Incredibly, he got a response, signed by the Scotland manager himself, on SFA-headed paper. Brown had compared the Champions League hammering with Scotland's two games with Italy – in which Gough didn't play – during the qualifying campaign for the 1994 World Cup. Rangers had lost eight goals while Scotland had conceded just three. Rangers lost to AEK Athens while Scotland had beaten Greece twice in qualifying for the European Championship, the finals of which were now imminent. Brown said, '[Gough] played 35 times while Andy Roxburgh and myself were with the national team and we won just 11 of these games. Without him, we have played 18 games, and we have still been able to win 11 of them.' Football, from the man who prepared his team for the opposition based on tip-offs from a taxi driver, was a simple matter of deduction. The style of the school teacher reigned supreme.

It was a style and sense of ambition that had diverged significantly from the Rangers support since Graeme Souness, covered in-depth earlier in the book, and was arguably at its apotheosis during this season. Gough, now in the best form for years, was the outstanding Scottish defender that year, yet his valid criticism of the previous manager's methods in his book made him *persona non grata* for the next man to own the company tracksuit. The two Colins – Hendry and Calderwood

– were steady and reliable options but the experience and form of Gough was not something that Scotland were in a position to dismiss so easily out of spite. Tosh McKinlay and Tom Boyd had both enjoyed a good season as Celtic continued their redevelopment, but none could seriously suggest that they had been better than David Robertson who remained at the door, if not yet out in the cold. He later would do so of his own accord, not content to waste his time if he wasn't getting a game ahead of weaker players.

And then there was the handling of the goalkeeping issue as both Goram and Leighton were left sweating it out by Brown until 'an hour and a half before the kick-off of our first game in England at Villa Park when we meet Holland next month. That's when the decision will be made public. To decide between two of the best keepers in Europe is not easy. You are looking at a really high level of excellence here. I only wish we had the same kind of competition in all the other areas of the team', the final line as inspirational as ever. In truth it should have been nowhere near as close. Leighton was a more loyal servant to Brown and surely it was only emotion that created a dilemma after a brilliant season from the Rangers number one, 47 games played and back to his best.

It wasn't difficult to see why Rangers fans – many of whom had been dealing with a conflict of loyalty or interest for some time now – struggled to feel a connection to a national team that seemed reluctant to include their players, with only the industry of Durie and McCall a guarantee to start. Add to this the handling of Duncan Ferguson by the SFA and the long line of disputes between the club and the national governing body and it was a relationship for many that was ready to break for good. Gascoigne, or more accurately his treatment, was a convenient reason to let it snap. Vilified from his arrival, Rangers fans were instantly keen to protect him from those in the fourth estate whom they saw as enemies, with no time for their club. Laudrup was a god who was almost too perfect and graceful, never a word out of place, let alone a pass. Gascoigne was *their* god. He was them on the pitch – imperfect, rash, vulnerable – and therefore the affinity during this season in particular was tighter than many Rangers heroes ever got close to. Even by 3 March, columnists like Gerry McNee were still writing from an early assumption and working their prose backwards, with caveats dropped in with great reluctance. 'The Gascoigne signing remains a gamble,' McNee wrote in the *Sunday Mail* on that day, 'and one which could blow up in Rangers' faces, but in fairness to the player he is scoring vital goals for them.' 'In fairness', as if he was bringing out a point of nuance that wasn't obvious to absolutely everyone who followed the national game every week. That tension between the two men – but one that personified something bigger at play in the country – would increase as the season reached its climax. With the Wembley showdown visible on the horizon, it was no coincidence that the song with which Rangers fans chose to serenade Gascoigne in the second half of the season wasn't a rip-off of a contemporaneous chart hit or another British terrace favourite. It was the old Negro spiritual – and unofficial anthem of the England rugby union team – 'Swing Low, Sweet Chariot'. For some it would be Albion over Alba.

As the season turned its final corner, both Rangers and Celtic went into the transfer market for some late reinforcements. Erik Bo Andersen's 13 goals for Aalborg in the first 20 games of the Danish Superliga season were enough to persuade Smith to spend £1.2m at the end of February, in addition to the earlier signing of Derek McInnes from Greenock Morton in November and the Aberdeen goalkeeper Theo Snelders, who would finally arrive a month later. Initially it appeared that Celtic hadn't learned their lessons from Maurice Johnston as they paraded the Portuguese striker Jorge Cadete at Parkhead under the assumption that no transfer fee was required. When it became clear that it did, the negotiations took a few more weeks before he was finally registered with the SFA. One day too late in order to be eligible for the Scottish Cup semi-final, which just so happened to be against Rangers. Despite Fergus McCann sending a letter to the SFA thanking them 'for their help and assistance in completing the signing', he furiously vented – in the club newspaper of course – that it was the association's chief executive, Jim Farry, who had held up the deal by that crucial day. Regardless, he wouldn't make it at Hampden but there was another league encounter to negotiate before that. One with some late drama but less raucous than others. One with another minute's silence, but one that was observed impeccably. Scotland's showpiece sporting event took place at the end of a week of national mourning. Rangers played Celtic in the shadow of a gunman.

At the start of the week, so much attention was being paid to arguably the most important Old Firm match in seven years. A Rangers win would effectively end the contest and a Celtic victory would bring them level on points and carry a lot of momentum going into the final seven games. When Walter Smith filled up his car on the Monday morning, the attendant asked him, 'Are you all set for Sunday?' 'Yes,' Smith replied. 'You'd better be,' came the response. The obsession with nine and ten titles in a row had created an incredible pressure on the manager and his team, with fans telling Smith at a summer function that they couldn't wait to celebrate ten. Smith said, 'They had completely forgotten that there were still the eighth and the ninth to win. They had skipped them completely. These two campaigns had already been taken care of and it was the tenth they wanted. Anyone from abroad would have wondered what was happening. But that is the way the fans think and we have to attempt to deliver.'

The language around this clash early in the week was 'do-or-die' and 'life-and-death'. By the Wednesday evening, much-needed perspective was delivered in the most horrific way as Thomas Hamilton walked into a primary school in Dunblane and shot dead 16 pupils, one teacher and himself. The language pre-match understandably changed and the action itself was noticeably less intense and slightly lacking the quality of the four that had already been played that season. Celtic had the ball but lacked any kind of invention against a makeshift Rangers defence with Moore at right wing-back and Brown deputising for Gough. Predictably it was Gascoigne again who grew into the game and dominated, blowing fake cigars in the face of Jackie McNamara – who was later sent off for two needless bookings – and sending in that most devilish of all deliveries, the in-swinging free kick, which Alan McLaren just had to guide into the corner of the goal four minutes before the break. With three minutes remaining Rangers had one hand on a 46th league title, but John Hughes escaped McLaren and equalised with a simple header. It was perhaps significant that Rangers, for whom a draw suited far better than Celtic, didn't retreat and see out the rest of the game. With the title there to be done and dusted, they surged forward again with McCall, the captain for the day, hitting the bar from a Gascoigne corner and McCoist blazing over with a great chance in the final minute, the defence-splitting ball provided by the English man of the match. Frustrating, yes but Rangers still held the three-point lead and, on this particular weekend, most understood that life went on.

With that lead and a superior goal difference of 13, any sense of advantage was balanced somewhat by the fact that Rangers had the tougher run-in with four of the seven games away from home. It was assumed by most that there were a lot of twists and turns to come and so it proved almost immediately. Rangers came out for the second half at home to Falkirk in their slippers – 2-0 up, playing great stuff and more individual masterclasses from Gascoigne and Laudrup – but were caught cold. The visitors, who had sacked the veteran coach John Lambie a few days before, played with total freedom to claw the game back to a single goal on two occasions, with Bo Andersen ensuring that enough cushion remained intact as Rangers eventually stumbled over the line with a 3-2 win. Nervy and stuttering it may have been but news of yet another Celtic stalemate, this time away at Motherwell, presented them with a five-point lead that evening. Surely, that was that.

With seven minutes remaining of the following match at Stark's Park, it was all back in the balance. Raith Rovers were 2-1 ahead and Rangers were floundering in a chaotic encounter. Another high, looping Gascoigne corner eventually found McCoist in the six-yard box and the same combination struck gold with a minute to go to win it for Rangers. This is a season packed full of moments of interest and drama and so it is easy for games of underrated importance to fall through the gaps of the collective memory, but McCoist's hat-trick that day is not talked about enough.[103] Celtic would win 5-0 at home to Aberdeen on the Monday evening and a two-point gap – with the potential of a one-game slip – would have tested Rangers' resolve, with a trip to Tynecastle up next. It is fair to argue that if Rangers had slipped up, Celtic may not have played with the same kind of freedom and possibly turned in another draw when their chance arose. It is fair because it is exactly what happened next. Rangers were poor in Gorgie as Jim Jefferies' side notched up a second straight win with a relatively comfortable 2-0 victory but Celtic failed yet again to really make it count. In fact they needed a last-minute Pierre van Hooijdonk goal to grab a point at home to Kilmarnock but it wasn't enough – as it hadn't been back in January – and a four-point lead that should have been two fuelled the title belief, with only one awkward game left.

---

103   Rangers would run out 4-2 winners in the end, a Durie penalty in injury time making absolutely sure.

The Hearts defeat and Kilmarnock draw wasn't an exact carbon copy of what had happened in the winter. There was another reason as to why Celtic were so dejected and Rangers a little flat. On the Sunday the two faced off for the sixth and final time that season in the Scottish Cup semi-final at Hampden, a match that pundits everywhere invoked the law of averages to predict, finally, a Celtic win. 'Only a fool would ever predict the outcome of an Old Firm game. So I'm taking Celtic to win 1-0 at Hampden this afternoon,' wrote Gerry McNee that morning. 'I don't think they'll need luck this afternoon because they are playing well enough to overcome their great rivals at last.' Gascoigne cut a brief pre-match chat with Radio Clyde short and refused to talk to them until they got rid of McNee. The following week's column was entitled 'Kiss off Gazza' as McNee counted the names of many big icons of Scottish football who had taken issue with him but were no longer around. 'Whenever you're ready to go home Paul I'll be glad to oblige – with a one- way ticket,' he wrote, before going on to lend his support to Hearts in the final, 'As I write, Greg Norman is chasing the Masters title. His record there is as heartbreaking as the Jam Tarts' in Scottish "majors". Norman and Hearts for a double? Lead me quickly to a friendly bookmaker!' Both would crumble, in the end.

If familiarity breeds contempt then it might explain why the sixth instalment was by far the worst 90 minutes of football between the two that season. Celtic were predictable in possession and Rangers more intelligent throughout, especially in clamping the wide threat from full-back that Celtic had enjoyed all season. It was only when Robertson and Durie limped off that Celtic used that freedom but by then it was too late. McCoist made amends for poor decision-making early in the game – he should have squared to Laudrup but dithered – when he pounced as Gordon Marshall could only parry a David Robertson shot into his path right before half-time. 'Rangers haven't pushed out very far,' said Martin Tyler on the Sky commentary midway through the second half, 'inviting more pressure.' It was a situation with which they were becoming increasingly comfortable. Celtic forced some corners and consistent pressure in the early stages of that half but with no real cutting edge. When another one broke down in the 66th minute, Alec Cleland threw the ball to Gascoigne deep inside his own half. Not for the first or last time, it was an exhibition of what this Rangers side could do so well when a game demanded it. Less than eight seconds it took. One touch from Gascoigne, one from Laudrup, one from Durie, a chest control as the great Dane took possession back and then a final touch to lift the ball over the onrushing Marshall. The contest ended and Sky's penchant for showing Celtic fans – young and old – crying in the stands commenced.

Celtic scored a late consolation but it made little difference to a result which, perhaps more than any other season, had the longer impact. With the law of averages not helping, Celtic were left to conclude that Rangers simply had something greater in play and it was an inferiority complex that would flow into the following campaign. They weren't at their fluent best that afternoon but they contained Celtic with ease and had two players in a totally different stratosphere who made the difference on the day.[104] His last realistic chance of success gone, Tommy Burns was noticeably deflated afterwards as he tried to spin the narrative of development – there is no question they were a better team than they were 12 months before – against the obvious loss of successful momentum following the Scottish Cup win in 1995 which they had promised would lead to more. 'I don't feel that we deserved to lose the game,' he said afterwards to Sky before following up with, 'At the same time I don't think we deserved to win it. But I definitely felt that we deserved to take something from the game.' Presumably he meant a replay rather than a point from a cup tie, but that hint of incoherence continued in his post-match comments, suggesting that Laudrup was offside for the second goal and assuring the media that Celtic would take the title to the last day. Within three days, that proclamation already sounded weak.

Rangers responded strongly to the hangover-related falter in Edinburgh with a 5-0 demolition of Partick Thistle at Ibrox. Bo Andersen scored a hat-trick but it was his more famous countryman who grabbed the headlines. He didn't score, but Laudrup – used in a more central role closer to Gascoigne – was involved in everything, dragging defenders wherever he wanted. It was another little glimpse into what was coming in the season finale. The only remaining test in the league came on Saturday, 20 April when Rangers travelled to Fir Park, a place where they had dropped points already in recent months and in four of the previous six campaigns, including most memorably at a similar stage in 1991. Celtic won comfortably at home to Falkirk in the hope that history would repeat itself but it only took five minutes for Rangers to deflate that when Stuart McCall's low drive put Rangers ahead. Bo Andersen made it more comfortable before the break and, of course, Gascoigne and Laudrup combined later to make certain, the former rolling home a pass from the latter. It was another big hurdle cleared. Unless their great rivals slipped up again, Rangers now just needed one win from their final two matches to win the league.

And so to Ibrox Stadium on Sunday, 28 April, for arguably the greatest match-winning individual performance that the old place had ever seen. Aberdeen had caused problems for Rangers twice in Glasgow already and interest was piqued for Celtic fans and neutrals when Brian Irvine was left in enough space to bundle the ball home inside 20 minutes.[105] Perhaps if the minutes had mounted up without an equaliser, it would have been an intolerable pressure. Perhaps Gascoigne would have done something special anyway. In the end it took him only two minutes to fire Rangers back level, picking up the short corner from Laudrup at the edge of the box before leading his merry way through what little space he had in the box and stabbing the ball high into the roof of the net. For at least the eighth time that season, Gascoigne had scored a solo goal that would have been remembered

---

104   It was Laudrup's vision and execution that set up the Robertson for the first goal.

105   Taking inspiration from Alex Ferguson the week before, Richard Gough likened Aberdeen to Leeds United in that they only raised their game for the champions. Unlike Kevin Keegan, who would have his famous meltdown the following evening, Aberdeen tried to make him pay the biggest price.

as one of the absolute greats by Rangers fans for years to come, if he didn't have the knack of continuing to better it. His next was voted the greatest Rangers goal of all time in 2018.

Not only was it so remarkable and important that it overshadowed the rest of his repertoire, it served as a single memory that dampens the overall quality of his team-mates that season. Rangers were good that day, nervy on occasion of course, but still impressive. Goram did what he was called upon to do, McLaren led an attacking threat as well as ensuring the solidity, McCall's industry was important as he was the only defensive-minded player in advance of the back three and Laudrup and Durie's runs were consistently intelligent.[106] But he still, even when so tired that he asked to come off, stood above them all with a solo run and finish that had all the hallmarks of his genius, energy, strength and bravery. Most of all it was the best of all when it was absolutely needed: ten minutes left to win the league and he did that, slaloming past those Aberdeen players who were willing to get close to him and striking fear into those who weren't, before caressing the ball into the top corner. Never has there been a more fitting way to win a championship.

Gascoigne's encore was from the penalty spot after Durie was fouled and he wrestled the ball from Ally McCoist. It took Gerry McNee on commentary too long to realise the overall significance and he tried vainly to get the words 'This for the hat-trick and the championship' out before the ball hit the back of the net. The man who appeared to lead the media's scorn and doubt was in place to narrate the conclusion to one of the most impressive individual seasons in Scottish football. 'Gazza and I spoke our first words – amicably – to one another on Sunday after the title decider,' he revealed the following Sunday, before adding with award-winning pomposity, 'so I'm now lifting my ban on him.' That was it. Twenty-five words and one sentence at the very end of his first column after one of the most remarkable performances in the history of the Scottish game and even then, there was enough room for self-aggrandisement.

The relationship would sour further the following season, leading to McNee refusing to refer to Gascoigne by name in his column but by the more dehumanising 'Number Eight' instead. Poignant then, as McNee described the sealing of the championship, that Gascoigne had covered his head by pulling his top up over it, just the number eight displayed on television screens around the country. The title of this chapter is both an obvious play on the eighth title in a row but also a reference to the media handling of the story of the man who inspired it. Because of its later use it was understandably a moniker that Rangers fans have found distasteful but perhaps now is the time to reclaim it. For, despite all the greats who have worn the number over the years, there is only one definitive Rangers number eight. With 19 goals – and nearly as many bookings – you would have to go back to Ally McCoist for a debut Rangers season with a bigger return, and that does not

---

106   Only Trevor Steven, very much at the end of his career and in an unfamiliar role of right wing-back, toiled that day against the pace and ingenuity of Stephen Glass.

include the assists and the life he gave back to a flagging and complacent dressing room. No player has had a debut season like it.

Interestingly, only 72 per cent of Rangers fans agreed with the nation's players and writers that he was the player of the year, with Andy Goram taking 11 per cent in the *Follow, Follow* end-of-season poll. Brian Laudrup had won 100 per cent of the previous season's vote but again, this says more about the general quality of this team than anything else and they were all to show this in a spectacular season denouement at Hampden Park, the venue for the Scottish Cup Final against Hearts. There was late disappointment for McCoist who was ruled out at the 11th hour due to a calf injury and many fans wondered if this had been a glorious swansong, bowing out with 20 goals and another league medal, as he cut a strangely disconsolate figure while walking around the Ibrox pitch during the title celebrations, a new contract not yet agreed. Not only that, the potential shadow of Mário Jardel was joined by Gianluca Vialli – with whom Smith and Murray had enjoyed positive talks with in Turin during the middle of April[107] – and Karl-Heinze Reidle, Mikkel Beck and Oliver Bierhoff among other centre-forwards. McCoist would very quickly sign a new deal but it was another man who had signed on for an extra year, Brian Laudrup, for whom the final would be most remembered.

As with Gascoigne's domination of the season, it feels somehow unfair that Laudrup owns this match for it was truly a superb Rangers performance, arguably the pinnacle of Walter Smith's time in charge in terms of sheer quality, balance and expression. For both Smith and his predecessor, cup finals were not a stage for entertainment, only results. Every single cup final that Rangers had been in since October 1986 they had either won or lost by the odd goal, the exception being the 1987 League Cup win on penalties. Where the Souness finals had at least provided enjoyable entertainment, every one of Smith's five finals had been cagey and tense. The natural confidence of a Hearts side who knew what it took to beat Rangers combined with the early loss of their captain Gary Locke to injury probably ensured a more open final in any event.

It was Rangers' movement though, without a natural striker and using Durie and Laudrup to great effect coming deep and linking up, that caught the eye and Laudrup's opening goal was a fine example of a Hearts defence who had prepared for McCoist and didn't know who to pick up, being brutally exposed by quick and clever interplay. Like the second goal in the semi-final, it was a rapid seven second move from inside the Rangers half that finished with an exquisite Laudrup volley. The party really started early in the second half when a fairly tame Laudrup cross was comically spilled through his legs by Giles Rousset – who earlier in the season had criticised Rangers' negativity in comparison with their rivals – and into the net. Durie helped himself to a hat-trick as Laudrup toyed with an exhausted Hearts defence but it was a genuinely brilliant team performance. He didn't hit the headlines, but Gascoigne ran the game from slightly deeper, supported by the

---

107   He would eventually say no and chose the lure of London and Chelsea.

engine of McCall and Ferguson, while both Cleland and especially Robertson bombed forward at every opportunity. Even John Brown – who had a later season cameo as both Gough and Petrić suffered some time out – was close to finishing one of the greatest team moves of all time. The 5-1 scoreline didn't flatter Rangers in the slightest as all associated with the club revelled in the late-spring warmth at the joyful expression of Smith's technically greatest side.

Judging by his face at the end, you may not have guessed that. His 13th trophy, his third double, his finest 90 minutes and yet, he knew that it would matter not if the following May did not bring home another championship. The BBC's Hazel Irvine barely entertained the post-match platitudes about how pleased he must be before asking about what was next. He was the man who had produced such a show but the only Rangers fan in the stadium who wasn't allowed to enjoy it. Thousands of others did however, although none could have realised that they were unlikely to see such a fine cup final performance again and certainly not the twin virtuosos at their best. They weren't to know that this was the aesthetic height of the era.

* * *

More of these players would surely follow. If it wasn't Vialli, it would be someone else. Somehow, the Rangers support at Hampden that day and all through the season couldn't fully appreciate what they were watching. They were taking it for granted. The mojo had returned and the push was on for the next stage of the development. Now that the laws had relaxed, the sky was seemingly the limit. Little did many realise that there was a new glass ceiling in place, not one dictated by unlawful directives, but by the power of market forces, television draw and an unrelenting pace of professionalism. How many really cared about Europe in any case? How much was all talk, from the chairman to the stands? Polls at the time asked Rangers fans if they would rather set a new domestic sequence or win the Champions League – the peak of footballing achievement – in the next two years. The result was conclusive and shouldn't have come as a surprise to anyone listening to the new favourite song in honour of their new favourite player.

Gazza wasn't here to make Rangers the champions of Europe. Gazza was here for ten-in-a-row.

Chapter Eight

Heroes

'Celebrity is a mask that eats into the face.'
John Updike

'When men are growing up reading about Batman, Superman,
Spiderman, these aren't fantasies. These are options.'
Jerry Seinfeld

In the March of 1996, two lifelong friends and Rangers fans in their early 30s were having a heated argument in a Motherwell house. Adam Caven had been drinking heavily for two days and had pushed his visitor, George Bunce, to the limit. As Bunce got up to get his jacket and leave, Caven attacked him with a knife that he had quickly grabbed from the kitchen and stabbed him in the stomach, after which he lost more than a pint of blood and needed a surgeon's skill to save his life. The argument wasn't about money or love or lifestyle. It wasn't the result of some long-repressed grudge that was finally coming to the surface. No, Caven nearly killed his friend because he didn't agree with him that Brian Laudrup was a more skilful player than Paul Gascoigne. Alcohol may have produced the extreme reaction – followed by a two-year prison sentence and £75 fine – but the more interesting question lay underneath. Why do we have such devotion to our heroes in the first place?

Ultimately, the answer is fame. 'There was always fame. It started in the cave,' said Clive James in the opening to the peerless documentary series *Fame in the 20th Century*, which aired on BBC1 in January 1993. It may well have been ever-present, he argued, but the century that was coming to its conclusion – propelled by the bottomless supply of and insatiable demand for mass communication – had transformed it into something different. The developing machinery of the moving picture had produced a kind of photosynthesis through which normal people were turned into gods and the ordinary people in the audience were left genuinely feeling as if they had a close relationship with someone who didn't know they existed. It's what psychologists call a 'parasocial relationship' and it had arguably never been as widespread as it was by the 1990s. At the end of the 19th century people still had to do things to become famous but by the 1990s it appeared to James that they could be famous just by being famous, leading to the fulfilment of the Warhol prophecy in the 21st century through reality television, YouTube and social media.[108] The 1990s acted as the final bridge between those two states as the cult of celebrity was so powerful that the ordinary masses had to touch its magic somehow. 'Docusoaps' such as *Airport* and *Driving School* made mundanity memorable as fame was sought for its own sake rather than being a byproduct of achievement.

The most prescient observation that James made was when he said that the lives of the truly famous people were 'our dreams come true, not theirs' and that they were effectively avatars for the life that we can't have. 'We all need to know the name of at least one person who can sing the way we can't,' James continued. 'It might as well be Pavarotti, who really does sing for the love of life.' He used Albert Einstein as someone who could think the way we can't, Adolf Hitler as evil the way we aren't, Martin Luther King as brave the way we aren't, Greta Garbo as beautiful the way we aren't, John Kennedy as doomed the way we aren't, Elvis Presley as famous the way we aren't. He could have gone on to show examples of those who can score goals the way we can't, dribble the way we can't, bowl leg spin the way we can't, serve the way we can't, drive the way we can't. Our need for the vicarious life is obvious.

In his play about the life of Galileo, Bertolt Brecht wrote a scene whereby his young pupil, Andrea, crestfallen at the great man's famous recantation under pressure from the church, bemoans that 'unhappy is the land that breeds no hero'. 'No Andrea,' Galileo responds, 'unhappy is the lands that *needs* a hero.' By its very nature, sport needs plenty of them. Individual pursuits are marked easily by that singular greatness but heroes in team sports can be a little different. The Ballon d'Or becomes seemingly more important with each passing year but how fair is it to assess one player's contribution on the basis of team achievement? How possible is it to extricate that from all the other factors happening on the pitch in the same game? Moments like Paul Gascoigne's second goal against Aberdeen make that argument more difficult as he appeared to suspend the nature of team sport in the balance for a few magical seconds. We could point to the impact of Brian Laudrup's dummy run but it makes little difference to the need for the heroic narrative. We all saw what we saw that day: a man picking the ball up in his own half and winning the league, the 34 previous games turning into mere scenery for his very own stage show.

---

108   The artist Andy Warhol was once quoted in the 1960s as saying, 'In the future, everyone will be world-famous for 15 minutes.'

Other Rangers heroes have lasted longer in the affections of the support, almost exclusively homegrown True Blues, but few have had as visceral an impact as Laudrup and Gascoigne. At the apex of such a period of dominance, here were two incredibly gifted players who were so far ahead of the rest of the country that you could almost build a new nation state within the gap. Laudrup's grace and balletic beauty was a welcome reminder of those wider creative players who had been so well-loved in the past but Gascoigne was different. Arguably the most naturally gifted player to ever play for Rangers, it was his everyday vulnerability that created the bond and pushed that vicarious pleasure to another level. Where he had come from and the way he lived meant that it really did feel as if his life was close enough to those who had paid to watch. Until he got the ball and the similarities stopped. The fact that he was so immediately hated by the rest of Scottish football and had an impact on the Rangers team as a whole – both in ways that Laudrup wasn't and didn't – only intensified that. As we shall see, it was a relatively brief affair but few, if any, have been as passionate. For Rangers fans, as it had been for England, he was living *their* dreams.

Fame creates a difficult persona for even the most balanced to wear and fulfil. When they are nowhere near stable however, it is almost always a precarious nightmare. Using clips of Diana, Princess of Wales, Clive James delivered an ominous voiceover near the end of the final episode, 'For the amateur actors who muffed their lines, the whole show threatened to come apart. They were human sacrifices, like those randomly chosen youngsters that the Aztecs would treat as royalty for a few nights and then cut out their hearts.' On the plane home from Italia '90, Gascoigne had been warned that the same people building his legend would not think twice about tearing it down. They wouldn't, but it was he who would make it very easy for them.

The details of that night in the Gleneagles Hotel in October 1996 will follow in the next chapter but Gascoigne's shameful domestic abuse of his wife Sheryl made for a very interesting reaction for those who loved him the most. As thousands of Rangers fans made their way to Ibrox on Saturday, 19 October, many will have gone through their normal routine. Had a drink at the same pub, grabbed some lunch at the same burger van, bought a programme or a fanzine. On that afternoon the 61st edition of *Follow, Follow* was hot off the press and, like six of the covers since his arrival, Paul Gascoigne was front and centre. This, however, was an edition like no other. In some of the others, 'HE'S LOST THE PLOT' could have been an accompanying headline that was ironic or full of mirth. What followed on the very first page was anything but. Forty-one of the 42 pages already seemed a little out of date, the week's news being too close to publication for the normal contributors to digest. As editor, Mark Dingwall had just enough time to ensure that the cover and first page editorial didn't miss. 'IBROX – NO PLACE FOR A WIFE BEATER' was the headline. After starting the piece with familiar moans about drink-driving and the miscellany of misbehaviour at Rangers, he followed up with some of the most remarkable language in the history of the publication, 'This latest episode is the final straw. Either he goes or Walter goes. Paying some of these clowns the money we do it's not too much to ask them to behave like human beings is it? Our beloved vice-chairman is quoted in Friday's *Scotsman*, "If Gascoigne plays on Saturday, scores a few goals and we win, ask the fans what they think." You can know what I'll think now Donald – I'll think he's a wife-beating bastard who is a disgrace and an embarrassment to us all.'

Over 25 years later, the reaction to it tells a story of a time that has long passed and perhaps one that was just coming to fruition. Officially, Rangers were more concerned with a recent red card in a Champions League match in Amsterdam, fining Gascoigne £20,000 – two weeks' wages – and with Smith heavily suggesting that this was the final chance on the park for his wayward genius. As for the off-field behaviour, the club effectively washed its hands of it. Smith said only, 'From the point of view of Rangers Football Club, I don't feel in any position to comment on their private life. Obviously I am disappointed for both of them about all that has happened.' Donald Findlay went further by saying, 'None of us here are going to get involved in somebody's private life. If Paul Gascoigne, or anybody else connected with the club, asks for help or advice we will give it. We are not going to interfere. It is entirely a private matter. We will stand by anybody who works for the club who gives us 100 per cent loyalty. They will get the same back. There is no reason to discuss it with him. I don't intend to discuss it with him, it's up to the lad – if he wants to speak to me or anyone else we are here.' None of our business, nothing to see here.[109]

Smith's focus was very much on his business and whether Gascoigne would feature against Aberdeen on the Saturday or indeed for Rangers ever again. The new England manager, Glenn Hoddle, was also under pressure from fans, media and women's rights groups around the potential selection of Gascoigne when the squad next met up in November. Even a temporary ban, some argued, would send a strong signal to millions of men that such behaviour will have consequences. To do nothing was a powerful statement that winning points was more important than the safety of women. Gascoigne started at Ibrox against Aberdeen and for England in Georgia but it is almost inconceivable in 2023 that such a high-profile player would feature so soon after allegations like that arose and weren't contested. Media condemnation was understandably and justifiably vociferous although some tabloid columnists seemed surprised that the domestic abuse story was bigger than the petulant kick at Winston Bogarde which had led to his dismissal against Ajax. What riled some Rangers fans was the barely concealed joy that such a story had landed at their feet so that their initial pronouncements of doom could finally be borne out. 'I am sick of Gascoigne and what he is doing to Rangers,' wrote Gerry McNee on the Sunday, before lashing out at the absent David Murray for failing to deal 'with a player I warned would unravel an entire club'. The apocalyptic 'I-told-you-so' having slightly less impact given what the last season had delivered.

---

109   Just the following month, Gascoigne would be the face of the new Rangers clothing brand.

The fan reaction was more interesting. Dingwall would later pedal back on his initial reaction but tabloid and radio polls suggested that his instinct was in the majority. A *News of the World* poll suggested that 65 per cent of Rangers supporters wanted him sacked, although any tabloid vote of Old Firm fans on a controversial issue must be treated with scepticism due to both sides getting involved for mischief.[110] Nationwide polls on Gascoigne's England future were perhaps a better indication. Sixty-four per cent of listeners to BBC Radio 5 Live, 76 per cent of Talk Radio, 71 per cent on Teletext and 67 per cent of readers of *The Journal* in Newcastle thought Hoddle was wrong to select him again so soon. In the following edition of the fanzine, the matter was given proper space. There were passionate critics of the club's inaction, with this story being the nadir of a constant period of embarrassing behaviour. One regular contributor, from the left of the Rangers support, 'Rantin' Robert Burns', encapsulated that perfectly, 'It seems ridiculous that an institution like Rangers, whose supporters regard Smith as the godfather of the club should seek to make light of, or cover up, such iniquitous behaviour by one of its players. Is the quest for nine or ten in a row to take precedence over all else? Will our players be allowed to do just as they please with OUR hard-earned cash, and live their lives according to the rules of the gutter? Where is the guidance? Where is the leadership? Where is the example to younger players? I'm fed up with the drink; the drink-driving; the philandering; the Rangers players on the front rather than the back pages; and it's about time the men at the helm of the club got a grip and reminded the players that without the fans they are nothing, and the patience of the fans, on-field performances notwithstanding, is being sorely tested. If ten in a row is achieved at the expense of the club being reduced to a haven for sewer rats, will we be happy? … I want players I can watch, can cheer, can applaud, without thinking I'm giving a mixed message.' Would cheering Gascoigne, he continued, be tantamount to saying, 'that it was all right to beat your wife as long as you put the ball in the pokey on a Saturday? If so, count me out.'

Gascoigne had support in print, of course. 'It's a sad day when the climate of retribution in this country can turn a black eye into a war crime,' wrote the 'Downhill Hack' – a Partick Thistle fan and old-school football journalist – whereas others pointed out the same behaviour had been so often ignored in other icons such as Sean Connery, John Lennon and Miles Davis and argued that drink-driving was far worse, and more dangerous, that 'giving the wife a skelp'. Some of this was a window into the mindset of time but it was also evidence of a natural defence of the worst behaviour of our heroes that would become so ingrained in social media discourse in years to come. Especially following the #MeToo campaign around historic and current sexual harassment and assault, the celebration of heroes whose status was once set in stone, has been an open cultural wound. Is it still OK to listen to David Bowie or Michael Jackson? To

---

110   This was also the time where both Rangers and Celtic launched their own official websites and unofficial fan forums started to appear and discuss matters like these in calm and measured ways.

watch the films of Roman Polanski or Woody Allen? To continue to celebrate the genius of Picasso and Hemingway? In her somewhat sketchy book, *Monsters*, Claire Dederer asked if genius can be a hall pass and quoted the American novelist Martha Gellhorn who said, 'A man must be a very great genius to make up for being such a loathsome human being.' Must the two go hand in hand or can we separate the art from the artist, a question that has been live since Wagner's antisemitism started to make the literati uncomfortable. Interestingly, Dederer paused her list of appalling male behaviour when she rhymed off the name of the boxer Floyd Mayweather, 'If we start listing athletes, we'll never stop.'

Sport, and especially football with all of its tribal loyalty, makes that parasocial relationship more intense than even art can create. The 'we' that fans talk about after a win of course includes the players. All part of the one group and different to – and better than – all the rest. Those initially furious with Gascoigne were no doubt driven by a sense of reflected shame and embarrassment in exactly the same way as the much more sought-after reflected glory. Fans in this situation feel let down as if they're part of the real human drama, which of course they're not. One reality-bending effect of fame is that it makes these people feel as if they are our friends. As if we know them, are close to them and therefore shamed by association when in fact, their only real relevance to us is what they produce. Only when fans realised that the strong condemnation placed them in harmony with those commentators whom they felt hated Rangers was there a need to tone it down and go back to supporting the player. For some, the need to downplay, excuse and compartmentalise was immediate on grounds of loyalty and pragmatism. There was a league to be won and Gascoigne was key to that so any internal tension was suppressed and the adulation continued as normal.

Gascoigne scored a free kick the following Saturday at Ibrox and was cheered from the rafters. Despite all the talk, the action from supporters was loud and clear. Morality is malleable in sport. The importance of success, less so. In the 2020s, claims of sexual assault can derail a career but the risk appears more likely in the lower leagues than if the player is highly decorated. Fans and sponsors are still inclined to look the other way when it suits but often divert that displaced anger down ridiculous paths such as in 2011 when Wayne Rooney was castigated for swearing directly into a live television camera. Rooney had succeeded as a footballer – he had just completed his hat-trick – but apparently had failed as a role model for children. Charlie Brooker, in a column for *The Guardian* soon after the incident, wrote, 'I don't have kids, but I know enough about parenting to state the following with confidence: any parent who is genuinely concerned that their child's worldview might be hopelessly altered by the unruly behaviour of a footballer has failed as a parent.' The limits of Rooney's example to others are his technique and decision-making on the pitch, not telling a cameraman to 'fuck off' and nor even the private life that so often became public.

'Those who become famous are up there for our use,' concluded Clive James. 'The most that they can hope for is to be used well but used, they always are.' This arguably applies more acutely to sporting heroes than any other as the impossible persona is measured on a weekly basis before we even get to the frail, fallible person behind the mask. I last wrote about Paul Gascoigne's behaviour in my first book, *The 50 Greatest Rangers Games*, 'Gascoigne was the loveable, footballing hero for his fans and the thuggish, overrated oaf for his detractors, but he was the troubled human being for far too few of us.' He is ultimately responsible for his actions and the career and life spiral that started that night in Perthshire, but the club's abdication of any responsibility looks increasingly worse with the passing years and so too is the sometimes corrosive pressure of worship in the stands, creating the fantasy for us and deconstructing the reality for him. The Greek origins of the word 'hero' tells the real story. Someone who is not quite a god but still greater than a mere human, this seductive but imaginary hinterland of existence that is tantalisingly tangible and yet still somehow supernatural.

There is nothing wrong with celebrating the lives of others. Their greatness really does light up much more than just their own existence. But a more mature way of understanding the reality of fame would do us all good. There really is no dimension between men and gods, even when they have a talent that appears to be touched by the heavens.

Chapter Nine

Destiny

Season 1996/97

'This is the crunch, the season when all the previous flags are either to be part of a glorious roll of honour, or become so much chaff in the wind. It's Bannockburn and the Boyne rolled into one.'
'The Blue Tfosi', *Follow, Follow, August 1996*

'Jim, we've got tae win it.'
Tommy Burns, August 1996

It took three calls before Mark Hateley accepted that his agent wasn't winding him up. The morning after he had made yet another substitute appearance for Queens Park Rangers, this time in a limp 2-0 defeat at home to Reading, he could have been forgiven for thinking that glory days and big games were long behind him. Once he knew that Dennis Roach wasn't pulling his leg, he was booking a flight to Glasgow. 'It took me a nanosecond to agree to come back,' he said. Walter Smith had raised an SOS and he was more than ready to answer the call. But why – at a club with so many new and exciting international arrivals – was there a need to go back into the past to invoke some old magic in order to seal the fate of history?

Two weeks before there was certainty – in this season of destiny – that all was in hand. Rangers were seven points clear as they raced into the lead at Pittodrie, just one of the four dangerous away fixtures left. Later that evening the gap would be just five points and then – finally, at the tenth time of asking – Celtic tasted victory over their old rivals, this time in the Scottish Cup quarter-final. Celebrations were as wild on the park as they were in the stands as Tommy Burns's side strangely recreated their pre-match huddle after the game. The momentum was now with them, they told themselves. Rangers were due back to Parkhead ten days later, where the lead could be shredded to just two solitary points, with six games left to decide and define the last decade.

With more players injured than available and with the two Old Firm heroes of the last 18 months – Paul Gascoigne and Andy Goram – included on the absentee list, Smith and Rangers were rocking as badly as they had ever been throughout the 1990s. At this time of all times. Season 1996/97 had taken its lead from the campaign just past with vibrancy and expression but was now faltering, the price of excess and unprofessionalism taking its toll. In a rare moment of linguistic competence, Hugh Keevins described the use of Hateley as 'more memorabilia than mobile' and it was something that resonated across a dressing room of bruised heroes, forced to eke out whatever they had left to give. What happened next enshrined a legend. What happened next reduced football to its most fundamental elements: will, effort, desire. It wouldn't be pretty but, even for the side's greatest artist, the time for painting pictures was over. Only winning mattered now. Failure was not an option.

* * *

If 1995/96 has been tense and exhausting then 1996/97 – the 'Season from Hell' as Gerry McNee called it in the August – was only ever destined to raise the levels of introspective claustrophobia. What better way to cleanse the palate than a three-week intermission in the form of an international tournament right over the parish wall. If Italia '90 had melted the cold continental resistance to English football then Euro '96 firmly established its place back in the fold. The trophy didn't stay there for long but football did come home as the tournament added credence to the Premier League's desire to host the game's best talent. It wouldn't all be done that summer but the influx of big names really started then. As for the seven Rangers players who took to the field, there were mixed fortunes but no disasters. Erik Bo Andersen and Brian Laudrup couldn't push Denmark's defence of their European title beyond the group stage, despite a win and a draw and the latter's three goals. Scotland too won four points but couldn't progress to the knockout stages, with only one goal to show for their hard work. Of course, it was Ally McCoist who scored it; his one and only tournament goal was a thunderous strike from the edge of Switzerland's box that put Scotland tantalisingly in pole position to grab that crucial second place until a late Patrick Kluivert goal at Wembley continued the same old hard luck story. Stuart McCall and Gordon Durie had impressed with their work rate and two clean sheets from Goram underlined the obvious merit in his inclusion as number one.

When Goram was beaten, he had little chance. The Scotland defence had, for reasons known only to them, left Alan Shearer in space in the box to put England ahead in the second group match and then, after a missed penalty from Gary

McAllister, came the moment of the tournament, one where fears and dreams up and down the United Kingdom were realised on the hottest day of the year. He may not have fulfilled the potential of his global introduction but Gascoigne was at the peak of his powers over the course of 1996. Despite Goram's pleading to Colin Hendry just to stand up and stall the England attack, the Blackburn Rovers defender took Gascoigne's bait. Within the seconds Hendry needed a ticket to get back into Wembley and Goram was picking the ball out of the net as Gascoigne's England team-mates recreated their infamous 'dentist's chair' routine at the side of his goal.[111] It was the moment that ignited a national festival, taken to new heights against the Netherlands where Gascoigne was sublime in a 4-1 battering of the Dutch. He was excellent in the semi-final against Germany too but didn't have the penalty box instincts of Shearer to gamble on a low cross. Had he done so, England would likely have won the competition and the clown prince been made a knight of the realm. Either way, the comedown from leaving that summer camp – a protected environment with people whom he loved – was still likely to be as dramatic and a problem with which Rangers would have to deal further down the line.

The tournament also provided Rangers fans with a window into what they could have won. For all the big names with whom they were linked – from Jürgen Klinsmann to Fabrizio Ravanelli to Mikkel Beck – none arrived. Fernando Couto looked impressive in more ways than one for Portugal, scoring once and being a central part of a defence that was only breached by Laudrup and a famous piece of invention by Karel Poborský in the quarter-finals, but he opted for Barcelona over Ibrox. Oliver Bierhoff came off the bench to score the final goal of the competition and win it for Germany but he stayed with Udinese as Rangers ended the summer without any fresh blood in attack.[112] There were reports of discussions with the tournament's top scorer but Alan Shearer was probably only ever going to head home to Newcastle United, his heart full if not his medal collection.

The Shearer deal was yet another stark reminder of where Rangers actually sat in the European pantheon as the world-record £15m fee was considerably out of reach for the Scottish champions multiple times over, in an era of record high sponsorship and commercial deals, but not for an English club who had only been promoted three years earlier and hadn't won a major trophy since man first stepped foot on the moon. Rangers could complete nine in a row and do another nine on the back of it and it wouldn't change the shrinking market reach.[113]

---

111   England's players were branded a national disgrace in their pre-tournament trip to Hong Kong where many of them were held down in a chair as spirits were poured down their open mouths, à la the position one would take on a trip to the dentist.

112   There was the extra disappointment of seeing Mário Jardel score in Scotland, but for FC Porto in their pre-season friendly against Hearts.

113   Rangers would announce a profit of £7m, the best trading figures in the history of Scottish football and second only to Manchester United in the United Kingdom. It attracted high-profile entrepreneur Richard Branson to consider a move but David Murray wasn't interested in selling his majority stake, although he was willing to listen to offers for a more minority holding.

One of the two summer signings was incredibly close to coming to Ibrox with a European Championship winners' medal. Jörg Albertz was the last man to be cut from Berti Vogts' squad and his star performance as captain of Hamburg the previous season was so good that it doubled the asking price. Albertz had a £2m release clause if the club didn't make it into Europe but, despite a dreadful start to the season, Felix Magath managed to steer them into the UEFA Cup. The final fee was £4m for a 25-year-old who, it was understood, had a ferocious left foot. It wouldn't take long for fans to appreciate just how potent it was as the German would prove to be some of the best value that Rangers ever got from a transfer fee. Joining him, for half the price, was the Swedish international defender Joachim Björklund from Vicenza. With Alan McLaren needing surgery at the end of the season, this was a matter of priority for Smith in order to maintain that three-man solidity that he had enjoyed for most of the previous campaign. It was a staggered start to pre-season work with so many returning late from their Euro exertions and, for Gascoigne, the added complication of his wedding, a typically overstated affair, complete with *Hello!* exclusivity to show the world how settled he now was. All would unravel within months of a season where Rangers didn't need distraction.

If anyone dared to suggest that Europe might be a distraction, they'd have been drowned out by the need to fulfil this war on two fronts, with two completely different requirements. War was something of the operative word as the qualifying draw for that season's Champions League threw Rangers close to the Chechen border. Down from the Caucasian mountains, Alania Vladikavkaz were the surprise Russian champions, wrestling the title away from the traditional Muscovite giants the year before. In the first leg at Ibrox they showed why, playing with the tempo and cohesion that one might expect from a team halfway through their season, to go into the interval one ahead. 'The way the team played in the second half was the best performance I have known since I came to this club,' said Brian Laudrup after the final whistle. 'I cannot remember seeing us create so many chances. I think an accurate scoreline would have been 8-2 or 9-2. That would have reflected the number of chances we created.' Rangers had to settle for a 3-1 lead with goals from McInnes, McCoist and Petrić.

The Russians had suggested that Rangers were 'running scared' as they waited for UEFA to confirm if they had to make the arduous journey into a city that neighboured a civil war. An itinerary that consisted of five city stops where the plane nearly crashed on the way home and a hotel with torn curtains and cold showers, where players had to bring their own linen[114] was not quite the land of luxury that one associates with football's greatest stage. The football itself, however, propelled dreams. Smith called it his 'best ever' result in Europe and the die was cast in 35 seconds when Ally McCoist headed home. 'I thought I'd score with every touch. I've never been in a game like it,' McCoist said afterwards. His

---

114   Some forgot, meaning a quick stop at Ian Durrant's mother's house to pick up some spares.

18-minute hat-trick started Rangers on their way to a 7-2 win on the night. It was a far cry from the tense and interminable battle with Famagusta and, although Richard Gough tried to dampen the excitement by describing the Russians as 'defensively pathetic, woeful', it didn't work, especially as the draw was a lot kinder than it had been the previous season. As seventh favourites for the Champions League at 16/1, expectations exploded. Ideally so would confidence at playing on that stage. As long as that didn't tip over into complacency, Rangers had a real chance of qualification out of the group stages for the first time.

There was a note of poignancy on the eve of a season where Rangers sought to underline the era since the revolution, that the last man to win a title before it passed away. Jock Wallace finally lost his battle with Parkinson's disease on Wednesday, 24 July, the news broken to many on the BBC's Olympics coverage from Atlanta by the presenter and former player of Wallace's at Leicester City, Gary Lineker. Fans of the generation that had gone before, for whom Wallace had broken the long winter of Celtic's success with three titles in four years, including two trebles, were caught in a period of reflection for what had been achieved in the period since he was replaced by Graeme Souness and what had perhaps been lost to modernity. Words such as dignity and fairness flowed from most of the tributes to a tough but just man and it is noticeable that, despite being the truest of True Blues, kind words were forthcoming from the Celtic board, former players and manager – a 'greatly respected' and 'lovely man' – as well as by journalists of a more senior generation such as Archie Macpherson and Gerry McNee, in contrast to the younger agent provocateurs such as Graham Spiers, whose obituary in *Scotland on Sunday* seemed to many to suggest that he thought Wallace a bigoted bully who was partly responsible for late-20th century sectarianism. Perhaps this grandstanding contrarianism to inflame the dying embers of religious animosity in a secular Scotland can in some way explain the origins of a climate almost three decades on where such basic human tributes to a Rangers legend across the divide would cause so much hostility. Nevertheless, this season was ultimately to lean less on Souness's modernity but something so synonymous with Wallace: character.

It was also appropriate that the man leading the media duties on the eve of the new season was Rangers' captain. Given his early success with Dundee United, Richard Gough already had nine league winners' medals in his collection and the season of destiny was given extra special resonance for him as it was his testimonial year. 'People suggest it is best not to talk about the record, but there is no use pretending we don't want to win this title desperately,' Gough said before making clear that his mantra for the season was 36 'cup finals'. Arsenal were the visitors for Gough's benefit match, the final friendly before the meeting with Alania four days later, and Rangers were absolutely magnificent, running out comfortable 3-0 winners. Brian Laudrup had to be taken off for his own good as Arsenal were increasingly frustrated by his trickery and, in their view, mockery. It was the introduction of Albertz, however, that got most fans talking as he glided around the Ibrox surface with an absolute weapon of a left foot. Arsenal may have been a couple of weeks behind in preparation and just a few months away from the introduction of their very own revolution under Arsène Wenger, but signs were good that Rangers were ready to pick up exactly where they had left off at Hampden in May.

In their first ten domestic games – in both league and League Cup – Rangers racked up ten wins, scoring 27 goals and conceding just four. If the opening day promised to tell the story of the season to the come then it was a familiar tale. Rangers weren't at their best at home to Raith Rovers, Celtic were very impressive on the ball up at Aberdeen but Rangers won, Celtic didn't and a lead was opened up immediately. It was at East End Park, Dunfermline, that Rangers really opened up the attacking valves in preparation for the trip to Russia with a fine 5-2 win and the first of McCoist's two hat-tricks in four days. Gascoigne and Gough were required to get the better of Dundee United and Motherwell with genius possession of the football and a crashing header respectively, before the visit of Hearts saw three more goals added to the tally. The match, however, would be more remembered for the number of red cards which, incredibly, outnumbered the Rangers strikes. Pasquale Bruno, David Weir, Neil Pointon, and Paul Ritchie were all ordered off as Hearts lost the plot, while chairman Chris Robinson turned up on the touchline appearing to gesture to his players to come off, not up to speed with the latest International Board directive which stated that play should only be abandoned when a side were reduced to six players. It was perhaps indicative that some Rangers fans complained at the team easing up when faced with such a weakened opponent. 'Celtic wouldn't do this,' one said before adding, 'This title could be settled on goal difference. We can't take these risks!' It was 14 September, only four league games in and with an early lead and nerves had already started to jangle. As it turned out, Celtic faced a seriously weakened Hearts side in the League Cup quarter-final at Tynecastle on the Tuesday night. They lost 1-0.

Rangers swept aside the other half of Edinburgh 4-0 at Ibrox to ease into the semis before encountering their first bit of domestic trouble at Rugby Park. Trailing 1-0 with 23 minutes to go and perhaps with minds wandering to two big fixtures on the horizon, Rangers blasted into top gear with Gascoigne and Peter van Vossen grabbing two apiece, both of their second goals being superb. Gascoigne put Rangers into a 2-1 lead with a trademark mazy run and controlled finish whereas Van Vossen's final goal, to make it four, was sensational in terms of the angle and distance he had to work with. It was the flying Dutchman's ninth of the season but, when he missed from a range a lot more traditional some months later, there would be no more.

That was all to come, however. On Saturday, 28 September Ibrox played host to the first Old Firm instalment of a season where the head-to-heads always felt as if they would be pivotal. Celtic had spent nearly as much as Rangers in the summer of 1996, just over £5m to £6m by Walter Smith's club. In Alan Stubbs from Bolton Wanderers, there was a recognised need at the centre of defence being serviced with quality. With Pierre van Hooijdonk, Jorge Cadete, Simon Donnelly and Brian McLaughlin already on the books, Tommy Burns sought more creativity in the shape of the Italian Paolo Di Canio. Although temperamental to say the least, he was a fine player for this level and would prove to be talismanic especially as Van Hooijdonk was already making strong noises about wanting away[115] but it is debatable that Celtic needed to spend more money in attack. With the loss of John Collins to Monaco on a Bosman, they did nothing to replace him and improve a central midfield of Paul McStay and Peter Grant. Two Celtic men who knew exactly what was on the line this season but nowhere near good enough to tackle a Rangers midfield that combined industry with brilliance. Add that to a refusal to replace Gordon Marshall in goal when fans were growing uneasy, early signs were there that an emotionally driven manager was not what Celtic needed in order to maintain the necessary focus.

'You all saw it and should write about it instead of trying to be clever and writing about other things,' Burns said in his post-match press conference, adding a touch of bitterness to the level of despondency that was consistent throughout these interviews during the previous season. Referee Willie Young was in the firing line for playing an advantage when Di Canio appeared to have been fouled by Gough in the box – he must have forgotten that Young failed to allow Rangers to play the advantage when he disallowed an Albertz goal and enforced a free kick instead – and then for sending off Tosh McKinlay for two first-half bookings. 'There's no way on God's earth,' Burns pleaded, that his player deserved to be dismissed. Given that it was deliberate handball while on a booking, it is unfathomable how any rational person could come to that conclusion while possessing a working knowledge of the laws of the game. The population of rational people in Scottish football that season was suddenly growing thin. Burns also said that his side's indiscipline was becoming a 'cartoon' without acknowledging that responsibility for seven red cards by the end of September may well have fallen at his door and the fervent tone that he was setting.

Many painted a familiar hard-luck story, especially when Goram touched a Grant effort on to the post before the ball seemed to defy physics by rolling across the goal line towards safety instead of the net. Celtic were already behind by the point when a thunderous Gough header from an Albertz corner early in the second half had given the home side a deserved lead. Smith spoke of tension after the game but it was very open – as the first encounter of the season often is – with flair and invention on display as often as crunching tackles and clearances. McCall was unfortunate with a backwards header from a gorgeous Laudrup free kick, Albertz was getting his Old Firm range in and, as always, Gascoigne was at the heart of it with bustling runs and 'Rabona' flicks. Celtic hit the woodwork again late in the game and any hopes that an equaliser was imminent were dashed within seconds. When John Hughes's header crashed off the bar, the ball fell to Gascoigne in

---

115   Later in the season, the Dutchman would reject an increased offer on his £7,000-per-week wages by saying, 'That might be OK for the homeless but not for an international striker.'

Rangers' box and, on the touchline, Burns's heart sank. The Englishman powered forward with the ball eventually being fed to the debutant Albertz. He waited for Gascoigne's run and delivered his cross with absolute perfection, right on to the diving head of the greatest player in the country.

It was only the fourth time in 21 Old Firm league games where the home side had won, and only Smith's second Ibrox league win against Celtic in 11 attempts, prompting some to suggest that his away plan of sitting in and breaking was now going to be used at all times. Why change a winning formula based on venue? Other fans disagreed. Rangers invited trouble once a lead had been established, they said, while ignoring the many chances that were created between the two goals. No, for them there was no masterplan, just the fortune of the woodwork and the fact that the ball had landed at the feet of a maestro. Again, nerves and anxiety were in evidence from the earliest point of this campaign but there is no doubting the importance of margins or indeed Gascoigne's role in this fixture. He had played in all seven since his arrival and starred in every one, directly contributing to six goals and rattling the crossbar himself. Like Jim Baxter before him, it seemed like a fixture that was tailor-made for him, one where he would go on to dominate for a few more seasons yet. Few would have believed that this would be his last Old Firm goal and arguably the last time that he excelled in the heat of that particular battle.

Even with a five-point lead at the top of the league and a perfect start, Smith was under pressure and yet again, it was Europe that was causing the strain. Smith had few complaints when he left the Champions League group stage draw at the end of August. All three sides were close by in western Europe and there was no way that it provided the footballing threat the previous campaign's group had. Grasshoppers of Zürich were not as good as Steaua Bucharest and although Guy Roux's Auxerre had surprised French football with their league and cup double, they could not be considered on the same level as Borussia Dortmund, already primed to go on and lift the big one. Ajax as a name were a huge draw – finalists only in May and winners the previous year – but this was not the same animal. Affected by injury and Bosman raids, only four members of the starting XI victorious in Vienna in 1995 took to the field when they faced Rangers in October. Grasshoppers were full of praise for Rangers after their technical director Erich Vogel took in the 1-0 win at Fir Park, when he admitted, 'I have never seen so many international players work so hard for two other members of the team the way that the Rangers men worked for Gascoigne and Laudrup. Gordon Durie demonstrated something that our own players must learn to do. He worked so hard. In Switzerland, our forwards will not make that kind of contribution. They are not in the same professional mode.' Manager Christian Gross increased the charm offensive on the eve of the match, 'They are the team who must be favourites in the group. It is a very interesting group, but I believe that Rangers want to do so much better than they did last season – and with the Scottish attitude that makes them dangerous. I've looked at Rangers and I see Goram, who is outstanding,

Gough, who is a leader, McCall, who works so hard, and then there are Gascoigne and Laudrup. We are not just playing the Scottish team. This is an international team. Any team which contains players like Laudrup and Gascoigne becomes special. That is why I believe they are the strongest team in the group.'

Then Gross watched Rangers train. 'I saw Rangers training at the stadium and left that session convinced they had come here for a holiday,' he said after the match. On only their second circuit of the playing surface, Gascoigne had spotted his old adversary Gerry McNee checking out the commentary position. 'McNee's a fat bastard!' Gascoigne shouted. 'Sit down fatty!' Smith had talked up the challenge of Grasshoppers, especially their prowess from set pieces, but Rangers, egos fuelled by the ease of their Russian expedition, were nowhere near sharp enough. Smith too could have been criticised for being carried away with what worked in the Caucasus as he chose to start with Gascoigne (who had been suspended for the qualifiers and was still rediscovering fitness), Laudrup, Albertz, McCoist and Durie for an opening night, away from home, in the Champions League. Sacrificing one of the forwards for McInnes or Moore in midfield and playing Laudrup in that free supporting role behind would perhaps have been better in hindsight but Smith would also have been conscious about the lack of confidence that Rangers had shown in Bucharest. Why hinder that? The balance is fine at the highest level and the evidence of that wasn't long in coming.

'It is the first time I have experienced this in football – a situation where so many good players are off form at the same time,' Smith said after the game, while McCall reflected years later, 'I think we were just too overconfident which was not like us. We thought we just had to turn up and get the points.' The warning signs from failures of old were there from the start as Goram was called into action twice before the crossbar saved him. Rangers had 60 per cent possession over the course of the game but looked ponderous with it, only Albertz showing any real threat as once again, Laudrup was left isolated and Gascoigne heavily marked. It was two Swiss players of Turkish descent who made the clinical difference on the evening. Murat Yakin and Kubilay Türkyilmaz scored the simplest of headers from set plays and the latter, who had impressed in the Euros, curled in a free kick in between.[116] Smith's answer to the 3-0 defeat was to ban his players from television appearances for one month. This immediately impacted on Gascoigne, who was due to appear on the very popular BBC sports entertainment show *They Think It's All Over*. The producer Harry Thompson wryly commented on the news, 'Now Gazza is not coming we will all be expecting a massive improvement in Rangers' performance as a result.'

There was but it wasn't enough. Rangers dominated the first half at home to Auxerre and, if Richard Gough's header had been inches either side of the man on the line or if Lionel Charbonnier (later to be of the Ibrox parish) hadn't managed to scramble to the ball after he was caught off-guard by a Gascoigne free kick,

116   Smith's mood and that of the Rangers support would not have been helped once they caught up with the rest of the Champions League action that evening. Trailing 2-1 to AC Milan in the San Siro, Mário Jardel scored two goals in six minutes to give Porto a sensational 3-2 victory.

then so much might have been so different. In the end, Thomas Deniaud scored two headers in 15 minutes – the first was brilliant, the second a result of the most appalling marking at a set piece you're ever likely to see when the Frenchman was the sole Auxerre attacker in the box at a corner and still managed to beat Goram to the ball while watched by five Rangers players – and that was enough. Laudrup and Gascoigne combined to get one back and both stars were the only Rangers players who could leave with pass marks – despite the close attention of Taribo West – as yet another continental side did to Smith what he so often did to Celtic: sit back, ride out the passionate storm and clinically exploit the increasing gaps.

With a double-header against Ajax to come, any realistic hopes were snuffed out in front of an Ibrox crowd well under capacity again. It was around this time that Murray defended the ticket prices by saying that one would have to pay the same to go and see Diana Ross in concert, ignoring the fact that even her greatest fans were unlikely to want to hear 'Endless Love' a dozen times a year. There was no mitigation for Smith on this occasion. It was a failure of preparation, attitude and approach rather than opposition, injuries or the break of the ball. The wider reaction was as familiar as the disappointment. A mountain of impassioned but confused opinion pieces following the two defeats, Celtic's elimination from the UEFA Cup by Hamburg and Aberdeen drawing with Barry Town of Wales lamented the death of the Scottish side who could be tough and aggressive against continental style for the entire 90 minutes while still managing to blame the wear and tear of the same domestic game for the lack of energy. A fairer point was the preoccupation with title number nine. 'They remain locked in an outdated combat,' one said. 'In a struggle which means less and less to the outside world, and which dissipates the energies which should be used in Europe instead of in the domestic environment.'

Importing foreign coaches? Some agreed that there was no point in having foreign players without European coaches working under the British manager but others were wary that it would lead to further dilution of what once made us 'great'. There was a fundamental incompatibility and one writer in the *Herald* warned, 'Frenchman Arsène Wenger will discover that when he arrives at Arsenal.' He would indeed before revolutionising it entirely, suggesting that the traditional attributes were still there, they were just far less effective than they once were, in a more professionalised game. This point would be made abundantly clear the following week, when Channel 4 aired the documentary *Gazza's Coming Home*. The traditional British dressing room culture was still very much in place.

The extent of the excess at Ibrox was laid bare as were the contradictions given to Gascoigne and others from the top. Smith dropped him because of his drinking but the player also said that he was told, 'If you do the business for me, you can drink as much as you like.' Airing after the Champions League defeats was one thing but there were numerous stories from the start of the season that added to a perception of unprofessionalism. In August alone, three Rangers players were in court. Charlie Miller had been charged with assault following a disturbance in a Bridge of Weir pub in March while Ally McCoist and John Brown were both found to be driving while having consumed twice the alcohol limit, the former banned for 15 months and fined £2,500, one of the highest at the time.

Fan anxiety about what was at stake this season was not helped by what some considered to be a dressing room which was losing its discipline and there was no question as to who was the biggest concern. Many still gave Gascoigne a free pass, such was the ingrained presence of alcohol in British life and his consistency of individual performance. What happened next challenged that natural protection as Gascoigne's life and career began to spiral out of control.

* * *

With the fallout from the Channel 4 documentary still creating news and a very lacklustre performance at Easter Road as Rangers suffered their first domestic defeat of the season, Paul Gascoigne took his new wife and family to Gleneagles for a quick break before flying to Amsterdam with the Rangers squad on the Tuesday. After a great day swimming with the kids and enjoying the wildlife, things turned nasty over dinner. As Gascoigne mixed champagne with whisky, arguments started, nominally around his family but he later admitted that the subject matter wasn't the real trigger. 'Sometimes I think I don't know how to be good,' he wrote in his 2004 autobiography, although it could easily have been something from a primary school diary. Alcohol was an easy escape from his inner demons and was one that he was using on an increasingly worrying basis. As the entire dining room could hear the marital row, Sheryl left the table. 'I followed her and attacked her,' he recounted in his book. 'I head-butted her and threw her to the floor. Her finger was broken, so she was screaming in agony. I tried to click the finger back into place, and that made her really shriek. Bianca and Mason, aged about ten and seven, were in the next room with the nanny, listening to it all. I found out later that Bianca was so upset she wanted to take a kettle of boiling water and come and pour it all over me. Fortunately, the nanny calmed her down. The next day, Shel took the kids and left, telling me she wasn't coming back. I did nothing to stop her. I just accepted it. And yes, I had pushed her around a bit before, but nothing as bad as this. What I had done the previous night was terrible, and at the time I didn't even say sorry. I knew I'd done wrong, but I couldn't bring myself to apologise.'

In other circumstances, Walter Smith may have taken him out of the limelight but even with a fully fit squad, it is unlikely he would have gone into a must-win match without one of his two best players by choice. As it happened, Rangers started with no recognised forwards and with Gascoigne effectively partnering Laudrup in attack. It didn't last long. His head still spinning at what he had done and knowing that the press were ready to go with it post-match, he was sent off after only 28 minutes when he kicked out at Winston Bogarde. Rangers were already one down at that point, with Dani escaping Stuart McCall's attention for one second to put Ajax in front. Now, with gaping holes everywhere, McCall was being pulled in all directions as the De Boer twins toyed with their future employer. Dani was left alone once again right before half-time and the game was out of sight. During the break Gascoigne hid in the toilet as Archie Knox berated McCall for not doing the one job they had prepared for. When McCall informed him that Gough had told him to move towards the middle and pick up Ronald de Boer, while he took care of Dani, Knox shouted, 'You're never fucking wrong are you?' That was it for McCall, whose knee was about to give way and require transplant surgery that would keep him out for the season[117], and he chucked an ice pack on the dressing floor, smashing it everywhere. A relative calm was restored until late on where two further Ajax goals sandwiched an Ian Durrant consolation to add another heavy defeat to the catalogue of continental catastrophe.

Gascoigne's ill-discipline rendered the inevitable European elimination somewhat redundant in the immediate aftermath. The fan and media reaction has already been detailed in the previous chapter but, where most of that was no doubt blind tribal loyalty, there was a contextual issue that should be taken into account. When Rangers played the League Cup Final at Parkhead in November, the women's rights pressure group Zero Tolerance was suddenly given exposure around the stadium. 'Where,' one wag asked, 'were the ChildLine adverts?'

On 5 April 1996, Strathclyde Police formally opened an investigation into historic sexual abuse allegations by former members of the Celtic Boys Club. By the end of October, Frank Cairney and Jim Torbett were formally charged and both would spend time in prison before fresh allegations about them and others associated with the club came to the fore. Although set up independently of Celtic Football Club, the links were intrinsically close and as such, the association and collective knowledge about the extent of the abuse was a concern. Tommy Burns rushed to Cairney's support when he was suspended in August. Sitting in Cairney's living room, he told the *Daily Record*, 'He has the whole of my backing and that of Celtic Football Club to a man.'[118]

Much of the reaction was a dark, homophobic black humour with 'Who shagged all the boys?' becoming a constant chant in the Rangers repertoire as well as cartoons in the fanzine about 'bum fondling hotlines'. That line of humour wasn't confined to some opportunistic rival-baiting. Celtic fan Tom Shields made mention of it in his *Herald* diary when on the road to Kilmarnock. Speaking of one man he met at the game, he wrote, 'Young McLaverty breaks the rule about Not Mentioning the Boys Club by saying that the UEFA Cup draw against Hamburg is a difficult one but it could have been worse. "We could have got Young Boys of Berne," he says. "And think what the Huns would have made of that."' Some of this was another example of what would eventually be known as deflective whataboutery but there is a grain of reasonable grievance. With such moralising in

---

117   It had been an 18-month time bomb that McCall and the club simply ignored to keep on keeping on.

118   Burns wanted the quote changed to 'he has my backing and I'm sure he will have the backing of several first-team members who played for Frank' but the Record stuck by its initial quotes.

the nation's sporting columns, why weren't those pages bursting with outrage that such a despicable series of acts could be perpetrated under the nose of one of the nation's biggest clubs and indeed, so vigorously defended by its manager?

In the end, Smith's response to the Gascoigne situation was utilitarian. He had already begun to wonder how he could control him and there is evidence of both the carrot and the stick being confused already that season. The player wrote that he turned up at Ibrox after a big night out where Smith told him to get dressed and go home. Given that Gascoigne played in every home game but two before the Gleneagles disgrace, and he was suspended for the tie with Vladikavkaz, it must have been the opening match of the season against Raith. The week after Aberdeen, Smith called Gascoigne at his home on the Friday night just to check on him. When Smith found him sober, he took him out for dinner with Knox, telling his midfielder that he had failed the test by having wine. That was a joke, they said, and Smith told him Gascoigne would play, which he duly did. He never came out for the warm-up against Aberdeen and looked sheepish at points throughout but on 28 minutes he whipped a free kick with a wickedly high dip and curl into the top corner to put Rangers ahead. There was no awkward silence or eerily muted applause. It was as wild as ever. 'The perfect answer to the troubles of the week,' Jock Brown said on commentary as if the violence of his head and fists could be washed away by the genius of his right foot. The truth is that for many it was, and especially when Laudrup put Rangers two in front with an equally brilliant goal, Donald Findlay's remark that all will be forgotten if he scores and Rangers win had a real resonance. The small problem was that they didn't.

Aberdeen grabbed one back before the break and controlled the second half, getting a well-deserved late equaliser through Billy Dodds. What had been a serene start to domestic bliss was now turning sour for Smith. All looked well away to Hibs on 12 October when Albertz got his free kick sights in with a blistering opener. Hibs, recently managerless following the dismissal of Alex Miller, rallied and a Darren Jackson penalty – from a Björklund foul outside the box – and a brilliant strike from Graham Donald suddenly put them in front. Incredibly Brian Laudrup missed not one but two penalties to at least keep the unbeaten record alive but the first hit the bar and the retake was saved by Leighton. A Pierre van Hoojdonk goal at home to Motherwell was enough for Celtic to take advantage but when further points were dropped at Ibrox the following week, they had the chance to go top when they faced Hearts at Tynecastle, live on television 24 hours later. After 51 minutes the whole momentum for the season was changing as Van Hoojdonk's two penalty-box strikes gave Celtic comfort and a surge of confidence. If they had held out for ten minutes, they may have ended the weekend at the summit but they could barely last for 60 seconds as Colin Cameron fired Hearts back into contention immediately and then the pressure started. The equaliser was late and from a former Rangers player in Davie McPherson, but there was something inevitable about it for those watching, and cheering, at home. If it was a let-off, it didn't last too long. The 5-0 hammering of Motherwell showed some old flair with that Gascoigne hat-trick and a Laudrup double but there was yet another 2-2 slip-up the following Saturday against a Raith Rovers side who were rock bottom of the table, with only one win. Celtic didn't falter that day, a 1-0 win against Aberdeen being enough to take them to the top on goal difference.

With only one win in four, it was the worst run of league form Rangers had suffered in 18 months and, with injuries to McCall, McCoist and Goram being added to the list and discipline far from under control, it yet again gave hope to many that this autumn was the changing of the guard and that a long era was finally coming to an end. This sense was underlined by the news on 25 October that, after ten years of service, Richard Gough would be leaving for foreign climbs at the end of the season. His intention was to go out while he was still successful, prompting many to question his confidence in a potentially record-breaking season next time out. Gough himself was starting to sound less than confident about matching Celtic's record, never mind going one better. In an interview with *Scotland on Sunday* he said, following this difficult period of form, 'The problem is that people now want instant success. It might actually do this club no harm not to have success for a few years and for the supporters who have jumped on the bandwagon to know what it's like from the other side of the fence. If we didn't win the championship, it wouldn't be a disaster but there are too many parochial attitudes here to appreciate that.' A far cry from the 36 'cup finals' that his side were 'desperate' to win at the start of the season but a sign of the pressure they were now facing. With a visit to Parkhead coming up next in the league, the feeling of being behind the eight-ball was new to many.

Sadly, the Champions League experience was becoming all too recognisable. Similar to the Juventus games, Rangers were far more organised and spirited at home to Ajax, despite selection issues forcing Smith to blood youngsters such as Greg Shields and Scott Wilson into a starting line-up that was missing Goram, Gough, McLaren, Ferguson, McCall, Gascoigne and Durie from that wonderful Scottish Cup Final side five months before. Interestingly his bench that night consisted only of forwards – McCoist, Van Vossen and Bo Andersen – but Smith opted to start without a recognised striker, Laudrup and Miller reprising a partnership that they had enjoyed at times during their first season together.

Unlike Juventus, Ajax were content to hold on to their 1-0 lead in the first half but it could well have been different. In the 59th minute the ball broke to Jörg Albertz just left of the penalty spot but, with players on the floor or out of range and just Edwin van der Sar to beat, he blasted it high and wide. In two minds whether to use placement or force, the German was nearly in tears afterwards. 'I made a big mistake. I think if we had scored we would have gone on to win the game. I think the team played well, but that was my worst game for Rangers,' he said. It is barely remembered as one of the big Rangers misses, perhaps because of the futility of the context or because of one that would occur a few weeks later, but what is known is that it was not allowed to ruin his career, which would be illustrious and heroic. Against group leaders Grasshoppers at Ibrox on 20 November, McCoist finally got his Champions League goals as they were beaten 2-1 in a game that proved fatal to the Swiss hopes of qualification and was Rangers' first win in the competition since that Scott Nisbet off-cutter against Brugge in March 1993. What was most telling is that this match, and the final 2-1 defeat in France, were not shown live by STV, instead opting to take the main ITV game, Manchester United's tie with Juventus in the first instance.[119] The increasingly peripheral role on the biggest stage was being further pressed home and Rangers' response was underwhelming. After years of big talk about how the club would be further modernised to compete with the game's best, David Murray's answer in 1996 was not a foreign coach, better discipline, new ideas or a breakaway league. It was to employ a former Celtic player to watch football on his television.

In the wake of the Ajax defeat at Ibrox, news broke that Kenny Dalglish – who had recently left his director of football role at Blackburn Rovers[120] – was due to take up the same position at Ibrox. That was quickly changed to a chief of scouting with a budget that could bring in Europe's best. The *Daily Record* ran a story which essentially threw darts at the continent's best established and emerging talent and included them – Marc Overmars, Patrick Kluivert, Raí, Eric Cantona, Sean Dundee and Emmanuel Petit – in a list of potential deals that Dalglish could help get done. In the end, the role was for Murray's Carnegie Sports International company to bring top names in sport and showbusiness to attend golf tournaments at the new and exclusive Loch Lomond golf club, which Murray's PR company had been involved with. Being an 'international super scout' while watching lots of football via a massive satellite dish at his Southport home was an added bonus if he happened to cast his eye over a player who could do Rangers a turn. It was another delusional farce – Dalglish became the new manager of Newcastle United in the January – and Walter Smith stormed out of a press conference following the 2-2 draw at Raith when he was asked about it. Far from ideal preparation for the trip to Parkhead where Rangers were going into the second Old Firm game of the season behind Celtic in the table for the first time since 4 November 1989.

On that afternoon, Maurice Johnston scored a late winner that burst Celtic's belief and optimism until Tommy Burns restored it six years later. Now it was in full flow, the chance to go three points clear and some more scoreboard pressure, with Rangers facing a trip to Aberdeen the day after league business resumed again for Celtic. If the game lacked the historical legacy of MoJo's dagger through the heart, it more than made up for it in quality, drama and exhaustive tension. Of the four league clashes between the two, it was the one most fondly remembered

---

119   The Auxerre tie was notable for Rangers not being allowed to wear their shirt sponsor of ten years, McEwan's Lager, due to French regulations on alcohol advertising. Center Parcs was used instead for this one-off occasion. Ironic that both the first and last group game had a holiday feel to them.

120   He had quit as manager the season before

by fans in a 2019 poll[121] and it was more akin to a game of basketball than an important top-of-the-table football match, with Sky being unable to show a replay of a chance in the first half for over two minutes because too much was going on and Andy Gray finally giving in near the end when he exclaimed, 'You carry on Martin, I'm absolutely speechless. This game is unbelievable. Un-be-*liev*-able.'

Almost everyone in the stadium that night presumed that Brian Laudrup would take another touch, including the new young replacement in the Celtic goal, Stewart Kerr. Just one more to gain more ground and perhaps open the angle. To shoot so soon would give him only a tiny part of the goal to hit. Hit it he did, however and within nine minutes Rangers had what they wanted: a lead and another punishing reminder to Celtic of the natural order of these fixtures. With Goram and Robertson back from injury – the former the latest Rangers player to be charged with a drink-driving offence – there was a much-needed settled feel to the backline and the use of Laudrup as a false nine before it was fashionable had proven its worth so soon. Even with a narrative so set in stone by now – Celtic with frantic possession and big mistakes (Brian O'Neil, the much-vaunted ball-playing prospect in their defence, struggled with the actual kicking of the ball and let Laudrup through) and Rangers looking as dangerous as they ever did – it was somehow still fresh and enthralling. Goram and Van Hooijdonk resumed their battle, Gough and Björklund swept up when needed and Rangers' breakaways were lightning quick.

How the match ended with just one goal defied belief. Albertz – whose introduction into Old Firm mythology was still yet a game away – passed up numerous chances, Gascoigne – perhaps desperate to reassert his hero status after a traumatic month – missed a weak penalty and then, with just seven minutes remaining, Rangers fans in the ground and watching at home on that Thursday night nearly passed out. Albertz found himself through on goal yet again but, with his previous misses still in his mind, decided to take Kerr out of the game and roll the ball to substitute Peter van Vossen who was eight yards from the empty goal. Somehow the ball wasn't where it should have been. Somehow a remarkable game wasn't over. Somehow those precious three points weren't yet safe. Somehow this tension continued. No one remembers or cares about the Dutchman's impressive start to the season, that impossible goal at Rugby Park or that it was his vision that beat the offside trap and created the chance of all chances. Possibly Kerr's scramble along the floor meant that he knew that the ball had to be lifted. Quite how it was lifted over the bar, only Van Vossen knows.

Less than two minutes later all those fears and cliches about making chances count were seemingly about to be realised when Gough crashed into Simon Donnelly in the penalty box, giving Hugh Dallas absolutely no option but to point to the spot. A share of the spoils would be a fitting way to end such a match,

---

121   The game was voted 26 in the Greatest Rangers Games of all time. The two still to come were voted 48 and 43 respectively.

some said. No side deserved to lose and, with Van Hooijdonk being so prolific and Goram not renowned for saving penalties, it was almost a given. Few things on this night could be taken for granted, a fox running a lap of the pitch providing a much-needed minute of respite for all concerned. It was a better penalty than Gascoigne's but still not great and Goram guessed correctly to turn the ball past the post; Celtic's last big chance was gone. Rangers, of course, managed to miss two excellent chances in the minutes that were left but mercifully it didn't matter. The pressure that was released that night was obvious as both sides knew the impact of yet another psychological blow.

Goram's reaction to the penalty save was one that didn't get a lot of traction at the time and surely would lead to parliamentary enquiries in the modern game. Goram could be seen on screen almost certainly calling Van Hooijdonk a 'black bastard' and in his book he wrote, 'When I saved the penalty, I lost it for a bit and shouted a few expletives that I regret now. We had a past, though, and he'd called me a lot worse than I called him. Didn't make me proud of it, though.' In the same pressure cooker, Tommy Burns was sent off for questioning the officiating that appeared to have been correct in all the big calls throughout the game. He had already been fined £3,000 for threatening a referee earlier in the season and, as much as Smith was more like a jack-in-the-box than he normally was up in the stand, he still maintained his composure and sense of perspective minutes after one of the greatest and important Old Firm victories he had ever managed. Burns was still wrapped up in his romantic ideals. Despite the glaring evidence of eight games without success, he said, 'Great things are built from perseverance and we will not change our style of play. It will one day get us to where we want to be.' After a very difficult six weeks, Rangers were renewed in their belief about where they were going. Top of the league again and back to Parkhead the following Sunday for the League Cup Final against Hearts.

With the national stadium in a new stage of renovation – a process that started in 1991 – Parkhead hosted a Rangers performance that both exemplified why this team were so great but also served something of a notice period for that greatness. After their Hampden humiliation, Hearts were always fancied to give a better account of themselves but it didn't look that way in the early stages of a freezing-cold afternoon. Gascoigne and Laudrup dragged defenders away from the arch-poacher McCoist to fire Rangers front and they managed to leave him free at a corner soon after to double the lead and equal the goalscoring record of 50 in a competition he had won more times than anyone else. But then Rangers turned to ragged complacency, allowing Hearts back into the game with a Stevie Fulton strike and a bizarre on-field row between Gascoigne and McCoist before the half-time whistle. The former's frustration at the latter's failure to be on his wavelength boiled over as Rangers' position of comfort was evaporating. As the fighting continued in the dressing room, Gascoigne's answer to the tension was to head to the players' lounge and get himself a brandy. It was the Rangers defence, especially Alec Cleland, who was replaced by David Robertson, and Craig Moore, who looked as if they had been enjoying a few as they creaked at Hearts' pace and pressure, in particular the skilful industry of Neil McCann down the left. When that finally resulted in an equaliser, the hope of the neutrals was fired up. The game looked to be heading in only one direction.

What happened next was Paul Gascoigne's career in microcosm. A constant state of hypertension which, when frustrated, led to lashing out and acrimony but when in control of a football, resulted in complete serenity and poise. Four minutes after Hearts drew level, he took the ball 40 yards from goal, shifted his body weight suddenly to wrong-foot Gary Mackay and then the old power returned as defenders were left with lead in their feet as he drove forward and curled the ball beyond Gilles Rousset. Two minutes later, he had won the cup before Hearts knew what to do. The instant control and bravery to run into where space was limited, only for the vision and skill to open it up to his will, using Charlie Miller as an accomplice, and poking it home. The two goals were just like the ones against Aberdeen in April both in form and importance.[122]

'The spark of genius, just when it's required,' said Jock Brown on the microphone, but he could have been talking about a lot of Rangers games since 1994. So often tired, missing key players, in trouble or bereft of creativity, this group battled hard to stay in touch and relied upon magic to do the rest. For this particular magician however, it was the final act. The common consensus that night was that a line had been drawn under a troubled period in the most emphatic way but everyone, including the man himself, was in denial. 'I haven't been myself for a few weeks for reasons you all know about,' he said afterwards. 'I am starting to come to terms with what happened. I am getting help and my personal life is not too bad. I feel I can concentrate on my football now and, hopefully, this is the start of good things to come.' He would, of course, feature in more wins and pick up another medal but Paul Gascoigne would never grab a big game for Rangers in that signature style ever again. He would remain a Rangers player for 16 more months but his days as an Ibrox star were over.

* * *

A century before this Rangers odyssey started, the face of football as we know it was created; England's Football League began in September 1888. Frustrated by the limitations of both cup football and test matches and exasperated by friendlies where some teams simply wouldn't show up, the league system was created with each club playing one another home and away, and so the perfect measurement in football was born. Consistency over caprice. The need to compete over 36 games and not a handful. Where a title is determined by the events that happen over 3,000 minutes and not just an isolated incident in one. At its best, it is the greatest kind of sporting tale. One with ebb and flow, jeopardy and joy. Long periods of

---

122   The final score was 4-3, the man of the match Neil McCann getting a deserved goal late on for Hearts.

calm and then a run that can derail to disaster or power to victory. The final six months of the nine-in-a-row saga were fittingly similar to the first six: a period of brilliant form and style that opened up a healthy lead and then a grim scrap to hold on. The ninth title was picked up in May 1997 but it was won over the course of this winter.

That famous Old Firm November win in 1989, when Maurice Johnston's late goal gave Rangers the points and sent Celtic into a psychological tailspin that arguably lasted for five or six years, wasn't quite matched by this November's victory but the effect was still significant. Celtic drew at home to Hearts on 30 November – another 2-2 which saw Paolo Di Canio sent off – and followed that up with a 2-1 defeat in the last minute at Motherwell on 7 December. Di Canio's red was Celtic's tenth of the season and it wasn't even Christmas. Burns refused to accept that the hysteria around nine in a row that he had helped stoke was the sudden cause of so much indiscipline from a side who were the best behaved in the league the season before. He did accept, however, that buying into the fans' obsession played a part in Di Canio's who, while on a booking lost the plot shortly after firing Celtic level from the penalty spot with 13 minutes remaining, 'He had a moment of madness at the weekend. He has told me he is sorry, and I am confident it won't happen again, but I have to be aware that he saw me being sent up the tunnel a fortnight ago.'

Rangers' response was emphatic. The following day at Aberdeen, live on television, they continued their flow from the cup final with a convincing 3-0 win over the side in third place, with Robertson, Laudrup and Miller on the scoresheet. The next week, as Celtic succumbed to that late winner at Fir Park, was exactly the kind of the day that fatalistic fans would point to as a sign from on high that it wasn't going to be their year. Rangers were twice in trouble at home to Hibs – Keith Wright putting them ahead early in the first half and the impressive Darren Jackson restoring the advantage after Ian Ferguson's piledriver of an equaliser – and the home crowd were baying for blood. This season really was a pressure like no other, with every fan seemingly lost in the present minute, unable to see the bigger picture unfolding. It was McCoist who relieved the tension with a six-minute double before Laudrup made sure. Rangers were coping, Celtic were folding. Just over three weeks earlier, Celtic had been top of the table with a home game against Rangers to come and carrying all the momentum. Now they were eight points behind and again the weather intervened to freeze them out of action for two weeks while Rangers had two opportunities to get more points on the board, one more suffocating than the next.

The first chance was spurned. Rangers never truly got going at Tannadice, perhaps with a subconscious foot off of the gas. It was only when Richard Gough diverted the ball into his own net with just under 20 minutes remaining that there was any urgency. Incredibly Erik Bo Andersen seemed to out-do Van Vossen's effort at Parkhead as he stretched to put the ball over the bar from three yards out. The failure to extend the advantage led one fan to demand that the player's wages that week were given to the children's charity, Cash For Kids. Were Rangers just as bad? Was this winter going to have as many spills as thrills? The answer was emphatic as Rangers won seven league games in succession and in so doing effectively made their grip on this precious title too secure to ultimately dislodge. Two regulation home wins against Dunfermline and Kilmarnock meant that the gap was 14 points (with three games more) by the time the two sides played again on the same day. Celtic ground out a 1-0 win at home to Dundee United and prayed that Rangers found the trip to Tynecastle as tricky as they had done.

'There were times when it was men against boys out there today,' bemoaned Jim Jefferies in the aftermath of a mauling. Walter Smith called it 'the best performance I can remember us giving at Tynecastle' as he watched Robertson do the kind of things that Gascoigne and Laudrup usually did in the first half, before the famous duo combined with two superb breakaway goals in the second period. Albertz was selected as the new man for penalties, although he did have a second saved, and it ended 4-1 to the runaway leaders. There were four more goals without reply on Boxing Day as Rangers defeated Raith – Bo Andersen getting a hat-trick and playing himself into a bit of form, timely as it would turn out – and Celtic came from behind to beat Aberdeen at Pittodrie later that evening to breathe some life back into their challenge. When it was Rangers' turn to be frustrated by the weather at Kilmarnock, Celtic eased past Dunfermline to make some inroads into the gap which stood at 11 points with Rangers having played two games more, before the two met at Ibrox for the latest do-or-die clash.

What some thought was an ideal week off to rest and prepare for the game turned into a bit of a nightmare for Smith as the flu ripped through the dressing room. Gough and Laudrup were ruled out while Gascoigne, Goram, Robertson and Bo Andersen made themselves available but were still feeling the effects. Björklund and McLaren returned to the defence but hadn't played a great deal of football and McCoist would be the captain. Rangers held an advantage on paper if not in energy. Celtic's only handicap on the night was self-inflicted. Pierre van Hooijdonk started the match on the bench as his contract dispute rumbled on in the public glare. There was no question that Celtic had to win this game. Given how poor they were when opportunities arose, a draw was of no use. It really was now or never for Burns to mastermind a win over Rangers or the jig was up for him. Live on Sky on the evening of Thursday, 2 January, it was another game packed full of drama, if the quality was perhaps reduced by the tired limbs.

The fuse was lit in the most explosive fashion through a combination of ferocity and accuracy when Albertz properly announced himself in a fixture that he would go on to enjoy for years. Martin Tyler said that he was getting a 'genuine reputation as a set-piece specialist' as he lined one up 30 yards from goal with the Rangers crowd singing his name in anticipation. It was a rocket: low, hard and on an immovable course towards the inside of Stewart Kerr's net at nearly 80mph. What followed was something of a fatigued slugfest until Burns relented on his principles by introducing Van Hooijdonk into the fray. It was only then that Celtic took a hold of the game as Goram was called upon to deny both the

Dutchman and David Hannah. The leveller was inevitable and it was Di Canio – a constant menace throughout – who was in place to drill one past Goram from close range. Depleted and rapidly tiring, Rangers were rocking on their feet, ready to be knocked out, bringing the race to life once again. And then Celtic stopped. All the energy and verve in chasing a glorious lost cause tightened and evaporated when they were presented with the chance to kill. Smith recognised the weakness and reacted by bringing McCoist and Moore off for Bo Anderson and Van Vossen, a very attacking gamble. In yet another moment of managerial naivety, Burns too made an attacking change when he replaced Alan Stubbs with Andreas Thom. Celtic needed to hold their shape and willingly disrupted it, with Hannah moving back into defence.

'I had the flu and a bad fever but on the day of the game I felt a bit better,' Bo Andersen recounted years later. 'Richard and Brian didn't make it but when we met at Ibrox, Walter Smith asked me how I was feeling. I told him that I couldn't play 90 minutes. I didn't feel well enough to do that. I said to Walter, "Use me as a substitute to finish the game." At half-time, Archie came to me and said, "Erik, you have to be ready. You have to go on and score two goals." I said, "Yeah, yeah – that would be fantastic but it won't be easy."' Thanks to some inexplicable head tennis along the Celtic backline with just seven minutes to go, it was. Albertz pounced on the comedic defending and presented yet another glorious opportunity for a Rangers forward. There was no mistake this time as the unlikely Danish hero took his acclaim. He got another minutes later   a result of another breakaway and brilliant vision and weight by Albertz – as Smith ran down the trackside to celebrate. No one would say it but a theoretical lead of eight points at the very worst and the bellwether new year win in the bag[123], the lead was now surely insurmountable.

Those weren't the headlines, however. 'WHY THE REFFIN HELL WAS THIS GOAL DISALLOWED' screamed *The Sun*, for some reason missing the question mark. In between the Bo Andersen strikes, a Celtic surge led to Jorge Cadete finding himself in too much space in the box and he hooked the ball past Goram to seemingly level the match up. The linesman's flag quickly put paid to any celebrations and so the distraction of the decision, the linesman's personal background and how this moment – among all the thousands of footballing decisions taken over the season and the millions not taken – was what it all boiled down to. 'I still can't believe the decision,' said Cadete 20 years later. 'The goal should have stood – 100 per cent. There was nothing wrong with it. It would have been a very important goal for us. It would have set us up to continue challenging Rangers. Looking back, that Old Firm win gave the title to Rangers. There was no way back for us after that.'

A key point missed in all the misdirection and convenient conspiracy theories is that there is a good argument that offside wasn't the reason at all. There was no

---

123   No side had lost the new year game and gone on to win the league since 1982.

question of offside and nor did Gordon McBride's flag go up when the ball was nodded down by Phil O'Donnell into Cadete's path. It was only raised as soon as the Portuguese striker controlled the ball and, given that his hand was pulled back immediately, there was a suspicion that the ball was unlawfully placed under that control. It may have been wrong or justified – the television angle and quality of picture are inconclusive by today's standards – but it was a call from the far-side position that could have been instinctively made. Given that a draw and yet another game without success against Rangers was of no real value to Celtic, the real narrative is that it was a defeat all of their own doing. To not start with his strongest side against opponents dragged out of their sickbeds because of an inability to manage contract negotiations and then to overload when in control of the game at 1-1 was negligence by Burns and Rangers took advantage, as they so often did.

Forty-eight hours later, Rangers took to the field with only four fully fit players – Snelders, Shields, McInnes and Cleland – due to 28 others suffering from the flu. Despite requests for the game to be postponed, the Scottish Football League forced Rangers to play on. When Hibs took the lead after only eight minutes, it was felt that this would be too much in a week full of exertion. Rangers rallied though as Bo Andersen equalised quickly and Albertz scored from the spot in the second half after Jim Leighton had brought Laudrup down. In two weeks – from Tynecastle to Easter Road – Rangers had shown brilliance and resilience in equal measure. With 13 goals in four games, this was a team able to be expansive or compact whenever the situation demanded. It was the adaptability required to win championships that their rivals simply didn't have.

Four more goals were rattled past Aberdeen at Ibrox as Bo Andersen made it nine in eight games with another double but it was a game marred by jeers from the visiting support and songs about the Ibrox disaster during the minute's silence for Rangers legend George Young, who had died two days before the match, aged 74. None of this was new as a growing tendency to rebel against decency was becoming prevalent throughout a lot of British fanbases, including Rangers who had disrupted the silence for Sir Matt Busby two years previously. This event, perhaps because it was an embarrassment live on television, prompted some— including Aberdeen chairman Ian Donald and local fan and sociology academic Dr Richard Giulianotti – to suggest a more Mediterranean show of reflective affection: a minute's applause, more in keeping with the nature of a noisy sport. There was something in the logic but more in the expedient need to cover up the lack of respect; nevertheless, a new trend in British football was born.

Given the claustrophobic tension coming from the stands during this season, either side putting together a long run of wins was always unlikely. Despite ten wins in 11, including two against Celtic that created comfort from a position of adversity, the first slip released all the anxiety that was being furiously repressed. Rangers controlled the re-arranged game at Rugby Park but were too guilty of being overelaborate and were stung early in the second half when Colin McKee put the home side in front. Gascoigne rescued a point, McCoist should have grabbed all three but it was the first wobble in eight games, reducing the gap to six points and, reading the thoughts of some supporters, one could be forgiven for thinking everything was back level. One fan wrote, 'Once again the collective attitude has to be questioned. Don't they want their own wee personal piece of immorality which comes with winning this season's league? I'd hit them in their pockets.' The best run of form of the season came to an end with a draw in an otherwise fine performance and the players should be fined! It wasn't a normal season. It was nine years squeezed into nine months and so often it was intolerable. A season where final whistles induced relief rather than joy. One more game chalked off on the road to history.

Another one followed on the Saturday as Rangers returned to winning ways at Fir Park but it wasn't the manner of the 3-1 victory that had fans excited – despite Gascoigne, Laudrup and Albertz all impressing – it was a substitute appearance of their new signing. Repeating his South American adventure of the previous winter, Walter Smith had better fortune with the Home Office this time but that was where his luck ran out. Sebastián Rozental was first mentioned as a possible target in November – around the time that Kenny Dalglish was rumoured to be helping Rangers out as a causal sofa scout – but it was thought that Sunderland, a club on the up at the time, and perhaps Manchester United would be ahead of the chasing pack. Rozental had scored 24 goals in Chile that season, was 20 years old and was featuring for the national team as they were qualifying for the 1998 World Cup in France. Free from the Bosman limitations, South America was becoming a bit of a fashionable place to shop for British clubs, with the Brazilians Juninho, Emerson and Branco arriving in Middlesbrough and the Colombian international Faustino Asprilla going to Newcastle over the last year. Smith and Knox didn't hang about, watching him closely and then forcing a deal for around £4m before Christmas. Again, the move was more dependent on the vagaries of Scottish football. With all ten work permit spaces all taken, East Fife's decision to terminate the contract of their Trinidadian international Craig Demmin freed one up. The chance that Rangers could have done with 12 months earlier was grabbed this time around. How well suited Rozental was to Scottish football was debated. Roy Hodgson – then manager of Internazionale, whose strike force included the Chilean hero Iván Zamarano – thought it was a bargain, 'I know a lot about Rozental. People in high places are extremely optimistic that he can go on to become the next big thing from South America. Rozental is highly rated, because Zamorano is an absolute hero in Chile and people there are talking about Rozental being a new version of him. He must be some player to be even mentioned in the same breath as Zamorano.' Meaning well but slightly clumsily, he continued, 'Contrary to what some people believe, Chileans are a very tough race and I am sure that will help Rozental, because everyone knows the Scottish league is a tough one. Rangers may well have got themselves a great signing.'

Gerry McNee wasn't convinced. He claimed to have spoken to Alex Ferguson about United's interest in the player and was told, 'The boy has a superb physique but he's not an out- and-out striker and not the answer.' McNee's bigger issue, it appeared from his growing weekly frustration, was with the continent of Rozental's birth. South Americans appeared to be trouble. They failed to settle, could be disruptive and spent too much time on flights in order to keep up with their international commitments at a time where the global footballing diary wasn't as synchronised as it would later be. 'Bearing in mind the problems foreigners are causing British clubs, is this Chilean Catolican worth the fuss?' was the question with which he opened his column on 15 December. There are similarities in tone with Alan Sugar's comments at the start of the year. Then chairman of Tottenham, Sugar had said, 'Pre-Bosman, Carlos Kick-a-ball, at the age of 23, comes over from Spain and costs £6m. But there will be some residual value. Now, he will not only come over here on high wages, but the transfer fee has no lasting value. He'll now arrive on a free at the end of his contract and claim all the money for himself.' McNee's wordplay is also worth noting here. Rozental was signed from the Santiago club Universidad Católica. The joke at the time was that only Rangers could go to a Catholic university team in a Catholic country and find the only non-Catholic player.[124] Usually so po-faced on the issue of sectarianism in the west of Scotland, it perhaps shines a light into his whole provocateur schtick.

In the end, McNee was correct about Rozental, but not quite in the way he imagined. He looked bright in his cameo at Motherwell, involved in Gascoigne's decisive goal, and then he and Bo Andersen both got a start at Ibrox in the following week's Scottish Cup tie against St Johnstone in a decision that had many speculating if this would be the partnership to move Rangers forward. Both scored in the first half as Rangers eased through to the next round, Rozental's coming from a Gascoigne pass into space where he showed calmness and precision to grab a goal on his full debut. When he came off, his face was a scowl instead of a beam as he looked up to his family in the Main Stand. Early in the match he had been challenged by Attila Sekerlioglu, a fairly innocuous moment but involving a fairly hefty contact at the side of the knee. Being keen not to come off on his Ibrox curtain call and the 'treatment' amounting to spray and being told to run it off, he played on and scored his goal before he was substituted as a precaution at the break. Rangers expected it to be minor and allowed Rozental to return to South America for altitude preparation in advance of Chile's qualifier in Bolivia in February. He was ruled out of playing in that game, sent home and then, on his first session back in Glasgow, broke down completely. Surgery was required and after only 58 minutes of football, Smith's struggle to plan for McCoist's retirement continued.

But what was £4m to a club now swimming in money? What was the loss of one international striker when there would be another one just around the corner? On 22 January – in between Rozental's two appearances that season – David Murray sold 25 per cent of his shares in Rangers Football Club to a Bahamas-based east London exile for £40m. Joe Lewis was the man and the real money

---

124   Rozental was Jewish.

behind restaurant chains such as Planet Hollywood and Hard Rock Cafe and had recently bought Arnold Palmer's Isleworth Golf Club for over $20m, upon which not only did he have a home but where one was recently bought by who the *Herald* described at the time as the 'new golf sensation Eldrick "Tiger" Woods'. The sale was sensational, not only because it now valued Rangers at £160m but because it would provide Smith with a transfer budget that even he could not have envisaged over his time at the club. With this investment and other commercial deals coming to fruition in the summer of 1997, Murray talked about clearing the £16m overdraft and starting work on a proper training facility – Rangers still trained at a cricket ground – and even a hotel at the stadium, like Chelsea were doing. But the majority would be on players.

Interestingly Murray made clear at the EGM in February, at which this deal was ratified by shareholders, that the club had to be smarter in the new Bosman market and that wages rather than eye-catching transfer fees may be more of a dealbreaker. By that point Rangers had already confirmed the signing of the Australian full-back Tony Vidmar who would arrive the following season, while Sweden captain Jonas Thern was soon to be announced, both on a free contract.[125] At a time when so many clubs were in a race to float publicly in order to upgrade their stadia, Murray felt that Rangers – although they were one of the only four clubs in Britain whom he felt could float sensibly – were on the right course. 'This business we have passed today gives us a balance sheet second to none,' he said at the EGM. 'That is not going to be the case with many other clubs in Britain, where fundraising is based on takeovers and buyouts. I think some of it is morally wrong and some of it is a house of cards that will collapse.'

Lewis's ENIC (English National Investment Company) group put two directors on Rangers' board with this deal – one of whom was Daniel Levy, later chairman of Tottenham – but demanded no extra control. 'Some other institutions made proposals to us which put unbelievable restrictions – on dividend policy, on management policy,' said Murray at the time. 'We have run Rangers with flair and that is why we are successful. We have a short chain of command. We make decisions on our feet as we go along. If we want to buy a player Walter comes to me, we have a meeting, and it is decided in two minutes.'

These were words that would eventually come to feel incredibly dated and ironic, but at the time it was a move that struck further despondency within the national game and especially the main challengers. Celtic had shown patient and steady progress off the pitch and, just when it seemed as if this Rangers side was growing too old together on it, Smith had the best part of £40m to spend rebuilding it. It was like 1986 all over again, only it was a club that already had a culture of self-assurance and dominance firmly established. Poignant then, that at the moment Rangers were looking towards new horizons, the man responsible for setting the revolution in motion was in trouble. Two weeks before the Lewis cash

---

125   In April, a similar deal would be done for the young Perugia midfielder Rino Gattuso.

was confirmed, John Lawrence (Glasgow) Ltd went into receivership with debts between £15m and £20m. Just like Lewis, Lawrence Marlborough – a tax exile recluse in the Americas – was not available for comment.

The motions carried that afternoon at the Royal Concert Hall in Glasgow really should have guaranteed many league titles beyond the current race. It was an incredible amount of investment and, although fans rightly caveatted any praise for Murray with the reminder that there had been no personal investment into the club itself, only directly to Marlborough, they knew that his ability to convince other rich men to do so was peerless. Murray was still talking about European super leagues – in December he assured listeners on Radio Clyde that 'Rangers will be at the party' and rumours abounded that Rangers were interested in buying AFC Bournemouth as a way into the English pyramid system, as were Celtic with Wimbledon – and the reality was that they would have to be for this kind of investment to make a much wider impact. Singular investments such as this – spectacular as it was – weren't a sustainable bulwark against the consistently increasing television revenue that the big leagues were creating. What is certain is that it should have assured domestic security for a generation. If, of course, the money was used wisely. The decision to offer a big deal to Thern was perhaps a warning that Ibrox was no longer a home to sharpness of analytic thought. At only 30 years old and highly regarded in his time there, Thern was leaving Italy for a reason and it was the same reason why his career would be over in two years. Even with some new blood, there were signs – hidden by the accounts and rhetoric – that it was a club for those on the wane.

None more so than its most famous player. Rozental wasn't the only injury worry after that St Johnstone cup tie; Paul Gascoigne left the field with nine minutes remaining due to a calf strain but Smith assured everyone that he would be making the trip with the team back to Amsterdam that midweek. It would have been better for all concerned if he was allowed to rest at home. Or even if Rangers hadn't bothered at all with the Sony Euro Sixes. A six-a-side tournament featuring Rangers, Ajax, Liverpool and Milan to formally open the new Amsterdam Arena, there was $200,000 for taking part and the same again for winning it. In the end it was scant consolation for the loss of Gascoigne, who injured his ankle in a collision with the Ajax goalkeeper Fred Grim and, despite attempting to join up with England a couple of weeks later, would be out for the best part of what was left of such a crucial season. For much the same reason, Graeme Souness had no time for the popular and mythologised Tennent's Sixes in the 1980s and early 1990s but a sense of prestige and status drove Rangers into unnecessary risk in a season with so much on the line.

Without Gascoigne there were stumbles. An insipid 0-0 home draw with Hearts was made easier by a Celtic defeat at Tannadice and Rangers then picked up the pace again with two comfortable wins away to Dunfermline and at home to Hibs respectively. With only six minutes gone at Pittodrie, Laudrup – captain for the day – had put Rangers in front on the breakaway and another big three points appeared to be in hand. With a comfortable lead and Celtic always appearing willing to spill any advantage they were presented with, Rangers stopped pushing for more and were punished as a result. Antoine Kombouaré's equaliser was irritating – he had far too much time in the box to get the shot away – but Jamie Buchan's goal was the kind of thing that spooks a dressing room and a support. It was a poor cross from the right that went straight into Goram's hands with no pressure around him. And then it was in the net. Whether it moved in the air – it was a blustery day in the north-east – or he switched off is unclear, but it was the kind of thing that only happened to Goram in those difficult early days. Now it was a total freak and Rangers did not need such omens as injuries were beginning to mount once again. Craig Moore headed the equaliser soon after but that was the end of the scoring. The gap was back to five points and fans moaned once more – despite the cushion and the impotence under pressure of that Celtic side – that this kind of form would blow the league.

Worse was to follow, both in the treatment room and the pitch. Of the nine games left of season 1996/97, Rangers won four and lost the rest. If this was the winter in which a most precious lead had been built, it would be a spring whereby Rangers hung on to it for dear life. Now was not the time for beauty. It was the time for bottle. Football at its most basic and rudimentary. For Rangers it was time to go back to basics. It was time to go back to the future.

* * *

On the morning of Sunday, 16 March, Walter Smith would have scanned the papers before making the short journey across the city for the biggest Old Firm match in a generation. It had seemed as if all of them had been billed as that for the last 18 months but this really was the one. A Rangers victory and the quest for nine was all but over. But a Celtic win at Parkhead, repeating their feat of ten days before, would reduce the gap to two points and grab all of that scarce momentum.

With a treatment room overcrowded and his side suddenly out of form, Smith was under the cosh but he still held the cards. He was the manager still on course for history. A surprise then, that Gerry McNee chose that morning of all mornings to make Smith the focus of his column. 'It gives me no pleasure to say this,' he started, 'but it's time for a parting of the ways between Rangers and Walter Smith. The entire backroom team has to go. No matter what happens in the final Old Firm derby of the season at Celtic Park this afternoon – and even if Rangers win the title – there has to be change.' Hours before an effective league decider, the nation's leading football columnist was not only calling for the Rangers manager's head, he was effectively saying that the prize at stake – a game that he would hype up from the commentary position that afternoon – was worthless. A parochial obsession, he felt. What's more interesting is that he wasn't necessarily alone as this was a nagging doubt shared by those for whom Rangers played a more important place in their heart than McNee's. In the days before the Parkhead battle, 'The Govanhill Gub' was more explicit than he had ever been in the past that Walter

Smith's time might be up. Criticisms of the backroom team were valid, of course, but he wrote in *Follow, Follow*, 'The buck stops with the manager … Do we really need to toss this league away before people will accept that there is something fundamentally wrong in our playing system and mentality?' Whether Rangers were losing their grip on this historic title was still up for debate but would be decided imminently. Whether some were losing their grip on reality really wasn't. That battle had been lost some time ago.

If there was ever going to be a way for Celtic to finally beat this Rangers side then a home tie in the Scottish Cup was most probably it. Rangers hadn't beaten Celtic at Parkhead in the competition since 1903 and had lost to them three times in a row between 1989 and 1991, the latter resulting in three Rangers red cards. On Thursday, 6 March Tommy Burns stopped ten in a row, in a way, with a well-deserved 2-0 win. Off the back of the Pittodrie draw, Andy Goram injured his ribs and failed a late fitness test. As he stood in the players' lounge with a drink in his hand, he was told that he would have to play anyway, Theo Snelders having broken down in the warm-up. Goram was in no fit state to perform his heroic repertoire even if his old foe Pierre van Hooijdonk was once more on the bench before he departed for Nottingham Forest shortly after, and his inability to move freely and come for a Paolo Di Canio cross in the first half led to Malky Mackay powering home a header before the Italian provided home comfort with a penalty shortly after.

Rangers were appalling, lacking all the grit and belief that had characterised so many performances there before. With no Gough or Gascoigne – and with Goram playing without his cape – too much was expected of the stand-in captain, Laudrup, and those miracles were beyond even him. The hero of the previous match, Erik Bo Andersen, wanted far too much time on the ball than this fixture provides and his contribution was over when he suffered a fractured skull during a clash of heads with Alan Stubbs. No, it was Celtic's night all right and their fans and players rejoiced. Many waited for the Rangers players to get back on their bus where they were greeted with abuse and reminders that they were, in fact, mortal. The home players did their celebrations on the pitch, strangely going back into their pre-match huddle after the final whistle, whipping up a crowd that needed no encouragement. The dragon had finally been slain and they'd soon get the chance to bury it when the stakes were even higher. They would have been better advised to hold back the outpouring until they were sure that the fire had gone out of it.

The race was now on for Smith to find some late-season cover at either end of the pitch. Snelders was clearly not reliable should Goram have more trouble so the journeyman veteran Andy Dibble was brought in on the off-chance that he was required.[126] His first day at training was up there in Rangers legend with that of Mário Jardel. 'His first training session was a bomb scare,' wrote Goram. 'He was letting them in from all angles. I could see the looks on the faces of the boys,

---

126   Dibble had enjoyed a short loan spell at Aberdeen in 1990 where he featured when Snelders was injured.

"What the fuck have we got here?"' Players joked that they had signed Officer Dibble and confidence was not high, should Goram be unable to shake off that rib injury, that this was the man who could be trusted to see them through to the finish line. Smith was left empty-handed on his return from Italy, however, as a deal could not be done with Bologna for the Swedish striker Kennet Andersson due to them not wanting to lose any players while still in the hunt for a UEFA Cup spot. The need to find someone – anyone – sharpened as the week went on.

Any reprieve from an emotionally drained Celtic defeat at Rugby Park on Tuesday, 11 March was wasted when Dundee United repeated that 2-0 scoreline at Ibrox the following evening. Somehow Rangers were even worse than they had been at Parkhead and what's more, Goram ripped a muscle in his thigh which ruled him out for the rest of the season. With Gascoigne's decision to recuperate from his injury by going on a three-day drinking session with Chris Evans and Danny Baker, Rangers fans were losing patience by the minute. It was this defeat that prompted Gerry McNee to call time on Walter Smith and replace him with the man who had just taken those three points. McNee – whose main objection to Smith's tenure was European failure – did not suggest Marcello Lippi or Johan Cruyff, but Tommy McLean, 'He [McLean] has the sharpest tactical mind in Scottish football and it deserves to be tested in Europe. Walter is a good and decent man but the truth of the matter is his time as manager is up. He is a man of honour and will know himself when to call it a day.' Any casual observer would conclude that Scottish football was losing its mind. There was more to come before the week was out.

'What is the difference between a panic measure and a stroke of genius? We find out tomorrow,' wrote one Saturday paper as the sensational return of Mark Hateley to Ibrox finally sunk in. His departure to Queens Park Rangers two years earlier had barely registered such was the excitement about new, fresher faces. Could he really be called upon to rampage at Parkhead as he once had done three or four years previously? Of course not. Hateley's presence was all that Smith needed. Something for the fans to rally behind – with 34 of 58 players on the books injured and a replacement for Goram who barely stayed at a club long enough to get his boots dirty, they were in need of one – and play on the minds of a Celtic side who weren't psychologically fixed after one good night. McCoist was the sole half-fit forward and could only make the bench as Laudrup was expected to play off Hateley's knock-downs. More than Hateley, it was the return of the captain that was most welcome. Three games Brian Laudrup had worn the armband for and all three were a disaster. Richard Gough's comeback – for what Archie Knox told the players was 'the most important game in the club's history' in the dressing room – was vital.

The biggest Old Firm fixture in the modern era was an absolute abomination. With no other choice, Smith drew battle lines and his team responded. The tackles were wild and the football non-existent. 'It was an awful game to play in and even when I've watched the video of it I've sat there in disbelief,' wrote Ian Durrant, a surprise starter that afternoon. 'Ever since Souness drummed it into me, I've always prided myself on the value of possession. I don't think I've ever given the ball away so much in my life as I did in that one game. Yes, it was a dreadful advert for football. But you know what? I don't really care. What mattered was the result.' The result came from one of the most basic goals one could ever imagine. An Albertz artillery-fire free kick from deep, a Hateley flick-on, Durrant barging his way in front of Stubbs to lob Kerr and Laudrup simply forcing the ball over the line. Celtic fans would have to go back to 1983 to find the last time Rangers took the lead at Parkhead and lost. With this fragile side, it was never going to happen.

Di Canio tried to conjure up something. An excellent free kick rattled the bar so hard that it was still shaking at the end but his frustration simply grew as the game went on, ending famously with a promise to Ian Ferguson that he would break his leg. He was nowhere to be seen when Ferguson walked up the tunnel. By that time all hell was breaking loose. Hateley had already been sent off for head-butting Kerr in a mass altercation that followed Laudrup being stepped on by Mackay[127]. Gough lasted for an hour before he was forced to come off but the Rangers rearguard was rarely tested by a side who didn't believe they had what it took when it really mattered.

Even McNee had fallen for it. 'Celtic's history is so much more romantic than Rangers' that nothing should surprise us in the season's remaining weeks,' he beamed in his column following the cup victory. Rhyming off the titles that Celtic had won from a position of adversity in the past, he claimed that Paul McStay 'the best player on the field in Thursday's Scottish Cup win, can do likewise'. Once the dust had settled on a match and a title – the importance of which McNee appeared to change his view on multiple times within the same column – he took a very different tone with the Celtic captain, 'Let's get one thing straight from the start – Paul McStay does NOT deserve another contract with Celtic. Frankly, he shouldn't have been given the last one. After signing it he hardly kicked a ball. And I'm kicking MYSELF that three weeks ago I fell for the same old McStay routine. He was the best player on the field against Rangers in a Celtic team which, to use his favourite word, was "buzzing". But it was a Rangers team which was appalling on that Scottish Cup night. Experience should have taught me not to join in the songs of praise.'

There was a great deal of dust to settle after this one. Joyous and relieved after yet another triumph over their most bitter rivals – this was the first time in history where Rangers won all four league encounters – the players decided to enact their own mock huddle on the pitch, just as their opponents had done ten days earlier. Bedlam ensued in the stands – as Rangers' players were pelted with coins at the tunnel – and in the media, where op-ed pieces entitled 'Ban this hate-filled match' were common and the prospect of all ten Rangers players in the huddle being booked was talked up. Tommy Burns, crestfallen at being at the wheel when his club's record was equalled, stoked the flames further when he stated that his side

---

127   He would follow Hateley 12 minutes later.

– who had preempted all of this in the aftermath of the cup match – were 'a class apart when it came to dignity in victory'.

Upon his return from a short break immediately after the win, Smith was in no mood to take any prisoners. First of all he took issue with Rangers being dragged into a narrative over discipline, 'Mark Hateley is the first player we have had ordered off in domestic football this season. As the manager of Rangers for the last six years, and considering the standard of games we play in and the motivation of the opposition, we have a good disciplinary record. Mark knows he was wrong and he was correctly ordered off by the referee. But I cannot see any other incidents in the game where Rangers were to blame. We had a player clearly stamped on. We had a player punched at that same incident, and at the end of the game we had another player punched.'

Smith then moved on to Burns and the wider insinuations, 'I take that as a personal insult. I have never acted in any way which would degrade the opposition. Ask any of my players, ask anyone who knows me. They will all confirm that. What we should look at here are our last three games against Celtic. At new year when we won we picked up the newspapers to be told that there was a "conspiracy theory" which was working in our favour. When Celtic beat us ten days ago all I said was that they were the better team and deserved their victory. Now we come to this game and we are accused of lacking dignity and blamed for incidents which took place during the match. When we lose a game there are no problems. When we win one then there are. That cannot be right. I would ask people to look at the three games and the publicity which followed them and then ask which was the dignified approach.'

As for the 'huddle', Smith pleaded a fair case, 'Why is it wrong for Rangers when it is OK for Celtic? Look, I think the huddle has been good for them. It has helped get their fans behind them when they have done it pre-match. But after the cup game they did it in the middle of the field and, as far as I am aware, it was the first time they had done it after a game. To my mind they did that to provide maximum embarrassment for Rangers' players and supporters. I did not complain or talk about that publicly but you can be sure that I did use it as a motivating factor for the league game. If our players wanted to show togetherness after the match on Sunday then why not?' One man he did not need to convince was Fergus McCann, who was angered at the reaction by Burns and added it to his list of internal verbal and written warnings to his manager, all in line with employment law and effectively the preparation of a defence should Burns claim unfair dismissal for a sacking that was now inevitable.

It came on 3 May, after Celtic failed to beat Falkirk in two attempts – at neutral Ibrox – to get to the Scottish Cup Final and cling on to something. Even if they had managed it, and if they had defeated the eventual winners Kilmarnock in the final, it is hard to see it being anything other than an anti-climactic washout. For five or six years Scottish football had one eye on this league campaign and now history was settled. It would not have been enough to save Burns from the chop.

The ceremonial part still had to be done but there were yet more tired slips to come. Kilmarnock won 2-1 at Ibrox on the Saturday following the battle of London Road before Hateley got a more fitting sign-off when he bagged the final goal in a 4-0 home win over Dunfermline. It was the 6-0 hammering of Raith Rovers at Stark's Park that put the champions in a position that could not be overturned by points alone and, with a goal-difference advantage of 17, it was the turn of Rangers fans to sing that 'nine in a row' song that had scarred a generation 23 years previously.

The stage was set for Ibrox on the bank holiday Monday, 5 May, when Motherwell visited and Rangers simply needed to avoid defeat to secure the most cherished title in front of their own support. Sky had moved the game to the Monday as far back as November, what with it being the final home fixture of the season, and had tied it up with Manchester United's match with Middlesbrough at Old Trafford, where they too could win the Premier League title with a victory. The two dominant British sides of the 1990s picking up their crowns one after the other. And it was LIVE! The signs of a flat afternoon should have been read from the rainy day in Manchester as United struggled to a 3-3 draw that did neither them nor Boro any favours. Further signs could have been picked up from Rangers' schedule. With no game in 20 days, many of the squad – some of whom were recovering from long-term injuries – took themselves down to Ayr for the Scottish Grand National on 17 April. McCoist arranged for a stretch limo to pick up 12 players at 9.30am and, according to Stuart McCall, a lot of tension was relieved, 'Not surprisingly none of the foreign lads were among the dozen or so out that day, which says a lot about the different attitudes there are.' More of that tension would be revealed in the summer but Rangers, seemingly just expecting to turn up and collect their medals – the new Ibrox screens showed videos of the other eight titles and then a large figure '9' at the end – were abject as Owen Coyle grabbed two goals to extend the wait and ensure that his side stayed in the division. Richard Gough assured the outside world that there was no complacency and that Motherwell just needed the result more. He was due to fly out to Kansas to start a new life on the day Rangers travelled to Tannadice for their penultimate fixture of a long and weary season. Gough would have to postpone his plans and get one more use out of his club suit.

Smith had warned his players and cut a frustrated figure but by the time the next game came around, he was more defiant. 'We will win it now,' he promised. 'A classic from Laudrup,' exclaimed Jock Brown on commentary, despite it being more of a collector's item than anything else. A header from the great Dane 11 minutes into a pretty entertaining end-to-end encounter was all that was required to seal history. It was his 20th goal of the season – more than his first two combined – and therefore fitting that it was he, the hero who arguably stood up more than any other in this season of all seasons, who was most synonymous with its conclusion. It would have been more fitting if Paul Gascoigne, starting his first game since January and talking excitedly about a contract extension, hadn't hit the post in the second half after some sublime work. The two of them on the scoresheet, the gods who finished the job, would have been narrative perfection. For their manager, it was only ever going to be a chance to breathe out. 'Now that it is over there is this strong, strong sense of relief. Now, of course, it starts all over again. The support was telling us it had to be ten long before we had won this one and these demands will continue,' Smith said. Typically understated and pragmatic for a man who had just enshrined his legend.

There were plenty of reasons as to why it wasn't a neat and tidy end to the story of nine, none more so than the heroes who were missing. Gough wasn't fit and had to lift the trophy in his full suit, tears streaming down his face but still proud to leave on a high, 'This is the way I wanted to finish. This may not have been our hardest season – maybe last year was in terms of closeness – but the pressure has been intense.' Durrant was in the stands too, his heart broken that Smith had left him out of the side on a famous night. Goram watched it in a Rangers pub in east Belfast because he couldn't handle not being involved. McCoist and Albertz were allowed on from the bench but were barely fit. With the game not live on television, fans had to tune in to the title-winning occasion by radio, something more redolent of the start of this journey in 1988 than how football worked in 1997, and what they listened to was a team of broken and tired men limping over the line. Warriors and heroes they most certainly were and who had collectively delivered so much joy to a generation of supporters but this was a triumph – their final one together – that had taken its toll.

* * *

And so, over 25 years later, we reach something of an *Alfie* moment about nine-in-a-row, one that is more Michael Caine than Morelos. In the final scene of the movie, Caine's character in the title role tries to find meaning in his life of accumulation, sexual adventure and achievement, 'So what's the answer? That's what I keep asking myself – what's it all about?' What *was* it all about in the end, this pursuit of a sequence? A symbolic and emotional triumph or a piece of local trivia? Since Walter Smith took over the reins, Rangers had spent £59.34m – or a net figure of £32.705m if you prefer – to be the undisputed kings of their own small castle. It wasn't the full intent of the outlay, but it was the end result nonetheless.

The Gerry McNee position, that Rangers were wasteful and parochial over this era, has to factor in two principal motivations. McNee was a Celtic fan and writer who kept Jimmy McGrory's medal as a prized possession[128] and was in thrall to the legend of Jock Stein. It would naturally have been in his own emotional interest for Rangers to have taken a break during this spell and focused on the Champions League where, incidentally, they could have furthered his own

---

128   McGrory was a legendary Celtic goalscorer from before the war.

broadcasting ambitions by allowing him the opportunity to commentate on the latter stages of European football's showpiece event. However, there is still some merit in his argument. As the big picture was getting bigger, Rangers' focus was undoubtably getting smaller. A time of record commercial revenue and market exploitation was not used to develop a modern football club with top-level training facilities and increasingly professional practices. By the end of the revolution, it had become the be-all-and-end-all that shaped and directed the club's habits and behaviour for the next phase, regardless of what soundbites were delivered every summer. Modernisation for the future would have to wait until the dying minutes of the 20th century as there was first an old score from the past to settle.

But what was so wrong with wanting to win the league championship every season? It is, after all, the primary objective at the start of every campaign for most big clubs. And to match and set new records, isn't that the kind of thing a club like Rangers should always be seeking to do? To be that dominant, that relentless – in any league – takes character to stay the course. It is easy to sneer at local success or take for granted what you are used to winning. As Rangers fans born in the new century would surely testify, winning is much preferable to not winning. This era provided more memorable moments than any other in the history of the club. The fans who saw it were luckier than those no longer with them and those who were still to come. But, especially as the years passed, there was an internal tension. There's almost certainly a generational fracture at play. Those who grew up enjoying this success set against the full exposure of the changing game around them, were more likely to feel some degree of dissonance and conflict. With so much exciting play happening elsewhere, their heads were more easily turned. For the generations before them however – those for whom 1960s dominance and European glory was supposed to be *their* birthright instead of Celtic's and those whose happiness, when they eventually got to enjoy the trebles of the late 1970s, was tempered by jibes such as 'aye, but you'll never see nine in a row' – this achievement was savoured to the limit. This really *did* matter. It was one symbolic achievement that they had ached to see and to turn one's nose up at it, is to ignore the reality of rivalry.

It is really a question of timing. Where the circumstances between 1986 and 1990 were perfect for the kind of revolutionary energy that Graeme Souness, David Holmes and David Murray brought to the table, they were anything but when the club was set on an almost unalterable path towards its perceived destiny. The years from 1992 to 1997 were not the ideal moment in the trajectory of European football for a club like Rangers to be caught looking within itself and back towards the past. It was incredibly difficult to do both. The style and practices that were trusted to get the better of Celtic and any transient challenger almost became too sacrosanct to rip up in the hope of better possession football getting the club to the quarter-finals of the Champions League more often than not. It was too much to risk.

If things had been different – say that second Dougie Arnott goal wasn't scored at Fir Park on the penultimate day of season 1990/91 and Rangers were blown away by Aberdeen at Ibrox – perhaps more could have been made of the position that the club would still have found itself in. More titles would have surely followed in any case – as would the revenue streams – but perhaps a healthier and balanced attitude to priorities would have ensued. A club with the headspace to invest sooner in facilities and infrastructure or to bring in European coaching earlier so that when the Bosman ruling came, it would have been ready to make the most of the newfound freedom. There is normally nothing wrong with making a league title a priority but there is when it is to the detriment of all else. Obsession of any kind is never healthy. With blinkers on, you can't see the world change around you. That die was cast in 1993. Once five had been knocked off – and the rest of the field beaten to a pulp – getting to nine became the holy grail. It was also the path of least resistance compared to matching Celtic's other great 1960s feat.

One big problem with the counterfactual history of Rangers being knocked off-course in the early 1990s and finding a more serene and well-balanced place in world football is that it is based on a major assumption: David Murray exercising cool judgement by the late 1990s. With the Lewis money burning a hole in his pocket, the summer of 1997 was the wildest in the history of the club. As offers were made for the world's greatest strikers while Rangers paid double the value for one of the world's worst left-backs, it was a manic scattergun approach that saw more players come through the door than at any other time in living memory. It wasn't a signing that Murray was most proud of, however. In the last year of his contract and making noises that he 'wanted to be with a good style and a good trainer', Rangers could have cashed in on Brian Laudrup for somewhere between £4m and £6m. Murray not only rolled the dice by choosing to renegotiate the following summer when Laudrup could have walked away for nothing, he doubled down by making him captain, a role he had only ever taken on a temporary basis for club and country and in which he had rarely looked comfortable.

There is a word that was later synonymous with Rangers in the 21st century but I would argue has rarely, if ever, truly applied up until now. The club had been arrogant at times, complacent too often and confident certainly, but never to this degree. The summer of 1997 – free from the suffocating cloud of necessity of the last few years – saw a free-wheeling sense of freshness that resulted in Rangers playing a pre-season friendly against themselves.

Hubris had well and truly arrived. What happened next should have been ultimately predictable.

Chapter Ten

Endangered Species

'I'll play for Rangers as long as I can, then spend the rest of my life being depressed.'
Ally McCoist

'The most beautiful thing is making the pass when you are in a position to score yourself. You know you're good enough to score but you give the ball. You share. And you see that joy in the eyes of the other guy. You know, he knows, everyone knows.'
Thierry Henry

Of all the myriad of stars that sparkled in the long sky that covered this Rangers era, only three were present for the duration. Walter Smith's took a while to be seen, dwarfed as it was by some bigger ones around him, before coming to the fore when needed and then establishing itself as the Rangers Polaris. One of those that shone the most during those early years was Ian Durrant's, but it was tragically invisible for over two years before regaining some of its insouciant twinkle. None however, shone as brightly and as consistently as that of Ally McCoist. Irrepressible, undimmed, he was the ever-present performer for these 12 unforgettable years and three more forgettable ones too. The ultimate Rangers goalscorer. The ultimate Rangers hero.

The time has surely come – now that his direct involvement in the game appears to be at an end and he has found a home as the nation's favourite pundit – for a proper and full biography of McCoist. One that pierces through the banter and the jokes and reveals the serious man beneath, which there simply has to be to have had the career that he has had. McCoist's real gift throughout the majority of his career was that of adaptability. Even his one big failure – management, a job he was never suited for and even back in 1991 told a newspaper, 'It's not for me. I couldn't wield the big stick. I'd only be fining my players if I heard they *hadn't* been out the night before' – was forgotten about quickly enough as he settled into the post-retirement role that he was made for, punditry. A colourful life that would have caused problems for other players barely made a dent on McCoist's carefully managed public image as the charisma of the loveable rascal could always be relied upon to charm the birds out of the trees. Unthinkable in the 21st century – when Old Firm fans have to treat the fixture with the utmost seriousness lest they face online ostracism – a Celtic fan in a Fighting Irish cap was filmed outside of Ibrox in 1991 saying on camera that he wished that McCoist played for Celtic. 'The guy's sharp, he's a nice guy, good personality,' he said, before another concurred with, 'He's a gentleman.' His campaign to be all things to all men did eventually grate on some hardline Rangers fans later in the 1990s but those gripes would be quickly forgotten after another important goal, just as Graeme Souness's frustration melted after another one-liner. There really wasn't another McCoist.

He was more than a joker on the field of play as well. An underrated header of the ball and not afraid to score from distance, McCoist was nowhere near as one-dimensional as some liked to make out. However, no player scores 355 goals for Rangers from 25 yards and that tally was mostly down to a penalty-box instinct that was second to none. McCoist scored 287 goals in 444 games between his arrival at Ibrox in September 1983 and his leg break in April 1993, which coincidentally may well have been the last hurrah for the British number nine, the penalty-box poacher. It was certainly the final years of the striking partnership, a fixture of British football, so wedded as it was to 4-4-2. McCoist's adaptability ensured he thrived, regardless with whom he was partnered. He was able to tailor his movement for those quicker colleagues such as Robert Fleck and Maurice Johnston – who called McCoist 'the best finisher I've played up front with' – equally as well as he could find the space created by more physical target men such as Kevin Drinkell and, sensationally, Mark Hateley, who he would watch from the bench to ensure he was ready to match the pattern of his play, when he finally got the opportunities to play alongside him.

It was more than just the duo at the top of the pitch, of course. Supply had to meet the insatiable demand for it to be successful, something that the retro football analyst Alistair Bain is keen to point out. 'While it's often thought that McCoist needed a target striker to partner him, I'd argue that the frequency, location and quality of delivery from wide areas was more important to him. It is no surprise that his big goal scoring years came during a time of Rangers playing 4-4-2,' Bain told me. 'Earlier in his career he would regularly drop deep to link the play wide, breaking away from the tag of just being a penalty box poacher, however his intent was to get on to the defender's blind side who had stepped out to pick him up. This bought him ten or 15 yards to assess where the defender was going to move back and block the cross, at which point he would nip in and often get first contact. Similarly I feel he also did his best work as a second striker when the ball was in wide areas.

'The vertical direct Hateley flick on has gone down in folklore, but he was far more successful when the ball was in wide areas again. This time allowing the first attacker (the head of Hateley or the runs of Durrant) to attack the front post, at which point he could position himself at the back post with the biggest field of vision, reacting to second balls and applying those instinctive finishes. Where I first noticed this skill set being tested the most, was during the games McCoist played in 1992/93 against European opposition. It is easy to say the lack of Hateley as a partner stunted his performances, but I would argue it was the depth of the crosses into the box. Walter Smith had to adjust tactically to counter each opponents use of 3-5-2, often doing so with an out-of-shape 4-4-2 that had Durrant out wide or deeper-lying wingers. McCoist therefore couldn't really get positioned on the blindside, as the angle of crosses rarely came from the final third, or in a position where he could pull away into space at the back end of the defender.'

What McCoist would have gone on to do if that night in Portugal had passed by without incident is one of the many open questions of the era. His tally of 88 goals in two seasons between 1991 and 1993 and a partnership with Hateley that produced 140 is a level that would have been almost impossible to sustain after the most purple of all patches in Rangers' history, but his struggle with injury on the other side of 30 would have been challenging enough if it wasn't compounded by the fact that McCoist returned to a game that was starting to change. More and more often the lone striker replaced the partnership and the images of touchline-hugging wingers soon belonged to a bygone time. The penalty-box striker – even one with other attributes – was becoming an endangered species. Even for the great chameleon, this would be the challenge of his career.

British football was slower to react, of course, but Smith was looking at one up front and Brian Laudrup in a free role rather than solely on the wing by the mid-1990s, if mainly in big domestic games and in Europe. Blackburn Rovers won the Premier League in 1995 with the most rudimentary approach that has ever lifted that particular crown. Alan Shearer – Britain's foremost centre-forward – was joined by another physical goalscorer in Chris Sutton and both fed off the work of out-and-out wingers Jason Wilcox on the left[129] and Stuart Ripley on the right. Operating in what the assistant manager Ray Harford called the 'magic box' – basically the 18-yard box if it was stretched to both sides of the pitch – the direct accuracy created enough chances for the partnership to get just under 50 Premier League goals that season. Even then it felt dated, with such cynicism leading to them being booed off the pitch in one game against Everton at Goodison Park, and that title was something of a farewell too as

---

129   Wilcox was also supported well by Graeme Le Saux who was a very modern full-back for the time.

the Premier League evolved from Eric Cantona's 'breaking the lines' to Arsène Wenger's impact at Arsenal, all brilliantly detailed by Michael Cox in *The Mixer*.

In the summer that Ally McCoist retired from Rangers, France won the World Cup without a contributing centre-forward.[130] The fact that they could and then add to that with an even more thrilling victory in the European Championship two years later was because of the weaponry that they had around that traditional space. In Thierry Henry and David Trezeguet, they had players who could thrive in the wider areas of a 4-3-3 and then cut in with devastating effect. Strong, athletic, intelligent and technically excellent, they had one attribute that was cranked up to new heights and shared by the other breakout star of that 1998 World Cup, Michael Owen: pace. Blistering, frightening pace.

McCoist had shown bravery and ability in playing as a lone forward under Graeme Souness when Rangers travelled behind the Iron Curtain in those formative years of the revolution, but that was more as a negative mindset to flood the midfield. The modern approach was to play with empty space, draw confused defenders out and then hit behind them at great speed. Even before the injury, McCoist was never the quickest – goalhangers didn't need to be – but this was a changing game. How much of a challenge was it? 'It's a brilliant question,' he told me, ever the charmer, even before going on to answer a slightly different but still interesting one. 'I used to chat for hours about this with Walter, as we were looking back. I asked him, "Nowadays, would you have left myself or Hateley out the team?" And he went, "I might have." And with the greatest respect, particularly away from home, it would probably have been me. He always said at the time that he would need to have a good reason for leaving one of us out and that you should always play to your strengths. He said that at that particular time one of our greatest strengths was our front two. But now, it has completely changed. False nines and all that carry-on.' And then the smile returned, 'But that's why I am delighted to see someone like Erling Haaland come back in. A proper old-fashioned centre-forward. He lives in the box as well as being strong and quick. I love it!'

One regular contributor to *Follow, Follow* wrote in the summer of 1995, 'Ally McCoist I would suggest is at the stage where he can no longer be thought of as anything more than a talismanic substitute. Still he's proved us all wrong often enough in the past.' He would do. The Champions League continued to be a struggle, with only two goals in 13 group games, both coming at Ibrox in the dead rubber against Grasshoppers, but even though his average goal per game had decreased by 0.5, the post-injury McCoist still found some goals at home in his final three seasons. Perhaps more significantly, it was moments rather than volume. The acrobatic return in the 1993 League Cup Final was one of four cup final goals, in addition to five more against Celtic – three of them important goals

---

130   Stéphane Guivarc'h was in the regular line-up but never scored – much like Olivier Giroud did the next time France were champions of the world. Guivarc'h would join Rangers later that same year.

in cup ties – and the screamer that was Scotland's only goal at Euro '96. Right until the very end, he was the man who was still liable to pop up with the goods and write his own script.

Graeme Souness's ultimate frustration with McCoist – beyond the soap opera battle of the egos – was that he felt that there was more he could bring to the table. That if he applied himself more, lived better, obsessed about his game, then the sky was the limit, with an instinct so naturally at hand. He had a point. So did the managers who shaped the game in the 1990s for the new century, who felt wary about relying on one talismanic individual. Their legs can break, you see. But fans need at least one McCoist who was the cartoon striker come to life and lived the life we wish that we could for just one night.

Far more important than treatises on transitions and exploitation of space, Ally McCoist was the boy who dreamed that one day he would score for Rangers and ended up doing it better than anyone else. It's doubtful if another will ever do the same.

Chapter Eleven

The Sense Of An Ending

Season 1997/98

'Nothing, it has been said, is true but change, nothing abides.'
'Sunset Song', Lewis Grassic Gibbon

*'Rangers have spent fortunes on second-rate players and they keep
getting knocked out in the first round of European competition.
For these reasons they deserve the title of the stupidest club in the
continent.'*
Christophe Larcher, France Football, September 1997

Of all the venues where season 1997/98 would pivot the most, no one would
have predicted a sports club based in a city-centre hotel. And yet it was
on a squash court in Glasgow's Hilton on the evening of Wednesday, 7 January
where fortunes were said to have turned the sharpest. One new Rangers player,
accomplished at the sport, was there due to an insatiable desire for any kind
of competition. Another, a novice playing only his second game, was there to
supplement fitness and improve his short-space reactions. When Marco Negri
took his eye off the ball, it thundered back with interest, detaching his retina and
disabling the goal machine, which had produced an incredible 33 goals before
the turn of the year. If Negri had been wearing goggles, or just fancied a night in
instead, Rangers would have won ten in a row.

There are countless stories like this. The tale of this season is a building with
dozens of sliding doors. If Lorenzo Amoruso's early achilles tendon operations
weren't botched, those crucial defensive errors would have been unthinkable. If
Diana, Princess of Wales, had escaped that tragic end in Paris, Rangers would

have likely beaten Celtic at Parkhead on the Monday night, such was the gulf in form at the time. If Paul Gascoigne hadn't been sent off by John Rowbotham in November and banned for five games, his spiral could have been avoided. If the same referee had shown Alan Stubbs a second yellow card in the same game he wouldn't have been there to score an injury-time equaliser, and a six-point lead would have been too much to claw back. If only Brian Laudrup had signed an extension or if Walter Smith, now an OBE, had kept his plans quiet, things would have been different. History would have been made. And with the ultimate margin so small, two points on the final day, those arguments remain convincing. Just one of the above would likely have made all the difference.

That, as now, however, fails to recognise the bigger picture. If one of those disasters hadn't occurred, something else likely would have. Despite the hubris, the noise and the advertising, Rangers were a mess from the very first day of pre-season. No amount of fresh paint or new faces would ultimately cover up the real story. That throughout it all, there was a permanent sense of an ending.

* * *

With the Joe Lewis money burning a hole in David Murray's pocket, there hadn't been a summer quite like it. Not 1995, 1991 or even 1986 had seen so much change, with nine players coming through the doors for around £15m and seven leaving for next to nothing. There was just as much noise about who Rangers missed out on than who they brought in. Italian defenders Massimo Paganin and Alessandro Pistone rejected Smith's advances as major work was now needed on a defence that had lost its historic leader, Richard Gough, and the presumptive future leader, Alan McClaren, had suffered another major injury setback. Swedish midfielder Stefan Schwartz declined the chance to team up with his international colleague Jonas Thern while the manager's anxiety about his goalkeeping options was highlighted with a thwarted chase for Georg Koch from Düsseldorf, Luca Bucci from Parma and Oscar Moens from AZ Alkmaar. It was Rangers' turn to reject a previous target, Gianluca Vialli, who was looking for a way out of his unhappy relationship with Ruud Gullit and Chelsea, but at 32 he was felt to be on the wrong side of the perfect transfer model.

Two other targets were about as perfect as you'd find in the summer of 1997. In May Rangers made a bid of £20m for the greatest player in the world. Superstar Brazilian striker Ronaldo was leaving Barcelona after just one season and the expectation was that the game's leading light would move to its greatest league, Serie A. He would, of course, join Internazionale but Murray insisted that throwing his hat into the ring was not a publicity stunt and nor was the apparent deal that Ronaldo didn't have to play in the more prosaic fixtures, instead keeping himself for the Champions League and the bigger domestic clashes. For fans, the offer produced a mixture of excitement about the level that Rangers could reach financially – there was no issue with the package on offer – but also discomfort around the 'choose-when-you-play' approach, in addition to the inevitable rejection. 'What is there for me in Scotland?' Ronaldo mused. 'What kind of league is that? What other clubs would I find interesting apart from Rangers? I did not want to move there. With respect to David Murray and Rangers I told them I did not want to proceed, no matter how much money was offered.'

There was one final deal that just escaped Smith and Murray but was a lot closer than Ronaldo. In early June, Smith flew out to Monaco to meet with the principality's outgoing captain, Emmanuel Petit. A bid of £4.5m was made which, given that he eventually rejoined his old boss Arsène Wenger at Arsenal for a lot less, led some fans to criticise the careless approach to spending. At that money, many argued, Petit was over-priced. In reality, at that price he would have been the signing of the decade and a midfield of Thern, Gascoigne and Petit would have raised excitement levels to dangerous new heights. It is also worth noting that clearly there was still a midfield space in Smith's mind, although many expected Petit or Schwartz to move back into defence when required and that it was that flexibility that was most attractive.

Joining Gough on the way out were Trevor Steven and John Brown into retirement and David Robertson, for £500,000, to Leeds United, all three such constant figures in that Rangers dressing room throughout the decade. When Davie Dodds left to start up his own decorating business in Dundee, Smith finally brought in some continental experience to the coaching staff in the form of Tommy Møller Nielsen, son of Denmark's European Championship winning manager, Richard. It was much-needed in principle but in practice, it would be too little, too late to continue the next stage of modernisation that was badly behind schedule. And it did not really represent the 'massive structural changes' that Murray promised, especially with Archie Knox signing a three-year extension.

The team, however, looked very different. Or teams plural, as it turned out. In July the *Daily Record* produced three different Rangers XIs that it suggested could win the title, at no time questioning whether this size of squad was too bloated or how easy it would be in practice to integrate so many new starters into the first team. The wealth of options was further illustrated at Ibrox on 13 July when the highlight of the pre-season saw Rangers play themselves. It was a hark back to an earlier tradition – effectively a public trial – last seen in 1966 with the blues playing the whites. This was less corinthian, however. The Nike Family Day was a commercial hit with ticket prices as low as £3 and absolutely free if you had bought the new Rangers kit the previous weekend. Nike's advertising strategy had already caused a stir, with billboards in the East End of Glasgow being attacked with chainsaws. Their campaign on the eve of the new season used a picture of Walter Smith next to a school blackboard. 'Nine out of ten – must do better' was the main title, with 'Rangers. Now pushing for top marks in history' underscoring it. It was both incendiary to those living in fear of a new record being set and heaped the pressure on a team that had been top of the domestic class for years.[131] On the day, the 'whites' – nominally a reserve side but not in reality – comfortably beat the 'blues' 6-1 but it should have been no surprise looking at the wild imbalance of the latter.[132] It was only an hour long and a few players – Gascoigne of course – played for laughs rather than using it to gain serious minutes but the fans enjoyed the spectacle and the first chance to see so many new faces.

Jonas Thern, Rino Gattuso and Tony Vidmar were already known to be arriving before the previous season was out but it was the other three Serie A stars who had grabbed most of the attention, at a combined cost of just under £13m. Joining Gattuso from Perugia was the striker Marco Negri and, with 15 Serie A goals for a relegated side, hopes were high that the curse of replacing Ally McCoist in the longer term would be lifted. Sergio Porrini was better known to Rangers fans after the clashes with Juventus two years before and his flexibility at both right-back and in central defence in addition to his tough, competitive spirit and pedigree, made him worth the £4m. For another million, Smith felt he had found the replacement for the huge presence left by Gough. Lorenzo Amoruso – sunglasses perched atop a head that looked as if it was carved from the Parthenon itself – had impressed for Fiorentina in the Cup Winners' Cup semi-final against Barcelona's attacking trident of Ronaldo, Rivaldo and Hristo Stoichkov and turned down Manchester United in order to keep his word to Walter Smith. He looked perfect. They all did. Former Scotland and AC Milan forward Joe Jordan – then a pundit on Channel 4's Italian football coverage – raved about the purchases, the strength and professionalism of the two defenders in particular, and said, 'I just never thought I would see the day when so many players of this quality would be playing in Scotland. I knew Walter and Archie were planning for this season when I saw them over there, I just didn't realise the extent of their plans and the level of their acquisitions.'

Others came in without the same fanfare. Smith settled on the Finnish goalkeeper Antti Niemi – on the recommendation of Møller Nielsen – and made it clear early on that he expected it to be a competition for places as Andy Goram yet again was missing appointments to aid his fitness and recuperation, on one occasion to go instead to watch golf's Open Championship at Troon. Another Scandinavian was the Norwegian left-back Ståle Stensaas, signed to replace the consistency of Robertson. Talk that he was reportedly touted around England for £500,000 and Rangers paid a million more was perhaps the first scratch on the overwhelming summer confidence. When Amoruso – who had gone for a clean-up operation in June for his achilles tendon – needed further surgery, more fans should have been worried. Some players were. Stuart McCall felt it was more 'strangers than Rangers', 'We were made favourites for the title before a ball was

---

131   Nike were by then accustomed to eye-catching billboards. The previous year they had featured Eric Cantona in front of a St George's cross with the tagline '66 was a great year for English football. Eric was born'.

132   The Blues lined up with no natural centre-back – Goram, Porrini, Vidmar, Wright, Thern, Durrant, Albertz, Laudrup, Johansson, Durie and Negri. The Whites had far more security in Niemi, Cleland, Björklund, Amoruso, Stensaas, Gattuso, Ferguson, Gascoigne, Bo Andersen, Van Vossen and McCoist.

kicked, but I wasn't quite so sure. My only fear for us was that three of the main figures from the defence would be missing. Davie Robertson had gone to Leeds, Alan McLaren was struggling with injury and Richard Gough had gone off to America. The back line was the part of the side that we built on and that was suddenly gone. People were getting carried away about our chances, but I had that doubt in the back of my mind. It was not going to be easy and with so many new boys from so many different countries it would take time to gel.'

Arguably the player with most interest around them that summer was Brian Laudrup. According to Ajax, an agreement was reached between the clubs for around £4.5m before the noise around the potential exit forced Murray to change his mind and hold his ground. An offer of £4m over the next three years was rejected by the player, who could – and would – leave in the following summer and potentially derail the season by talking to new clubs from the winter onwards. Laudrup – whose brother Michael was already at Ajax – was quoted as saying that he 'wanted to be with a good style and a good trainer', placing further scrutiny on Smith's capabilities in European competition. An agreement was eventually reached – although the correct word would be impasse – whereby Laudrup's contract situation wouldn't change but he wouldn't be going anywhere during the season and furthermore, he would be the new Rangers captain. With the loss of Gough, the uncertainty over the state of mind and professionalism of Gascoigne and Goram and some of those stalwarts reaching the end of their time, it is understandable that Murray changed course and stuck to it. But there was still a clear level of denial about how simple contractual situations like that can be when a player evidently no longer wishes to be there. Laudrup's first job on day one of pre-season was to clear the air with Gascoigne, whom he had publicly criticised during the summer about his lifestyle. An uneasy start then for two creative linchpins, around which so much was expected.

Still, confidence was huge and one reason for that level – as it so often is in Glasgow – was as much to do with the state of affairs across the city. With no football manager in place nor a general manager by the start of June and with the attacking trio of Pierre van Hooijdonk, Jorge Cadete and Paolo Di Canio either out the door or heading for it, Celtic were in the type of mess their support had hoped was part of the past. 'I have heard Rangers spent nearly £6m on players last week, yet Celtic do not even have a manager,' complained Cadete. 'It will be impossible for Celtic to match Rangers if they do not buy quality players, but nothing is happening. Celtic are being left behind. There are even good players at the club who do not know if they are staying.' Despite Bobby Robson's name being strongly linked as well as Craig Brown – brother of the new GM, Jock Brown – it was the former Dutch midfielder Wim Jansen who was plucked from Japanese obscurity at Sanfrecce Hiroshima. His announcement was underwhelming to say the least with one Celtic season ticket holder complaining, 'We have got second-best once again. I don't think he will be any better than the man they sacked, which means we are no further forward.'

A couple of cup wins for Jansen at Feyenoord was not enough to worry Rangers fans that Celtic now finally had what it took to get the better of the experienced Smith. Celtic did eventually start to do some business, however, and had their own influx of numbers with which to deal. Darren Jackson arrived from Hibs, Craig Burley moved back north from Chelsea, former Rangers target Marc Rieper signed from West Ham in the September, Jonathan Gould was a free upgrade on Gordon Marshall in goal, Regi Blinker came as part of the Sheffield Wednesday deal that rid them of Di Canio, Stéphane Mahé transferred from Rennes and Henrik Larsson was reunited with Jansen with the pair having worked together at Feyenoord. At over £6m, this was new summer territory for Celtic but Rangers had spent nearly £10m more and had all of the structural advantages bedded in.

For a former great from the distant past, Celtic was the wrong focus. 'Next season is not about ten in a row for Rangers,' said Jim Baxter as he helped promote the Nike day. 'It is about Europe. We all know there is a European league coming and Rangers have to be part of it.'

Walter Smith left the Champions League draw relatively pleased. GI Gotu of the Faroe Islands were the opposition in the first round and then, if successful, Rangers avoided Parma, Barcelona, Paris Saint-Germain, Newcastle United and Bayer Leverkusen but would face the awkward opponents of IFK Göteborg, well up and running in their domestic season. As was the norm by then, the first-round matches were played before a domestic ball had been kicked but there were no nasty surprises on the pitch with Rangers scoring 11 goals without response over the two legs – Negri, McCoist and Gordon Durie helping themselves to nine of those. For the fans, however, there was no sign of the pricing tension being relieved as they were charged £18 to see a second leg of a contest that was done. More controversy was to follow in the next round.

When the league campaign started on the first weekend in August, it was like nothing had changed despite all of the new faces. Larsson's dithering on the edge of the box allowed Hibs to take all three points against Celtic on the Sunday and then Rangers made their bow the following evening, live on Sky, as they welcomed Hearts to Ibrox. The first half an hour was perhaps all that should have been expected for a side with five players making their domestic debuts but inside two minutes, Negri had announced himself to the Scottish stage. The first was possibly the worst goal he had ever scored as he bundled the ball over the line – Sky used their new computer graphics to show that it was a goal – but a minute later his chip over Rousset from just inside the box was absolutely exquisite. Alec Cleland made it three late on – Negri technically assisted but that is stretching it – and Martin Tyler made the point that it was a 'goal from a Scotsman' as the natives tried hard not to be forgotten in this united nations XI.[133]

---

133 That evening's fanzine could hardly contain the excitement and the cover included all the flags now represented in the dressing room but inside there was still evidence of uncertainty and loss over what was disappearing as a cartoon was published of Murray showing someone pictures of Porrini, Amoruso and Negri on the wall with the text at the bottom reading '…and should a suitable one become available – we wouldn't shirk

The quaint farce that is Scottish football was demonstrated over the next few weeks. With the international calendar still not yet synchronised with club football, Rangers were due to be without three international players for the following weekend trip to Rugby Park[134]. League rules meant that clubs could get a postponement if they were missing two or more and Rangers did so on that occasion. In the League Cup, however, organised by the same organisation of course, no such rule applied. Rangers played under those conditions comfortably in the second round with a 4-1 home win over Scottish Cup holders Falkirk but the quarter-final against Dundee United at Ibrox on 9 September was too much. With seven internationalists unavailable, Rangers crashed out to a brilliant Gary McSwegan strike in extra time. Paul Gascoigne may have shone for England at Wembley on the same evening but that was of no consolation to his employer.

United turned up that evening with renewed purpose as their first visit of the season, on 23 August, could not have gone much worse. For all the false dawns of Ferguson, Salenko, Jardel and Rozental, it finally looked as if Rangers fans had their new goalscoring hero. Negri scored all five in a 5-1 battering, the hat-trick goal being the pick of the bunch with his control, skill and vision combining to devastating effect as he bamboozled defenders and goalkeeper alike. It was the second league game of the season and Negri had scored seven goals already. It was more than Gordon Durie had managed in 24 matches the previous season and more than Brian Laudrup had scored in 33 appearances during the campaign before that. A sensation was born and what's more, Celtic were an early 1990s shambles. Their second 2-1 league defeat on the bounce – this time at home to Dunfermline – caused some celebrity fans such as Billy Connolly to question the appointment of a Dutchman who it was said, with some black humour among the Celtic support, was the 'second-worst thing to hit Hiroshima'. With such a gulf in league form – Celtic had managed a win away to St Johnstone as Negri was terrorising United – Rangers were red hot favourites for the first derby clash, scheduled for the evening of Monday, 1 September at Parkhead. What happened on the Saturday evening, however, overshadowed everything.

The death of Diana, Princess of Wales, in that Paris car crash stopped the country in its tracks. The Sunday English Premier League game between Liverpool and Newcastle was postponed immediately and the Old Firm was not far behind it, with the added fears of any minute's silence being disrupted by a hostile home support. The issue in Scotland intensified later in the week as the SFA refused to re-arrange their World Cup qualifier with Belarus at Pittodrie, scheduled as it was on the same day as the funeral. Eventually, on the Thursday, there was a move to delay it by 24 hours which meant that Goram, McCoist and Durie would play, having said they would not if it was held on the Saturday.

---

from signing a Proddy'.

134   Had Brian Laudrup not contracted chickenpox it would have been four.

Hysteria ruled for a week or so before life returned to normal but few noticed that it had bought Celtic some valuable time before they first faced their great rivals that season.

They took advantage of it, going on an eight-game winning run in the league as Rangers inexplicably started to stutter. Two away wins against St Johnstone and Kilmarnock were sandwiched between two home draws with Aberdeen and Motherwell. This spell in September was a portent for the season to come. The attacking play was generally excellent with Rangers scoring ten goals in the four matches, Negri producing six of those as his tally reached a ridiculous 16 goals in all competitions by the end of the month. One of the goals against Aberdeen – the one that put Rangers 3-2 ahead – would be in the top ten or 20 of all time had it eventually led to a successful season. Laudrup excelled himself; with the ball having been dragged out wide, he somehow managed to flick it high over the head of Jim Leighton and into the net. It was absolutely stunning but it was what happened next that was more telling, as Aberdeen equalised again minutes later. The marking for that goal and the two that had dragged them back from 2-0 down was appalling and similar would allow Motherwell to take the lead twice on 27 September. With no Goram or Niemi due to injury, Theo Snelders was between the posts against Aberdeen and the back three of Vidmar, Porrini and Craig Moore were devoid of any direction. 'We were missing the leadership and organisation of Goughie,' wrote Stuart McCall in 1998. 'I noticed the difference in my first game back. We were looking around for someone to take the lead. It used to be all for one and one for all, even in our bad times, but everyone was looking at each other for leadership.' This was highlighted most acutely, as always, in Europe.

It's very easy to forget that for the best part of an hour, Rangers were the better team in Sweden. The attacking fluency that was in evidence against Scottish sides early in their season wasn't quite the same against a well-organised Göteborg defence but there were signs there that Durie's work rate would be the ideal foil for Negri's awareness. Rangers had most of the ball and made the running, Gascoigne going very close with a header early in the second half. And then the same old story unfolded. Porrini wasn't tight enough to his man when the Swedes worked the ball into the Rangers box and no one was near Stefan Pettersson at the edge of the box as he drilled the ball high into the top corner. Two minutes it took for the damage to be doubled. No leadership or a calm reset, just more unease from Porrini in dealing with his man in the box, Cleland was too late to read Pär Karlsson's run and Goram made a mess of trying to keep the resulting shot out. At this point in history Rangers had only ever qualified via away goals once in European competition – seemingly of the belief that it was a technicality only used by foreign types while they would try and bluster their way through for Blighty – and the chances of a vital one here were thin. The Swedish champions held most of the remaining play and, just when fans thought that a two-goal deficit was the task at Ibrox, an even more comical third was conceded with a minute to go.

With the expectations so high, the criticism was only ever likely to be crushing. Jonas Thern was the latest in a long line of imports whose comments to his home media were translated very differently to a Scottish audience and he had to backtrack quickly, 'All I attempted to say to the Swedish newspapers was that we did not have a good enough understanding in the team yet because we had played so few games together. Rangers have brought in a lot of new players and it is always the case when that happens that there is a period when you have to get to know each other. That was our big problem in Gothenburg, that and the lack of real match fitness, which, again, is normal at the beginning of a season.' Years later, Negri would be less diplomatic. 'It was unforgivable,' he said in Jeff Holmes's book, *Moody Blue*. 'The day before we left – just 48 hours before the tie – there was no practice. Instead we went to a huge gym for a bizarre session based on sauna, Turkish bath and Jacuzzi. We were to leave at dawn the next morning and stayed in a hotel near Glasgow airport. We were up at 4.30am and faced a long and arduous journey. At the same time, the technical-tactical preparation left much to be desired. We were told very little about our opponents, and knew nothing about their current form, how they would play or their star men. It was such a shock to me, as just a couple of months beforehand the complete opposite had been the norm. In the build-up to games in Italy, you were given every last detail on the opponent.'

In Negri's mind, it was Smith's assistant that took most of the blame, 'In the dressing room after the match, our assistant manager Archie Knox exploded with rage. It was ten minutes of hell as the attack was aimed especially at me. He was gruff and rude. Often, while he spoke, he would burp loudly before grinning from ear to ear. On other occasions, it was much worse as he would spit on the floor when we were getting changed. He was the exact opposite of Smith, who was always the epitome of elegance. I had serious doubts about his technical preparation. He treated players like horses. If you were playing well, you got a "carrot" and were praised and pampered. If you weren't up to scratch, he would come out with the whip and scream and shout at you, with more than the odd "fuck off" in there for good measure.'

It wasn't known at the time of course, but if it had been, it would simply have confirmed many supporters' fears. Møller Nielsen was a token gesture in lieu of genuine coaching reform. The same lack of preparation existed, the same reliance on blood, sweat and tears persisted, the same humiliation was the result. When Murray dismissed it in the Sunday papers that weekend, tensions between him and the support boiled over again. On the field, his view was that it was a crazy 30 minutes and that 'these things happen', especially with so many new players. But when the discussion moved back to ticket prices, fans were less understanding. 'Fans want Champions League football for £6' was a patently ridiculous thing to say when very few were suggesting such a low tariff and his comment that fans had to 'dig deep' because supporters produced only 35 per cent of revenue was careless, even if true. The commercial, advertising and television revenue can only be generated when there is a strong fan base to begin with. The price range for the home leg was £20 to £23, which Rangers did not allow to be televised live and the club had Ally McCoist doing radio adverts with soundbites out of North Korea – 'Your passion is our strength, you are our fuel!' Despite going back to a 4-4-2 with McCoist and Negri up front and with Charlie Miller grabbing an early goal, the match finished 1-1 and Rangers were out of the Champions League, if not Europe altogether. Season 1997/98 was the first in which parachutes to the UEFA Cup were offered for those big clubs tumbling out right before the group stage began.

RC Strasbourg was the safety net but it provided nothing but the same. A 2-1 defeat in France – with Negri dropped to the bench and all three goals coming from the penalty spot – was bizarrely treated as a positive due to the slender deficit and the away goal. Within 11 minutes of the second leg at home, Rangers were in control of the tie with Rino Gattuso putting them ahead. It was short-lived. Two Strasbourg goals either side of the interval ended the contest and Rangers' European campaign on the final day of September with the match most remembered for the sight of captain Brian Laudrup pleading openly with Smith on the pitch for some tactical instruction. Before the first leg, *France Football* had described Rangers as the 'stupidest club' in Europe. For many supporters now, it was the final embarrassment, especially as it was the first time where their team could be knocked out twice in quick succession. Change had to come.

Pressure was affecting everyone. Stuart McCall openly admitted between the two UEFA Cup legs, 'This is the biggest level of pressure surrounding the team now than I have ever known before. You always get pressure with Rangers, I've never known it like this since I joined the club,' before hinting that all was not well with the new players in terms of digging in for one another and getting out of this jam. Celtic too were feeling it. Early in the month, both Fergus McCann and Jock Brown – whose background was a serious bone of contention for many fans – were lambasted at the AGM for not spending enough money. 'Why have you sold all our stars,' asked former director Willie Haughey, 'and torn the hearts out of this place?' They would end the month out of Europe too although with their heads held higher from an away-goals elimination to Liverpool and the run of league wins started a much-needed uptick in momentum, albeit two points behind their rivals.

Smith's response – not for the first time – was to return to the past in order to shape the future, as an SOS was sent to Kansas City pleading for the return of the dressing room king. With Lorenzo Amoruso now sidelined until the spring, Smith needed someone on whom he could rely and few players, if any, fitted that bill better than Richard Gough. He would return in the coming weeks but it was Rangers' AGM – back in the Royal Concert Hall that had seen such a triumphalist and optimistic vision of the future earlier in the year – that would play host to the real story of the season. On 28 October, with Rangers now behind Celtic in the title race, Walter Smith addressed a packed auditorium and confirmed that this season would be his last.

* * *

'Gascoigne produced one of the most controlled performances of his career,' beamed *The Times*, 'and played with a sustained quality and maturity, illuminated by flashes of technical brilliance.' 'Doesn't quite sound like me, does it?' the player wrote years later. It certainly didn't – not in any of his performances in the calendar year at any rate – yet there it was right in front of the watching world. A 'grown-up fuck you', the sportswriter Rob Smyth called it. Intelligent, composed and canny, Gascoigne was brilliant in Rome, back in the city where he was once adored, as England managed the storm and qualified for the World Cup, to be held in France the following year. It would prove to be, of course, one of the greatest false dawns in modern British football and these sporting mirages – so seductive to fans despite the build-up of evidence to the contrary – littered the autumn of 1997 for Rangers. By then fans knew that the story was definitely coming to an end but so many were so dazzled by the brightest lights and in turn believed that it was one destined to have a happy ending.

So many simplistic narratives of this era endure and this season is no different. The story of Gascoigne is 18 months of brilliance and 15 of disgrace. Off the field, it is hard to argue, with too many Chris Evans and Danny Baker-related incidents to count. On it, he was almost certainly performing below the standard which he had set but the notion of a constantly poor contribution has a little hole in it and that can be found in the October and November of 1997. Gascoigne was brilliant, shockingly so. Central to the play, directing the tempo, the odd bit of magic, it was enough to convince many that he was back to his best just when club and country required it.

The trip to Easter Road on 4 October once more showcased the glaring contrast between Rangers as an attacking force and the special offers that were available to the opposition at the back. With 46 seconds of the second half gone, Rangers were 3-1 down, with all the Hibs goals highlighting the gaps and poor movement in the three-man defence. Stensaas for example was relatively impressive as an attacking force, involved in a great deal of Rangers' goals and dangerous moves on the left, but he was not a wing-back, lacking either the engine of David Robertson or his awareness and defensive intuition, thus leaving his team badly exposed. Porrini had predominantly played right-back for Juventus and any move inside was part of a back four, not a three. He looked lost too often. Gordan Petrić – the ball-playing centre-back of the three – only played one in four that season but the absence of a leader was all too obvious. Nevertheless, Rangers won. Gascoigne caressed a free kick into the top corner before Jörg Albertz hit the same spot with a great deal more force from further out. It was Negri, of course, who grabbed the winner, running on to a through ball from Gascoigne and finishing superbly.

The following weekend was a successful one for both of the biggest home nations. Scotland's 2-0 win over Latvia at Parkhead – with Gordon Durie scoring the second – was enough to secure the only second place that brought about automatic qualification for the World Cup, finishing two points behind Austria. Later that night it was England's turn, displaying excellent game management – save for a crazy final few end-to-end minutes – to get the point they needed in football's Colosseum. Gascoigne, with Paul Ince and David Batty in England's midfield, produced the most mature and disciplined performance of his career. It wasn't the carefree childlike wonder that lit up the same nation seven years earlier, but instead a more pragmatic, while still cultured, display.

When Dunfermline – five points behind Rangers in fifth place – arrived at Ibrox, there was a reassuring familiarity on show. Ten years to the month since he first signed, Richard Gough answered the distress call and returned to the heart of the defence, slipping the captain's armband on as he took his place. 'I doubt if Walter Smith has ever given me any bad advice,' said Gough. 'He wanted me to stay last season, but I just thought that it was right for me to go. Now it could be right for me to return and help him through the injury problems he has at the moment and help the club which did so much for me. Walter wants me back and I can only repay him by trying to organise the defence and, perhaps, provide the leadership people seem to think the new team needs. I will be trying to do that with Walter, working with him to help Rangers Football Club. I owe him and Rangers and the supporters that much.'

Smith now had a kind of balance he hadn't had for some time. Porrini and Joachim Björklund were free to do their own thing now that the back three had its leader. Gattuso, McCall and Miller gave Gascoigne that room and Laudrup and Negri up front were always going to be a handful. Negri scored four that day but he wasn't the star attraction. Gascoigne was, scoring twice and involved in everything. His first was reminiscent of the wonder goal that won the league in 1996. His second was a 20yard chip that he took on the up step without missing a beat. It was a beautiful goal to cap off a virtuoso performance. It would be his last for Rangers. Neither he nor Negri were to blame the next weekend at Tannadice – always looking dangerous and combining brilliantly for the only Rangers goal – instead it was Goram who took the rap for the defeat. Messing around with the ball at his feet, he was robbed by Robbie Winters who put United ahead – the kind of error fans hadn't seen since those fraught early months – and later he was slow to come off his line to stop a United breakaway and in so doing, brought down Steven Pressley, who converted the resulting penalty to take the points. Celtic were now one point clear at the top of the table at this stage of the season for the first time since 1989. If that provided Rangers fans with a sense of discomfort about all that they knew to be true, what happened next shook those assumptions to their foundations.

Walter Smith had to fight back the tears as he took the microphone on the stage of Glasgow's Royal Concert Hall. 'When your time is up, it is up,' he told Amoruso later in the week, hinting that, if all of his boys were leaving at the end of the season, then it was right for him to do so too. What he delivered to the shareholders on Tuesday, 28 October was less succinct and distilled. Unusually for Smith, normally a very good public speaker, it was an address that was a little wayward and disjointed. Who could blame him, however? The ovation that greeted him was heartfelt and genuine. And now, the man who lived his boyhood dream was preparing to say goodbye. As is always the case with the comings and goings of Rangers managers, the picture is never entirely clear. Smith said at the time that he had made the call at the start of the season – without any encouragement from Murray – that he wanted to have a crack at ten in a row and see all the new players bedded in before departing with so many of the heroes who had served him well. Neil Drysdale's *Silversmith* notes Murray's observation in the summer of 1997 that his manager was exhausted with life in the hotseat but wouldn't dare suggest taking away his chance at confirming immortality. What is clear is that, after Strasbourg, an agreement was reached between the two men in early October. Drysdale states that Smith offered to leave immediately but that Murray rejected it, not wanting Smith to have the indignity of leaving so soon in the season, as well as ensuring that he had time to arrange the successor. A decade or so later – on the eve of Smith's crowning renaissance, the 2008 UEFA Cup Final – he admitted, 'I was nicely sacked.' His inference was that the Strasbourg defeat prompted a discussion about the timing of his exit, which would be at the end of the season. This runs contrary to the idea that this was the plan all along. Tired he may have been, but there is a chance that Smith wasn't entirely desperate to leave.

His speech recognised the pressures and failures of Europe and that him leading Rangers into another campaign would likely be counterproductive. Media criticism was nothing new but the vociferous nature of the Ibrox reaction to two European exits in two months was a new dynamic that had a clear impact on Smith. His weariness in the job was all too clear. He had given a bizarre interview shortly before with *The Times* when he said, when questioned about his tactical nous, 'What is a tactic anyway?' But there was more to it than that, 'There was a growing sense of anticlimax about the job. Rangers were not given any credit for beating Hearts in the Coca-Cola [League] Cup last year. I went to the press room after the game, and it was like a morgue. There was no sense of achievement. It was, "Oh, they've won it again, now let's get on with it." There was a realisation on my part that things were changing for me. The next day's papers all focused on complaints that a foul had been committed on the halfway line in the build-up to our fourth goal. That had an effect on me. I didn't get any feeling of a great sense of achievement. But I decided to carry on because of nine in a row, and what it meant to everybody.' Smith felt that he hadn't been afforded the credit that he deserved and he had a point. This never-ending circus would take it out of anyone.

It wasn't an easy AGM for Murray, even though the main story took most of the attention away. Following his post-Göteborg comments, he was forced to apologise, but with the natural caveats, 'I unreservedly apologise to real Rangers' supporters if they took offence, but my remarks were directed at those who have jumped on the bandwagon and who are too ready to get on phone lines and hammer our players. They are not the genuine Rangers supporters and I have the right to say so.' Murray had gone further in *Scotland on Sunday* with Graham Spiers when he said, 'Rangers supporters are different from Celtic's in this respect. Celtic have gone public, many of their fans have stumped up hard money to buy shares, which in turn has helped to finance their stadium, and as a result, I sometimes think their supporters feel greater loyalty to the cause. They actually feel a part of what's been created. Rangers fans still have to buy their season tickets, and I'm not dismissing that, but they basically got the stadium for nothing, and some of them have had it too easy for too long.' This was news to those who had paid their money for years into the Rangers Pools in order to bring Ibrox into the future after such a traumatic past. It was the final straw for *Follow, Follow*'s 'Govanhill Gub'. 'Our club is now at the crossroads,' he wrote in November 1997. 'David Murray's blinkered management has brought us to that point. What I will say is if the thought of European and financial oblivion appeals to you then just keep on swallowing the chairman's bullshit.'

It was hoped that the AGM revelation would bring clarity on an issue which was rumbling away. It may have done but it inevitably created more speculation which was already in plentiful supply on a weekly basis. Usually it was around Paul Gascoigne's future – either through bad form and Rangers wanting to sell or through good form and English clubs such as Aston Villa, Everton and West Ham United wanting to get him back down the road, much in line with Glenn Hoddle's wishes – but Marco Negri had to confirm his desire to stay more than once before November, the interminable Laudrup saga continued despite him saying that he wouldn't think about it until 'March or April' and even the future of the old boys such as McCoist – who was linked with Falkirk in November[135] – and Durrant and McCall was an ongoing story. Now, it was who would replace Smith.

Despite the clear signs from Murray's AGM address that it would be European – 'northern European' would technically encompass British managers but the stress should have been obvious to anyone paying attention – Kenny Dalglish, Terry Venables, Bobby Robson and especially George Graham were all linked in the early weeks. None of this, albeit part of football's daily life, was helpful to a squad still trying to find consistency. One other part of Murray's speech that day was well-received for those looking forward but tinged with regret for those who believed action should have been taken sooner, 'There will be changes because we have to move with the times, and these changes mean there will be no more bouts of indiscipline at the club.' Standards would change at Ibrox. But not for seven months.

A Negri hat-trick got things back on track in a 4-1 win over Kilmarnock at Ibrox before the Old Firm met for the first time that season. Celtic had the better of the build-up as they finally secured the signing, for £1.9m, of Paul Lambert from the champions of Europe, Borussia Dortmund. Rangers-mad as a child, it

---

135   Where McCoist was going was into television as a new chat show with the comedian Fred MacAuley.

was a player who they could have got if they had wanted to move sooner. There are arguments as to why, by the autumn of 1997, this wasn't viable. Smith had lots of midfield options from experienced players (McCall, Ferguson, Thern), those in the middle of their careers (Gascoigne, Albertz, Miller) and genuine prospects (Gattuso and Barry Ferguson). It is also unlikely that Smith would have been allowed to spend money on players that Murray had no idea if the new manager would want. But there was almost certainly a sniffiness around Scottish players – even one with a Champions League medal in his pocket – when the restrictions were down and the money was available. Longer term, there is merit in the argument that Lambert may have curtailed the career of Barry Ferguson into the new century but, of all the 20 signings that both clubs made that season, none were as significant in deciding the outcome of the title.

It made no immediate difference at Ibrox, with Lambert seeing only 14 minutes of action as a late substitute. What is most obvious watching it back is the clear move to compact conservatism of Wim Jansen's side compared with his predecessor. Rangers, usually playing the role of reactor, were dominant and well worth the three points on 8 November. Goram had to make a brilliant double save in the first half but Rangers could and should have had more goals than the solitary Gough strike before the break – Negri's record-breaking run of scoring in ten consecutive league games came to an end – but it was enough to send Rangers two points clear of Celtic, while still a point behind Hearts with that re-arranged game at Parkhead in hand.

The lead over Celtic had been extended to three by the time the two met again 11 days later, but not by as much as it could have been. The defeat at Ibrox had ended Celtic's eight-game winning run in the league and their wobble continued with a 2-0 loss at home to Motherwell. Coupled with Tosh McKinlay breaking Henrik Larsson's nose with a training-ground head-butt before the Ibrox game, it was clear that results were something of a veneer. This was not a side who were obvious champions-in-waiting. Rangers didn't capitalise fully up at Pittodrie. Once more the ridiculous rules around international matches meant that Paul Gascoigne played for England in a friendly against Cameroon at Wembley while his side were in a crucial battle in Aberdeen. There were chances created but Rangers lacked the fluency they had shown over the previous month. Eoin Jess put Aberdeen ahead with a long-range effort in the first half – it was all Aberdeen were reduced to – and Albertz finally made Rangers' pressure pay when his header brought the sides level. Laudrup missed a good chance later on but there was a lot of huff and puff and little reward.

On the Wednesday night, Rangers were greatly improved. Missing Laudrup through injury, they weathered an early Celtic storm and went on to dominate the game and create the best chances. With McCall called back into defence alongside Gough and Björklund, the midfield was Gascoigne, Gattuso and Thern with Albertz and Cleland providing the width for Durie and Negri up front. Negri missed a great chance in the first half and then an even better one with just over

20 minutes to go as Rangers sought a record sixth consecutive Old Firm win. By that point in time they were down to ten men and a career and a season turned again. John Rowbotham had only taken care of a handful of Rangers games since that infamous match against Aberdeen at Ibrox two years previously and certainly none as high profile as an Old Firm match. Given that there were seven bookings in the first half at Parkhead – five for Rangers and two for Celtic – the signs were clear that he had lost the run of this game too. With just over 30 minutes left, Morten Wieghorst became the latest player to try and rob Gascoigne of the ball by tugging his shirt and nibbling at the back of his legs. Gascoigne's response was always to use his arms and, sometimes his elbows, to protect himself and, more importantly, the ball. Much had been made of this since his arrival and, with Rowbotham still under pressure to show retribution for his failure to give him a red card against Aberdeen, the risk was high. When the midfielder presented him with the opportunity, he didn't hesitate. Gascoigne first tried to shake the Dane off by returning the desire to swap shirts. Then there was another attempt to hold off his marker on the chest before his arm was raised and came down on the side of Wieghorts's face. Of all the altercations that Gascoigne was involved in of this nature, this was by some distance the softest and most innocuous. However, it was a red card that was very much in the post and, technically, correct. As was the reaction by the authorities who banned Gascoigne for five games in total because of an accumulation of bookings. 'I thought the red card was harsh,' Wieghorst said afterwards. 'I was pulling his shirt and naturally Gascoigne became frustrated. I am sorry he was sent off.'

Rangers players were less diplomatic. One unnamed player said that night, 'The referee was a joke from the first whistle. There is no doubt sending Gazza off was payback for that Aberdeen game. He was being fouled all night, but you could see the ref's eyes light up as if it was a chance to get even. Some of the stuff that was happening was outrageous. When Gazza went to take a corner he was pelted with missiles and fans were running down stairs to try and get on to the pitch to get at him. Yes, we are furious. All Rangers have had to listen to in recent years is that Old Firm refs are biased towards us, but I don't think you'll hear much of that today.' With uncharacteristic bluntness, Smith was even more direct when he said, 'There was no way he [Rowbotham] could have refereed in an impartial manner and he should not have been appointed to the game.' It was the last night when Paul Gascoigne was anywhere near his best and this coda – seven weeks of vibrant but mature exhibitionism – was a hauntingly sad finale.

The drama wasn't over and neither were the season pivots. Another breakaway found Negri in space for the third time and he didn't miss on this occasion, arguably the hardest of the three, his hard left-footed drive wrong-footing Gould and putting Rangers ahead. Rowbotham then made a decision that was arguably more significant to the outcome of the season. With ten minutes remaining, Alan Stubbs – on a booking – clattered into Negri at waist height on the touchline. It was wild and out of control and a clear yellow card, if not more. Rowbotham, perhaps because of the fact that he had so recently cautioned the defender, decided to do nothing. Jansen kept throwing Stubbs up to provide a focal point for Celtic's late aerial bombardment and Rangers, on the whole, dealt with it comfortably. There was one more chance for Thern on the break but he was exhausted by the time he swung his foot at the ball. From the clearance Celtic won an injury-time corner and Richard Gough held his head in his hands. Goram dealt with the set piece but the danger wasn't fully cleared. When Jackie McNamara sent in one final cross, Stubbs found himself on the right side of Gough for once and steered the ball into the corner of the net. The Rangers dressing room was in despair as well as fury, even though it was a record unbeaten ten game Old Firm league run without defeat. A six-point gap and a third defeat on the spin for Celtic would have been almost certainly too much for a side with no league-winning experience to deal with. It gave them a lifeline – from a player who should have been in the shower – and the race continued.

It is interesting, in the weeks leading up to these games – the type of situation where Rangers had routinely held on to a 1-0 lead – that prominent players were playing down the quest for ten. 'If we had failed to get to nine, it was as though the previous eight titles did not matter, and that put a lot of pressure on us,' said Gough before the clash in the East End. 'This year, for me the pressure of going for ten is not as great.' Laudrup had said similar a few weeks earlier, 'I must say that I feel less pressured this season than I did last year … We knew that we could not fail. This season I think the intensity is less. Obviously, we all want to beat the Celtic record – but it will not be such a sense of failure if we don't win the championship this time.' That intensity had previously produced concentration levels in these fixtures that Celtic couldn't match. It might have been coincidence but it furnishes an established belief that the hunger was no longer sufficient to keep pushing these players to the end.

The ponderous state of life without Gascoigne was evident immediately as Rangers dropped two more points with their third consecutive 1-1 draw, this time at Fir Park. A lesser-spotted league goal from Ally McCoist opened the scoring – Rob McLean on commentary for BBC Scotland said 'there's number one', a clear assumption that there would be more to come from the visitors – but, despite some Goram heroics, Rangers were done again on the left flank and Tommy Coyne was left with the freedom of the penalty box to scramble a cross home. What could have been six points was now only one. How quickly and often this season would chop and change. The goals flowed against St Johnstone at Ibrox – a quick reprieve for Gascoigne before the extra four games were enforced – as Gattuso and Negri with two were enough to counteract the two St Johnstone replies and it was Negri, eventually, who got the only goal against Hibs at home the following Sunday, live on television. His penalty was saved but he managed to force home the rebound. The day before, Celtic – now the holders of the League Cup following their comfortable victory over Dundee United at Ibrox the previous Sunday – had drawn 0-0 at Kilmarnock to open that gap back up but Rangers duly returned the favour with a meandering goalless draw away to Dunfermline on 13 December, on a pitch that was so waterlogged the game was close to being postponed.

All of this meant that, on the morning of Saturday, 20 December – the final match before Christmas – Hearts, Rangers and Celtic had all played the same amount of games and were separated by only two points, Hearts with 37, Rangers 36 and Celtic 35. An unexpected third party was very much in the race and Rangers visited Tynecastle that day – where Hearts had only lost one in eight that season – with many expecting the champions to be sat in third place during the festivities. Instead, Rangers were absolutely magnificent, even without the suspended Gascoigne, Laudrup only making the bench as he came back from injury and illness, McCall standing in as captain for Gough and Gattuso sent off in the second half. Two first-half Gordon Durie penalty-box strikes sandwiched a John Robertson equaliser but the gears were shifted in the second half as Albertz drilled one in the bottom corner from range and Negri – who else? – scored another before Durie grabbed his hat-trick, Rangers ran out 5-2 winners and returned to the summit. Of all the mirages during this period, this was arguably the most seductive and tantalising. Supporters had seen all of this turmoil before. Pretenders to the throne excelling early, Celtic being all talk and no action, early European exits and choppy autumn form but now it was the winter and Rangers – this Rangers – knew how to put the foot down. It was a huge statement that order had been restored and even the scoreline was reminiscent of the start of the revolution, where Rangers won there by the same margin in early February 1987 after some disappointment and kickstarted a run towards the title. It had been something of a tradition ever since.

Negri's penalty at Tynecastle brought his total for the season up to an incredible 31 goals before the arrival of Father Christmas. He had actually been carried off in the 1-0 win over Hibs at Ibrox but Smith dismissed any suggestions that he would be on the sidelines and he was duly back in time for the next match. Negri was a quick healer, apparently. Robust, resilient. He would have to be. He had scored nearly 60 per cent of Rangers league goals. The nearest was Albertz with four and it was clear, especially without Laudrup and Gascoigne contributing in the same way that they previously had, that Rangers couldn't afford for the Italian goal machine to suddenly malfunction. Fortunately he seemed impervious on the football field. Unfortunately, as it would turn out, that wasn't where the problems would occur.

* * *

On the face of it, the 2-1 victory over St Johnstone at Ibrox on 21 March was very much routine for Rangers but nothing about this season was ever exactly as it looked. Negri scored, of course. His 36th and, eventually[136], 37th in an incredible season – but his last. Not just of the campaign, but for ever.

Late in the game there was that familiar slaloming, bustling run from one half of the field to the other, three players left in his wake before he got the shot in. But by then he was number 15, not number eight, and the shot was weak and saved with ease. It was the last attack that Paul Gascoigne would ever make in a Rangers shirt. He would leave within the week. One genius gone, the other definitely going. A new manager confirmed, the current incumbent enjoying his testimonial. A four-point lead over Celtic as the bells rang in 1998 was now a five-point deficit. A winter of collapse that, despite signs of promise from some other players, would ultimately prove decisive.

Wednesdays are very different for footballers in Italy than they are in Scotland. Instead of the day off here, it is usually the hardest slog of the week for Serie A players and Marco Negri liked to keep that habit going, whether through going for a run or visiting the gym with Sergio Porrini. They had played squash once before – Negri's first attempt, whereas Porrini was an old hand by then – and they perhaps fancied that fast-paced intensity to work through the disappointment of the stinging defeat suffered the previous Friday. When Negri missed the line of the ball coming back at him, his detached retina derailed a team who were so heavily dependent upon him. Unlike many operations on Rangers players around that time, this was excellently handled and without complication. The striker was given a month of recuperation with no training and was ordered to wear dark glasses whenever he was out during the day.

Arguably even more damaging was the chain reaction that it set off in other areas of Negri's life as internal doubts and demons were given credence, tensions in his relationship with his girlfriend Monica were opened and a breakdown in relationships with Lorenzo Amoruso and Walter Smith – the former getting involved as an unwanted intermediary in his domestic strife and telling the manager that his compatriot wanted away – which were never properly resolved. He perhaps had a point when he asked himself why Smith didn't put an arm around him at this time in the way he did numerous times with Gascoigne but regardless, he was allowed, and he allowed himself, to become more distant and introspective.

When this is used as the main reason for or at least a key part of the collapse, a wider view is imperative. Injuries happen regularly in sport and this was effectively a four-week pause, not a ligament injury that ruled him out for the season. How players respond is the key and Negri simply didn't. The real story is the various weaknesses that such moments expose. Twenty-three goals in his first ten league games is the standout headline but seven in the next ten is less-quoted. Although still impressive, it is perhaps a sign of a tapering back towards a less-spectacular norm. Negri would score four more goals for Rangers after his return, all of them

---

136   The goal was initially credited to Jonas Thern but Negri was later awarded it. A modern-day Dubious Goals Panel would have probably left it with the midfielder.

from close range. His variety as well as his volume of goals dried up, in addition to the increasingly sullen and unkempt image that he portrayed that winter. Negri's inability to deal with the lay-off and respond – he felt that his peripheral vision was badly affected even when the pain had passed – was more than matched by his team-mates who were too heavily reliant on him for goals. That is the real reason for such a costly implosion, a more reliable truth than the freak barrowload of goals that filled that early season promise. It wasn't Negri's loss that was most damaging, it was the lack of firepower elsewhere.

The replacements had their own injury worries to deal with and, ironically, there was one loss that would eventually provide Rangers with hope and some degree of glory. Ally McCoist was all set to go out on loan for the rest of the season in order to give himself one final shot at a World Cup place. Newcastle, Fulham, Sunderland, Everton and Birmingham City were said to want him down south and Smith was happy to give him his wish. The day before Negri's squash match, McCoist damaged knee ligaments in training and was ruled out for six weeks. It put paid to any loan but, although no one could know at the time, it would be an injury that would eventually be of benefit. Smith was waiting on more concrete assurance that Sebastián Rozental's latest treatment would bring about a return before he gave McCoist the final approval. He would eventually return but – despite hope given from the Chilean national team camp, with whom Rozental trained in preparation for a friendly with England – there would be another setback soon enough. Within a couple of days he was left with Gordon Durie as the only recognised striker and the following month at Rugby Park, even he would suffer as a horrendous collision led to serious concerns about his consciousness which thankfully came to nothing.[137]

Paul Gascoigne's early departure was probably sealed as he warmed up as a substitute at Parkhead. 'When I was warming up, all the Celtic fans were giving me a load of stick, most of them shouting variations on the wife-beater theme,' he wrote in 2005. 'They wound me up so much that to annoy them in return, I pretended to play the flute again. Mad? It was suicidal. I was just so furious with them for shouting abuse at me that I did the only thing I could think of that would shut them up.' The reaction to this incident was a different world from the misplaced joke in the summer of 1995. Rangers fined him £20,000 and Fergus McCann took the opportunity to make some moral and political capital from the incident while demanding that the SFA take some disciplinary action. Gascoigne had death threats at traffic lights and in the post, some from fans and one, allegedly, from the IRA. It was yet another unnecessary chapter in a life that was spiralling even faster out of control.

Smith's patience was now nearing the end. 'People think Gascoigne and I have a father-and-son relationship,' he said in 2000. 'Well, I've got two sons and I have

---

137   Added to the injury crisis was yet another setback for Lorenzo Amoruso during a collision with Joachim Björklund in training. Thankfully, it was just another month on the sidelines for the Italian.

never felt like hitting them, but have certainly felt like smacking Gascoigne a couple of times.' Gascoigne wrote in his book that he was technically sacked by Smith on several occasions – told not to come back the next day and that he was finished – but that quasi-paternal relationship always came to the fore, with Smith so often doing what he could to keep his genius in check, even taking him on a helicopter ride over the city to try and make him appreciate the place that Ibrox Stadium had. But there are limits to every relationship and Rangers and Gascoigne were at theirs. David Murray and Walter Smith had always made it clear during the constant speculation that the choice was always with the player. When offers of nearly £3.5m were on the table and the chairman made it clear that the figure might not still be there in the summer, Gascoigne took the hint. Needing to feel loved at all times, he chose Bryan Robson and Middlesbrough but changed his mind three times on 25 March before signing the following day. Team-mates like Stuart McCall were convinced that he would stay, and felt the blow personally, 'Everybody in the dressing room was very disappointed – the players were as upset as the fans. Everybody wanted him to stay. The boys were amazed and I was one of them. When I spoke to Gazza he said he wasn't totally happy with the decision, he didn't want to go. For the first time in years he had found happiness on the park and truly loved the dressing-room craic and the gaffer. It was a love affair with the club as a whole.'

Fans and media saw Gascoigne's exit as a sign that Rangers had effectively chucked the season. 'That was my initial reaction too,' wrote McCall later that year. He wouldn't be the only player or supporter to make the argument that, although Gascoigne was clearly way past his best, and that others were coming into far better form in midfield, some of those vital games at the end could have been broken by one of those moments of magic. In the autumn certainly but he had shown so little after coming back from his ban that it was a forlorn and ethereal hope. It was another mirage.

The main reason that Gascoigne chose to go was that it was made known to him that the incoming manager didn't want him. 'I am not moving to Glasgow Rangers and any talk of me going there is absolute nonsense,' the Dutch coach Dick Advocaat said on 22 January. 'I know that there was some talk about me joining Rangers in Glasgow last week, but I do not want to go there. I am happy in my position with PSV. An official from Rangers told me they would be interested for me to become their head coach two weeks ago, but I declined that offer. I do not have any reason to leave my post as coach of PSV as I am perfectly happy and settled with my life.' By the middle of February, he was announced as the tenth Rangers manager. Any hopes that a line had been drawn that wouldn't be looked at until May were fanciful. Not only Gascoigne, but Goram, Petrić, Björklund and others were speaking openly about whether or not they'd be wanted the following season just as the current one was disintegrating. In nearly every newspaper piece on the new arrival, the magic word was 'discipline'. A heartening noise for fans looking forward but it only served to highlight the issues within the current dressing room, which was far from helpful.

One player Advocaat didn't need to worry about was Brian Laudrup, making his move to Chelsea official, just as the deal for the Dutchman was announced.[138] It was a deal that even Murray couldn't do, such was the lure of playing in a Premier League that was just about to start challenging for primacy in world football. This announcement, Gascoigne's sale and Smith's testimonial against Liverpool on 3 March[139] were mostly symbolic in reality but it is difficult to downplay the impact they had in creating an atmosphere of a long, slow goodbye to an era. Conscious or not, this constant reference to the past is almost always counterproductive when trying to energise a dressing room for the challenges that lay in front of them

The health of Negri and his striking colleagues was only part of the explanation as to why Rangers fell from leaders to also-rans. The final match of 1997, a 4-1 win at home over Dundee United, was nearly as explosive in attack as the victory over Hearts had been the week before with two more for Negri and Laudrup rolling back the years with a balletic run and shot into the top corner but it had started badly as more defensive creaks were exposed before control was regained. Celtic lost in Perth on the same day[140] with injuries hitting just as Rangers were free-scoring and Smith had almost a full squad from which to choose. What happened on 2 January was something of a role reversal of that gritty Old Firm narrative that Rangers had enjoyed so often.

It was a fixture that had long been seen as a bellwether for the season. Neither side had lost the January game and then ended higher than their rival in May since 1981. Win this and you'll win the title, it was said. Although true, we should perhaps be wary of painting this particular match as a decisive point in the season. Rangers were bright and confident in the opening stages, ten league games unbeaten against Celtic and Smith going into his final league visit there with a record of seven wins, three draws and only one defeat. Laudrup and Albertz lost their composure in the box and the retreat gradually happened as Celtic – knowing that it was likely win or bust – found more bravery in attack. Their start to the second half was incessant and it was Andy Goram who was called upon to be the hero once more as Rangers were shaking. He had no chance when Craig Burley was left in space by Gough, who rushed out from far too great a distance to stop McNamara either shooting or feeding the ball through and the Rangers response – aided briefly by the late energy from the Gascoigne substitution[141] – was finished by Lambert when he smashed the ball into the top corner from the edge of the box. A darkly poetic moment but it didn't have the pivotal impact that some have since believed. Celtic dropped two points at Fir Park in the next match

138   Laudrup was surprised to meet with Gianluca Vialli and not the manager Ruud Gullit when he had his initial talks. This was because Gullit's time was very limited and the new man was getting in early.

139   Rangers were four points adrift at the time and for many, it was not well-received.

140   The defeat caused the normally quiet Wim Jansen to blow his top and some dressing-room truths were shared and the air cleared.

141   This was his only taste of Old Firm defeat. He had previously started 11 games, with six wins and five draws.

as Rangers toiled to two wins against Aberdeen and Motherwell at Ibrox. A three-point lead had been re-established and it could have been more with Celtic one down at Tannadice with 14 minutes to go. Burley's winner three minutes from time was equally as significant as breaking the deadlock against Rangers.

Minutes from being six clear, Rangers finished January by giving Celtic the opportunity to go level, which they took. The shaky performances all month came to a head at McDiarmid Park with a 2-0 defeat to St Johnstone and it opened up a six-game run in the league where Rangers could only win once. The goals conceded were comical. John O'Neil's first in Perth was the result of far too much space yet again being afforded on the left while the second and the costly injury-time equaliser for Dunfermline at Ibrox the following week were down to a lack of sharpness in the penalty area. The opposition were consistently being first to the ball. Goram's only error during this period – apart from a poor clearance against Hearts which Neil McCann took advantage of – was exacerbated by Joachim Björklund as the two failed to communicate on how to deal with a long ball, leaving Paul Wright to put Kilmarnock ahead, and the second Hearts goal in a 2-2 draw at Ibrox was redolent of that Bobby Williamson winner at Ibrox in 1993 as Björklund – previously such a reliable performer – failed to keep control of the ball in the box and Jim Hamilton could not have been provided with an easier chance. Without the Negri of old and Rozental looking a shadow of the player that had attracted Smith in the first place, Rangers no longer had the firepower to negate the defensive frailty. Instead it was Albertz and Thern who were asked to come up with long-range heroics to salvage what they could. Thern's cool chip rescued a point at Kilmarnock; Albertz twice equalised against Hearts and his rocket won the only three points in this run late on against Hibs. It was valiant but it wasn't enough.

Ally McCoist's resurgence had been primarily the preserve of the Scottish Cup, where he saved Rangers from a quarter-final exit in a replay in Dundee, until he opened the scoring in a league match at Motherwell on 14 March, but the increasingly familiar weakness in dealing with cross balls was punished twice as Owen Coyle and Willie Falconer took all of the points and presented Celtic with the opportunity to go seven clear when they faced Dundee United at home the following day. That they didn't fully capitalise – a 1-1 draw being all that they could manage – is telling about the quality of this title race. On the evening of 28 February, after Rangers had scrambled to that draw against Hearts at Ibrox, Celtic were four points clear with nine games remaining. They would only win four of them. This was not a side swashbuckling its way to the title and putting others to the sword. It was one seemingly just waiting for the rest to fall. Many Rangers players certainly had. Their race had ended the season before and they had little left with which to give. But there were exceptions. Despite how grim the picture looked in the middle of March, this was still a season very much in the balance and a handful of Rangers players, new as well as old, were about to show just how close it could be.

* * *

At around 5.20pm on Easter Sunday, a resurrection was confirmed. As the snow fell from a murky grey sky, he did it again. Powering through a helpless Celtic rearguard before shaping himself on to that trusted left foot and ending the match there and then. It was the week that made Jörg Albertz as a fully fledged Rangers hero and it was one that validated an unlikely story of recovery. Incredibly – from a position of despair a month before – Rangers were top of the league table with only four games remaining and a double was on the cards with which to send off this legendary manager and team. In the end, it would be a legend that caught up with itself right before time was called.

The comeback from that awful six-week period began with the home win over St Johnstone on 21 March but really kicked into gear the following weekend. Rangers won 3-2 at East End Park but it was yet again hard work. McCoist's two predatory goals were both cancelled out by Dunfermline before Thern scored a brilliant long-range strike that they couldn't match. The Swede was very much getting his range in but, even though Negri showed signs of good link-up play despite clearly not being in the correct state of mind, Archie Knox decided to dig him up by asking if he was going to claim that goal of Thern's too. It was yet another fracture in an increasingly distant relationship between the man who had driven the early season and his management. Despite that, the mood was enhanced by yet another home draw for Celtic on the same day – this time a stalemate against Hearts – which brought back the lead to a tantalising three points. By midweek, Rangers had played their re-arranged game and sat at the top, a 3-0 home win over Hibs that was only comfortable in the last 30 minutes once the deadlock had been broken. It was broken by McCoist and the comfort provided by Thern and Durie but the first two goalscorers were starting to show some real form just at the right time.

The reason for the re-arrangement was the Scottish Cup semi-final on Sunday, 6 April, where this chaotic season was thrust into yet another new direction. 'The day before the game Walter told me I was on the bench,' wrote Lorenzo Amoruso years later. 'I thought it was a big decision for him to make but he told me that if I played as I had done in training I could handle it no problem.' Indeed he would. Amoruso had just rejoined the squad at their training camp in St Andrews and felt the confidence rushing back quickly and he took his place as a substitute trying to take it all in. It was an Old Firm game at Parkhead with a difference as the equal split of tickets negated the traditional vociferous backing that Celtic would expect to feel when walking out.

The game – perhaps let loose from the shackles of a suffocating title pressure – was wild and free, with both sides going at each other constantly in the first half. Rangers were slightly wasteful, Celtic stopped, yet again, by Goram. The pace was too much for Gordan Petrić, whose hamstring gave way after 19 minutes. Enter

Amoruso, roared on to the park by a support that had been itching to see him play a game of competitive football. He strolled through most of it and nearly made the debut of all debuts when his free kick from 40 yards fizzed and dipped in front of Jonathan Gould's eyes. By that time, Rangers were in front. In truth they owned the second half, with that dangerous counterattacking fluency that had characterised Smith's time in charge coming back to life. Thern had already released Laudrup with a stunning ball from deep but he couldn't quite get the shot away that he wanted. Albertz had two other efforts go amiss before he took control of another raking diagonal ball from the Swedish captain on the left. With tired legs aplenty in the Celtic defence, the German had all the space in the world with which to find the ultimate Old Firm marksman.

It was McCoist's unbeaten 27th and final goal for Rangers against Celtic, the one record that he 'really wanted to get'. His celebrations through the years ranged from the raw aggressive roar to the smiling jester but none – even the stunned look to the heavens as they opened over Hampden in March 1992 – were as iconic as this. With 15 minutes to go, he couldn't miss as he was left to ghost into the space that Albertz had delivered the ball towards and headed home from six yards. And then, it was as if he didn't really know what to do, spinning in a circle before falling to his knees, almost in tears, in front of a packed Rangers support. Without a goal against Celtic in two years, he must have feared there wouldn't be another moment like this. The one that Rangers strikers can never get enough of. And now he had his last. On his knees he pulled his jersey outwards and appeared to speak to the support; *his* support. Thank you and goodbye. And then he was joined by his captain in an even more emotional embrace, their tears and words captured for ever in a photograph that remains one of the most iconic of the entire era.

Perhaps too much has been taken from it and indeed this McCoist encore as a whole. He was certainly part of a group which breathed life back into a season – his two goals at Dens Park in the quarter-final replay being so vital as well as opening up the two wins over Dunfermline and Hibs – but his impact on the league was arguably more minimal than has been made out in the subsequent years. He and Goram were the two old boys who most deserved that final applause but the real engine for this short revival came from midfield. The glimpse into what Thern could have given the season was all too brief but the dramatic denouement could not have happened without him and it certainly could not have have happened without the man who drove at the Celtic defence with a couple of minutes remaining, side-stepping desperate lunges before blasting the ball into the roof of the net to make sure that Smith's farewell would be a cup final, despite Burley's very late consolation. Albertz was quick to give McCoist all the praise afterwards, admitting, 'When he came back he lifted us all. In my view there is no question that he has to go to the World Cup after these performances. I just love him,' but he should have ditched the modesty and accepted the key role that he had played in rescuing a lost cause. Albertz enjoyed his introduction in the new year of 1997 but it was here that he crashed his way into genuine folklore. A bona fide big-game Rangers player.

By the time the two sides met again at Ibrox seven days later, Celtic's lead was back to three after an impressive midweek win at Rugby Park. The tempo was down and the caution up a little, with more at stake. Celtic had perhaps the best of the chances but Lambert was too often trying from range and, when he did work his way into the box, he fluffed his lines badly. By then there had already been something spectacular. It was arguably better than the Ray Wilkins goal from a similar spot in the same fixture ten years before. Wilkins hit his full on the volley but it didn't have the shape and power of Thern's as the Swede scored his third goal in as many league games to put Rangers ahead in the sunshine before Albertz scored an almost carbon copy of his cup goal in the snow to put them back on top of the table by the slender margin of just one goal with all clubs having played the same amount of games. Even the bookies were split, with William Hill making Rangers odds-on favourites to win the title at 8/11 and Celtic at even money while Ladbrokes offered punters exactly the same odds but with the two giants swapped around. For Smith it was still Celtic's to lose, with three of their remaining four games to come at home and with his side having to go to Aberdeen, Hearts and Dundee United, outside of Celtic the toughest fixtures in the calendar. He was keen to press home the weight of expectation after what he thought was his final Old Firm battle, 'Celtic have three home games and an away match to go, and if you don't do well in that situation, you don't deserve to win a league. They could have been seven points ahead a few weeks ago, and if they don't lift the championship they will look back and believe that they threw it away. The pressure on Rangers was in not being top of the league. That was something new for us and we responded well to that.' Alan Stubbs responded defiantly, 'We know what he is trying to do. He is trying to pass on the pressure to us; take it away from his own place and put it at ours. We have seen it all before.' The question was now all about pressure. 'Who would blink first?' the captivated Scottish footballing asked.

They should have been asking who would blink most often. The final four games captured the wild swings of inconsistency that had scarred Rangers' season and the frail, nervous grip that Celtic had held on the race since January. One feature of this climax is that all ten clubs in Scotland's top flight had something to play for. Hearts weren't yet technically out of the championship fight, four points back behind the Old Firm; both Kilmarnock and St Johnstone were chasing the final European place and incredibly five clubs were not yet safe from relegation. One of those was Aberdeen, in eighth place, just five clear of bottom side Hibs.

The need for points was intensified with the stoking of some old fire. The previous week, Ian Durrant's book *Blue and White Dynamite* was released and serialised in the *Daily Record* in which he wrote at length about the hate campaign waged by Aberdeen fans since his sickening injury at Pittodrie ten years earlier. Safety fears were raised as the Rangers bus had been smashed with bottles and glasses the previous season, T-shirts depicting Durrant's injury had been on sale in the city and an Aberdeen fanzine had recently had to apologise after celebrating the death of Davie Cooper. The origin story for so much of the modern animosity was back in the news and the tension couldn't have been higher in a bitter battle on 19 April, with Celtic back on top after their win at home to Motherwell the previous day. It was Stephen's Glass's goal – rising above the diminutive Stuart McCall who had been dragged back deep into defence to deal with the cross – that made the difference on a day that saw Amoruso sent off for laying his hands on the face of an opponent, a few missed Rangers chances and even fewer displays of fluency. That Aberdeen would be motivated to play Rangers would have been of no surprise – Eoin Jess said later that beating them that day meant more than him going to the World Cup[142] – but it was perhaps telling that Smith's team simply could not repeat the same intensity that they had displayed in the Old Firm double-header. All of that work, wasted at the next opportunity. As if the freedom that Rangers had shown while being a chaser had disappeared when back at the summit.

And then, true to form, they were brilliant at Tynecastle. It took until the second half – there was no McCoist to do any damage as he was ruled out with an small injury – but Rangers were well worthy of their 3-0 win, with Rino Gattuso showing more evidence of what was to come in his career with two brilliant goals before Albertz wrapped it all up.[143] Over at Parkhead, Celtic faltered again to a goalless draw, this time against a Hibs side clinging on to their Premier Division status by their fingertips. It was back to a single point with Rangers finally back with home advantage for the penultimate weekend.

Ironically, 2 May is a date so synonymous with Rangers' title glory. It was on that day in 1987 that the revolution was underlined up at Pittodrie and in 1999, the greatest of all domestic victories would be won. But in 1998 it was the last hurrah for ten in a row. It was supposed to be a day where Rangers could pile the pressure on Celtic as they went to Dunfermline in second place on the Sunday. Instead, it was the champions who felt it tighten. 'We were nervous right from the start and we could not string three passes together,' wrote Amoruso. 'The pressure had got to us and we gave probably our worst performance of the season.' Once more, the preparation could be questioned, with Durrant's testimonial – a 2-2 draw against Sheffield Wednesday with a strong Rangers line-up on the park – taking place on the Wednesday night. With three cup finals on the horizon, requiring full focus, Rangers were playing first-team players in friendlies. On the Saturday, Rangers had all of the ball but no incision or composure. They huffed and puffed and then, in injury time, Ally Mitchell scored the killer goal on the break. Of all the weird results that season, of all gut-punch defeats, it is difficult to think of one greater. Everyone knew instantly that it was over.

It was back in the February edition of *Follow, Follow* – when the wheels were starting to come off – that Mark Dingwall wrote, 'Immortality awaits those who

142   It was after this game that Richard Gough said that Aberdeen 'only play four times a year', something that has stuck ever since.

143   More signs of poor discipline were also in show as Craig Moore became the second Rangers player to be sent off within the week.

win ten in a row. Those who lose it will not be forgiven – from David Murray down. Players and staff at Ibrox should not fool themselves over this – if they think that throwaway lines in their biographies will explain away the pain then I say – think again.' As Bobby Tait – the latest in a line of referees alleged to be part of the grand masonic conspiracy – blew for full time, that same frustration and anger at yet another wasted opportunity manifested itself in the booing around Ibrox. But only for a matter of seconds. Almost instantly there was an immediate realisation of what the supporters were witnessing and an applause suddenly broke out, with 20,000 staying longer to accept the final lap of honour around the Ibrox pitch for those who had helped forge the greatest ever era. It had been a long, slow acceptance of reality that was punctuated by brief moments of hope but now it was dawning on everyone that these heroes wouldn't likely be seen in Rangers colours again. Time, they thought, to bid an Ibrox farewell to Walter Smith, Archie Knox, Andy Goram, Richard Gough, Ian Durrant, Stuart McCall, Brian Laudrup and Ally McCoist. Men who between them alone had won 109 medals for Rangers and filled this stadium time and again with happier days. When the dust settled, those were always likely to be the lasting memories.

And still, it wasn't put to bed. 'Cheerio to ten in a row' was ringing around the bright Fife skies as Celtic fans could almost touch their first title in a decade. And then, with seven minutes remaining, the 20-year-old English striker Craig Faulconbridge, on loan from Coventry, sent a looping header over Jonathan Gould, pegged Celtic back to 1-1 and silenced the party. So, as Walter Smith – who would enjoy his own surprise party arranged by the squad and full Rangers staff that evening – had predicted after the final league win over Celtic, it was a title race destined to stumble and falter all the way to the last day. The picture was simple; if Celtic defeated St Johnstone at Parkhead then they would be champions but any other result would leave the door open for Rangers to make history with a win at Tannadice. Modern readers may view such a scenario as being the most outside of bets, that Rangers needed a miracle instead of it being a tense conclusion in store. Surely it was almost inconceivable for Celtic to not win, comfortably? This needs context. St Johnstone under Paul Sturrock were a team in the ascendancy, only a point behind Kilmarnock in the chase for that last UEFA Cup place and had beaten both Rangers and Celtic that season, admittedly both times in Perth. More important was the fact that Celtic had only won once at Parkhead in their last five games and had spilled 14 points there across the campaign. This was not an impenetrable fortress, defended by a team of seasoned winners. And besides, Rangers were at Tannadice where titles had been won before. Plenty of fans – either making their way up the A9 or taking their seat at Ibrox to watch the game beamed back on the giant screens – had convinced themselves once again that it was all still possible.

The hope was punctured early, Henrik Larsson's third-minute strike filtering through on radios as 29,000 people strained to make out the television pictures. False hope was raised when a Brechin City equaliser at Clydebank was confused for drama at Parkhead but Rangers' comfort against United – 2-0 up via Brian Laudrup's final goal and an Albertz penalty – was shrugged off by an increasingly fatalistic crowd. When Harald Brattbakk's late goal finished the contest, those thousands began to pour out of the weirdly silent stadium. There would be no further twists to create that agonising hope. Those younger fans – for whom the league title now felt like a birthright – grappled with the new reality in life as they wandered back home, watching new colours flying out of car windows. There was a pitch invasion of sorts at Tannadice but again, thousands stayed and sang in defiance as Smith and Gough both led dignified congratulations to Celtic and bemoaned the chances that their side had passed up.

The greatest of all eras had one final stage left in its journey and again, the noise around the Scottish Cup Final was full of acrimony, injury and sentimentality. When Smith wrestled with recalling Negri into the squad, he asked him to play a midweek reserve game in which to prove his fitness. 'I told him bluntly it was out of the question,' wrote the striker in 2016. 'I was fit and ready to play and that was the end of it. I demanded some respect and insisted I had nothing to prove to anyone. Certainly not among a group of kids.' He would watch from the stands as one of his primary *bête noires* at Ibrox, Archie Knox, was given the honour of leading out the team in his final match, the last leg of a gruelling, and now very saccharine, farewell tour that had ultimately sucked the energy and focus from an important season.

In truth, Rangers had played far worse in cup finals during this era and won. They weren't at their best but they were still the better side on the day, just without the luck. Perhaps Hearts were due some given their consistent pushing at the door in recent years and their day got off to the best possible start when they were awarded a penalty inside 30 seconds for a challenge on Steve Fulton by Ian Ferguson that either started outside the box if Willie Young felt that there had been a clip on his legs or was a dive inside the box under no pressure from Ferguson's hand. Either way, Colin Cameron was cool from the spot and Hearts were ahead. Rangers took control and Laudrup hit the post before the break and McCoist – a half-time substitute for Ståle Stensaas – hit the side-netting not long after play resumed. From the resulting goal kick the cup was effectively sealed. Lorenzo Amoruso had shown moments in his first month of action that would continue throughout his Rangers career. A dominant leadership swagger at the heart of defence, the occasional blemish in discipline and here, as he was forced to deal with Gilles Rousset's long kick, the odd aberration of concentration as he let the ball bounce and allowed Stéphane Adam a shot at goal which Goram could ultimately do little to keep out.

With the scripts for this season looking increasingly faded, Rangers threw everything at glory. McCoist missed from four yards and then seemed to be pushed inside the box by his old team-mate Dave McPherson before, with nine minutes left, he latched on to a brilliant Gattuso through pass and did what he had done so often before, when he swept the ball instinctively into the bottom corner of the net. It was his 355th and final Rangers goal – so fitting that it was he who scored the last goal of this era as he had netted the first, at Easter Road on the first match of the Graeme Souness regime – but there was still time for more pathos to the concluding chapter of a remarkable personal story. McCoist was robbed of the chance to take the game into extra time from the spot when Young awarded a free kick right on the edge of the box instead of the penalty which should have been given. Craig Brown – who had chosen to omit both McCoist and McCall from his World Cup squad – had a bit of a nightmare on co-commentary when he said, 'Yeah, it just looks as if it's outside,' when the pictures couldn't be clearer that the foul was right on the 18-yard line and therefore a spot-kick. McCoist looked desperate, clinging on to the final minutes of the job of his life, not yet ready to give it up.

When the end came, he and others looked bereft on that Parkhead pitch as they collected runners-up medals for only the fourth time in 12 years. Fans stayed back in their thousands yet again – this really was the last stand – before disappearing into the hot spring evening, just waiting for a World Cup and a new broom to come and remove the bitter taste of defeat. For the players, the tears that were kept in check on the pitch flowed in the dressing room. 'We got back to the dressing room and a river of tears was released,' wrote Amoruso. 'Coisty was inconsolable. He was sobbing and he wasn't the only one. It was a terrible moment and if I needed a reminder of what this club means to people I got it in that dressing room that afternoon.' 'We went back to Ibrox for a party with the staff, wives and families,' wrote Stuart McCall, of a long-standing cup final tradition regardless of the result. 'The boss pulled us all into the dressing room before we went upstairs to the function. It was a tear-filled end. Most of us were caught up with the emotion as he thanked us for our efforts down the years. Goughie replied on behalf of the lads and somehow managed to keep his tears in check. Coisty and I were crying our eyes out and even when I went up to see my wife later I was unable to control myself. I said a couple of words to her and just broke down again. Coisty and Durranty stayed behind in the dressing-room for one last wander down memory lane, alone with their thoughts and tales.'

Later in the week, Walter Smith sat down with journalists to have one final look back at his time as Rangers manager. He understood where the future of football was going and that he, and many of the players who had left with him, were a dying breed of long-timers. Shorter contracts for players and coaches was the post-Bosman future, which would necessitate a freshness of message from his seat. That, more than anything, was what he felt had gone over the previous 12 months. When giving his assessment on what went wrong in his final year, he made a pertinent observation on the running theme of the season. 'The basic problem that we had during the season – apart from the injuries we suffered, and I am not making these an excuse – was that we had nine players who were going to be out of contract this summer and, because the club was in a state of flux and changes were going to be made, most of these players realised that they would be leaving,' he told the *Herald*. 'Therefore, when I made my decision public in the autumn, it was never going to affect the lads. Their futures were already uncertain and anything that I did could not change that. In essence, I suppose, what it told them all was that I was in the same position as they were. I was going to be leaving, too, and it simply underlined to them all that this was an end of the good times we had all enjoyed together.'

Of all the theories for the lost Rangers season – Smith's announcement, Negri's eye, Amoruso's ankle, Diana's crash, Gascoigne's sale, Laudrup's uncertainty, passing on Lambert, Stubbs's missing second yellow – none are greater than the situation Smith set out to the written press. The end of his second spell was announced in advance and yet his side pushed on to win him a title and a fitting farewell in 2010/11. There was no 'lame duck president' creating inertia there and it was because Smith wasn't leaving with half of that squad. There was youth in there and a lot of players in the prime of their career, willing to stay and win more. The XI that finished the Scottish Cup Final of 1998 had an average age of 30 and that included a 20-year-old Rino Gattuso. The Celtic side that finished with their hands on the title had an average age of 27 and with so little variance around that mean. The failure of 1997/98 was the legacy of poor squad management. A lack of ruthlessness to get rid of a player just as they had turned the corner on the way down. A need to hold on to the boys whom the manager felt he could trust. Smith was left – by choice – with too many players who were simply too old and too tired to find the necessary consistency and tried to do too much in one summer to alleviate that. It didn't work. Rangers were better than Celtic that season – the head-to-head demonstrates that quite conclusively – but it wasn't that which cost them dear. Five points out of 12 against Aberdeen and Motherwell – sides that only escaped relegation late on in the season – was evidence of a lack of that necessary incessant drive to win and keep winning.

The plan that was put in place to win nine was that which ultimately cost ten.

Chapter Twelve

My Generation

'It was the age of wisdom, it was the age of foolishness.'
Charles Dickens

'If I hadn't seen such riches I could live with being poor.'
Glennie/Booth/Whelan/Gott

I stood at Tannadice on a cold, but sunny, February afternoon in 2022, watching Rangers limp to yet another 1-1 draw in the league. Days after heroically disposing of favourites Borussia Dortmund from the UEFA Europa League, here we were, witnessing another title challenge slowly disintegrate. The Union Bears – the pulse and conductors of the Rangers support both home and away – never let up in their singing throughout. One song in particular rekindled memories of another visit to the same ground 25 years before. The story of Charlie Miller's cross and Brian Laudrup's header was invoked, so as to try and inspire the current crop. 'Whoa oh oh, whoa oh oh, Glasgow Rangers nine in a row.' Time hadn't been kind to these young men. Their formative years being characterised by shame and struggle and even the long-awaited league triumph in 2021 was not the overture for a permanent shift in power that many had hoped for. The younger Rangers fans of the 2020s have had to cling on to the past in order to keep them going, proud of their lineage if not what was being served up in front of them.

I didn't. Sure, there were songs sung of bygone days of yore, but mainly about 300 year-old battles and constitutional skirmishes. Barcelona in 1972 or the spirit of Bill Struth would be acknowledged on stadium tours or in history books but it wasn't something we felt necessary to celebrate on matchday. We didn't need to romanticise history because we were making it. In reality, I had as much choice about the football team that I support as I did about being born at all. It is like that in the west of Scotland. Your club is a matter of heritage, bestowed upon you at birth. But it was *when* I was born that made all the difference. Being a football fan always has its challenges. Your team is never on top for ever. There are always bad times to suffer and being a Rangers fan over the last decade or so has brought about an awful lot of suffering. But to be a Rangers fan and born in 1980 – as I was – was as perfect timing as you could possibly wish for.

At the time of writing, I have just witnessed the conclusion of my 37th season of watching football and only now, at the age of 42, have I reached the point where I have seen Celtic win more league championships than Rangers. If I had been born even a year earlier, that depressing sensation would have been my immediate introduction to life as a Rangers fan as I would almost certainly have been conscious of Celtic's last-gasp snatch of the championship from the hands of Hearts. Realistically, for a Rangers supporter to have been born before 1980 and taken longer to be overpassed, they'd have had to have come into the world in 1932. Those coming of age in the 1920s, such as my grandfather, would never experience it, even if they had lived to be 100. He, however, grew up in a global depression and fought in a world war whereas I had Super Soakers and *Sensible Soccer*. If not part of the 'Greatest Generation', then I was almost certainly part of the most fortunate.

We had no scars that needed to properly heal. Nor did we approach the success that the revolution brought with any hint of caution, the kind of which some who had enjoyed the mid-1970s could have been forgiven for having.[144] No, for us, right away, this was an intravenous line through which flowed triumph, hope and heroes. A bad year for us was only winning the league. A really bad one – 1987/88 – was only a cup and the final such year, the sad novelty of nothing, was passed off as a farewell chapter before we started it all over again in 1998. The sun shone every day during our summers, most notably when Rangers paraded big signing after big signing. And if the science is correct – that our outlook and expectations are fundamentally formed by the time we reach our teenage years – then our perception of Rangers as a dominant, title-winning machine was set in concrete. At the age when our imagination is possibly at its most malleable, the possibilities seemed endless.

One younger Rangers fan I spoke to once bemoaned the fact that not only had he missed out on nine in a row but, 'I missed the music too.' It isn't just Rangers collecting trophies that provides our nostalgia with such warmth. I am technically not a Millennial as that generation is often marked by births between 1981 and 1996 but, given that I am only a couple of weeks outside of the zone, I think it is fair to say that the same influences still apply. If Millennials are indeed affected more than any other generation by immaturity and some form of arrested development, then is it really any wonder? With our childhood in the analogue

---

144   Rangers finally ended Celtic's dominance by winning their first league title in 11 years in 1975. Two trebles followed in the next three seasons before a sudden and painful jolt back into the wilderness. Any fan who lived through that may have taken longer to accept that this spell of success was going to last for a lot longer.

age and our adulthood in the digital, we grew up in a kind of Goldilocks zone following a technological and entertainment explosion.[145] Before a time when the options became too disparate, saturated and overwhelming, this felt like a time of plenty but with portions that could still be consumed appropriately. The late 1980s appeared to produce more and more affordable toys, home entertainment, foreign holidays and satellite television brought the American Dream into our homes via *The Simpsons* or WWF wrestling. Critics lamented Hollywood's infantilised output but it was a golden time for feel-good escapism, adventure and comedy. When that wide-eyed childhood innocence turned into a more moody teenage angst in the 1990s, a homegrown cultural explosion arrived at the perfect time as British music, comedy, fashion, art and movies had a brief window of beautiful imperialism. Even if your diet was full of Oasis, Reeves and Mortimer, Steve Coogan, *Dazed and Confused* and *Trainspotting*, there was still room for a controlled – if a great deal more cynical – fix of Americana through Tarantino and Seinfeld or, if your younger sister had the remote control, *Friends*. It lacked the political posturing of the 1980s and was far better for it. This complacent, fun, hedonistic age set between the Cold War and global terror. It was all a show about nothing. And it was fucking brilliant.

Imagine my surprise then, when it became clear that not quite everyone shared the same kind of memory. One of the most enjoyable things about recording a year-long podcast on the era – *Dominant: The Souness and Smith Years* – was the generational differences that the contributors weaved through the weekly narrative. David Edgar and Andy McGowan were both born in the mid-to-late 1970s and the Rangers to which they were introduced was a bad joke. The sad preamble they endured only intensified all of the imminent excitement that was to come. Alan Bradley and John Cowden had endured longer pain but had seen glory too – European as well as domestic – and so their tone was often more one of appreciation than infatuation. Cowden, born in 1966, leaned on Dickens to accurately describe the era as 'the best of times', but never indulged the hero worship of Graeme Souness that myself, Andy and David often would. He already had his heroes of course and it is often impossible to feel quite the same way again about the figures who appear on the scene later in life. That generation simply had a perspective that we lacked. They knew the value of these trophies. They were savoured but not taken for granted. It was on the day that Rangers paraded the sixth title in a row around Ibrox that I admitted to my father that this was getting a little boring. The response was curt. And, when it all ended and some of us were in a huff about how the final stage had been handled, our elders were more able to show genuine gratitude for years that they must have feared would never arrive. We, on the other hand, in the words of Cowden, were 'spoilt brats'.

---

145   Some have argued that there is a 'micro generation' called 'Xennials' for those born between 1975 and 1983.

Where both generations failed was with what happened next. As is writ large throughout this book and *Revolution*, Rangers fans were never slow to moan and complain during this era, whether about players, managers or the chairman, but *action* was very different. Even though the writing was on the wall in the years preceding the events of 2012, there was a generation and more unable to conceive of the impending nightmare until it was too late. David Murray had his faults but he was still so closely associated with the most golden of times. Rangers were too big and too successful to fail. We were inculcated from the real-world threat of collapse. The biggest cost to those who lived through the era was the ingrained foolishness to assume that the state of football can ever be permanent.

And what of those who paid the real price of 2012, the youngsters who grew up with little to cheer about and whose memories of any success were either hazy or non-existent? Jordan Campbell, 27 years of age when we spoke and a writer for *The Athletic* who covered the club for five years before heading down south to be an Arsenal correspondent, once described this era to me as 'a romantic age' whenever he saw clips and videos, 'There is a certain mystique and myth about the period to people my age. Did this really happen?' Growing up with Rangers from 2002 onwards with a sense of parity, a brief hint of dominance during Walter Smith's return and then the humiliation of the lower leagues, Campbell remarked how it was 'impossible to imagine how it must have felt to be so far in front'. Years later, it arguably provided a sense of realistic patience with Steven Gerrard's three-year plan to win the title when older fans – those who had seen Graeme Souness, Walter Smith, Dick Advocaat and Alex McLeish achieve success instantly – lost patience and nerve immediately before Covid-19 changed the dynamic in March 2020. Campbell talked about a 'normality' around the equal share of titles between 2002/03 and 2005/06 and, whereas most non-partisan fans would look dispassionately at foreign leagues and agree that a different winner each year would be healthy, Rangers supporters of my generation would rarely see that in Scotland as something that should be the norm.

'Seeing a league table consistently showing Rangers at the top doesn't feel normal,' said Ross Hutton, born in 1999, a podcaster on the Heart and Hand network and whose secondary school life was ruined by the crash of 2012. 'I'm not accustomed to seeing it. In fact, I've been conditioned to the opposite. This is why celebrating history is so important. It's a lineage that you can cling on to until better days come back around.' This was part of a discussion around the 55th title-winning season of 2020/21, which Hutton described as still meaning 'the world' because it was all he had in recent memory. As understandable as that is, it highlights another difference in the legacy of perspective. The initial emotional reaction to that league win – for fans of any age – was visceral and most likely surpassed the intensity of those other dam-busting seasons of 1987 and 1975. However, for those in their 30s and above, the historical significance was dependent on that team winning more. Titles plural is the benchmark for us and as such – even though they were a couple of penalties away from immortality in Seville in May 2022 – it is a success that is not looked back upon with the fondness of those before which led to floodgates being opened.

And perhaps that unrelenting need for more is the cost of my generation's childhood and adolescence. I may envy those fans 20 years my junior for their hair and faster metabolism but they didn't see Brian Laudrup, Paul Gascoigne and all the silverware you could ever hope to polish. One of my younger interviewees asked if I still expected that level of success and had that made the last decade or so doubly difficult. I don't believe that to be the case; in fact I expect less and less from the club as the years go on and the wider footballing landscape makes my formative years feel even more distant. I think, however, that it may be more existential than that. That there is an unshakeable feeling that I'm left with – a small one that is easily managed – that unless Rangers are truly dominant, unless they are winning two trophies a season, three leagues in every four and that they are the only possible answer to the question 'who is the top dog in Scotland?', then they're not really Rangers at all. As we shall see in the final chapter, of course they are, but the characteristics of the club I first met and loved are undeniably different than they are now.

Some years ago, while undergoing a short period of counselling, I offered up a throwaway line when asked to list the things in my life that were causing anxiety, 'I feel as if I'm losing my football club.' That wasn't in the spring of 2012 but ten years before, after nearly two years without a trophy, a clear sign of downsizing and the emergence of a genuine and constant threat from the other side of the city. As it happened, Rangers won the next five available, but even the disproportionate and borderline hysterical comment that it was, there was something in it. The club as I knew it, that I had only ever known it – utterly and crushingly dominant – was disappearing with absolutely no guarantees that it would be back.

Which, of course, is how it works. Apart from successful German penalties, there is nothing permanent about this sport. The game is never won or lost for good. At the end of our interview, Jordan Campbell called this era – and indirectly my childhood – 'an anomaly'. Which it was. Even at a club as decorated as Rangers, this was the best of times. A beautiful aberration.

And I am so grateful to have lived through every minute.

Epilogue

Dominant *(noun)*: **occupying or being in a commanding or elevated position**

'A natural order felt restored.'

This was the last sentence I wrote In *Revolution*, a time where new ideas and energy were used to infuse old notions of superiority, those handed down by grandparents who had grown up in the Bill Struth era and could hardly conceive of any other club to naturally reign supreme in Scotland. The 1990s only intensified such a belief. Even the eras of Scot Symon and Jock Wallace appeared to be very bright, but ultimately false, dawns. What they were living through was Rangers as it should be, as it used to be, but now even better. As one caller on Radio Clyde's *Open Line* said, less than an hour after the treble-clinching 1993 Scottish Cup win, 'The bad old days are long gone. We'll never be back there.' He meant the early 1980s and no one on the panel countered the point, even with a general long-term warning against hubris. In 1993 such a statement felt like fact more than prediction.

Bad days would return, however, and much worse than had ever been seen before. The chaos of 2012 wasn't directly caused by this era – the infamous Employee Benefit Trust payments came later – but the roots of mismanagement can be found there, as standards of corporate governance dissolved into ad-hoc phone calls and meetings in passing and when the club's focus shifted away from the future just at the worst possible moment.

How do we judge this era – the six years that came after that initial revolutionary period – 25 years on? Even though it brought about the exact same number of titles and trophies, there is an undeniably different feel and pace to the years after 1992. More complicated, more nuanced, with all the change happening around the club rather than being driven by it and the language used feeling more and more like fantasy than a genuinely grounded plan for success. Glory, yes, but not as big or as important as was happening elsewhere and as was being shown all the time on television. There was another party happening, at which Rangers couldn't hang around for long enough.

The cold-hearted and detached football historian perspective must be that the success delivered in that time was no more than par. Given the strength of Rangers' position in 1992 both on and off the field of play, and the fact that they spent over double what Celtic did between then and 1998[146] – and three times their net spend – getting to nine was an absolute minimum. As ridiculous as it sounds, eight titles would be viewed as a failure now as it would have then and the tenth could and really should have been delivered too. Europe – despite one thrilling season and one very difficult group draw – was a massive let-down. Although it was rarely accepted at the time, the game had changed so quickly that winning the Champions League really was that one-shot affair in 1993 but more consistent and further adventure should have been achieved.

The financial situation upon Smith's departure – thanks to investment, retail and sponsorship – was very healthy but the work needing done to the training infrastructure, neglected when Rangers were on top and the wild and wasteful spending to try and catch up with the European express train after so many years of domestic swaggering, wasted that advantage and led to ruin. It was not inconceivable that Rangers could have kept Celtic at arm's length from 1998 to the present day, forgoing the odd championship in the 21st century and possibly even one in the mid-1990s as they made more long-term investments instead of spending millions on players that kept them ahead of already weaker sides, but 'the hairy old beast, history, big with memories' as the historian Simon Schama once described it, locked them into a different future.

Writing near the start of season 1996/97, Hugh McIlvanney described Rangers' quest as a 'double exorcism', an attempt to kill both European and domestic ghosts from the past by winning the Champions League and, at least, equalling the nine titles. There are many Rangers fans who still bristle at such an analysis and feel that Rangers shouldn't be defined by Celtic in any way. Noble, for sure, but it ignores the inescapable reality of the nature of rivalry that one side's success is always compared to the other's. That is just how it works.

In theory there was another line for Rangers to tread throughout the 1990s. Cooler heads would have said that winning titles consistently is generally a good target but shouldn't blind a club against planning for the longer term, or that Rangers had a lot to do in Europe to make up for their own past misses, more so than trying to overcome any other club's highlights. Cooler heads would also have noted that the ghosts that McIlvanney and others wrote about – smitten

---

146   Walter Smith spent around £52m between 1992 and 1998 while Celtic paid out just over £25m in that time. Rangers brought in over £16m in transfer fees whereas Celtic recouped £13m.

as they were by Jock Stein's Celtic – were as fictional as any other. This was now a different sport than it was 30 years before. A sequence of titles where half the league was part-time is not the same thing. By 1998, the Champions League was also unrecognisable from the competition where Celtic could reach a final by getting the better of four sides who had never previously gone beyond a European quarter-final and from countries that had never produced a winner in these tournaments. It wasn't like for like but that reality didn't matter.

Cooler heads would have pointed out that a genuine focus on Europe would potentially risk a quiet and unsuccessful domestic season and that it would also have meant the need for a new manager in 1995. But cool heads were nowhere to be seen. History can be a very emotional draw and the fervour increased with every passing year. With that in mind, there is a notable element to the achievement during the decade that doesn't come out in mere results. Walter Smith's handling of that pressure and his ability to recharge and reinvent his side in 1995 was no mean feat and is much more complicated than outspending rivals. Few managers could have navigated that as he did and keep the dressing room in the right kind of place to deal with those big domestic matches. His over-reliance on those men who would walk through fire for him, however, was ultimately his undoing. In different circumstances – ironically perhaps if he had lost that title in 1991 and kept his job – he would have been willing to be more ruthless with succession planning within the squad and happy to risk the odd failure for the greater good. In truth, he wasn't allowed to look much beyond 1997 and everything that it meant. And neither were the fans.

And this touches on something that the purely analytical footballing histories so often miss. There is nothing wrong with historical revisionism. It is a dirty word in modern common parlance but it's also an important tool in re-assessing and better understanding events with the benefit of perspective, and this glorious period in Rangers' history should not be protected from that. However, what we should not forget is how it was experienced by people at the time, totally absorbed and living every moment. One tabloid poll in the summer of 1997 found that over two-thirds of Rangers fans would choose to win the Premier Division that season rather than the Champions League. A frankly ridiculous mindset when viewed from today's perspective but some evidence that the rhetoric about further modernisation was often as empty in the stands as it was in the boardroom, consumed as everyone was by the more accessible glory at home.

Rangers were lording it over their rivals, winning all the key battles and the support absolutely lapped it up. For thousands, history only provided future targets rather than the need to heal. When I spoke to David Edgar about the 5-1 victory over Celtic in 1988 for the first episode of my *Time Capsule* podcast, he dismissed the need of others around him that day to avenge the famous 7-1 League Cup Final defeat back in 1957, 'I hadn't seen anything like this in my lifetime. 1957 didn't happen to me, it had no relevance. This did. And for any Celtic supporters around my age, it happened to them too.' There is something in that, for my generation at least. The ghosts of Celtic's success in the late 1960s and early 1970s and Rangers' misery of the early 1980s were all too ethereal for us. This *was* real, as was the other side of the coin for our contemporaries on the other side of the divide, and as such the joy and excitement of those 20 trophies in 12 years and the hedonistic, gloating, 1990s narcissism that followed should never be erased from the story. It could and should have been more, as many fans complained at the time, and it could and should have ensured stability for generations – although too few warned about the potential catastrophe – but it was thoroughly enjoyed by all who were there in the moment. Abstract analysis, for all of its worth, doesn't erase the rush that was felt on those nights.

It was actually 25 trophies in 14 years. Two more titles and another treble and double were delivered by Dick Advocaat in his first two seasons and could easily be seen as part of the same era, characterised as it was by success and bravado. Sadly, it was more of a coda than a new movement. If the 1990s really did end for the western world when the World Trade Center collapsed, then they ended for Rangers just over a year earlier as notions of natural supremacy were given a shuddering thud after a 6-2 defeat at Parkhead in the August of 2000. Nothing was quite the same again as the plan to fast track the side to compete in Europe – despite some early signs of promise and reputational reconstruction – was very quickly found to be highly unsustainable and a tough period of downsizing, dark-horsing and demotion followed. A very different Rangers emerged.

Different to those who had known only greatness for sure, but how different was it really? The major takeaway for me is how much this era still echoes into the present as 21st-century Rangers fans have focussed on the running total rather than the current state of play. Fifty-five Scottish titles to Celtic's 53, 117 major honours to their 116 as of the summer of 2023, that gap is becoming perilously close. Those supporters, at the time of writing, can still just about hang on to overall superiority but that claim owes a huge debt to Bill Struth, Graeme Souness and Walter Smith, with the three men responsible for over half of the league titles won and Souness's creation of modern Rangers being of more importance than simple numbers. This era, much like the 1930s, was not the norm. It was special for those who enjoyed it but a dangerously oppressive bar for the club to clear in the future.

The past truly is a foreign country and making gods and monsters out of the key actors in both of the dramas that encompass this 12-year period does no one any favours, least of all those currently trying to achieve whatever success they can for the club. If there is anything to learn from this story, it is the importance of opportunity in history, the creation of which has so often nothing to do with those on stage at the time. The open window in 1986 that made the revolution possible for Graeme Souness is just as important as the one that was closed throughout the 1990s which made life so much more difficult for Walter Smith. Rangers exploited plenty of chances but wasted many too. A better understanding of what was possible then and now would do everyone the world of good.

And if, at some point in the future, a window opens again that allows the club to get back on top for a sustained period of time, then I trust that Rangers fans will savour those years to the fullest. I would also advise them to listen to those a lot older who might warn them that there's no such thing as a rightful place at the top, just as there is no guarantee that the party will last for ever.

It never can, of course, but if those in charge understand their history well enough then there's no reason why – perhaps with the volume turned down a little and the bar tab rationed – that it can't continue for a lot longer than this one did.

Acknowledgments

As with *Revolution: Rangers – 1986–92*, the book which directly precedes this one, I am eternally grateful for the input and insight of David Edgar, Andy McGowan, John Cowden and Alan Bradley. The debates and discussions we shared on the podcast *Dominant* – a 55-part series that covered the whole Graeme Souness and Walter Smith era – gave me the ideal sense of perspective from which to complete this history. There are few things in my life of which I am as proud.

I must thank, once again, Prof Graham Walker for continuing to act as a sounding board on the political context which shaped the era; Rob Smyth, firstly for providing me with his experience of being a fan of another big club that was outgrowing its home nation during the same decade and secondly for our podcast conversation on style and substance; and also to Alistair Bain for his tactical expertise, an essential factor in understanding the game at the time. Special thanks on this occasion must go to Jamie McCabe, a Rangers fan and Tartan Army foot solider, for his view on an era where both appeared incompatible. Alan Pattullo of *The Scotsman* for his help with all things Duncan Ferguson. James Dixon for his contacts, insight and research on the Marseille affair. Finally, to Jordan Campbell and Ross Hutton, for their reflections on what this era means to those who didn't experience it.

I can't let the moment pass without thanking my editor, Gareth Davis, for all of his hard work tidying up my prose and offering some well-researched suggestions.

My final thanks has to go to my long-suffering wife Helen. With a new arrival imminent, this may well be the final book that I have the time to pen for a while, but she has supported my desire to capture the greatest era in Rangers history in my own way. Over a quarter of a million words later, I am ever grateful for her encouragement and patience.

Bibliography

Books

Lorenzo Amoruso, David McCarthy & Keith Jackson, *LA Confidential* (First Press Publishing, Glasgow, 2003)

Michael Bond, *Fans* (Picador, London, 2023)

Alastair Campbell, *The Blair Years* (Arrow Books, London, 2008)

Michael Cox, *The Mixer* (Harper Collins, London, 2017)

Michael Cox, *Zonal Marking* (Harper Collins, London, 2019)

Claire Dederer, *Monsters: A Fan's Dilemma* (Sceptre, London, 2023)

Tom Devine, *The Scottish Nation: A Modern History* (Penguin, London, 2012)

Neil Drysdale, *Silversmith: The Biography of Walter Smith* (Birlinn, Edinburgh, 2011)

Ian Durrant & Iain King, *Blue & White Dynamite* (First Press Publishing, Glasgow, 1998)

Ronnie Esplin & Graham Walker, *The Official Biography of Rangers* (Headline Publishing, Edinburgh, 2011)

Ronnie Esplin & Graham Walker (Eds), *Rangers: Triumphs, Troubles, Traditions* (Fort, Ayr, 2010)

Ian Ferguson & Ken Gallacher, *Fergie: The Ian Ferguson Story* (First Press Publishing, Glasgow, 1999)

Francis Fukuyama, *The End of History and the Last Man* (Penguin, London, 1992)

Paul Gascoigne, *Gazza: My Story* (Headline, London, 2004)

Michael Gibbons, *When Football Came Home: England, The English and Euro '96* (Pitch Publishing, Durrington, 2016)

Andy Goram & Iain King, *The Goalie: My Story* (Mainstream Publishing, Edinburgh, 2009)

Richard Gough & Ken Gallacher, *Field of Dreams: My Ibrox Years* (Mainstream Publishing, Edinburgh, 1993)

Mark Hateley & Alistair Aird, *Hitting The Mark: My Story* (Reach, Liverpool, 2021)

Mark Hateley & Ken Gallacher, *Top Mark!* (Mainstream Publishing, Edinburgh, 1993)

Jeff Holmes, *A Season To Be Cheerful: Glasgow Rangers 1992/93* (Pitch Publishing, Durrington, 2017)

Jeff Holmes, *Moody Blue: The Story of Mysterious Marco* (Pitch Publishing, Durrington, 2015)

Raphael Honigstein, *Englischer Fussball: A German's View of our Beautiful Game* (Yellow Jersey Press, London, 2009)

Archie Knox & Roger Hannah, *The School of Hard Knox: The Autobiography of Archie Knox* (Arena Sport, Edinburgh, 2017)

Sid Lambert & Chris Scull, *Can We Not Knock It?* (Conker, Leicester, 2021)

Archie Macpherson, *More Than A Game: Living with the Old Firm* (Luath Press, Edinburgh, 2020)

Andrew Marr, *A History of Modern Britain* (Pan, London, 2009)

Stuart McCall & Alan Nixon, *The Real McCall: Stuart McCall's Own Story* (Ally McCoist & Crawford Brankin, *Ally McCoist: My Story*, (Mainstream Publishing, Edinburgh, 1998)

Ally McCoist & Crawford Brankin, *Ally McCoist: My Story* (Mainstream Publishing, Edinburgh, 1992)

Hugh McIlvanney, *McIlvanney on Football* (Mainstream Publishing, Edinburgh, 1994)

Alan Pattullo, *In Search of Duncan Ferguson: The Life and Crimes of a Footballing Enigma* (Transworld Publishers, London, 2014)

Daniel Rachel, *Don't Look Back In Anger* (Trapeze, London, 2020)

Walter Smith & Ken Gallacher, *Mr Smith: The Fan Who Joined The Ibrox Legends* (Mainstream Publishing, Edinburgh, 1994)

Daniel Storey, *250 Days: Cantona's Kung Fu and the making of Manchester United* (Harper Collins, London, 2019)

Alwyn W. Turner, *A Classless Society: Britain in the 1990s* (Aurum, London, 2013)

Jonathan Wilson, *Inverting The Pyramid* (Orion, London, 2008)

Other sources

Rangers season DVDs

Walter Smith – The Story of a Rangers Legend

Rangers TV archive

Rangers matchday programmes

Various newspapers (titles cited in text)

Follow, Follow fanzine

The Rangers Historian magazine

ND - #0278 - 270225 - C0 - 234/156/14 - PB - 9781780916538 - Gloss Lamination